CANADA AND CHINA

A Fifty-Year Journey

MW00805733

CANADA AND CHINA

A Fifty-Year Journey

B. Michael Frolic

UNIVERSITY OF TORONTO PRESS
Toronto Buffalo London

© University of Toronto Press 2022
Toronto Buffalo London
utorontopress.com

Library and Archives Canada Cataloguing in Publication

Title: Canada and China : a fifty-year journey / B. Michael Frolic.
Names: Frolic, B. Michael, 1937– author.
Description: Includes bibliographical references and index.
Identifiers: Canadiana (print) 20220155135 | Canadiana (ebook) 2022015516X |
    ISBN 9781487540883 (paper) | ISBN 9781487540876 (cloth) |
    ISBN 9781487540906 (EPUB) | ISBN 9781487540890 (PDF)
Subjects: LCSH: Canada – Relations – China. | LCSH: China – Relations –
    Canada.
Classification: LCC FC251.C5 F76 2022 | DDC 327.71051 – dc23

ISBN 978-1-4875-4087-6 (cloth)   ISBN 978-1-4875-4090-6 (EPUB)
ISBN 978-1-4875-4088-3 (paper)   ISBN 978-1-4875-4089-0 (PDF)

Printed in the U.S.A.

We wish to acknowledge the land on which the University of Toronto
Press operates. This land is the traditional territory of the Wendat, the
Anishnaabeg, the Haudenosaunee, the Métis, and the Mississaugas of the
Credit First Nation.

We acknowledge the financial support of the Government of Canada, the
Canada Council for the Arts, and the Ontario Arts Council, an agency of the
Government of Ontario, for our publishing activities.

 Canada Council for the Arts **Conseil des Arts du Canada**

 **ONTARIO ARTS COUNCIL**
CONSEIL DES ARTS DE L'ONTARIO
an Ontario government agency
un organisme du gouvernement de l'Ontario

Funded by the Government of Canada Financé par le gouvernement du Canada  **Canada**

To Irene.

Contents

Contents

Preface

When I stepped off the train in Beijing in 1965, I did not expect that China would occupy my life for the next half century. It has been a remarkable adventure in understanding a unique culture and a civilization that has emerged from economic backwardness to become a superpower. I experienced the establishment of Canada's diplomatic relations with China in 1970, the Cultural Revolution, the aftermath of the Tiananmen crisis, lectured in Chinese at Peking University and to Communist Party officials, taught about human rights to Chinese students, and shook the hands of some of China's leaders. I began teaching one of the first courses in Canada on Communist China in 1968. A stint as first secretary in the Canadian Embassy in the 1970s introduced me to our decision-makers, and I was a participant observer as our government made China policy. Over the following years, I read classified materials and had access to over 100 Canadian and Chinese officials working on Canada-China relations.

The ten stories that follow are the result of two decades of research and behind the scenes discussion with prime ministers, ministers, ambassadors, members of the Foreign Service, and China specialists. They begin with the negotiations with China for diplomatic recognition in 1968, and they end during the leadership of Justin Trudeau in 2021. For most of those fifty plus years, Canada and China had a good working relationship, but in the recent period, relations struggled as China pursued more aggressive policies towards Canada. The book concludes with guidelines for a strategic framework that may help us reset relations with China.

Acknowledgments

Thanks to the three universities that provided the support to complete this book: York University, Harvard University's Fairbank Center for Chinese Studies, and the Munk School of Global Affairs and Public Policy at the University of Toronto. I am grateful for funding from the Social Sciences and Humanities Research Council of Canada, and the Asia Pacific Foundation of Canada. The Department of External Affairs – now called Global Affairs Canada – opened its classified files, and its officers and staff took days of their time to talk about current and past relations with China. My thanks to the fifteen Canadian ambassadors to China who agreed to be interviewed, in particular, Howard Balloch, Fred Bild, Earl Drake, Arthur Menzies, David Mulroney, and John Small, and to the over 100 politicians, public servants, and members of the China policy community who talked about their China experience.

The People's Republic of China's Ministry of Foreign Affairs provided an official Chinese perspective, especially from the nine Chinese ambassadors to Canada whom I interviewed. Special thanks to State Councillor Yao Guang, Vice Minister Liu Huaqiu, Ambassador Zhang Yijun, and National People's Congress advisor Lu Congmin. I am also indebted to the students in the Beijing Foreign Studies University from whom, during my five years teaching there, I learned how China sees Canada.

Special thanks to my colleague, University of British Columbia professor Paul Evans. In the 1980s, we launched our joint research project on Canada-China relations at York University, and since then he has become Canada's leading specialist on these relations. I am also deeply grateful for the advice and support I received from Harvard University professor Ezra Vogel – from the time I began to study China in the late 1960s, until his passing in December 2020. Senator Jack Austin also provided important insights from his rich experience as an advisor to three prime ministers, and as president of the Canada China Business Council.

No book is complete without the help of those who have read the manuscript and assisted with the final editing. My thanks to Daniel Drache, David Zweig, Jeremy Paltiel, John Dirks, Gong Yan, Alan Middleton, Gregory Chin, Julia Bentley, Susan Spronk, and to Alicia Filipowich at the York Centre for Asian Research. Their assistance was invaluable. Of course, I assume full responsibility for the final product.

chapter one

Telling the Story

Many of the major world issues will not be resolved completely or in any lasting way, unless, and until an accommodation has been reached with the Chinese nation.

– Pierre Elliot Trudeau, 1968

First Encounters

In 1965, China was a Cold War opponent, isolated from the Western world, different and far poorer than the Soviet Union where I had just spent the previous year. During my time in China, I saw an immobile population, with peasants living in straw huts without drinking water, a truck factory without an assembly line – one truck being built on a dirt floor by hand labour, the skeleton of a bridge across the Yangtze River abandoned by China's former Soviet friends, a tiny urban population (12 per cent), no automobiles, steam locomotives, bicycles and horse drawn carts, and airports with dirt runways and recycled Russian airplanes. Annual per capita income was about US$200, and 80 per cent of its massive population lived below the poverty line. It was economically backward, closed off from most of the developed world, armed with a revolutionary ideology, and especially wary of outsiders.

The contrast with the China of today is remarkable. The population has doubled, and skyscrapers line the streets of its cities. China now has over 100 cities with a population of one million or more, and it is 60 per cent urban. Shanghai and Beijing each have populations of over twenty-five million. Private cars clog city streets, high-speed bullet trains connect large parts of the country, and its people are on the move everywhere as tourists, exploring their own country, and if possible, the outside world. China has become "the workshop of the world." It is today's second superpower, and its manufactured goods are everywhere. In 1970, its exports were less than 3 per cent of its gross domestic product (GDP); now they are close to 20 per cent. As China's economic strength has grown, so has its political and strategic influence. No longer content with what Deng Xiaoping forty years ago called "biding our time" before China was ready to challenge the Western multilateral system, China is now an aggressive international actor, barely responsive to criticism of its internal and external policies, and ready to confront the current multilateral world order to satisfy its economic and strategic needs.

How Canada has dealt with this changing China is the story of this book. It tells us how we first engaged with this isolated communist state and developed significant political, trade, and people-to-people links. We started as strangers, with a bilateral relationship that sought to set aside the substantial differences, political and developmental, that existed between us. As the relationship grew, both sides talked of "friendship" and also of "partnership." What we have learned after fifty years is that China is unique and does not easily fit our Western categories, and that its leaders are unwilling to adopt many of our norms and values. It has been a challenge for our government to develop a policy that can account for these differences and win the approval of Canadians, especially when it involves China's human rights practices. Prime Minister Pierre Trudeau said in conversation in the 1980s: "I never thought it would be easy to work with China. It is an authoritarian state. But after I had been there, I realized China had to become part of the rest of the world, and we needed to know much more about it."[1]

In the mid-1960s the Chinese knew almost nothing about Canada, and we, in turn, knew little about China. For most Canadians, China was the Far East, a mysterious part of the world visited by a handful of people, a few missionaries, traders, and curious travellers. It was also a Cold War opponent tied to Moscow and the communist world. Back then, my hosts knew one big thing about Canada. It was the home of Dr. Norman Bethune, a Canadian doctor and a communist who was glorified by Mao Zedong in an essay in little red books read by hundreds of millions of Chinese. Bethune, almost unknown in Canada, became a Chinese hero for the medical help that he gave to the Chinese communist soldiers during the Second Sino-Japanese War. It cost him his life, and he died in China in 1937. Today, Bethune is still remembered as "the Canadian – a foreigner who helped us."[2]

Bethune was one of the few ties Canada had with China. Traders took Canadian sea otter skins and ginseng to China in the late eighteenth century. In the nineteenth century, clipper ships sailed from Vancouver to Asian ports, carrying goods from Canada and returning with silk, rice, and tea. Once the railroad had reached the Pacific coast, shipping times shortened, and trade expanded. In 1909, Canada established a window on East Asia by opening a small trade office in Shanghai. By the 1920s, two-way trade between Canada and China reached $22 million, a small figure when compared to the trade that the Americans, the British, and the Japanese then had with China. After the communists took power in 1949, trade shrunk to a few million dollars, where it remained until the great Canadian wheat sales of the 1960s.[3]

Beginning in the latter part of the nineteenth century, around 1,000 Canadian missionaries went to China, and over 15,000 Chinese workers came to Canada. This was the principal link between the two countries. Missionaries preached the Gospel and spread Canadian values. Some built hospitals and founded schools that still exist in China today. They provided glimpses of China from their lives there, and they told us that bringing Western values to China was no simple task. After the Communist Party took power in 1949, they were expelled, returning home with mixed views of the new communist government. Their children, called the "mish kids," would later play an important role as advisors to the Canadian government, and as our first three ambassadors to China.

On Canada's Pacific coast, Chinese workers provided cheap labour in the gold mines and helped to complete Canada's transcontinental railroad. They came, they stayed, and they became the object of racist policies that drove them into Chinatowns, where they worked in hand laundries and Chinese restaurants. By 1923, the Canadian government halted Chinese immigration to Canada. In 1947, they were finally granted the right to Canadian citizenship. The treatment of those early Chinese residents in Canada is a shameful legacy that has not been forgotten, neither by the two million Canadians of Chinese ethnic origin living in Canada today, nor by the Chinese people.[4]

In 1949, Canada was about to recognize the new communist government of the People's Republic of China (PRC), but once the Korean War broke out, Canada and China remained enemies on opposite sides of the Cold War for the next twenty years. Canada tried to recognize the PRC four times after 1949, attempts that were stymied by a combination of fear of US economic retaliation, Canadian anti-communist sentiments, and what appeared to be Canadian indifference.[5] In 1961, John Diefenbaker's Conservative government decided that Canada could do business with Communist China and sold it $160 million of wheat on credit. We did not know that millions in China were starving and that they desperately needed food. Premier Zhou Enlai later thanked Prime Minister Pierre Trudeau, stating: "You gave us wheat when no one else would do so."[6]

Selling China that wheat was a landmark decision. Many Canadians concluded: "If we can trade with them, why not also have diplomatic relations?" By the mid-1960s, Canadian public opinion now supported closer relations. South of the border, the Americans, committed to a hard-line anti-communist policy of "isolating and containing" the PRC, were also starting to think about loosening that policy. Future US president Richard Nixon, foreshadowing his famous 1972 visit to Peking, said it was time to rethink relations with China. If Nixon, the consummate American anti-communist, was thinking about engaging with the PRC, so why not Canada?

In 1966, we were holding teach-ins at Canadian universities in support of diplomatic recognition. The business community saw opportunity ahead in a new China market. I was getting a steady stream of requests to share with others what I had seen in China. The change was palpable, yet the Canadian government was hesitating. Prime Minister Lester B. Pearson said: "Better to have peace with Washington than relations with Peking." He did not want to upset the Americans, who, in his opinion, were not ready to come to terms with the PRC, their sworn enemy since the beginning of the Korean War.

Then Pierre Elliott Trudeau arrived on the scene. He had been to China twice, in 1949 and 1960, and had co-authored a popular book about his second trip. As prime minister, he wanted to move Canada in a new direction, with less dependence on the Americans and a more assertive foreign policy that resonated with Canadian domestic interests. Unlike Pearson, he was prepared to recognize China right away. Trudeau later said: "We had waited too long. I knew it was time to bring China into the world community." In 1968, he announced that Canada intended to enter into negotiations with the PRC, and he instructed the Department of External Relations to prepare the necessary documents.

In 1970, after almost two years of negotiations, the two countries established diplomatic relations. This act was celebrated by both the Canadians and the Chinese, and also internationally, as a diplomatic achievement. Without Trudeau's intervention, recognition surely would have been delayed. Other countries, possibly even the United States, could have achieved it before Canada. The opening to China might have turned out differently, with Canada following behind a large pack led by the Americans, rather than Canada standing at the front, ahead of most Western countries.

A Fifty-Year History

This book describes how the Canadian government made China policy with ten stories that describe key bilateral decisions, beginning with Pierre Trudeau's recognition of China in 1970, and ending fifty years later with his son Justin's attempt to reset a struggling relationship with China. Using official documents, many of them closed, and drawing upon interviews with members of our government, we show how our China policy was made and implemented. We observe how we approached our counterparts in the Chinese Ministry of Foreign Affairs when making policy, their reaction to our initiatives, and what happened when relations struggled in the last decade.

Canada established a one-China policy, gave development assistance to Beijing, formulated a trade strategy, dealt with human rights, discussed important multilateral issues, and worked together with Chinese counterparts on a range of other issues. We can see how our government acted, and can identify some of the key individuals who shaped our China agenda.

Three narratives tell the story. First, and most important, this book looks at China policy through the eyes of our government. I interviewed five prime ministers, thirty-five ministers and heads of departments, ten foreign ministers, and all fifteen of our ambassadors to China. Over forty members of the Department of External Affairs in Ottawa – now called Global Affairs Canada – and its officers in the Beijing Embassy and the Shanghai Consulate made valuable contributions. The principal material in this book comes from those hundred plus interviews, and from the Department's detailed files that I viewed on a restricted basis.

The Department of External Affairs, whose name was changed several times, from "External Affairs" in the 1960s to "Global Affairs Canada" in 2015, carried out the negotiations for recognition in 1968, managed the Tiananmen crisis in 1989, organized the great Team Canada trade mission to Beijing in 1994, helped Stephen Harper to recast our China strategy in 2009, and took charge in 2020 of the Canadian response to China's more aggressive behaviour.[7]

A second narrative places the author within the book as a participant observer, first in 1965 in Beijing, and then as first secretary in our Beijing Embassy during the latter part of the Cultural Revolution. For a short time, I was a part of the structure and process of diplomacy. One learns how foreign service officers think and act, and one gains long-term access to those making the decisions and to the Department's files. Afterwards, I became a full-time academic observer of our relations with China. I was a professor of politics at York University in Toronto, lectured in a number of Chinese universities, administered an educational exchange with Jiangsu Province for the Ontario government, and participated in several

Canadian International Development Agency (CIDA) projects in China. Over the past twenty years, I trained thousands of Chinese officials, corporate executives, and educators in Canada and in China – teaching them about Canada. The challenge was to maintain objectivity and understanding while experiencing China from multiple perspectives. I visited China over sixty times and have been in almost every one of its thirty-one provinces. My observations about Canada's relations with China are recorded in a personal diary, from which there are excerpts in this book.

Over a thirty-year period, the Department connected with those of us in the China policy community through consultations, roundtables, and short-term secondments to the government. From 1973 to 2001, it appointed thirteen sinologists – China scholars like me – to serve as full-time foreign service officers in the Beijing Embassy for one- or two-year terms. I participated in trade strategy sessions in 1987, foreign policy roundtables to discuss sanctioning China in 1989–93, human rights consultations in 1995 and 1996, discussion of Prime Minister Harper's new China policy in 2008–10, consultations in Ottawa dealing with Beijing's policies in the Justin Trudeau period, and meetings and dinners that Canada arranged for visiting senior Chinese officials.

The third narrative comes from PRC sources. Important bilateral decisions required collaboration with our Chinese counterparts, for example, the creation of the CIDA aid program for China in 1981, the fifty-page 1987 China trade strategy, the 1994 Team Canada mission, and Prime Minister Harper's state visit in 2009. However, China's published data on relations with Canada are thin, and the files of the Chinese Ministry of Foreign Affairs (MFA), the Department's equivalent, are closed to both Canadian and Chinese researchers. Their officials rarely give out information about how they make policy, and there is no book written by any PRC scholar on the fifty-year history of relations with Canada.

Despite those limitations, this book presents a Chinese perspective on the bilateral relationship. Contacts made with Chinese officials in the 1970s provided access to MFA officials in Beijing, and with PRC diplomats who served in Canada in the years that followed. Their ministers and ambassadors have sought me out, and I them. Together, we talked about the collapse of international communism, discussed human rights and trade, the effects of American China policy, and had dinner conversations in Ottawa. Each of the stories in the book contains contributions from the Chinese side, especially the chapters about diplomatic recognition, Taiwan, trade strategy, the Tiananmen crisis, human rights, and the resetting of relations. In addition, the Department's files contain summaries of China's position on bilateral issues, details of what Chinese leaders have said during high-level visits, and voluminous reports by Canadian diplomats about their discussions with MFA counterparts.

As with all political histories, it is impossible to cover every part of a bilateral relationship. I have chosen the most representative decisions – those that have the best documentation and, I believe, have captured the story of our engagement with China.

The Main Observations

Relations with China are divided into three periods. The first period lasted twenty years, from diplomatic recognition in 1970 to the Tiananmen crisis of 1989. It is often referred to as the time when Canada helped China open up to the outside world. In 1987, Ambassador Yao Guang proclaimed to his Canadian counterpart: "We see a beautiful (*meihao*) future – a Golden Age with our relations." Ambassador Richard Gorham replied: "More has been accomplished in the past three years than in any other period since diplomatic relations were established."[8] After the Chinese army crushed the demonstrations at Tiananmen Square in 1989, relations changed. China's leaders did not respond positively to Canada's criticism of its actions, and Prime Minister Li Peng bluntly told Ambassador Drake: "We don't need you."[9] According to one Canadian ambassador, the killings at Tiananmen ended Canada's brief love affair with China: "The days of romanticism in our China policy are over. We have to be realists now."

The second period began when Jean Chrétien became prime minister, and both sides were re-examining post-Tiananmen relations. In 1994, he went to China with the largest trade delegation that

Canada had ever assembled. Called "Team Canada," it secured a record $8.5 billion in agreements. Chrétien was criticized for focusing on trade instead of human rights, but he said that, since he was not even able to tell the premier of Saskatchewan what to do, how could he make China's leaders change their policies? Relations settled down, and by the end of the decade, Premier Zhu Rongji said that Canada was "China's best friend." But the boost in trade was fading, and there was growing public pressure to hold China more accountable for its human rights practices and its invasive activities inside Canada. China, rapidly acquiring superpower status, also needed less from Canada.

Stephen Harper and the Conservatives launched the third period when they took power in 2006. The government changed course, treating Beijing as an adversary. China's leaders were almost apoplectic when Prime Minister Harper received the Dalai Lama in his office with a Tibetan flag on his desk, and when Parliament officially made the Dalai Lama an honorary Canadian citizen. Relations soured for the next two years, but in 2009, Harper reversed course and travelled to China in search of trade. Relations were still fragile when Justin Trudeau and the Liberals returned to office in 2015. Trudeau said he would restore full relations, but that did not happen. A hoped-for free trade agreement never materialized, and China's behaviour towards Canada became more aggressive. Then Canada detained Meng Wanzhou, the chief financial officer of the giant Huawei Corporation, at the request of the United States for possible extradition to America. Relations plummeted when the PRC retaliated and took two Canadians hostage, accusing them of espionage, sentenced another to death, and banned the import of several key Canadian agricultural commodities. By 2020, relations were at their lowest point in fifty years.

America has had a strong influence on Canadian China policy. In the 1960s, many Canadians viewed negotiating with China as a declaration of independence from the American policy of isolating and containing China. We established full diplomatic relations with China almost ten years before the Americans. China's leaders first claimed that we were acting as an American surrogate, but then

Beijing decided that "Canada had a somewhat independent for-eign policy." We liked to say that we were ahead of the Americans, but after the 1970s, we knew that America was China's prize, not Canada. Canada's fiction was that we stood on our own, separate from American policy, but that was never the case. China's fiction was to look the other way until it had a good reason to complain. That happened in 2017 when the United States unexpectedly put tariffs on Canadian exports and renegotiated the North American Free Trade Agreement (NAFTA). The United States inserted a clause that would give it veto power over any future comprehen-sive Canadian trade agreement with the PRC.

Canada was caught in a US-inspired trade war between the two superpowers that unravelled Canadian links with China. The PRC foreign minister, Wang Yi, visited Ottawa and spoke belligerently in front of the Canadian foreign minister. In 2018, the MFA increased its invective, saying that "Canada is a satellite of the United States." This more aggressive Chinese diplomacy, which emerged in the mid-2000s, was coined "wolf warrior diplomacy," named after a popular Rambo-style Chinese action film. South of the border, the Trump regime escalated its attacks on Canadian trade policy and imposed sanctions on Canada. The American economic security blanket, which had comfortably enveloped Canada for so many years, was now under threat and it would require a significant effort in the future to restore full relations with Canada's American ally. Then in 2018, the United States asked Canada to detain Meng Wanzhou, in Vancouver, for extradition to America. The PRC responded by taking two Cana-dians hostage, sentencing another to death, and banning imports of Canadian canola, pork, and beef, and relations between Can-ada and China plummeted. In 2021, after three long years, it was Washington that brokered the deal that released Meng and the two Canadian hostages.

Several individuals played a key role in shaping our China policy. While diplomacy and decision-making is a collective enterprise, a feature of this book is the focus on individual decision-makers, from prime ministers to foreign service officers, who made it happen. In several stories, an individual takes charge and makes an impact. Pierre Trudeau was the architect of our engagement with China. Joe Clark stepped in for Brian Mulroney to direct China policy in the post-Tiananmen period. Jean Chrétien "owned" China policy, and he went to China six times while he was prime minister. Stephen Harper took relations in a new direction by treating China as an opponent, while Justin Trudeau has borne the brunt of the most difficult period in our relations.

Several ministers took leading roles. Mitchell Sharp managed the negotiations for recognition and the establishment of the one-China policy in the early period; Barbara McDougall opposed closer relations in the 1990s; Michael Wilson's objective was to reopen the gates to trade; Lloyd Axworthy tried to hold China accountable on human rights; and Stockwell Day helped restore relations in 2009. We expected this leadership from prime ministers and ministers, but senior officers, such as Arthur Andrew and Howard Balloch, also made important contributions – Andrew in negotiations with Beijing in the 1970s and Balloch for our post-Tiananmen China policy. Senator Jack Austin helped to organize the 1994 Team Canada trade mission, and he advised Liberal governments for thirty years. Canada's fifteen ambassadors raised our profile in China, especially Arthur Menzies, Earl Drake, Fred Bild, Howard Balloch, and David Mulroney.

We have had failures as well as successes. Did Canada make the right decisions? As we dig more deeply into the bilateral relationship, we should acknowledge our failures. We thought that recognition was an achievement, yet it is possible to conclude that Canada was out-negotiated by the Chinese, had to abandon Taiwan, and was forced to accept Beijing's agenda. In 1976, Canada was roundly criticized for refusing to allow Taiwan to participate in the Montreal Olympics, an unpopular decision both inside Canada and internationally, since it put politics ahead of sport. For four years, Canada tried to sanction China for what it did at Tiananmen, but was unsuccessful in changing Beijing's behaviour. The Canadian government spent the 1990s searching for a viable human rights strategy, and after a decade essentially gave up.

Ottawa made trade a priority, but was unable to expand exports of our value-added goods or reduce our trade deficit with China. Canada tried to maintain a "helpful fixer" role with China in international affairs, but it brushed us off. We began as a pioneer and mentor to China and ended in a distinctly unbalanced relationship, with Beijing in command, taking Canadians hostage and banning our exports. Could we have pursued better strategic options?

China policy begins with trade and human rights. Trade was our first point of contact and today serves as the principal rationale for preserving links with China. Increasing Canadian economic links with China is one of the main themes in this book. We developed a strategy in the 1980s, sent large trade delegations to China in the 1990s, and attempted to establish a free trade agreement in the 2000s. The PRC is Canada's second largest national export market, and we benefit from imports of China's low-cost manufactured goods. By 2020, annual two-way trade reached over $100 billion and continued to rise, even when political relations had stumbled for several years.

Human rights are the other side of the bilateral coin. In this book, we see how Canada attempted to change China's human rights practices and how we have consistently failed. While distressed by China's suppression of individual freedoms, Canada nevertheless could not persuade China's leaders to change their policies. The twin themes of human rights and trade run together throughout the post-Tiananmen era. After 1989, we made rights a priority, but during the Chrétien period, trade was the principal focus. When the Conservatives took power in 2006, human rights briefly dominated, although in the recent period, trade re-emerged as Canada's principal objective. Canadians who want their government to act more decisively on human rights believe that our traders have had too much influence on the government's relationship with China. Traders, on the other hand, argue that good relations with China enhance trade and will bring Canadian values to China.

What does the book leave out? It contains limited information about recent events in Hong Kong, where 300,000 Canadian citizens are living under China's heavy shadow; consular matters; immigration; and China's links with the two million Canadian citizens of ethnic Chinese origin. The focus on national-level engagement also does not highlight the many provincial and local-level ties that we have with China. There is just a brief discussion of collaboration on environmental issues, ethnic policies, security concerns, educational linkages, and other people-to-people initiatives.

The focus is upon the domestic determinants of the bilateral relationship, rather than on how Canada and China interacted on international security matters. Canada's "Golden Age" in foreign relations was already passing when it helped China to join Western international institutions in the 1970s and 1980s, and its capacity to work with China on international issues has continued to recede. We were not a participant in the Six-Party Talks on Korea; have no real role to play in the South China Sea; cannot mediate between the Americans and the Chinese; have almost no voice in the security of Taiwan or Hong Kong; have lost our position on the United Nations Security Council; and fewer than 100 Canadians are involved today in peacekeeping, once Canada's pride. We have some influence and a modest role to play in certain areas, for example, global warming, nuclear disarmament, counterterrorism, refugee policy, and cyberwarfare, as well as in track-two diplomacy, where we have created useful Canadian links with Chinese officials over the past twenty-five years. However, we have become a marginal partner for China geopolitically, one that the PRC can bypass whenever it chooses.

Future Directions

Today Canada and China have an unequal, asymmetrical relationship. In the early years, we had the advantage. China could come to Canada and learn from us, and we brought our expertise to China. We helped it to enter international institutions, including the United Nations, the Asian Development Bank, and the World Bank. Relations then were asymmetrical in our favour. Now Canada is the subordinate partner, and we have to be clear about who we are: a smaller second-tier country, tied to the Americans, with declining leverage in international affairs. We had to come to terms with American dominance, and now it is our turn to do the same with China. Are we prepared to step back, swallow hard, and treat China like we do the Americans, deferring to a dominant partner with the power to control a large part of our relations? That may be a bitter pill, especially for those Canadians who cannot forget Tiananmen and for those who don't trust China.

It took a long time to adjust to the Americans, and some say we still have not got it right. Where to begin with China? Two areas catch our attention: trade and people-to-people links. After each crisis in the bilateral relationship, trade and people-to-people links continued almost unabated. With over $100 billion in two-way trade, close to 200,000 Chinese students in our schools and universities, two million Canadians of Chinese origin, and extensive travel by Canadians to the PRC, we must keep these avenues open.

Canadians want their government to act more decisively on human rights, but China does not respond to our criticism of its practices. One option is to engage China with low-cost initiatives that have a long-term perspective, hoping for liberal value change over time. Canada developed such programs in China through institution building, grassroots participation, and encouraging the development of civil society. We can have a small impact, but the impetus for value change comes from within a culture and society, and is not imported from abroad.

When China was "over there" and not yet showing up here, we did not pay it much attention. China is now in our farmlands, our oil fields, our schools, our Canadian ethnic Chinese communities and their media, and our corporations. We are aware of significant PRC encroachments upon Canadian sovereignty, penetration of our security and intelligence operations, and attempts to compromise our politicians and public servants. Now that China is "with us" and no longer remote, should we ban investment by Chinese state-owned enterprises because they have an in-house Communist Party cell inside them reporting directly to Beijing? Do we heighten our surveillance of Chinese activities that encroach on our sovereignty? We are confronted by a large authoritarian state that is looking for an edge wherever it can find one, and a civilization that will do what it can to promote its rebirth as a great power.[10]

Our decision-makers have to become more knowledgeable about China. One of our recent ambassadors to China said: "We urgently need to invest in China competence in Ottawa, where that commodity is alarmingly scarce. Future leaders in key departments, in the security agencies, and in the Canadian Forces need to be far more aware of how China works and how it thinks. That investment includes intensive Mandarin language training and the organization of special programs to help our foreign service officers learn how to manage China relations more effectively."[11]

Much of what passes for "public opinion" about the PRC is based on incomplete knowledge. The images that we have of China – a communist country with a different culture and an authoritarian government – need to be complemented by a deeper understanding of that culture and of the living conditions in that large over-populated country. We have to be better educated about China, with stronger reporting from our media and expanded people-to-people relations. China also needs to learn more about Canada. My graduate students in Beijing knew almost nothing about us. They said we were underpopulated, resource-rich, racist, and controlled by the Americans – that we have Niagara Falls, Banff, red maple leaves, blue skies, and not much else. Could they identify any important Canadians? Just Norman Bethune, Pierre Trudeau, Justin Bieber, and Celine Dion.

When I stepped off that train in Peking in 1965, Canadians knew little about China. In less than half a century, China has become a superpower competing with the Americans and asserting greater control over its bilateral partners. This astonishing hyper-growth has put tremendous pressure on our relationship, making us realize there is a substantial disjuncture between Canada and China. Today we are dealing with a party-state that is challenging in its needs and wants. In this book, we can see how far the two sides have travelled together, yet still remain apart, especially when China chooses to flex its new muscles with hostage taking and aggressive diplomacy. After the release of the hostages in the fall of 2021, Canada and China have to reset relations, and it will take some time to return to the friendlier days of the past. There is still much that we need to learn about each other if we want to preserve our bilateral relationship: China has to accept the responsibilities that accrue to its new superpower status, and Canada's challenge is to find a suitable pathway to maintain a partnership with China based on equity and mutual respect.

chapter two

Diplomatic Relations

In 1968, Prime Minister Pierre Trudeau decided to establish diplomatic relations with China. The negotiations took almost two years. The sticking point was what to do about Taiwan. The Canadian government did not want to sacrifice diplomatic relations with Taiwan in order to establish relations with China, but that is precisely what happened. Canada agreed there was only one China, the PRC, although it refused to acknowledge PRC sovereignty over Taiwan. Canada chose to "take note" of China's position, "neither challenging nor endorsing it." The final agreement was announced on October 13, 1970, and it was celebrated as a Canadian success story. However, less than two years later, US President Richard Nixon went to Peking. While full American recognition of the PRC did not actually occur until 1979, once Washington had engaged with Peking in 1972, Canada's moment of glory was already fading.

Why had Canada waited so long to recognize China? Since 1949, it had sought to recognize the PRC four times but had always backed away. American opposition and Canadian ambivalence were the principal deterrents. However, by the mid-1960s the context had changed. A majority of Canadians now favoured recognition. The Cold War was changing; China was facing a possible war with its former partner, the Soviet Union, and it needed new allies. The Americans were trapped in Vietnam and looking for a way out. That included a possible rethinking of the US policy of the isolation and containment of China.

Enter Prime Minister Pierre Trudeau, who had been to China twice, first in 1949 and again in 1960. He had co-authored a book in which he supported the recognition of the communist government of China, even *if its policies were unpalatable for most of the Western world. In May 1968, he announced that Canada intended to recognize the PRC "as soon as possible ... taking into account that there is a separate government in Taiwan." The two sides chose Stockholm for the negotiations. Each country was represented by able professional diplomats, the Canadians by Ambassadors Arthur Andrew and Margaret Meagher, and the PRC by Wang Dong, who was later appointed ambassador to Canada. The twenty sessions took twenty-one months. The Canadian negotiating team reported to Prime Minister Trudeau's foreign policy advisor, Ivan Head, and to his foreign affairs minister, Mitchell Sharp. Every document had to be approved by the Communist Party's nine-member Politburo and by Premier Zhou Enlai and Chairman Mao Zedong. When final agreement was reached, Mao said to Zhou: "We now have a friend in America's backyard."*

Not everyone agreed that recognition of China was a Canadian achievement. Ottawa was criticized for terminating diplomatic relations with Taiwan, in particular by the Conservative opposition. The Canadian negotiators were unable to settle the "practicalities" of recognition: protection of diplomats, trade, consular matters, settlement of claims, and immigration. The PRC refused to discuss these issues until agreement was reached on Taiwan, and it took three more years, until Prime Minister Trudeau made a state visit to China, for the two sides to settle those issues.

Canada had shown its independence from American policy, and for the moment it had become one of China's "best friends." By the end of the decade, however, the Americans had also recognized China, and the other Western countries had joined them. Canada then became just one of many "favoured" foreign petitioners in the newly opened Chinese court.

We now have a friend in America's backyard.
                                        – Mao Zedong to Zhou Enlai, October 1970

Prelude

It was May 1965, and I had arrived in Peking after a year of doctoral research in Moscow. I wanted to see whether the Chinese brand of communism was any better than that of its struggling Soviet "Elder Brother." Canada and China did not have diplomatic relations,[1] and we were on opposite sides of the Cold War. The two major communist countries, China and the Soviet Union, were preparing for armed conflict with each other, and the United States was caught up in an unwinnable war in Vietnam that was exposing its strategic vulnerability. A decade-long Cultural Revolution was about to change the face of China, where politics had taken command over daily life and Mao Zedong's words were everywhere. China had just become a nuclear power, and my hosts said with pride that China could now defend itself in any war, against either the Russians or the Americans.

In my diary I wrote:

> After a year in Moscow, China is a startling contrast. It's poor and loaded with ideology. Where are all the foreigners? My hosts don't know anything about Canada. Just Dr. Norman Bethune, who is celebrated by Chairman Mao for helping China in the 1930s. He's my lifeline. They are worried about the Russians and the Americans. They ask why we don't have relations. I tell them things may be changing, but I don't know what Ottawa has in mind.[2]

For almost twenty years, the United States, the dominant world power, had been carrying out a policy of "isolating and containing" China. In 1961, President John F. Kennedy briefly toyed with revising that policy; however, he backed off, saying that the time was not ripe. With the deepening split between China and the Soviet Union, and with America trapped in Vietnam, perhaps the United States could "play the China card" and detach China from the Soviet Bloc. President Lyndon Johnson flirted with the idea, but he was too preoccupied with the Vietnam War. In 1967, Richard Nixon, soon to become the thirty-seventh president, unexpectedly said that America's China policy needed a reset, and a growing number of Americans were ready to drop the isolation, but keep the containment of China.[3] Did that foreshadow possible American recognition of the PRC and its admission to the United Nations? The United States was not prepared for such big steps since it had to overcome many obstacles: what to do about Taiwan, the opposition of the powerful American anti-China lobby, China's involvement as an opponent in the Vietnam War, and an American public that was not ready to accept state-to-state relations with its Cold War enemy.

Canada did not have those concerns. It had no imperialist history in China, no strategic commitment to Taiwan, no troops in Vietnam, no Canadian anti-China lobby, and no urgent pressure to do something about containing China. Canada had sought four times to establish relations, in 1950, 1955, 1958, and 1964, and each time had failed. The conventional explanation was that Canada always yielded to American pressure not to engage with the PRC, but Canada also held back due to domestic opposition to communism and because of Canadian indifference – China just was not that important to Canada. Until the large 1961 wheat sale, our links with China were stuck on the back burner. Then Canadians began to wonder, if we were now selling China hundreds of millions of dollars of grain, why not also have diplomatic relations.[4]

The Department was reading the signs carefully. A 1964 Gallup poll reported that more than half of Canadians advocated recognition, up from 32 per cent in 1959. Paul Martin Sr., the foreign minister, said: "The increasing ostracism of Communist China from the world community may be self-defeating and a potential threat to international stability." If not diplomatic relations, then why not admission to the United Nations? Even John Diefenbaker, the former leader of the Conservative opposition and a fierce anti-communist, said: "You cannot forever deny the existence of a nation of so many millions of people if the United Nations is to be the institution representative of all nations. The time has come when fullest consideration should be given to this question." Former minister of trade, Alvin Hamilton, who had negotiated the large 1961 wheat sale to China, met with Premier Zhou Enlai, who told him that China wanted comprehensive relations with countries like Canada, not just a relationship through trade.[5]

In mid-1964, Vice Premier Chen Yi, in an interview with the Canadian Broadcasting Corporation (CBC), said China was ready to develop "friendly relations" with other countries:

CBC: Mr. Vice Premier, the world at large knows little about your country, and the people of China do not have much contact with the world at large. How long do you think it will be before you can confidently open up your country to more visitors?

CHEN YI: There has never been a question of a lack of confidence on the part of China. The countries that lack confidence are those that hinder their own people from coming into contact with the realities of New China.

CBC: Have you a word for the Canadian people?

CHEN YI: I would like to take this opportunity to extend my greetings to Canada. The Chinese people have always been friendly towards the people of other countries, and the same holds true for the Canadian people. We hope that the friendship between the peoples of Canada and China will develop further. *It will be a good thing if relations between China and Canada could be normalized.* (emphasis added)

France and the PRC had established diplomatic relations at the beginning of 1964. That was a shock for those who supported the isolation and containment of China, especially for the Americans. Secretary of State Dean Rusk worried there could be a chain reaction, with other countries "getting on the French bandwagon." Belgium and Italy had recently established trade offices in Peking, and the pressure was mounting at the United Nations to admit the PRC as a member. The obstacle was what to do about Taiwan, which occupied the China seat at the United Nations. Talking with President Johnson in Washington, former trade minister Alvin Hamilton suggested that trade could lead to better ties with China. Hamilton told Johnson: "The quickest way to achieve peace with your enemies is to start trading with them – why not end the American trade embargo with China?"[6]

In Canada, the Department of External Affairs was putting together scenarios for a possible engagement with China, either by establishing diplomatic relations, admitting it to the United Nations, or creating trade offices in both countries.

We got the message. We had to see what was possible. Were the Chinese talking friendship, but didn't really mean it? Were the Americans ready to step back and let us connect with the PRC? Was Prime Minister Pearson, who had said, "Surely peace with Washington is more important than praise in Peking," willing to risk American anger and possible economic retaliation against Canada?

China might be ready for closer ties, and the Americans might not impose economic sanctions if Canada acted. Opening a trade office in China seemed to be a possibility, and

Canada explored the idea of establishing a trade office in China, similar to what the Belgians and Italians had done. But staff in trade offices abroad did not possess diplomatic immunity, so how could Canada provide protection for them? Canada was doing well enough with its wheat sales to China, which amounted to several hundred million dollars a year, so did Canada really need an office in Peking, and did China need one in Ottawa? The Americans objected, because a trade office in Ottawa would give Communist China a base from which it could conduct intelligence operations in North America, and didn't Canada have similar concerns?

In the fall of 1965, I returned home. Back in Canada, change was in the wind. Several universities were holding seminars and conferences about China, and the media were suggesting it was time to engage with Peking. My hosts back in Peking had told me that China wanted to have closer relations with us. Was this an opportunity for Canada, and was the PRC ready to follow up on its 1964 French initiative and discuss possible diplomatic links with Canada?

In my diary I wrote:

> Back home. Everyone is asking about China. The *Globe and Mail* says we should connect with them. Don't wait for the Americans. They've gone off track with the Vietnam War. Better to have relations, even if we don't have that much in common right now. Need to be careful. It's a communist country and our links are fragile.

In 1966, Foreign Minister Martin decided that Canada's best course for engaging with China lay in admitting it to the United Nations. He proposed that Canada should support a "two-China" policy so that both the PRC and Taiwan could be members of the United Nations. Canadian recognition could likely follow. Admitting the PRC required overcoming several major hurdles: Were there enough votes in the United Nations to accept the PRC as a member, and was China ready to join? If the PRC were admitted, what would happen to Taiwan, which also called itself "China?" The UN vote was the key, and its members had two options: either to vote for admission using the "Albanian Resolution," which required a simple majority, or to vote for the "Important Question Resolution," where admission would require a two-thirds majority. The United States insisted that the PRC's admission was an "Important Question," knowing that the PRC did not yet have the votes of two-thirds of the UN members. Those supporting the PRC said it was only a matter of time before a simple majority of members would be prepared to vote for its admission using the Albanian Resolution.[7]

The Americans were against having the PRC join the United Nations, where it would occupy the China seat on the Security Council and could veto American-sponsored resolutions. They mounted an intense campaign to stop Canada from supporting the PRC's admission. Secretary of State Dean Rusk, a dedicated anti-communist, was determined that Canada should wait until the Vietnam War had ended, since China was a Cold War opponent and supported the Vietnamese communists.

Martin did not wait. In 1966, Canada surprised the Americans by abstaining on the Albanian Resolution, rather than opposing it. This stand was called "the first substantive change in Canada's China policy since 1949."[8] However, the Albanian Resolution did not win a simple majority of the votes cast because of strong American arm-twisting of UN members to vote against China. The motion was defeated, and the PRC was not admitted. Ottawa was discouraged by the outcome, since its efforts to admit China had apparently reached a dead end. The admissions option was put aside until the Canadians began negotiations for diplomatic recognition in 1968.

Enter Pierre Trudeau

Pierre Trudeau was Martin's parliamentary secretary, and he joined the Canadian delegation for the 1966 UN vote. The experience convinced him that diplomatic recognition of China was the best way to proceed. He recalled:

> If we were going to move forward I did not think the United Nations was the way to go. We needed to control the situation. Recognition was in the Liberal Party platform. If we could make the proper contact with

Peking, we had to take that road. It would be harder for the Americans
to stop us. Look, De Gaulle and the French did it. Why not Canada?

Pierre Trudeau was no stranger to China, having been there in 1949
and again in 1960. His first trip in 1945 had made a big impression
on the thirty-year-old Trudeau. He felt China would eventually take
its place in the world as a great power. After his return to Canada, he
supported the recognition of the new communist government, even
if its policies were unpalatable for much of the Western world. Following his second trip in 1960, he co-authored a popular book with
Jacques Hébert, *Two Innocents in Red China*, in which he wrote: "The
two-China policy is based on ignorance of the Chinese mentality."
American policy supporting Taiwan "was based only on a question of
prestige." China could afford to wait: "Time is on its side and China is
in no hurry." Trudeau was convinced that it was in the world's interest
to bring China out of its isolation as soon as it was possible to do so.[9]

Trudeau took over as the new leader of the Liberal Party, and
after the 1968 election he became prime minister. In contrast to
Lester Pearson, his predecessor, Trudeau cultivated an image of
change, signalling a departure from policies of the past. He felt
that Canada was too closely aligned with American interests.
Under Trudeau, improved relations with the PRC would become
an example of Canadian emancipation from American influence.
To burnish his foreign policy credentials, he held small meetings
at his residence to talk about international issues. Ivan Head, who
was his foreign policy advisor, and a less dramatic Canadian version of Henry Kissinger, recalled:

> We invited a mix of people from in and out of Ottawa, politicians,
> mainly Liberals, and civil servants. Much of the content of the govern-
> ment's 1970 foreign policy review came from these discussions. We
> were ready to strike a new course for Canada. We ate sandwiches and
> chocolate bars, and just kept talking. We talked about China policy, and
> about our relations with the Americans.

Ivan Head mirrored Trudeau's thinking, and he was the link
between the prime minister and the Department of External Affairs.

There had never been anyone quite like Head, and the senior mandarins in the Department were unnerved. Their discomfort suited Trudeau, who was critical of the Department. He later said, in conversation: "It wasn't the 1950s anymore. Foreign affairs could no longer be the preserve of a small elite. If we were going to change things, we had to change how our diplomats worked. Look how we were mishandling our China policy." The installation of Head as his foreign policy advisor was intended to put the Department on notice that both the content of policy and the decision-making process itself were up for review. In addition, the new foreign minister, Mitchell Sharp, a former public servant *par excellence*, could be counted on to follow the wishes of his leader and the Office of the Prime Minister (PMO). With the support of these two men, Trudeau was well positioned to carry out his plans.

What did the Department think of the new direction in foreign policymaking? One deputy minister later said: "Frankly, at the beginning I was upset. How could they do this to Canada's crown jewel? People said we were the best in the world. How was I going to work with this Ivan Head?" That was in 1968. A few years later, however, he admitted: "It wasn't that bad. We learned to live with each other, at least I did. Not sure about some of my other colleagues." Head was critical of the slow progress made on the China file. "It had been several years, and where were we? A majority of Canadians were saying it was time to recognize China. The Department had all those 'mish kids' [the children of Canadian missionaries born in China], and it had all that diplomatic expertise, and we couldn't move forward."

The PRC was not making it easy for Canada. In mid-1966, Mao Zedong launched the Cultural Revolution, and China was soon wracked in violence and anti-foreignism. The world was transfixed by the spectacle of young Red Guards attacking Party officials, shutting down government offices and universities, and destroying almost anything of traditional value. Foreigners were a particular target. The *Globe and Mail* reported that "a Chinese mob" smashed its car and attacked its three occupants outside the Ministry of Foreign Affairs in Beijing: "For almost 45 minutes they pummeled our car and shouted anti-Soviet and anti-imperialist slogans at us. Then a new group arrived, and with clubs and bars they began to pound the car. They smashed the windshield, the rear window, bashed in the roof ... Then they began to spit on us."[10]

At the British Mission, a gigantic crowd formed. "They were wielding crowbars, mattocks, hammers, poles and other heavy weapons. Soon a large part of the building was on fire. The mob just on the other side of the thin wooden windows hammered fiercely on them, and shouted in Chinese, "*Sha! Sha!* (Kill! Kill!)." They also attacked the embassies of Indonesia, Mongolia, India, and the Soviet Union, ignoring their diplomatic status. The Reuters correspondent, Anthony Grey, was put under house arrest in solitary confinement and kept imprisoned for over two years.[11]

China had regressed. At the United Nations, the same Chen Yi, who had preached friendship and openness to Canada a year earlier, now spoke of violence and imminent conflict between China and the West. China had shut down and was turning nasty. Red Guards had immobilized the Chinese Ministry of Foreign Affairs: the phone rang in the ministry, but no one was answering. How could Canada get any response if it wanted to talk to China about recognition? Did the PRC, so wrapped up in its internal crisis, have time to think about foreign relations? Did it have any inkling about Trudeau's intentions? Aside from a recently arrived New China News Agency (NCNA) correspondent, whom did the PRC have in Canada to report authoritatively back to Beijing?[12] The Department now felt that, given all those questions, the time was not right to pursue recognition and Canada needed to wait for China to reopen. One Department official later said: "China was a black hole. We didn't know what was going on there, and we figured that China was too busy with other matters to try to learn more about us."

In mid-1968, Trudeau acted. He later said: "I decided Canada wasn't going to wait any longer for either the Chinese or for the Department to do something." Recognition was in the Liberal Party platform, and it had popular support, although, according to Trudeau, "China would probably say no unless Canada agreed to break relations with Taiwan. We wouldn't do that."

A few days later Trudeau gave more details:

The present situation, in which a government which represents a quarter of the world's population is diplomatically isolated even from countries with which it is actively trading, is obviously unsatisfactory. I would be in favour of any measures, including recognition on suitable terms, which can intensify the contacts between our two countries, normalize our relations and contribute to international order and stability.

On May 20, he stated:

The China which the United Nations Charter speaks of is the PRC. That is the China we will recognize ... I am saying now it is time not to continue doing it through the back door. Instead, we should try the front door.

A few days later, he said:

I feel our hands are free. I feel that there are two facts of life in international politics in this particular area, the fact there is a government in Peking which represents 700 or 800 million people, and the government of Taipei [Taiwan] which represents – what is it, 10, 12, or 14 million people? These are two facts. Now what will happen, what Peking will answer me, how Taiwan will react, we will see.

Trudeau said China was "both a colossus and a conundrum, about which we have incomplete information, which opens an area of unpredictability." China must become a member of the world community because "many of the major world issues will not be resolved completely or in any lasting way, unless, and until an accommodation has been reached with the Chinese nation." He then announced that Canada intended to recognize the PRC as soon as possible:

We shall be looking at our policy in relation to China in the context of a new interest in Pacific affairs generally. Because of past preoccupations with Atlantic and European affairs, we have tended to overlook the reality that Canada is a Pacific country too. Canada has long advocated a positive approach to mainland China and its inclusion in the world community. We have an economic interest in trade with China – no doubt shared by others – and a political interest in preventing tension between China and its neighbours, but especially between China and the United States.

Our aim will be to recognize the People's Republic of China government as soon as possible and to enable that government to occupy the seat of China in the United Nations, taking into account that there is a separate government in Taiwan. (emphasis added)[13]

Preparing for Recognition

For the previous one and a half years, China had withdrawn in inner turmoil from the rest of the world. It ignored diplomatic conventions and immunities by humiliating foreign diplomats and journalists in Peking. Indulging in acts of anti-foreignism and isolating itself from the outside world in a revolutionary posture, the PRC did not appear to be a candidate for the normalization of relations. It was conceivable that Peking would not respond to the Trudeau initiative, thus putting Canada in the embarrassing situation of unilaterally recognizing an unwilling partner.

Since past attempts at establishing relations had come to grief, why would Canada expect that this latest venture would succeed? The government had considered recognition at least four times since 1949, and each time the initiative failed. Canada had given up on joint trade offices and been rebuffed at the United Nations over the admission issue. Was the time ripe for Canada to embark on a China policy that differed sharply from that of its American neighbour? Canada's abstention on, rather than rejection of, the Albanian Resolution had elicited strong criticism from US State Department officials, especially from Dean Rusk. Would Trudeau's attempt at accommodation with China, in the midst of the Vietnam War, provoke an angry American reaction and the imposition of economic sanctions against Canada?

For many Canadians caught up in the Cold War, the establishment of diplomatic relations was issuing a licence for spying and subversion. The Chinese were communists, and like their Soviet "Elder Brother," they were expected to use their diplomatic missions to promote revolution abroad. Equally important, the PRC would have a golden opportunity to infiltrate the Canadian ethnic Chinese communities. Those communities largely supported the Republic of China (ROC, also called Taiwan) and were generally apolitical on other issues. With the establishment of a Chinese embassy in Ottawa, that situation might easily change, and the ethnic Chinese communities in Canada could become fifth columns for communist revolutionary work in North America.

Most important was Trudeau's instruction: "*taking into account the fact that there is a separate government in Taiwan.*" Was Canada formulating a "two-China policy" or a "one-China, one-Taiwan policy?" The PRC was insisting on a "one-China policy," and it adamantly opposed any arrangement that gave official diplomatic status to relations with Taiwan, which continued to call itself the Republic of China. If so, prospects for any PRC agreement were gloomy at best, because Peking soon made it clear that "taking into account the fact that there is a separate government in Taiwan" was the key sentence in Trudeau's speech, and that China would be closely watching how Canada intended to interpret it.

The Department later claimed that it never received detailed direction from above as to how it should interpret Trudeau's qualification about Taiwan. Indeed, had Trudeau consulted the Department before making this statement, it would have recommended against seeking relations at that time. The Cultural Revolution was creating political chaos inside China, and Canada's anticipated point of contact, the Ministry of Foreign Affairs, was under attack from Red Guards and was essentially immobilized. The Department felt it was better to wait until China got its house in order. One official said: "Maybe the Far Eastern Division and the mish kids were pushing for recognition, but others in Ottawa were less enthusiastic. The trade group was hesitating, and the security people were very concerned. Not everyone was on board."

The Department was entrusted with the difficult task of taking what appeared to be a "one-China, one-Taiwan" policy and repackaging it into a "one-China" policy without losing credibility in the process. That it managed eventually to do so was a testimony to its skill at developing a political formula and negotiating plan that enabled Canada to "derecognize" Taiwan without losing too much Canadian face. Trudeau was the catalyst, the one person able to make the dramatic act that would change Canadian China policy, but it was the Department he was criticizing that provided the necessary expertise to make it happen.

Well before Trudeau's May 1968 speech, the Department had been collecting material for a general review of China policy. Reviews on potential recognition, done between 1963 and 1966, were available in the Department's files. Several of its members had lived in China before 1949 and had special knowledge of China, for example, "mish kids" such as Ralph Collins, Jack Maybee, Chester Ronning, John Small, Arthur Menzies, and Robert Edmonds. In June, the Department prepared a memorandum for Foreign Minister Sharp, listing the various options open to Canada and assessing the legal and practical implications of each one. Based on the experience of other countries, it was reasonable to assume that it would not be possible for Canada to have diplomatic relations with both the PRC and Taiwan.

Asked whether Canada intended to follow the course taken by General Charles de Gaulle in 1964, when France had recognized "Red China" and ended diplomatic relations with Taiwan, Sharp replied that, once France recognized the PRC, Taiwan had simply withdrawn its ambassador and gone home, and France did not have to commit to a "one-China" policy, making recognition of the PRC an easy task. When he was asked if that could also be Canada's strategy, Sharp replied: "I hope we can bring about a situation in which the existence of a separate government in Taiwan is recognized, and that we can at the same time accept that the government of the PRC is effectively in control of the mainland area."

Did Sharp expect opposition from the American authorities? He replied that, shortly after his appointment, he had met with Secretary Rusk, who had strongly opposed any Canadian attempt at engagement with China. "I wanted to acquaint Secretary Rusk with our plans to review these patterns, and quite explicitly, so there would be no misunderstanding." Sharp noted that the American position on China was becoming more flexible, with a discernible inching towards a possible one-China, one-Taiwan policy.

In Washington, Assistant Secretary of State William Bundy called in the Canadian ambassador, and told him that while Canada's policy was for Canada to decide, Washington wanted to make Ottawa aware of the problems that would occur if Canada moved towards recognition. Unlike the French experience, after establishing relations with Peking, Canada would have to force Taiwan (the ROC) out of Ottawa. Bundy emphasized the importance of supporting Taiwan for American prestige. "We have to prevent Taiwan from falling into the hands of the communists." He also spoke of the unfortunate effects that recognition would have for the ongoing Vietnam peace negotiations, since recognition would increase Peking's influence at talks in Hanoi and Paris, and would strengthen Hanoi's intransigence. Bundy expressed US concern that recognition would upset the political-strategic balance in the Asia-Pacific region, not only because it undermined the security of the ROC but also because it would have an unsettling effect on China's neighbours, especially Japan.

According to Bundy, if there was any change in US relations with the PRC, it could not be at the expense of Taiwan. That was the official US position and reflected American public opinion at the time. Canada's "America watchers" in the Washington Embassy, and in Ottawa, cautioned the Department not to underestimate the possibility of a punitive US response to Canada. While a growing number of Americans were prepared to accept some form of engagement with China as a "necessary evil," they were not willing to sacrifice Taiwan. One would expect a vigorous American official reaction to any Canadian negotiations with China that derecognized the ROC.

In the first week of July, the Department submitted a draft of its latest China Policy Review, now referred to as the "Black Book," to Foreign Minister Sharp, and to senior officials in the Departments of Finance and Industry, Trade and Commerce (ITC). By August, the final version was sent to Ivan Head, the PMO, the

Privy Council Office (PCO), the prime minister, and all members of Cabinet. The document assumed that relations with Taiwan would probably change, but it made no specific recommendations regarding the nature of this change, and it was expected that Cabinet would consider the document in September, although it then waited until December. One can suggest several reasons for the three-month delay. The Department of Finance was raising objections to the proposed new China initiative because it paid insufficient attention to economic factors, in particular, to the threat of American economic retaliation. Also, the Department was still searching for a formula that could solve the PRC-Taiwan dual recognition problem. Behind the scenes, Canada was trying to gauge China's reaction to Trudeau's announcement, but it had not received any response from Peking.

The Wheat Board decided that recognition would protect Canadian wheat sales to China and stimulate further exports. It also wanted to continue selling grain to Taiwan, although if Taiwan had to be sacrificed to appease the PRC and if Canada had to lose the Taiwan grain market, so be it. Since 1961, the Board had been responsible for the sale of up to several hundred million dollars of grain annually to the PRC, as well as sales to Taiwan. It preferred to keep its delicate trading operation with China separate from the equally sensitive political operation carried out by Ottawa. The Department pointed out: "We talked with the Board's representatives before they left for China, and this was done informally, at the deputy minister level."

What about American economic retaliation? The Departments of Finance and Industry, Trade and Commerce pointed to overland oil imports, balance of payment guidelines, and the interest equalization tax – all areas in which Canada was receiving preferential treatment from the Americans. Congress could pass legislation limiting Canadian imports, and the Americans could also reduce defence purchasing contracts from Canada. However, these threats seemed to have lessened. Canadians were reminded that Washington had not punished Canada for continuing to trade with Cuba after the United States had placed an embargo on trade with Cuba's new communist government.

By the fall of 1968, Sharp said Canada would recognize Peking as the only government of China without accepting its territorial claims over areas in which it did not exercise jurisdiction. At the same time, the government was prepared to say that Canada considered it desirable and necessary to deal with whoever controlled Taiwan for matters concerning the island. Canada would take the position that such relations were not intended to constitute recognition of Taiwan as an independent state or to imply any other position as to the status of that "territory." That strategy also envisaged the possibility that Canada might permit representatives of the Taiwan government to have a trade mission in Canada, if they chose to do so, to facilitate Canadian dealings with Taiwan on matters of mutual interest. This constituted *de facto* relations with Taiwan, but not *de jure* (full diplomatic) recognition.[14]

The proposal to seek recognition was submitted to the Cabinet Committee on External Affairs and Defence in December 1968, and it was approved by Cabinet on January 27, 1969. It stated that Canada would not make any commitment to Peking that prevented Canadian recognition of an independent state of Taiwan. The Taiwan ambassador called on the Canadian Foreign Minister on the same day. Sharp outlined the basic thrust of Canada's thinking. When the ambassador declared that Canada's move would represent the failure of his mission in Ottawa, Sharp told him that the Canadian decision "in no way reflected upon the Ambassador's distinguished service in Canada."

The first stage of implementing the prime minister's statement was now complete. There was sufficient support from senior government officials, and the three major political parties were in favour of recognition, although a portion of the Conservative Party, led by John Diefenbaker, was suspicious of any formula that sacrificed Taiwan. The government had clarified its position on Taiwan and was cautiously optimistic that Canada might be able to recognize the PRC without giving up its official relations with Taiwan, or alienating its American neighbour. Now it was up to the Canadians to persuade the Chinese to meet with them to see if the two sides could reach an agreement.

Negotiating in Stockholm

Peking had not responded to Trudeau's announcement for six months, and Trudeau was asked if he intended to abandon the attempt. He responded: "I told the media we could wait, the Chinese have a reputation for patience, and I was in no hurry." The Department felt that Peking was not responding because of the Cultural Revolution, and its preparation for possible armed conflict with the Soviet Union. The Chinese Foreign Ministry later gave a different, if not entirely convincing explanation:

> Our government was definitely interested in meeting with the Canadians. We did not reply because Canada did not follow up the May statement by Trudeau. We were canvassing all our posts abroad to see if they had been approached by Canada; they had not, so we were waiting and wondering why there was no follow up from Canada.[15]

In the end, Robert Edmonds, counsellor in the Canadian Embassy in Stockholm, found a channel of communication with the PRC. Both Canada and China had diplomatic missions in Stockholm, and the Department decided that would be the best place to negotiate with the PRC. According to Edmonds, "the Swedes could be counted on to be benevolently disposed towards our initiative; and secondly, Stockholm was sufficiently removed from the international media centres to escape the glare of constant press scrutiny." The Canadian ambassador to Sweden, Arthur Andrew, had substantial negotiating experience, and Edmonds, a mish kid, spoke Chinese. But could Canada make the initial contact in the Chinese Embassy "when Canadian diplomats are forbidden to communicate with diplomats from any country with whom they do not have relations"?[16]

Edmonds finally managed to connect with the senior political officer from the PRC Embassy at a reception in Stockholm, and he invited him to see a documentary about Norman Bethune in a private showing at Edmond's house. The PRC political officer accepted, watched the film, and said: "Chairman Mao has proclaimed Canada's Dr. Bethune as a great hero for the Chinese people." Once again, Norman Bethune had come to Canada's rescue. The Embassy reported to Ottawa that it had succeeded in establishing contact with the PRC, but Edmonds said that, oddly, there was complete silence from headquarters for another two months.

Why the continuing delay on the Canadian side? The Chinese had made no indication that they were ready to negotiate, and the Department later said: "We could not be seen as being too eager. If Peking didn't respond, we had to wait. We were not in a hurry." The PMO also thought it was better to wait until after the American presidential elections and the inauguration of a new US president in January 1969: "Then the American position would be clearer, and then Peking might respond."

Edmonds said:

> The Embassy had no idea as to the state of play in Ottawa. We knew it had gone to Cabinet and we just waited. Then a telegram from External Affairs suddenly arrived in Stockholm on February 4.
>
> The purport of our telegraphic instructions was that the Embassy should contact the Chinese Embassy forthwith to apprise them of the Canadian government's intention to enter into negotiations about mutual recognition and the establishment of diplomatic relations, and to advise them of our flexibility as to how and where the substantive discussions should be conducted, although Stockholm, as a venue, would be acceptable.

Ottawa instructed Ambassador Andrew to call upon his Chinese counterpart and propose talks. The Canadian Embassy in Washington was instructed to tell the State Department that Canada was ready to proceed with negotiations with China, and reassure the Americans that, even if Canada might ultimately break diplomatic relations with Taiwan as the price for establishing relations, it planned to maintain *de facto* relations with the island. Ottawa said it would break off discussions with Peking if Canada was forced to sever ties with Taiwan, and it would also stop the negotiations if Peking insisted that Canada had to endorse the PRC's claim to sovereignty over Taiwan. The Canadian intention was to refrain from expressing any position on

Taiwan, arguing that this issue was an internal Chinese matter and not a condition for recognition.

In the House, John Diefenbaker asked the government "whether it intended to carry out the undertaking the Prime Minister gave in May of 1968." He noted that the prime minister had said Canada would not end relations with Taiwan as a price for recognition. "What I am asking the Government is, are they going to keep the undertaking that was given by both the Prime Minister and the Secretary of State for External Affairs (the Foreign Minister) that there would be no breaking of relations with Taiwan as a condition of the recognition of Communist China?" Sharp replied: "The question, which is in issue, of course, is who speaks for the government of China? The question is which government of China do we recognize?" Pressed by Diefenbaker to be more specific, Sharp admitted: "Relations between Taipei and Canada will, of course, be affected, since the government of Taiwan does claim jurisdiction over the whole of China, and we cannot have two conflicting authorities."

A few days later, Sharp added:

> I doubt very much that the Canadian Government would recognize or challenge the sovereignty of Peking over Formosa [Taiwan]. That is a matter of dispute. When we recognize other countries, we do not necessarily recognize all their territorial claims or challenge them.
>
> The Government's policy with respect to the recognition of China has been expressed by the Prime Minister and myself in recent days. *That is our policy and if it varies in any respect from what has been said previously, it varies.* (emphasis added)

The Canadian shift from a "two-China–" or a "one-China, one-Taiwan policy" to a "one-China policy" had just become part of the public record. Whether this admission would now be enough to persuade the PRC to enter into serious negotiations remained to be seen.

The PRC was in the midst of appointing a new ambassador to Stockholm. Ottawa instructed Andrew to contact the PRC chargé d'affaires to arrange a meeting. However, he turned out to be unexpectedly elusive, and the Embassy tried several times to establish contact without getting a reply. Apparently the chargé was waiting for guidance from Peking. After several days, Canada chose not to wait any longer, and Sharp announced that Canada was proposing that the two countries begin negotiations to establish diplomatic relations. Finally, on February 19, the chargé called to arrange a meeting with the Canadian ambassador.

The first session was held on February 21, 1969, lasted forty-five minutes, and was extremely cordial. Following some talk about the weather and after tea was poured, Ambassador Andrew informed the Chinese chargé that the Canadian government wished to meet the PRC at a convenient time and place to discuss mutual recognition and an exchange of ambassadors. During the discussions, Andrew hoped they could explore the possibilities of concluding consular and trade agreements, as well as other areas in which relations might be developed.

The chargé immediately informed the Canadian side of China's "Three Constant Principles" on which the PRC would agree to establish diplomatic relations with all foreign countries:

1. A government seeking relations with China must recognize the central People's government as the sole and lawful government of the Chinese people;
2. A government which wishes to have relations with China must recognize that Taiwan is an inalienable part of Chinese territory and, in accordance with this principle, must sever all kinds of relationships with the "Chiang Kai-shek gang";
3. A government seeking relations with China must give support to the restoration of the rightful place and legitimate rights in the United Nations of the PRC, and no longer give any backing to so-called representatives of Chiang Kai-shek in any organ of this international body.

The Canadian team considered that the "Three Constant Principles" were an expression of the PRC's general position, rather than a red-line precondition for further discussion. Agreement on the first and third principles was in the realm of possibility, but the second one, which required Canada to agree that Taiwan was "an inalienable part of Chinese territory," was definitely unacceptable. Also, Canada first wanted to discuss "the practicalities of recognition," that is, consular matters, privileges and rights of diplomats, compensation for properties confiscated by Beijing after 1949, questions of dual citizenship, immigration, family reunification, trade, and civil air agreements. The Department pointed out:

> That was standard operating procedure when we established relations with new states after World War Two, and into the 1960s. We thought that was the correct strategy for talking with China. After what had just happened to Anthony Grey and the foreign diplomats in Beijing in 1967, we needed to be reassured that our diplomats would be protected. As for "our practicalities versus their principles," that did catch us by surprise. We had assumed, based on the more than one hundred US-PRC talks in Warsaw since 1956, that China never began negotiations with a statement of principles, tipping its hand so directly. We expected that it would always hold back to see what its opponent had to say, and wait for the discussion to unfold.

Ambassador Andrew talked about his first encounters with the Chinese side:

> When we finally met we were the *demandeur*. According to diplomatic practice, the *demandeur* speaks first. Once we had said our piece, the Chinese immediately put forth their Three Principles. They wanted to start the negotiations right then. That was unexpected. We knew from the American experience in the Warsaw talks that the Chinese had a special negotiating style. That was never the case with us. The Department just followed its basic procedures for diplomatic negotiations. We did not think they were a "different breed of cat" – that ordinary rules did not apply for them. If there was a difference between Chinese and other negotiating behaviours, it may have had to do with style, rather than substance.
>
> As someone trained in the Department, I felt confident I could handle any sort of negotiation. Of course, these negotiations were special. We were well briefed from the material in the Black Book.[17]

The six-week delay between the first meeting on February 21 and the second on April 3 raised speculation that Canada had encountered Chinese indifference. The *Washington Post* reported on March 7, 1969: "The Peking Government had shown itself cold to Canadian overtures looking to the recognition of Communist China. After a first meeting between Canadian Julian [*sic*] Andrew and Chinese Embassy officials, Robert Edmonds, Counsellor of the Canadian Embassy remarked, 'We were not talking on the same wave-length. The stumbling block is understood to be Canada's relationship with Taiwan ... There can be no compromise on this issue.'" In the House, Sharp was asked to comment on the negotiations; however, he could only report that the two sides had met and that they would continue to do so.

Several possible explanations were put forward to account for the slow Chinese response. Decisions of this importance had to be referred to Premier Zhou Enlai personally, and he had his hands full with more urgent matters: the Cultural Revolution, possible armed conflict with the Soviet Union, and preparations for the critical Ninth Communist Party Congress in 1969. Other explanations were of a tactical nature, for example, the PRC did not wish to be too eager, or it felt Canada had committed itself and it was in China's interest to delay as long as possible to gain a better bargaining position. There was speculation that Peking thought Canada was acting as an American surrogate, so China wanted a delay to get a better picture of Canada's real motives, to see if Canada was negotiating on America's behalf. The Italians and Belgians were also interested in establishing diplomatic relations with China, and it was possible that Peking was waiting to see what those countries had to offer before entering into substantive discussions with Canada. The MFA later provided more details, drawing on information from its closed files:

Yes, our Ministry of Foreign Affairs was under great pressure because of the Cultural Revolution, so we slowed down. We were understaffed, and Zhou Enlai had to do everything. He received approval from Mao to go ahead in early February, and the MFA sent a telegram to Stockholm on February 11 to make contact and explain our basic principles.

Once we had met with Canada, Zhou and Mao sent instructions to our Chargé on how to begin.

We delayed replying to Trudeau's May 1968 statement for several reasons. We had to decide if this was a genuine Canadian action, or if Canada was acting as a surrogate for the Americans. We still had doubts about Canada's relationship with the Americans. We finally decided you had a *somewhat independent foreign policy*, and it was possible we could deal with you over the Taiwan issue.

We wondered why you took so long to contact us. Were you having second thoughts? We had to choose among Canada, Italy and Belgium, all of whom were interested in establishing relations. We could not handle all three at one time. Since Canada was linked to the Americans, and because the United States was our main target, we preferred Canada. (emphasis added)

The Department felt Peking would respond in a positive fashion. Failure to continue the negotiations would remove the possibility of Canadian recognition in the foreseeable future, which could affect the likelihood of recognition of China by other countries as well. The PRC surely wanted to repair some of the damage wrought by the Cultural Revolution, and the Canadian initiative could refurbish the PRC's tarnished image in international affairs. If China was indeed interested in better relations with the outside world, and especially with the Americans, then Canadian recognition was a step in that direction, given Canada's close relationship with the United States.

Canada asked to hold the next meeting in May, at which time discussion could begin on the practical matters of establishing diplomatic relations. Later, the two sides could focus on the more difficult political issues contained in the "Three Principles." The Chinese side referred the "practical" questions raised by the Canadians about trade, consular agreements, and the operation of an embassy back to Peking, pointing out that Canada had not responded to the statement of Three Principles made at the first meeting.

The Canadian team now took stock of its position. In the course of a year, Canada had moved from a one-China, one-Taiwan position to one that derecognized Taiwan without accepting the PRC's territorial or political claims regarding the island. Ottawa hoped this would be enough to secure Chinese agreement on terms acceptable for Canada. Two of the "Three Principles" seemed to be covered: support for Peking's admission to the United Nations and agreement that there was one China. Based on these first encounters in Stockholm, Canada was guardedly optimistic that an agreement might be secured without prolonged negotiations.

It was now well into 1969, and Canadians were aware that the negotiations had started. The media, both Canadian and international, were trying to find out what was happening in Stockholm, but the two sides had agreed to negotiate *in camera* without media briefings. In the House, Sharp provided a brief update on the negotiations with the PRC, and the opposition wanted assurances that Canada would not sacrifice Taiwan. While it was not possible immediately to gauge the public's perception of the negotiations, it is fair to say that informed Canadians were intrigued by this apparent declaration of independence from American China policy, and by the prospect of achieving an important diplomatic success. The business community saw increased opportunities for trade, and Canadian universities were holding teach-ins and conferences recommending that Canada recognize the PRC.

In my diary I wrote:

> Started teaching a course on modern Chinese politics at York. May be one of the first in Canada. Student interest is high. Went to China teach-ins at the University of Toronto and at Guelph. Lots of enthusiasm. Recognition is where it's at. Not just in Canada. Was at several American universities, and they also support the Canadians. Pressure is rising in America to do something decisive about relations with China.

Searching for a Formula

At the next meeting, Canada invoked the spirit of Norman Bethune and again raised the "practicalities" issue, presenting an *aide-mémoire* that outlined the rules and principles of diplomatic relations in some detail. The Canadians asked about compensation for the former Canadian Embassy premises that had been requisitioned by the PRC after 1949. Canada wanted repayment of an outstanding loan for six ships belonging to the Ming Sung Company, which had been seized by the PRC government after it took power in 1949. In addition, an assortment of private claims against China had been made by individual Canadian citizens. The Canadian shopping list also included a consular agreement to cover dual citizenship, reunification of families, and access of consular officials to nationals who might be detained or arrested. Canada referred to trading arrangements currently in existence between the two countries, and stated that it was Canada's intention to negotiate a trade agreement and to establish a civil aviation link between the two countries.

The Chinese insisted that, before discussing these "practical" matters, Canada first had to accept its Three Principles. The Canadian negotiators said that they had already dealt with them. But the PRC said no, because Ottawa was not ready to break off all relations with Taiwan, and it refused to acknowledge PRC sovereignty over the island. Some Canadian leaders were saying in public that Canada could have *de facto* relations with Taiwan after the current *de jure* relations had ended. Canada's position in the UN debates was also unclear. While the government now supported China's entry into the United Nations, Ottawa insisted that there first had to be agreement on recognition before Canada voted in favour of Peking's admission. The PRC complained that not voting to approve China's admission to the United Nations meant that "Canada still supported Taiwan's Chiang Clique, which is propped up by the bayonets of American imperialism." It was apparent the two agendas were not the same, and the encounters between the two sides revealed significant differences in assumptions and tactics.

In a later interview, Ambassador Andrew talked about PRC negotiating strategy and tactics:

> The Chinese always referred everything to Peking. So they were quite inflexible. We were able to say, "I know Ottawa will oppose this." The Chinese could not do that. So it took much longer for them to reply.
>
> We were told the Chinese were masters of patience and time. We were also in no hurry. We did not feel we were under the gun, although

the media kept pushing us to make a decision. The Prime Minister was willing to wait.

We were also told that a favourite PRC tactic was to put their opponents on the defensive. We never felt on the defensive. It was just as important for them to succeed as for us.

I remember one area where they did put us on the defensive. They compiled lists of quotations by Canadian political leaders to show that the Canadian position was either pro-Taiwan or that we supported a two-China policy. To stop this, Sharp made his July statement in the House, saying we had a one-China policy.

And one time they pointed out a contradiction between what we were saying and what the Prime Minister had said in 1968. I had to tell them: "Never mind what our Prime Minister said then, what we say now is our policy." I had to contradict my Prime Minister's own words, a diplomatic no-no, to be sure.

They didn't like our reference to proper diplomatic practices, rights, and immunities. They said: "We follow normal practices in all diplomatic relations and don't need to discuss that." I said: "We remember the burning of the British mission in Peking just last year." They replied: "But you won't behave like they did," referring to the British suppression of the 1967 pro-Cultural Revolution demonstrations in Hong Kong.

That Canada had asked for an explicit PRC statement about protecting diplomatic privileges and immunities was seen by the Chinese as "an expression of unfriendliness." This attitude carried over into the sixth meeting, which was held in July. The Chinese negotiating team was now headed by Ambassador Wang Dong (later to become ambassador to Canada), fresh from Peking. During this difficult session, the Chinese side demanded that Canada recognize Taiwan as an integral part of Chinese territory and said that Sharp's statement in the House, "neither challenging nor endorsing the Chinese position on Taiwan," was insufficient. Andrew recalls:

At the sixth meeting we used our Arctic claim tactic. "We don't expect you to support Canada's claim to the Arctic, and you should not expect us to support your claim to Taiwan." The Chinese said: "We will support

your claim to the Arctic, so why not support our claim to Taiwan?" That
was unexpected.

Ambassador Wang Dong declared: "You have the Seventh Fleet
patrolling the Straits of Taiwan and preventing unification with China."
I replied vigorously: "We are Canada and this does not refer to us. If you
feel this way, maybe we should not continue. If you think we are negotiating for another country, then there's no future for these negotiations.
We are not a cat's paw for the United States."

I closed my folder conspicuously.

Wang Dong then said he had been mistranslated and the meeting
continued. Was this a deliberate Chinese challenge to see our reaction,
or just a slip of the tongue?

In the House on July 21, 1969, in response to a planted question from Liberal MP David Anderson, Sharp further clarified the
Canadian position on Taiwan with an explicit message to the Chinese side:

> We are not promoting either a two-China or a one-China, one-Taiwan
> policy. Our policy is to recognize one government of China. We haven't
> asked and do not ask the government of the PRC to endorse the posi-
> tion of the government of Canada on our territorial limits as a condi-
> tion to agreement to establish diplomatic relations. To do so might cast
> doubts on the extent of our sovereignty. We do not think it would be
> appropriate, nor would it be in accordance with international usage,
> that Canada should be asked to endorse the position of the government
> of the PRC on the extent of its territorial sovereignty. To challenge that
> position would, of course, also be inappropriate.[18]

The Chinese negotiating team reacted positively to what Sharp
had said:

> Foreign Minister Sharp's statement was important. It settled a number
> of issues. Until then we were not sure that Canada was acting indepen-
> dently. It told us three things: that Canada was serious about establish-
> ing diplomatic relations; that you would sever relations with Taiwan;
> and that Canada supported China's admission to the United Nations.

However the MFA still had some doubts about Canada's independence from the United States.

The MFA was doing its best to carry on with the negotiations, and even though things were progressing in Stockholm, Zhou was under attack. He had to step in and do Foreign Minister Chen Yi's work.

In the ensuing nine-week interval between sessions, Margaret Meagher, an experienced career diplomat and skilled negotiator, replaced Arthur Andrew as ambassador and head of the negotiating team. This switch was a routine replacement. Andrew had served his time abroad, and the Department needed him back in Ottawa. When asked later why she was chosen to go to Stockholm, Meagher said it was probably because she had handled difficult negotiations in Israel, Cyprus, and Austria. Were the Chinese surprised that Andrew left? "I don't think so, since Wang Dong had also just replaced the Chinese chargé." Did being a woman make any difference? "Some people in Ottawa wondered whether the Chinese thought we were diminishing the significance of the talks. I was used to being the first woman to do things in the Department, and the Chinese quickly realized absolutely nothing had changed." Ambassador Meagher continued:

> We were negotiating on political issues that had international significance. One didn't think about personal relations with the other side. However, I liked Wang and he liked me. We had a good relationship and tried to be friendly to each other. Never a raised voice, never a banging of anything on the table. He was the epitome of courtesy all the time. Later, he became Ambassador to Canada, and he and his wife visited me in the Maritimes.

Wang asked how Canada could claim it had a one-China policy, yet it was abstaining on the Albanian Resolution and continuing to vote in favour of the Important Question Resolution. The latter required a two-thirds majority, which China did not yet have, preventing China from being admitted to the United Nations. Was not admission to the United Nations one of the Three Principles, and didn't this abstention show that Canada was not supporting the PRC's claim to be a member of the United Nations? Ottawa replied that, until relations with China had officially changed, the Canadian position on United Nations admission would remain the same. This stance became a sticking point for the PRC, which said that Canada was reneging on its promise to support the PRC's admission to the United Nations.

At the seventh meeting, the focus shifted to a discussion of the form and content of an agreement. The Canadians declared their preference for a simple communiqué announcing the establishment of diplomatic relations, and the Chinese side agreed to prepare a draft communiqué, which it submitted at the eighth meeting on October 18. The draft communiqué contained three paragraphs. One of them outlined the position Peking expected Canada to take on Taiwan, and it read:

> The government of the PRC reaffirms that Taiwan is an inalienable part of the territory of the PRC. The government of Canada expresses respect for the above stand of the government of the PRC, and will not pursue the policy of so-called "two-Chinas" or "one-China, one-Taiwan" and, therefore, decides to sever all relations with the Chiang Kai-shek Clique.

Beijing had moved closer to the Canadian position of *neither challenge nor endorse* by inserting the words "expresses respect for the above stand of the government of the PRC." But Canada would not accept the statement that "Taiwan is an inalienable part of the territory of the PRC." At the ninth meeting, Canada proposed a draft modelled on the Sino-French communiqué of 1964, simply announcing mutual recognition and the decision to establish diplomatic relations, without mentioning the sovereignty issue. Also, prior to this session, the Canadians had submitted a document wherein they simply *noted* the position of the PRC – that Taiwan was an inalienable part of Chinese territory. This "note" was a step towards the eventual agreement months later, which stated that Canada *"took note"* of the PRC's position on Taiwan.

Developments in the fall of 1969 looked promising, but then Zhou Enlai decided to slow down the negotiations. According to Zhou, both sides needed "to pause and reflect on what it would take to reach a proper agreement that would serve as a model for others to follow." The MFA later gave a more detailed explanation:

> In September, Ambassador Margaret Meagher had joined the negotiations, and she said Canada would not be following a two-China policy. After months of tough negotiations, we had finally reached a tacit agreement on the Three Principles. But Canada did not want to make this public.
>
> Other countries were watching. We wanted a joint statement which embodied our Principles, so others could follow. In Premier Zhou's words, "we should have a better statement, higher than the French."
>
> As for the United Nations vote, we were close to agreement on admission. But Canada did not vote in favour of China's admission. So Premier Zhou instructed us to have a "cooling off" period. We needed to know Canada's intentions. This lasted for five months.

The Chinese negotiators said they would not use the 1964 Sino-French model again, and that any future recognition agreement had to be based on the "one-China principle." The Three Principles had now become one: accepting the Chinese position that there is only one China, the PRC, and that the island of Taiwan is part of China. Ambassador Meagher sat next to Ambassador Wang at the opening of the Swedish Parliament in early January 1970, and all that he said to her was "Happy New Year." Was this a Chinese snub because Canada had not voted in favour of China's admission to the United Nations? The Department interpreted his comment as a signal that the PRC was unhappy with Canada's stance, but Ambassador Meagher was more positive: "He spoke in English. He said it with a nice smile. I knew he was trying to learn English. It wasn't a rebuff. If anything, it was the reverse."

After months of negotiations, was Canada getting anxious and ready to make additional concessions? The Department cautioned its minister to put the delay into a proper context, saying there were no grounds for pessimism. There was no public pressure to make a decision, and Canadians seemed inured to the possibility that the negotiations might go on forever. Ottawa had shifted from a one-China, one-Taiwan position to what was, essentially, the abandonment of Canada's *de jure* relationship with Taiwan. There was now enough support in Parliament, Cabinet, and among the public for this position, although a minority, led by the Conservative opposition, objected to the likely derecognition of Taiwan. American President Nixon had met with Trudeau in 1969 and told him that "the timing and tactics of the Canadians are unwise, and Canada should have waited until a joint US-Canada initiative could have been orchestrated." Neither then, nor at any time later, did Nixon and the Americans say they would take any punitive action against Canada. Department officials later said that, when the Americans began to contact China secretly in 1970 to begin their own negotiations to establish relations, "the Americans never contacted Canada. It was like we did not exist."

Had the prime minister become weary of the encounters in Stockholm? Having distanced himself from Taiwan, was he prepared for further compromise? In an appraisal of the Canadian position during a press conference in December 1969, Trudeau said: "I am optimistic, in the sense that nothing until now has shown to us that we should break off the talks or give them up as hopeless ... It is taking a lot of time, more than I would hope for, but there is nothing in the talks which gives us cause to be discouraged, or to say that the whole thing is finished and we shouldn't continue them."

After almost a year of meetings and a further delay in the negotiations, the Department remained positive about the negotiations:

> We were satisfied. The talks were dragging on, but we had settled some difficult problems. We agreed there was one China. We said we would support UN admission. We had a defensible position – that we were prepared to end *de jure* relations with Taiwan. We had told the Chinese we would neither challenge nor endorse the PRC's claim to sovereignty over Taiwan, and we were about to discover the phrase "take note," which we hoped would bring about a successful conclusion.
>
> The Prime Minister was supportive from the first day, and we were able to coordinate with Ivan Head, his foreign policy advisor. The Americans were not threatening us, and Canadian public opinion remained supportive.

Resolution

Mitchell Sharp expected that the talks would be prolonged and deliberate. He had stated: "This is the way the Chinese negotiate. Of course, we won't let them go on indefinitely. If the talks look as if they are bogging down, we will suspend them." In reply to questions asking about Taiwan, he again said that Canada neither challenged nor accepted the sovereignty of Peking over Taiwan, and he repeated the phrase: "We don't ask the Chinese to accept our sovereignty over the Arctic." Nevertheless, that had not been enough to satisfy the PRC, which continued to insist that Canada had to agree that Taiwan was an inalienable part of Chinese territory.

How concerned were Canadians over the likely termination of official relations with Taiwan? The Conservatives continually raised the issue, saying that Trudeau and the Liberals were selling the island out to the communists. Most Canadian ethnic Chinese also supported Taiwan, and the Canadian companies trading with it lobbied the government to preserve their markets there. The majority of Canadians, however, had little or no interest in Taiwan. In taking the pulse of Canadians, the Department realized that Canadians knew almost nothing about Taiwan, and they had a generally unfavourable view of the island's authoritarian government: "We looked at the polls. In Canada, unlike in the United States, Chiang Kai-shek did not have a good image. Taiwan was seen as a nasty dictatorship with few meaningful ties to Canada."

What did Trudeau think? In conversation, he told me:

> I did not dislike the people of Taiwan, only its government, which I experienced first-hand in 1948–49, and in 1959, when passing through Taiwan on my two visits to China. I did not want to alienate the Canadian Chinese community or to turn my back on Taiwan. The actions of my government did not mean that Canada had to pretend Taiwan did not exist. We could still have a relationship, just not an official one.[19]

In trying to end the stalemate, Canada had discovered the phrase "taking due note," or simply "taking note." The Department experimented with the wording: "The Canadian government, while *taking note* of this position of the PRC government, nevertheless considers it inappropriate ..." However, *"taking note"* did not appear path breaking at the time. The Canadian side thought that the phrase might be inserted in the joint communiqué if it made a difference between success and failure. Later, the phrase became the key to breaking the deadlock over Taiwan because *"taking note"* did not imply agreement with the Chinese position, only that Canada was aware of what it was. The PRC could thus loudly claim sovereignty over Taiwan, while Canada could artfully avoid commenting on the Chinese position. With such a compromise, both sides could preserve their respective positions on the status of Taiwan without losing political face. Later, as many as a half-dozen Canadians took credit for discovering the phrase.

In the House on June 18, 1970, Minister Sharp spoke about the state of the negotiations: "We are waiting for the Chinese representatives to make another appointment with our Ambassador in Stockholm ... [T]he Chinese are very patient, and I think we have to be the same way." He was asked if Canada was withdrawing diplomatic recognition from Taiwan:

> MR. SHARP: Yes, Mr. Speaker. I have made it quite clear on a number of occasions that we have a one-China policy now. We will have a one-China policy in the future.
>
> MR. LAMBERT (EDMONTON WEST): You used to have a two-China policy.
>
> MR. YEWCHUK (ATHABASCA): Does this mean that Canada will be asking the Taiwan Ambassador to withdraw from Canada, and has he been informed of this clearly?
>
> MR. SHARP: Since we have a one-China policy, we will recognize one government of China and will not recognize two.[20]

At the fifteenth session in August 1970, the two sides agreed upon the wording of the first and last paragraphs of the communiqué, leaving only the controversial second paragraph that dealt with Taiwan. The PRC still wanted Ottawa to acknowledge PRC sovereignty over the island, but Canada refused. Finally, on October 3 the Chinese accepted the "takes note" phrase. Both parties then agreed on the text of a four-paragraph communiqué, the second paragraph having been separated into two parts at the suggestion of the Canadian side. The four-paragraph communiqué was released in the House on October 13 by Foreign Minister Sharp in a speech announcing mutual recognition and the establishment of diplomatic relations.

The key second and third paragraphs read as follows:

> 2. The Chinese Government reaffirms that Taiwan is an inalienable part of the territory of the People's Republic of China. The Canadian Government *takes note* of this position of the Chinese Government.
> 3. The Canadian Government recognizes the Government of the People's Republic of China as the sole legal Government of China. (emphasis added)[21]

The negotiations were over. After almost two years, the two countries had agreed to establish diplomatic relations with a one-China formula that many other states would now employ when they established diplomatic relations with the PRC. Prime Minister Trudeau sent his congratulations to the Canadian negotiating team: "We had a consistent position and carried it out right to the end. I like consistency. Like Frederick of Prussia, I act first, and then I find learned men who will prove I was acting out of right."

Foreign Minister Sharp proclaimed: "It is not often that Canada leads the world. Our recognition led a procession of some 30 other countries who very shortly thereafter followed our example."[22] Ambassador Andrew praised the negotiators and said that he never had any doubts about reaching an agreement: "It is a great achievement, and Canada deserves full credit." Ambassador Meagher thought the negotiations were the most memorable experience in her career: "It was a great achievement, and I am proud to have contributed to it."

The *Globe and Mail* made the following comments in an October 14 editorial:

> The long negotiations between Canada and the People's Republic of China have at last been concluded successfully; the fiction that the

government of Chiang Kai-shek controls the destiny of China's 700 million people is no longer part of this government's foreign policy.

This should be a source of satisfaction to all Canadians, and especially to Prime Minister Pierre Trudeau who personally decided on the approach to Peking before the last election.

Official U.S. reaction to the Sino-Canadian diplomatic recognition has been low key. Publicly Washington can hardly expect to be enthusiastic, but privately White House officials probably see it as a help in their own attempts to achieve a meaningful dialogue with China.[23]

The *People's Daily* wrote about "the traditional friendship between the Chinese and the Canadian people ... Doctor Norman Bethune dedicated his life to the revolutionary cause of China. The recent years have seen development of the intercourse between the two countries. The decision of China and Canada now to formally establish relations reflects the common aspirations of the two peoples, and conforms to their interests."[24] The MFA said that the final agreement showed that the two sides were flexible, had a far-sighted perspective, and had drawn world-wide approval: "The agreement with Canada had a big impact on other countries who wanted to establish relations with us, especially other 'middle-ground' countries similar to Canada."

Zhou Enlai took the final agreement to Mao Zedong, and the Chairman gave his personal blessing:

Among the pile of documents on the desk of Premier Zhou Enlai late at night on October 7 was the telegram from our Embassy in Stockholm with the text of the joint communiqué. Actually, the negotiation was led by Premier Zhou from beginning to end. He had to see all the documents. The other members of the Politburo had to sign off on them. And also Chairman Mao.

Premier Zhou read the telegram and was relieved. He had a big smile on his face.

The next morning he raced to Zhongnanhai and showed it to Mao who, expressing much satisfaction, said to Zhou, "*We now have a friend in America's backyard.*" This was an important day for all of us!

A Moment in History

The journey towards recognition, first attempted in 1950 after the Communist Party took power in China, had come to an end. Trudeau thanked Mitchell Sharp and Ivan Head for bringing the negotiations to a successful conclusion. In Stockholm, the weary negotiators drank sherry and had dinner with their Chinese counterparts. Mitchell Sharp congratulated Ambassador Meagher for her successful efforts on Canada's behalf. The Taiwanese ambassador was asked to close his embassy in Ottawa and consulate in Vancouver, and expedite the immediate departure of all Taiwanese diplomats, their staff, and their families. The international media generally applauded the Canada-PRC agreement for accepting the reality of the existence of a country with one-fifth of the world's population.

In Canada, the recognition of China was considered a diplomatic coup. The government had pursued a difficult strategy without alienating Canada's neighbour, even though the American government at the time was officially opposed to the recognition of the PRC. Canada had occupied a part of the centre stage of world diplomacy for almost two years, showing off an independent foreign policy, fine diplomatic skills, with the potential to be more than just a middle power. At the time, Canadian recognition of China stood out as a Canadian success story by any standard, and it deserved to be recorded in history in those terms.

The Stockholm discussions, while conducted *in camera*, were monitored by several other countries, especially the United States. The Department kept as many as a dozen countries informed of the progress of the talks. "We distributed sanitized summaries after each meeting to a dozen selected countries, including the Americans, the Japanese, the Russians, and Taiwan. We also kept the Belgians and the Italians, who were negotiating with China at the same time, informed of our progress." Three weeks after Canada had established relations, the Italians, who had been negotiating with the PRC in Paris, announced they had recognized the PRC using the identical Canadian formula. Later one of the Italians said to me: "You Canadians were better organized. We are Italians, after all, and the Chinese wanted Canada to be first."

The first question to ask is, "Is this the full story?" What has been left out, either by accident or by design? For example, we lack information about the behind-the-scenes debates concerning the potential security threat of a Chinese Communist Embassy in Ottawa. Also, what was said behind closed doors by the Americans about possible reprisals for establishing relations with Peking, and how did Canada reply? Would we ever find out if Canada and China had used secret emissaries to contact each other during the negotiations?

Conversations with Pierre Trudeau, Mitchell Sharp, Ivan Head, Ambassadors Arthur Andrew and Margaret Meagher, Counsellor Robert Edmonds, and American officials and China specialists filled many gaps. Interviews with key Chinese officials, who either participated in the negotiations or who later had access to the MFA's closed files, were invaluable. Given that we were able to draw on these authoritative individual sources beyond the written files, we can say: "Yes, we have the main elements of the story, if not all its secrets and subtleties."

The second question concerns the decision itself. One can say that Ottawa was driven by a mission to bring China into our world, and it failed to see the limitations of the Stockholm agreement. Should Canada have bowed to Chinese pressure and sacrificed Taiwan so swiftly? Canada abandoned the island with little public discussion, and the Americans and Japanese later found better solutions, managing to retain some official ties with Taiwan while at the same time recognizing the PRC. Could it be said that Canada was "out-negotiated" by the Chinese? Ottawa took pride in its tough bargaining stance, yet Canadian diplomats at the outset were forced to debate the Taiwan issue with their Chinese counterparts, even though that was not the intended Canadian strategy.

Canada wanted to avoid discussion of "principles," which really meant Taiwan, by focusing on "practicalities," that is, securing agreement on diplomatic immunities and privileges, consular agreements, and trade. All these practical matters were pushed aside during the negotiations, and only several years later, after diplomatic relations had been established, were the millions of dollars of claims that Canada had against China settled, with somewhat disappointing results. It may have been unrealistic to expect Chinese settlement of claims, or discussion of the practicalities of diplomatic relations, until the political questions had been settled. Both sides could wait for Trudeau's state visit in 1973, when practical matters were discussed and a full range of bilateral programs was established.

What does the recognition decision tell us about Canadian politics and the Canadian decision-making process? In 1968, recognition was not a contentious political issue in Canada. The major political parties supported closer relations with the PRC, as did a majority of Canadians. The prime minister used the China decision to distance himself from Lester Pearson, his predecessor, and to stake out a popular claim for greater independence from the Americans in foreign affairs. By combining the China initiative with an ongoing major review of foreign policy, Trudeau and his advisors sought to take control of the foreign policymaking process.

In the short run, the Department's authority and expertise were challenged by Trudeau; yet in handling the negotiations with the PRC, the prime minister and his advisors relied upon the very public servants that they had been criticizing. The Department's historical memory, professionalism, and discretion were vital for the successful completion of the negotiations. Once the talks were under way, Trudeau "let the professionals do their job." He made the big foreign policy decisions, but he had no patience for the day-to-day administration of foreign relations. He had confidence in Mitchell Sharp, whom he described as "a loyal soldier," and he had Ivan Head as his key advisor. Only occasionally was Trudeau directly involved in the twenty-month negotiations.

For many Canadians, recognition was an act of emancipation from the embrace of bad American policy. While American pressure undoubtedly had been a major factor preventing Canada from establishing relations with China in the 1950s and again in the early 1960s, by 1968, the United States had realized it could not prevent Canada from engaging with the PRC. American protests over closer links with China had a hollow ring: the Vietnam War had diminished American credibility, and its China policy would soon change. The bogeyman of economic sanctions against

Canada had been dispelled by changing circumstances, and by the fact that Canada could no longer blame the Americans for its own hesitation to engage with the PRC.

Reflecting on their experience, the two heads of Canada's negotiating team, Ambassadors Andrew and Meagher, said that the Stockholm discussions were not much different from other diplomatic negotiations in which they had participated. The official language of the talks was English, and the reference points were universally held principles of international diplomacy. The impression given by the Department, its negotiators, and the Canadian ministers and politicians who were involved was that Canada was negotiating with a large, stubborn power, which had an authoritarian government, was a Cold War opponent, and did not know very much about Canada.

Many Canadians at that moment, and for some time afterwards, referred to an emerging "special relationship with China," a relationship that in their minds was confirmed by expanding wheat sales, the celebration of Norman Bethune, the legacy of Canada's past missionary experience in China, and, perhaps most important, an image of China that was different from the one held by the Americans. Were Canadians more flexible and open to China than the Americans, and unburdened by imperialist history? Canadians felt they were positioned to break down the barriers between China and the outside world, and a variety of public figures, starting with Trudeau and the mish kids, contributed to this idealization of Canada's special role.

This attitude led to exaggerated assumptions by some Canadians about the significance of having established diplomatic relations with the PRC. In 1970, Canada basked in the glow of friendship, international acclaim, and increased trade prospects. A decade later, Canada had become one of a rapidly expanding group of foreign petitioners at the newly opened Chinese court. The period of Canadian prominence was brief. Once President Nixon visited China in 1972, the Americans had arrived to stay, and while it took seven more years before the establishment of full relations between the United States and China, the die was cast. America was always China's prize, not Canada.

By the late 1970s, Canada's "China moment" had passed. Trudeau's goal had been to bring China out of isolation so that the mystique of its culture, and the roughness of its communist authoritarianism, could be tempered by the conventions and practices of the modern Western state system. That is in good part what happened, and Canadians could point to a moment in time, in 1970, when relations were unique and on the cusp of history.

chapter three

The One-China Policy

In this chapter, Canada defends its one-China policy by barring Taiwan from the 1976 Montreal Olympics. Trudeau is called a Nazi, and Canada is accused of "bowing down to Communist China so it can sell Peking more wheat."

After recognition, visitors from Taiwan no longer could say they were from the "Republic of China" (ROC). This led to a cat and mouse game after they arrived in Canada waving the ROC flag. The Chinese Embassy would immediately protest, and officers in the Department would order the Taiwanese visitors to stop calling themselves "China" and take down their ROC flag.

In 1974, the PRC applied for membership in the International Olympic Committee (IOC) so that its athletes could compete in the 1976 Montreal Games. The PRC said that, if it became a member of the IOC, the ROC had to be expelled. The IOC was unwilling to expel a member in good standing, especially since Taiwan had the support of a majority of its members. However, the IOC president, Lord Killanin (Michael Morris, the Third Baron Killanin), knew that sooner or later the PRC would have to be admitted. Was there a way to accommodate both the PRC and the ROC? Taiwan would not surrender its name of "Republic of China" (ROC), and the United States, Taiwan's major supporter, opposed any attempt to expel it from the IOC, or force it to change its name.

In 1974 and 1975, I was in charge of negotiating Canada's sports exchanges with China at the Embassy. At every meeting, the Chinese Sports Federation declared that it was Canada's responsibility to ensure the PRC's admittance to the Games and exclude Taiwan. I replied that Canada supported the PRC's admission, but it was up to the IOC to settle membership issues.

Lord Killanin and the IOC delayed acting. By the end of 1975, the PRC had retreated from its push for membership since its team was not ready to compete at a high level, but it continued to demand Taiwan's expulsion from the IOC. Canada said that Taiwan would not be allowed to participate in Montreal if it called itself "China." Backed by the Americans, Taiwan said it intended to participate in the Montreal Games as the Republic of China (the ROC).

The IOC said that it would move the Games elsewhere if Ottawa did not change its position, and it accused Canada of putting politics ahead of international sport, and of caving in to Beijing's demands. The IOC then proposed a compromise: a version of the 1960 Rome Olympics formula, when Taiwan had participated as "Formosa," its name under Japanese occupation from 1895 to 1945.

Taiwan refused. Prime Minister Trudeau then offered a last-minute solution: Taiwan could fly the ROC flag and sing its own anthem in Montreal, but it still would be denied entry to Canada if it called itself China. This concession was acceptable to the Taiwanese athletes, but their government in Taipei ordered them to return home. As a result, neither Taiwan nor the PRC participated in the 1976 Montreal Games. In 1979, the PRC finally became an IOC member, and in 1984, both the PRC and Taiwan participated in the Los Angeles Games, with Taiwan calling itself "China (Taipei)," the name it uses today in international organizations.

Afterwards Trudeau said: "We made the right decision. Our officials handled it well. Canada took criticism from other countries, and from the media. We had a clear policy, and we observed it." More than a few Canadians felt Canada had unnecessarily put politics ahead of international sport. The Americans continued to criticize Canada for having sacrificed Taiwan in order to maintain good relations with China. Beijing grudgingly acknowledged that Canada had observed the "one-China" policy, but Taiwan was still a member of the IOC, and the PRC had not yet been admitted. Foreign Minister Sharp said Canada had not banned Taiwan to please the PRC, but to honour its policy commitments: "It is clear that we are going to have our ups and downs with China."

Of course I had to tell Taiwan it could not attend the Montreal Games if it called itself China. We had spent almost two years in Stockholm arguing over Taiwan, and we came up with the right solution, that there is only one China, and it is the PRC. After 1970, they could not say they were from China when they were in Canada. That was our policy. It was logical and consistent.

– Pierre Elliott Trudeau, 1988[1]

Prologue

On October 13, 1970, after twenty months of negotiations, Canada and China established diplomatic relations, having agreed that there was only one "China," the PRC. It was a significant achievement, although at that precise moment Canadian attention was focused elsewhere – on the abrupt implementation of the War Measures Act. The federal government, fearing an insurrection by the Quebec sovereigntist group, the Front de libération du Québec (FLQ), had brought in the troops to maintain order, and thoughts of China were temporarily eclipsed by the Quebec crisis. In any case, not many Canadians had been keeping track of the long negotiations in Stockholm. China still remained a distant place, remote from their daily lives. In the Cold War context of that time, it was communist, exotic, unfriendly, economically backward, and far away.

The first Canadian ambassador arrived in Peking in the spring of 1971. Ralph Collins was born in China, a "mish kid" who had lived there before the communist revolution. In June, he arranged a reception for our group of twenty-eight visiting academics and China watchers. We were the first such Canadian group to visit the PRC after recognition. Collins provided tea and peanuts, and he asked us "to excuse the barebones. We are starting from scratch here and it isn't easy." Marooned by the Cultural Revolution, foreign diplomats were isolated in their Beijing embassies, guarded by PRC soldiers, and plainly marking time. That was not the best way for Canada to begin a significant new relationship.

Canada had a modest agenda: helping China to gain admission to the United Nations in 1971, as promised in the 1970 recognition agreement; developing economic links between the two countries by holding a large trade exhibition of Canadian goods and services in Shanghai; encouraging China to find its own path in the midst of its split with the Soviet Union; and laying the groundwork for the upcoming state visit by Prime Minister Trudeau. China was admitted to the United Nations in the fall of 1971, and Taiwan was expelled. When Foreign Minister Sharp visited Shanghai in 1972 during the first Canadian trade exhibition ever held in the PRC, he remarked that working with China was not going to be easy, although he was optimistic about the progress that already had been made in the new relationship:

> We do not always agree with the Chinese. Many times we are diametrically opposed. It is no surprise that we differ ... Canada has argued that it was foolish and dangerous to exclude one-quarter of humanity from the counsels of the world. We're making progress in breaking down the barriers that have existed for almost a generation between the People's Republic of China and Canada.[2]

Prime Minister Trudeau's state visit in 1973 was a defining event. His meetings with Mao Zedong, Zhou Enlai, and Deng Xiaoping captured the attention of the Canadian public and the international media. While his visit did not match the drama of US President Nixon's trip a year earlier, he set the tone for future relations by developing strong personal ties with China's leaders; securing China's commitment to make Canada its first source for grain; and settling the "practicalities" that had been put aside during the recognition negotiations – such as consular matters, people-to-people links, a trade agreement, and an agreement on diplomatic rights and conventions. Zhou Enlai called Trudeau, who had first travelled to China twenty-five years earlier, "an old friend" and Canada "a country with whom China wanted to work more closely." Trudeau later said that "opening relations with China was the right decision. I knew it was controversial at the time, given the strong American support for Taiwan. It was logical. I did not expect that later on Taiwan would cause Canada all that trouble."

Canada and Taiwan

When Canada established relations with the PRC in 1970, it severed its diplomatic links with the Nationalist government in Taiwan. Canada had established relations with the Nationalists in

1943 during the Chinese Civil War, when they still governed mainland China. By 1949, the Communists had taken control on the mainland and renamed it the PRC, and the Nationalists had fled to the nearby island of Taiwan, where they called themselves the Republic of China (ROC). For twenty years, Canada did not recognize the PRC government in Peking, nor did it have much to do with the ROC government in Taiwan. Until 1970, the ROC ambassador performed perfunctory duties in Ottawa, but Canada did not have similar representation in Taiwan. Ties between Canada and Taiwan were minimal: a modest trade relationship and limited people-to-people links, mainly through immigration to Canada.

Canada's post-1970 policy towards Taiwan was based on the avoidance of official ties. The Department of External Affairs put it this way:

> The Canadian Government discourages contact with Taiwan that would be inconsistent with Canada's recognition of and good relations with the PRC. In practice, this policy means restricting entry to Taiwanese whose official position, representational role or activities in Canada would result in the promotion of the identity and claims of the "Republic of China."

This restriction notwithstanding, Taiwan and Canada were free to develop *de facto* economic and cultural ties. In the five years between 1969 and 1974, Canadian exports to Taiwan grew from $12.1 million to $41.5 million, an annual growth rate of about 28 per cent, almost exactly the same rate of growth as Canada's exports to the PRC during the same period. In absolute terms, however, Canadian exports to the PRC in 1974 were eleven times greater than exports to Taiwan, with wheat comprising 80 per cent of the total.[3]

Contacts with Taiwan were kept to "an absolute minimum" to avoid acts that could be interpreted as recognizing that Taiwan was also "China." Canadian officials could travel to the island, but they could not use their diplomatic passports. The two governments maintained a few basic links, such as the negotiation of annual textile import restraints, which they carried out in "neutral territory" in Washington. The PRC was aware of these meetings, but it did not object. Every effort was made to keep these contacts hidden from view. The Department made it clear that visits by Canadian officials to Taiwan were proscribed, and that neither Canadian trade promotion activities nor immigration interviews could be carried out on Taiwanese soil.

Taiwanese activities placed a strain on the Canadian government. The ROC operated small "private" trade offices in Toronto and Montreal, employed lobbyists in Toronto and Ottawa, and posted journalists in both cities. It conducted extensive propaganda, claiming that Taiwan was the rightful government of China, and it targeted influential Canadians, such as members of Parliament and leaders in the Canadian ethnic Chinese communities, to support Taiwan. The Canadian government was always scrambling to prevent its officials from accepting offers of all-expense-paid junkets to Taiwan: "The government discourages formal visits to Taiwan by Canadian officials, federal, provincial and municipal, to avoid misrepresentation by the Taiwanese as *de jure* recognition, and to minimize offence to the PRC."

Ottawa was concerned that visitors from Taiwan were arriving in Canada waving the ROC flag and saying they were from China. Almost every group from Taiwan referred to itself as from the ROC, which resulted in angry protests by the PRC Embassy in Ottawa. Most Canadians were puzzled by the fuss over the ROC name and flag, except for members of the small ethnic Chinese communities in Canada that supported the Taiwanese.[4] Ottawa was acting as a police officer for a policy that most Canadians did not understand or care about very much.

The word often used by the Canadian government to describe its policy towards Taiwan was "consistency" – upholding the one-China principle that had been established in 1970. Taiwanese were free to visit Canada as long as they did not claim to represent "China." Prime Minister Trudeau deemed this policy "eminently logical," and it was reinforced by the PRC, which protested each attempt by the ROC to call itself "China" when in Canada. One member of the Department reported:

> Every Monday morning it seemed that someone from the PRC Embassy was pounding on the door at the Pearson Building in Ottawa with an

angry protest about a visiting Taiwan group somewhere in Canada calling itself "China." Either we were constantly tracking these Taiwan groups to make sure they behaved properly in Canada, or we were fending off protests from the PRC.

In 1971, the PRC, with the support of Canada, joined the United Nations, and Taiwan was expelled over American objections. During the rest of the 1970s, the United States was preoccupied with how to manage its relationship with Taiwan. For the United States, unlike for Canada, protection of the Chinese Nationalist government had been a priority after Chiang Kai-shek fled to Taiwan in 1949. The Americans sided with the Nationalists during the Chinese Civil War, providing them with military support, and then treated Taiwan as a Cold War ally against Communist China. The United States could not abandon Taiwan, and it looked for a way to preserve America's ties with the island. The Americans were disappointed with Canada's decision in 1970 to end official relations with Taiwan, and were concerned that Taiwan would be prevented from participating in the 1976 Olympics, as well as losing its seat in the United Nations. As we will see later in this chapter, most of the criticism that was levelled at Canada for threatening to exclude Taiwan if it called itself "China" was driven by the Americans and their proxies in the Olympic movement.

After 1973, the Canadian "one-China formula" that had severed diplomatic links with Taiwan was supplemented by a "Japanese formula," which permitted the establishment of a Japanese multipurpose semi-official trade office in Taiwan. The trade office allowed for a wider level of economic and cultural interaction with Taiwan, while still affirming the existence of only one China. This arrangement was also a template for Sino-American normalization in 1979, enabling the Americans to keep an office in Taipei, where it could maintain a semi-official relationship with Taiwan. The Japanese formula was an exception to the rigid application of the one-China policy until well into the 1980s, when several other countries, including Canada, established semi-official trade and cultural offices on the island, with corresponding Taiwanese offices in their respective countries.

China Applies for Membership in the IOC

China applied for membership in the International Olympic Committee (IOC) in late 1973, so it could qualify for the 1976 Montreal Games. During the 1960 Rome Games, Taiwan was not allowed to call itself the ROC, and it participated under protest as "Formosa." Following the 1960 Rome Games, Taiwan participated in the next three Olympics as the Republic of China, displaying its ROC flag and playing its national anthem. After the Munich Games in 1972, the PRC had four years in which to do three things: assemble a team capable of competing in Montreal in 1976, gain readmission to the IOC, and expel Taiwan from the IOC.

The Asian Sports Federation expelled Taiwan from the 1974 Asian Games in Tehran, and the PRC was admitted to the Asian Sports Federation without formally applying for membership. For this act, China publicly thanked Iran, and also Japan, Pakistan, Afghanistan, Bahrain, Burma, Hong Kong, India, Kuwait, Malaysia, Nepal, Sri Lanka, Singapore, and "other friends." The IOC, which had sanctioned the Asian Games, a regional sports event, first threatened to withdraw its patronage because of the expulsion of Taiwan, but it finally accepted the Asian Federation's decision. Most of the twenty-six International Sports Federations had opposed Taiwan's expulsion, declaring that the Asian Sports Federation's decision to expel the ROC and recognize the PRC was illegal.

The decision to award the 1976 Olympics to Montreal had been made in 1970. When Canada applied to host the Games, Foreign Minister Mitchell Sharp assured the IOC on November 28, 1969, that "all parties representing the National Olympic Committees and International Sports Federations recognized by the IOC will be free to enter Canada *pursuant to the normal regulations*. I should be pleased to provide any further information respecting these regulations should you desire it" (emphasis added).

No one could have imagined that a rapid politicization of the Olympics was about to occur, beginning with the killing of eleven Israeli athletes in Munich in 1972; followed in Montreal in 1976 by a boycott by twenty-eight African countries who opposed New Zealand's participation because its rugby team had played

in apartheid South Africa; then Moscow's refusal to admit several
IOC members to its 1980 Games, for example, Israel; and finally the
American-inspired boycott of those same Moscow Games. Back in
1970, no one expected any trouble from benign Canada, with its
reputation as a model of openness and commitment to international sports competition.

In the summer of 1974, I was appointed first secretary in the
Canadian Embassy. Part of my duties included administering
sports exchanges between Canada and China, and we soon discovered that the Chinese had a larger agenda than negotiating
routine exchanges of basketball, volleyball, badminton, table
tennis, hockey, and swimming teams. At each meeting, before we
could discuss any exchange of sports teams, my Chinese counterpart would remind us that Canada was the PRC's new friend. He
expected Canada, as host of the 1976 Montreal Games, to lobby on
China's behalf, so it could be admitted to as many of the twenty-six
international sports federations as possible, and to expel Taiwan.
To be considered for IOC membership, a country had to join at
least five of the twenty-six sports federations. Then it could form
its own National Olympic Committee and apply for admission to
the IOC. I was subjected to a steady diet of rhetoric to persuade us
to intervene on China's behalf, and our PRC interlocutors made
it clear: "Since the Games are in Canada, we expect our Canadian
friends to help us gain IOC membership and to expel Taiwan."

To stop this pressure, we reminded the PRC that states could
not lobby the IOC. It was an independent sports organization, and
Canada could not force the IOC to admit the PRC or to expel Taiwan. We were not permitted to talk with our Canadian representatives on the IOC or to any members of the Canadian Olympic
Committee. In fact, Canada was not even the actual host of the
upcoming Olympics – that was the city of Montreal. These points
having been made, the PRC nevertheless persisted.

Our Peking interlocutors said it would be "regrettable" for Sino-
Canadian relations if Canada did not take action. Ottawa cabled
us that admission of the PRC to the Olympics, or any change of
Taiwan's IOC status, was solely the responsibility of the IOC, and
that the latter was avoiding a decision while hoping to deflect the

problem onto Canada's shoulders. Ottawa then sent the Embassy a second cable: "You will continue to reply that Canada has no role to play in determining IOC membership. Listen carefully, and promise them nothing."

The IOC was torn. Advocacy for the PRC's admission at the expense of Taiwan was not a popular option for most IOC members. After the killings at Munich, many members were appalled at the consequences of the politicization of international sport. Taiwan was a legitimate member of the IOC, and it had competed as the representative of China since the 1960 Rome Olympics. It was already 1975, China had still not formally applied to the IOC, and there was a strong possibility it would not get admitted in time for the 1976 Games. It also had not behaved well in Tehran, where it had snubbed the Israeli athletes. That did not sit well with many IOC members. Why expel Taiwan, a member in good standing, in favour of a state that might cause the IOC as much trouble if it were admitted, than if it were not?

> At Tehran, aside from the issue of expelling Taiwan, China had joined the Arab states in refusing to compete with Israel. A Chinese refused to fence with an Israeli, and was banned from the Games. The Chinese refused to face the Israelis in the tennis final, and they acted quite discourteously at the podium when the Israeli national anthem was played during the basketball award ceremony.

In April 1975, the PRC made a direct approach to the IOC at the urging of some of its supporters: Iran, Japan, Pakistan, and Tanzania. The head of the IOC, Lord Killanin, dubbed this gesture "somewhat short of a formal application." At the IOC meetings in Lausanne in May 1975, the issue of PRC admission was raised by Iran and supported by Japan and Tanzania. Killanin said with concern: "Their initiative in support of the PRC has sufficient potential to split the IOC down the middle." The IOC decided "to further study the matter," and Killanin said he would address the problem again before the Innsbruck Winter Games in February 1976.

Prior to that IOC meeting, Killanin, along with James Worrall, the IOC representative from Canada, met with Arthur Andrew, the former Canadian ambassador in Stockholm, now the deputy minister of foreign affairs. Andrew reminded Killanin of the terms of Canadian recognition of the PRC. Canada recognized the PRC as the sole legal government of China, so Taiwan no longer could call itself "China" when it was in Canada. Andrew also expressed hope that the PRC would become a member of the IOC in time for the 1976 Games. He did not say explicitly that a Taiwan team could not participate in Montreal if it called itself China, although when pressed by Killanin for an assurance that Canada would admit Taiwan, he replied: *"That is a ministerial decision."* Andrew could not say what that decision would be.

The reason why Ottawa did not say anything further to Killanin was clear. The PRC was trying to occupy the Chinese seat at the Olympics. The PRC's application was on the agenda of the IOC, and Killanin was scheduled to visit Peking later in 1975 to discuss China's application. Stating Canada's position categorically a year before the Games would have strengthened Killanin's hand and diminished pressure to have the IOC deal with the Chinese application. It would have given him the latitude of moving the Games elsewhere if Canada did not modify its position. Montreal had already spent hundreds of millions of dollars on site preparation, and if the Games were cancelled it could be a financial catastrophe.

By admitting the PRC to the Olympics, the IOC might be forced to expel Taiwan, an IOC member, since the PRC said it would not participate in the Olympics together with an entity over which the PRC claimed sovereignty and which also called itself "China." Perhaps Peking could participate if Taiwan called itself something else? If the issue could be settled among the PRC, the IOC, and Taiwan (the ROC), then Canada would not have to take action. Andrew expected that Killanin would take the initiative, go to Peking, and settle the issue within the IOC. The longer he took, the better it was for Canada, since then it would be too late to cancel or move the Games from Montreal.

In conversation, Andrew later recalled:

We knew Montreal was going to be a problem. We had to defend our position, our one-China policy. The Americans had other ideas. They had not established relations with the PRC, and did not yet have a one-China policy. They wanted the ROC to go as "China" to Montreal, and they had support in the IOC. Killanin thought Canada would give way to all that pressure, but Trudeau was adamant.

The IOC Does Not Act

The positions of the various participants were hardening. The Taiwan National Olympic Committee reminded Killanin that it was a member of the IOC and that it was entitled to compete in the 1976 Olympics. Its National Olympic Committee was called the "Republic of China National Olympic Committee," and its athletes intended to show up in Montreal, calling themselves "China" or the "Republic of China" (ROC).

Meanwhile, the PRC had now acquired membership in nine international sports federations, qualifying it to apply for IOC membership. If Peking had not coupled its membership bid with a demand for the expulsion of Taiwan, the IOC would most likely have approved China's application for membership in late 1975. But the IOC was not going to expel one of its present members in good standing, and there was substantial IOC support for having both the PRC and ROC as members, by adopting either a "one-China, one Taiwan" or a "two-China" solution, both of which the PRC opposed. Within the IOC, the American representatives took a predictably strong position by resisting any attempt to remove "China" from Taiwan's name. The United States was preparing for the 1976 presidential elections, and the Republican Party supported the continuation of full diplomatic relations with the ROC. Ronald Reagan, who was challenging President Gerald Ford for the Republican nomination, emphatically stated that he opposed any change in Taiwan's name when it competed in Montreal.

Governments and individuals looked for a solution in the history of previous Olympics. In 1960, the IOC had required Taiwan to participate in the Rome Olympics as "Formosa." Taiwan had threatened to boycott the Games, but the head of its delegation marched in the opening parade in 1960 at Rome, holding a placard with the name "Formosa" written on it, closely followed by a second team member with a sign that read "Under Protest." Taiwan was allowed to fly its ROC flag and play its national anthem. It was at Rome that C.K. Yang, the famous Taiwanese decathlon athlete, won a silver medal in a memorable competition with American Rafer Johnson. In the 1968 and 1972 Olympiads, Taiwan participated as the ROC. One Taiwanese later said: "That was our official IOC name. Of course we had to participate as ROC and not somebody else."

In Peking, discussions with our PRC counterparts took an interesting turn. A new interlocutor had taken over. He was aggressive, yet sympathetic and understanding of my position at the lower level of the decision-making process. He complained that "Canada was not doing enough to further the friendship between our two countries." While he continued to talk about China's future admission to the Montreal Games, he now focused on why Canada had to exclude Taiwan for the 1976 Games. When I reported this shift to our ambassador, he said it was probable that the PRC was giving up on admission for the Montreal Games since China did not have enough time to field a competitive team. The ambassador instructed me "to cable Ottawa that the main issue now is Taiwan and the preservation of our one-China policy, not the PRC's admission."

One evening we learned how sensitive the PRC was about Taiwan. It was Embassy policy to show Canadian films to Chinese guests. The films, produced by the National Film Board and delivered to the Embassy in the diplomatic pouch, were watched at the Embassy by an audience of a dozen or so guests, usually PRC government officials. This particular film was set in Ottawa. As it panned over the city skyline, our Chinese guests suddenly jumped up and announced they were leaving. We discovered that the film, produced before recognition in 1970, had a brief shot of the ROC flag flying over its Ottawa Embassy. Three of us had vetted the film before showing it, and none had taken notice of the flag. We were embarrassed, Ottawa was not amused, and we had acquired a better understanding of the important role that names, flags, and anthems were playing in the PRC-ROC confrontation.

After the May IOC meeting, the intensity of the situation temporarily subsided as all sides retreated to explore their positions. Killanin said that he was ready to travel to Peking to talk directly with PRC officials, yet months passed and no meeting took place. He had hesitated to go earlier, but now the PRC was not ready to meet with him. It was apparent that everyone was waiting for someone else to make a move. In November, the Canadian government told a group of Taiwanese boxers who intended to participate in a pre-Olympic event in Montreal that they were welcome in Canada "provided you do not claim to represent the ROC." They declined to come. The Department said that this was "an application of Canada's normal policy on Taiwanese entry." On December 8, the Canadian IOC representative, James Worrall, said he had informed Killanin that Canada had applied its "normal regulation" as per Foreign Minister Sharp's 1969 letter to the IOC. Worrall reminded Killanin that Deputy Minister Andrew had said that any policy change would require "a ministerial decision," and the implication was that such a change was most improbable.

The Department asked to meet with Killanin, but that could not be arranged until early 1976 during the Innsbruck Winter Games. Canada wanted to learn what action the IOC had taken on the question of PRC/Taiwan participation to ascertain the IOC's thoughts on a possible boycott or disruption in Montreal by the PRC or Taiwan. The Department did not intend to go beyond these points, since no final decision had been announced by Canada regarding the Taiwanese team's participation. Ottawa did not want to ease the pressure on the IOC "since it was up to the latter to find its own solution."

In a later conversation, Arthur Andrew said the Department did not think that the IOC would vote to admit the PRC before the Montreal Games. The best that Canada could expect was a compromise solution requiring Taiwan to change its name from ROC to Taiwan or to Formosa, as in the 1960 Rome formula. One problem was that "the PRC had not formally revealed its final position on the Olympic question, if indeed it had one." China might accept the barring of the Taiwan boxers as a symbolic victory, drop its efforts to participate in Montreal, and instead continue to build up support among the international sports federations so it could be admitted for the 1980 Moscow Games. Andrew said:

> The PRC has clearly indicated to us that it expects us to do something. Not to take action would be a very serious problem in our bilateral relations. The PRC has not raised the question with Canada at the highest level, and has not made clear exactly what it expects us to do. It appears to be awaiting the results of the Innsbruck meeting, like everybody else. There are indications that the PRC is less interested in participating in Montreal than in denying Taiwan's participation.

The Department then listed four options for Canada if the ROC remained a member of the IOC and planned on sending a team to Montreal:

1. Allow entry to a team designated as ROC. (Unacceptable)
2. Allow entry to a team called Taiwan or Formosa, but not ROC. (Acceptable)
3. Refuse entry to a Taiwan team under any circumstances. (Not current Canadian policy)
4. Allow entry to a team designated as Taiwan or Formosa only if a representational/symbolic formula is negotiated to permit both a Taiwan/Formosa and a PRC team to participate in Montreal. Otherwise no Taiwanese entry. (Desirable but probably unlikely)

At Innsbruck, Killanin confirmed that it was unlikely that the IOC would resolve "the China problem" during the Winter Games, possibly not even prior to the 1976 Montreal Games. It was also now clear that the PRC was no longer pressing to get IOC membership to compete in Montreal. However, Canada still could not count on Killanin, or on the IOC, to prevent Taiwan from participating as the ROC or as China.

The Department stated that participants from Taiwan could take part in the 1976 Games, "but only if they do not try to use the name of the ROC, or under any other designation which includes the word 'China,' and that they will not use any flags, anthems, emblems or other descriptions of the ROC. We will need to secure

Killanin's support, or at least his understanding, if we hope to have it applied during the Games. Consequently, arrangements should be made for an early meeting by the Prime Minister, or the Foreign Minister, with Lord Killanin."

However, another month passed before Killanin was informed by letter of Ottawa's decision. No reason was given for this delay, although based on later conversations, the government had decided, "at the highest levels," that Canada should continue to delay. On May 2, Prime Minister Trudeau approved the decision to refuse the Taiwanese Olympic team's entry to Canada if it called itself China. Mitchell Sharp, now head of the Privy Council Office and leader of the government in the House, told Trudeau that he would be meeting on May 26 with James Worrall to inform him of this decision and to request IOC cooperation in carrying it out. Sharp restated Canada's rationale: "We permit the entry of persons from Taiwan, including sportsmen, to take part in conferences, sports events, and other gatherings provided they do not proclaim themselves as representatives of the ROC, display ROC flags, or other emblems and propaganda on behalf of the ROC."

Sharp also said that "any solution had to give equal weight to the importance of maintaining reasonably good relations with both the IOC and the PRC." This was "the most defensible position, whatever happens this summer." He concluded with the observation that, "if we alter our policy towards the ROC for the sake of the Olympics, what are we left with as a policy *after* the Olympics?" Worrall immediately informed Killanin, who asked for a written statement of the Canadian position. It was provided by letter on May 28, signed by Sharp. The letter, which arrived in Lausanne on June 1, provided the background and rationale for "the intention to apply Canada's *normal regulations* governing Taiwanese entry to Canada to those persons from Taiwan who will participate in the Olympics" (emphasis added).

Sharp said the question of membership in the Olympic movement was "a matter that can be settled [only] by the IOC ... But since this question has not been resolved so far, it has become necessary for the Canadian government to take a position, insofar as the summer Olympic Games are concerned, because our China policy is involved. Back in 1960, the Taiwanese had participated as Formosa – the Rome formula – so a solution was obvious." Sharp added: "We hope that some such name might be adopted on this occasion."

Crisis

Sharp's remarks precipitated a crisis that lasted from early June until the July 17 opening of the Games. Canada took an almost merciless beating in the international media, especially from the Americans, including President Gerald Ford, future president Ronald Reagan, and Secretary of State Henry Kissinger. The Canadian government was also criticized by the Conservative Party opposition in the House, the Canadian Olympic Committee, and the Canadian media. In their view, aside from again sacrificing Taiwan, Canada had intruded into the realm of international sport, uncharacteristic of a democratic nation such as Canada, and it should not have crossed the boundary between national political interest and Olympic sport.

When it became apparent that Ottawa was not backing down, Canada's actions were compared to Hitler's policies during the 1936 Olympics. Killanin linked the Canadian action to the exclusion of Jewish athletes in the 1936 Berlin Olympics, although he stopped short of actually equating the two situations or of directly comparing Prime Minister Trudeau to Hitler. At the peak of the crisis, the Americans said they would pull out their entire team of 467 athletes. ABC threatened to cancel its television coverage – the loss of US$25 million in broadcast fees would have dealt a deadly financial blow to the IOC. There was also serious talk of a last-minute relocation of the Games to Mexico City or to California. Canada was excoriated in the European and American press, accused of reneging on its promises and of kowtowing to Peking, so it could sell more Canadian wheat to China.

Much of this hostility stemmed from Killanin's reaction to Sharp's letter. On June 8, he issued an official reply, stating that the suggestions made in the letter were "in complete conflict with Olympic rules and contrary to the conditions under which Montreal was awarded the Games. Had this been indicated at the time, the IOC, supported by the international sports federations, would not have selected Montreal." Canada was "in direct conflict with fundamental principles," and "no discrimination is allowed against any country or person on grounds of race, religion or political affiliation." He also noted that recognition of an Olympic committee does not imply political recognition, which was outside the IOC's competence, but it is dependent upon the "area" – the words "country" or "nation" were deliberately not used – having a stable government for a reasonable period. He also added that the Taiwan National Olympic Committee no longer claimed sovereignty over any sport in the area governed by the PRC, and it did not purport to represent any athletes on the mainland.

Killanin referred to a "protocol" involving the Olympic Games, which held that Olympic territory was sacred and that, during the Games, the IOC was the supreme authority:

> I must point out that since Hitler endeavoured to interfere in the Berlin Olympic Games, it has always been made clear to and accepted by all organising countries that all Olympic areas are considered "Olympic territory," and any actions which include nomenclatures of Olympic Committees, flags and anthems, are the prerogative of the IOC. During the period of the Games, the IOC is the supreme authority.

Killanin claimed that he had explained the IOC position to Canada several times, specifically in April 1975 and at Innsbruck in 1976. "No Canadian objection was raised. Therefore, the proposals you now make are in complete reversal of the conditions under which Canada was awarded the Games." On June 24, Killanin sent a telegram to Sharp, saying that, since he had not received any reply to his letter of June 8, "I therefore assume that you are in agreement with my views and will comply with Olympic rules and regulations." Foreign Minister Allan MacEachen immediately cabled back that the position of the Canadian government had not changed and that "therefore, I am unable to confirm that we are in agreement with your views." He said that a meeting between Killanin and Department officials should be held as soon as possible, and he restated the Canadian government's position:

> Clearly it would be in Lord Killanin's interest in some circumstances to attempt to persuade us to his position through public pressure. We should not allow him to choose either timing or method. We therefore propose to go public on this issue with a comprehensive statement of our position if Lord Killanin makes a public statement on the subject, or if the outcome of our exchanges with him or other publicity suggests such a statement is imminent. We would take the approach that we are proposing a reasonable solution to the problem.

On July 2, Killanin did "go public," revealing the exchange of letters and harshly criticizing Canada. The *New York Times* announced that "Canada Bans Taiwan Team." The *Globe and Mail* was more cautious, with a headline that read "Canada May Lose Sanction for Olympics." The press quoted an IOC representative in Lausanne, who said: "We are in a position one step removed from cancelling the Olympic Games. We would remove the name 'Olympic' from the Games and cancel all ceremonies and medal presentations. They would just become a Canadian sporting event." The US Olympic Committee sent a telegram to the Canadian Olympic Committee, saying that the Americans would probably boycott the Games if they were no longer officially sanctioned.

Killanin backtracked, claiming that he had not threatened to decertify the Games. It was reported that the Taiwan athletes, most of whom were training in California, "were depressed by the whole affair" and that their track coach, C.K. Yang, "was in tears." China announced it was sending a large delegation of officials from the All-China Sports Federation to the pre-Olympic IOC meetings in Montreal to ensure that Peking had a voice in any Olympics decision. In Peking, Chinese officials cornered Canadian Embassy officials at a diplomatic reception to remind Canada of its agreement to observe the "one-China" policy. "In view of the good relations between China and Canada, Chinese authorities express the hope

that the Canadian government will not give credence to any misguided attempt to implement a 'two-China' or a 'one China, one
Taiwan' solution."

In the House, the Conservative member Otto Jelinek, a former
Olympic competitor, pointedly asked: "Why the flip flop on the
Olympics?" Prime Minister Trudeau replied that there had been
no change in Canadian policy. The IOC could solve the problem
by asking Taiwan to use the 1960 Olympics formula when it had
participated as Formosa:

> Mr. Speaker, the Hon. Member may not have been listening. The Sec-
> retary of State for External Affairs said there was no sudden flip flop.
> This problem has been in discussion with the IOC for more than a
> year. They apparently have not seen fit in one way or another to solve
> this problem as of yet, but they have indicated to the Secretary of State
> for External Affairs the very obvious answer. It is the one they them-
> selves gave to Italy in 1960 ... [The problem] had already been solved
> 16 years ago.[5]

Ottawa took steps to prevent members of the Taiwan team from
entering Canada in advance of the Games. Those who held dual
US and Taiwanese citizenship could use their American passports
to enter Canada at any time, but most of the team held Taiwanese
passports, and they needed tourist visas to enter Canada. "At this
moment we haven't issued any visas, and until assurances from
the IOC have been made that they won't compete as ROC, none
will be forthcoming." The Department advised posts to be on the
alert to intercept members of the Taiwan team who were applying for Canadian tourist visas. All points of entry received a list
of the names of the Taiwanese team members to ensure that this
policy was enforced. Despite taking these measures, the Canadian government was concerned that even if Taiwan agreed to
participate under a different name, "there is a substantial risk
that, while in Canada, the Taiwanese will deliberately violate the
intent of our policy and carry out some public activity, embarrassing our government, in order to promote the identity and
claims of the ROC."

Resolution

It was now July 10. Killanin referred again to Mitchell Sharp's letter of 1969. He claimed that the intent of the letter was that Canada agreed to admit all athletes from IOC-sanctioned Olympic committees without reservation. He dismissed Sharp's qualifier in the letter, "pursuant to the normal regulations," as a meaningless phrase.

The IOC vice president then asked if Canada might accept a compromise whereby Taiwan could participate "under IOC patronage." That would have permitted Taiwan to carry the Olympic flag with its five rings and march under a placard with the initials "IOC," without any national anthem. Canada said it was interested, although it again enquired about using the Rome formula. Killanin replied that the Rome formula was not "neutral," since it would mean an actual name change of an Olympic committee, from "ROC" to "Formosa" or to "Taiwan." Canada would be seen as interfering in the IOC by telling it to change the name of one of its members. He said there were two choices: either neutral participation under IOC patronage, or the Rome formula – and the former was preferable. According to Andrew, what the IOC was suggesting with the "neutral formula" was for Taiwan to fly the Olympic flag, have no name, and use the Olympic anthem. That could be acceptable to Canada.

Taiwan refused. The head of its delegation said: "There is no possibility that we will take part in these Games under those conditions, but we will wait and see what the full session of the IOC says." That day, twenty-five members of the Taiwan Olympics team showed up in Boston, having waited for three hours in Detroit, unable to enter Canada. Another twenty went back to California, and still others returned to the American Midwest, where they had been training. On July 11, US President Ford went to Plattsburgh, New York, to give an elaborate send-off to the first of the 500 American athletes and officials going to Montreal. His press secretary, when asked about the status of Taiwan and America's position, replied: "It's too soon to consider the question of withdrawal." The next day, however, Ford announced that he opposed the IOC decision, and although he claimed he had no power over the US Olympic Committee, he said that he hoped it would vote against the proposal.

In a subsequent press conference, Foreign Minister MacEachen remarked:

I was surprised the head of any government would suggest to the representatives of his national Olympic Committee how they ought to vote. We have been scrupulous in avoiding talking with, or even suggesting to our own national Olympic Committee what position it ought to take in any of these matters. When the head of a government suggests to representatives of a national Olympic committee how they ought to vote, that really is bringing politics into the international Olympic movement.

Within a week to go, the Executive Board of the IOC recommended that Taiwan could compete under the Olympic banner – the so-called "neutral formula." Taiwan had already indicated this solution was unacceptable, but it was hoped that the United States, its strongest supporter, could persuade Taiwan to accept a compromise. Julian Roosevelt, one of the two American members on the IOC Board, said that it would probably be rejected. He stated: "I am sure ninety percent of the IOC members are opposed to this capitulation. I think we've got to call Trudeau's bluff. Let him call this the Montreal Games if he wants, but not the Olympic Games."

It was speculated that the Mayor of Montreal, Jean Drapeau, also opposed the Canadian government's position, partly because of the serious economic repercussions for his city if the Games were cancelled and also because Quebec could interpret this stance as unnecessary federal intervention at a time of surging Quebec separatism. Killanin called on Drapeau on July 10, seeking his support. The next day, however, Drapeau wrote a personal letter to Killanin, which Drapeau later read to Arthur Andrew on the telephone, supporting the Canadian government position without reservation.

The IOC members voted to support the Executive Board's recommendation to disallow Taiwan's participation if it called itself China. The *Globe and Mail* headline read: "IOC Rules against

Taiwan, Threat to Games Removed." Killanin said that, while the IOC had ruled that Taiwan could not compete if called itself the ROC, it was still unclear whether Taiwan would reconsider the IOC's compromise proposal, the "neutral formula," whereby its athletes could compete under the Olympic banner. The Taiwanese Olympic Committee informed him that "our government in Taipei is considering the proposal, and will give us their answer tomorrow." The Americans reacted with anger to the IOC decision that prevented Taiwan from competing as China, and the vice president of the US Olympic Committee said that the American team should either withdraw from the Montreal Games or compete under protest: "There has to be a strong stand on the principle involved. The situation doesn't look very good."

The next day, Taiwan announced that its team would not participate if it had to give up its name and the right to bear its flag and play its national anthem. The neutral formula was now dead. From its ashes, however, emerged a last-minute phoenix put forth by Taiwan and supported by its principal advocate, the United States. This solution was the short-lived "Taiwanese Already in Canada Formula," wherein Taiwan proposed that its two athletes and three officials who were already in Canada because they held US passports would parade in the opening day ceremonies under the ROC flag and name. Then they would immediately withdraw and return home to Taiwan without competing in the Games. The IOC said it was willing to support this compromise as a gesture to reassert IOC control and to save face for two of its members in good standing, Taiwan and the United States. However, the Canadian government immediately rejected this formula out of hand as a political stunt that violated Canadian policy.

Killanin said he had telephoned Prime Minister Trudeau to tell him that the IOC had gone as far as it could and that he was ready to discuss any other last-minute possibilities. "I had to phone the Prime Minister in the morning to tell him that I would not be able to make it to Ottawa for the Olympics flame lighting ceremony. While I had the chance, we went over the whole situation. An hour later he called me back to say the flag and anthem situation would be okay." However, Trudeau had no recollection of this conversation – "I never spoke directly with him," he said – although he did offer the IOC a final compromise: that Taiwan could fly the ROC flag and play the ROC anthem, but it could not call itself the ROC. The prime minister said the next day: "They can fly whatever flag they want, and play whatever little tune they want, but let them not call themselves representatives of China."

The Cabinet decision of July 17 stated the final Canadian position: athletes from Taiwan were welcome in Canada as long as they did not claim to represent the "Republic of China" or "China." The Cabinet further agreed:

> In order to assist the International Olympic Committee in meeting some of the difficulties caused by the refusal of the Taiwan delegation to participate under the Olympic banner, the Secretary of State for External Affairs is authorized to agree to a formula such as used in Rome in 1960 whereby the delegation from Taiwan will be identified in writing by the word "Taiwan" to the exclusion of any mention of "China" or "Republic of China." That, preferably, the flag to be used by the delegation be the Olympic flag or the flag of the "Republic of China" with Olympic motif added; that in the last analysis the flag of the "Republic of China" be accepted as long as all written identification refers exclusively to Taiwan.
>
> Members of the Taiwan delegation who have gained legal admission to Canada will be allowed to remain. The members of the Taiwan delegation that have not yet entered Canada will not be authorized to enter until a final agreement is reached concerning the status of the delegation and the modalities of its participation.

The IOC Board reluctantly approved "the final IOC compromise offer." The vote was fifty-eight in favour, two opposed, and six abstentions in support of the revised "Rome formula." Taiwan withdrew immediately after the vote. Its government could not relinquish the name ROC, and the Taiwanese, with eighty-seven pieces of luggage plus their equestrian horse, immediately returned home. Roosevelt, the American IOC representative, said the members of the ROC team "were ready to participate with the unwanted name of Taiwan, rather than dropping out, as long as they would have their own flag and anthem. They knew they'd be heroes, but they just couldn't convince the people back home." Killanin told IOC members he was bitterly disappointed that Taiwan had chosen to leave and felt that "Taiwan had let us down."

The IOC said its decision "did not constitute a precedent" and was valid only for the Montreal Games. In fact, the modified Rome formula became the basis for the participation of both Chinas in future Olympic Games. Neither of them participated in the 1980 Moscow Games, but in the 1984 Los Angeles Olympics, they resolved the China name issue by competing as two separate teams, with Taiwan calling itself "China (Taipei)." The Canadian stand that had caused such a backlash in 1976 was settled less than a decade later.

The Department said the experience had been unique and challenging:

> [Our position] represented the application of certain basic features of our China policy for the first time in a unique area of international activity, the Olympics. It was a forum in which our action was highly visible, and inevitably in collision with the general firmly held belief that politics plays no part in the Games. Criticism from the information media, at home and abroad, was not surprising.

From Ottawa's perspective, Canada's position was logical, based upon the application of the "one-China" policy that Canada had agreed to after establishing diplomatic relations in 1970. In a "normal" bilateral situation, Canada would have been capable of pursuing this policy without incident. The Montreal Games had moved Canadian China policy squarely into the international arena, where it encountered entrenched interests that were protecting Taiwan and targeting the PRC. This opposition had dug itself into the International Olympic Committee. Taiwan's principal protector was the United States, the most powerful IOC member. It was a strong supporter of the political status quo for the island, and it was determined to defend Taiwan's sovereignty to the bitter end. Behind the scenes, the PRC repeatedly reminded Canada of its commitment to a one-China policy. At times, it seemed the weight of these forces would overwhelm Canada's capacity to defend its position. By imposing a national political agenda onto an arena of international sport, Canada was defending an unpopular position. Mitchell Sharp pointed out: "Of course we were right. As the Prime Minister said, our policy was consistent, and it was logical. We knew it was unpopular. Had we overreacted? We never thought so. Trudeau made the final decision, and he had the Department's support. We were just observing our one-China policy."

In my diary I wrote:

> Taiwan isn't going to Montreal and China isn't yet a member. After those many months negotiating with the PRC sports people in Beijing I didn't expect such an outcome – that neither China would show up. Maybe I've underestimated the PRC. The PRC does not seem satisfied with Canada's efforts. This also looks like another setback for the Americans.

A Post-mortem

The exclusion of Taiwan from the Montreal Olympics was a political drama played out by five actors: Trudeau and the Canadian government; Killanin and the International Olympic Committee; the United States and its Olympic Committee; and "the two Chinas," the ROC and the PRC. The outcome supported Canada, but not the other members of this *dramatis personae*. Taiwan was not allowed to participate as the ROC, and its antagonist, the PRC, still remained outside the IOC. The Americans lost prestige by failing to protect Taiwan, and the Canadian government had to endure a barrage of international criticism. In this post-mortem, we take a closer look at these five players and their programs.

Trudeau and the Canadian Government

For Trudeau, a "one-China" policy was an absolute condition of Canadian recognition of China. It put Taiwan where it belonged, as a protectorate of the United States, and it gave to Canada symbolic, if not real, independence from American policy. The prime minister's position was clear: "I intervened directly at the end on the grounds that our government's decision was logical. We could not allow the Taiwanese to perform in Canada under a flag that made a claim to a territory they did not rule. We had no choice if we wanted to stay on the right side of Peking, and it was consistent with our 1970 recognition decision."

Ivan Head, the prime minister's foreign policy advisor, recalled that "the Prime Minister's technique was to stay out. In Trudeau's view, Prime Ministers get in too early and could be criticized for influencing events prematurely. Don't use up your energy if you can avoid it. Save it for when it is absolutely necessary." Trudeau said he was not involved in the early stages of the Olympics issue and only stepped in when there was a crisis in the last couple of weeks. "I can remember Ivan Head sending me some of the more outlandish editorials. They even called me Hitler. This probably helped mobilize Canadian support for our position. When the Americans took an active role in support of Taiwan, and when Ford criticized Canada, that helped our side. Canadian sympathy for the Olympics was replaced by Canadian anger at American intervention."

Trudeau said he did not talk with Ford personally about the Olympics. He had a good relationship with him. The American president's actions criticizing Trudeau and Canada "were obviously the results of election pressures on him." Head confirmed that Trudeau and Ford did not communicate directly on the Olympics issue. "The Americans were stuck with Taiwan. The Taiwan lobby in Washington, the Committee of One Million, was powerful and continued to exercise a strong influence on US policy."[6]

The Olympics crisis was played out in the international media as a confrontation between the IOC and the Canadian prime minister. Killanin claimed to have discussed the issue with Trudeau. This was apparently confirmed by the minutes of the July 17 Cabinet decision, and Trudeau may have forgotten that he had spoken with him. "I can remember arguing with someone from the Olympic Committee, but not Killanin. I don't recall either meeting with him, or talking on the phone."[7]

Who made the final decision? The prime minister said there was no real discussion in Cabinet. It was unanimous. Head added a qualifier: "The trade and commercial people – the public servants – they were concerned that Canada was going to lose trade with Taiwan, but they did not have the final say." Trudeau said the decision was consistent with Canadian government policy right to the end. "I said they could fly whatever flag they wanted and play whatever anthem [he called it "their little tune"], but we could never deviate from the principle that you cannot pretend to call yourself something else."

Lord Killanin and the IOC

For many Canadians, Lord Killanin was the villain of the piece, a master of indecision and dissimulation. After he took over as president of the IOC, there were high hopes that he could settle the China issue by reinstating the PRC, and keep both the ROC and the PRC as members. He represented "a younger generation, aware of the cleavage in the Olympic movement and more amenable to change." He resolved "to do my best to solve the Chinese puzzle and get the PRC back into the Olympic arena." Yet he did not go to Peking, and he waited too long to deal with the Taiwan issue. He said that the problem was finally resolved because of the talks he had with Prime Minister Trudeau just before the Games were to begin, conversations that Trudeau did not recall. At the press conference following the Games, he condemned Canada for acting like Hitler in the 1936 Games, and he also criticized Taiwan for "being far more interested in making a political point than engaging in athletic competition."

Killanin was under enormous pressure from all sides. The PRC refused to give an inch on its demand to exclude Taiwan, and opinions were divided within the IOC on the need to disallow Taiwan from competing as "China." The Americans and their allies had formed a powerful group inside the IOC in support of Taiwan, and Killanin's vacillations are explained, in good part, by the split within the IOC between the American-led group defending the ROC and the bloc of representatives from the developing countries that supported the PRC. Furthermore, the Taiwan issue was only one of several urgent matters confronting him in 1976. There were doubts that the construction of the new Olympic facilities in Montreal would be finished in time for the opening ceremonies, and over twenty African nations were threatening to boycott the Games if New Zealand participated. Even the prospect of the Queen's appearance at the opening of the Games posed a problem: would she speak in English or in French? Eventually the latter was chosen to satisfy Quebec, on the grounds "that French takes precedence over English in the Olympic movement."

Those in the Canadian foreign policymaking process who sought to engage Killanin felt he didn't take Canada seriously. His occasional arrogance, and his insistence on comparing Canada's actions with that of Nazi Germany, did not sit well with Canadian officials. A Departmental analysis later questioned why he had not asked sooner for clarification of Sharp's 1969 phrase "pursuant to the normal regulations." Was it that Killanin was confident Canada would give way in the end and do what he wanted? One Department official referred to "a British colonialist mentality that he carried with him wherever he went. He forgot we were no longer a colony." Killanin had assumed Canada would back down, as many other governments had done in the past when facing international condemnation, especially when it involved a sporting event. He may have thought that international opposition to Canada's actions, and the support of the Americans, were his trump cards.

The United States

The Americans exercised their muscle, weighing in with a barrage of criticism of Canada. It came from President Ford, because supporting Taiwan had become an American presidential election issue. Siding with Taiwan against the PRC was deemed an American responsibility. Respectable newspapers, such as the *New York Times* and the *Washington Post*, wrote editorials harshly critical of Canada and Trudeau. American representatives in the Olympic movement condemned the Canadian action. They organized support inside the IOC and threatened to withdraw from the Games. ABC television reminded everyone that if the American team withdrew, ABC had the right to abrogate its US$25 million contract, and at least three American cities said they were ready to host the Games if the IOC took them away from Montreal.

The usually measured *New York Times* wrote a tough editorial condemning Canada, suggesting it was "obviously acting under heavy pressure from Peking." The editorial concluded that "Prime Minister Trudeau would be well advised to reconsider his apparent willingness to cave in to Peking's demand that the Olympics be subservient to international politics." The Canadian Consulate in Los Angeles reported a bomb threat on July 13. The *Washington Post* referred to Prime Minister Trudeau as "the grand censor of the Olympics," and then added: "By the way, when do you think the Olympics might be held in Canada again?"

The Canadian Embassy in Washington said there was reason to worry "when the best papers such as the *New York Times*, the *Washington Post*, and the *Los Angeles Times*, and others have all lost their objectivity." It added: "Essentially we were seen to have come down on the wrong side of the motherhood issue, i.e., the supposed immunity of the Olympics from 'political interference.' The baser motives then imputed to us, such as kowtowing to communists and concern for Canadian wheat sales, were rounding out the picture."[8]

The key battleground was not in the American media or in exchanges between the two governments. It was in the Executive Board and Council of the IOC, in the international sports federations, and with Taiwan, where the Americans played the key role. If the United States had not committed itself to supporting Taiwan's presence in the Olympics, it is fair to say there would not have been a crisis. A large part of Taiwan's team had been trained in the United States, attending schools there, and Taiwanese athletes were a part of the American sports scene. For years, the IOC had acquiesced to US wishes in international sport, and American television revenues fuelled Olympic budgets.

Was Canadian exclusion of Taiwan an example of Canadian anti-Americanism, the government knowingly choosing a path that put Canadian sovereignty in direct conflict with American interests? Trudeau did not see it that way. He stated: "I had my arguments in the past with the Americans, Nixon in particular, but Canada's position on the Olympics was not anti-American. We knew they would lose face if Taiwan was excluded, but they were on the wrong side of history."

The American administration found itself in a difficult situation as it played out its political battles with the PRC behind the scenes, in the Olympic Committee and in backrooms, with its Taiwanese allies. It had kept its public criticism of Canada more or less under control until just before the Games. It was harder to assess the damage caused by the emotional overreaction from the US media, although the expectation was that most of the criticism of Canada would fade away once the Olympics were over and other national and international issues commanded attention.

The People's Republic of China

China shaped the issue that brought about the crisis. The PRC's determination to replace the ROC in the Olympics created the context in which Canada, if it wished to retain its one-China policy, had to support the PRC. The Chinese made their position known at every opportunity, beginning in early 1974. Initially, the Chinese wanted admission to the Montreal Games in 1976, but by the end of 1975, as admission appeared doubtful, they focused on Taiwan's exclusion. The PRC expected Canada to be its ally. It refused to accept that there was any formal separation between the "independent" Canadian Olympic Committee and the Canadian government. One PRC Sports Federation official, seemingly puzzled, asked: "But you are all Canadians aren't you? How can the Canadian government have no control over its own citizens in this matter?"

The Chinese Ministry of Foreign Affairs outlined its basic position on the Olympics issue:

- The "Chiang Kai-shek clique" [Taiwan] has no right to participate in the Games.
- The Sino-Canadian Agreement of 1970 recognizes the PRC as the sole legal government of China, and Taiwan is an integral part of China.

- Relations between Canada and China "have progressed satisfactorily," and China hopes this will continue by Canada "taking measures to prevent the Chiang clique from entering Canada to participate in the Olympics."
- The Chinese Government and people oppose any "two-Chinas" or "one-China, one-Taiwan" policy.

Not being a member of the IOC, the PRC could not participate in the final decision. However, it continued to act as a watchdog over the participants, reminding Canada that it must not compromise its "one-China" policy. On July 17, China objected to the modified Rome formula that would have permitted Taiwan to compete under the Olympic banner. Zhang Wenjin, the PRC ambassador in Ottawa, complained that the Rome formula would still allow Taiwan to use the ROC flag and play the ROC anthem, and he demanded that "Canada prohibit totally the participation of Taiwanese athletes under any circumstances."

The head of the All-China Sports Federation said the whole affair was a plot to gang up on China. The two superpowers, the United States and the Soviet Union, "were conspiring to prop up the Chiang clique to perpetuate a two-China policy." In fact, in the IOC debates, the Soviet Union had defended the PRC's position. While China did express a measure of gratitude to its "friends," it was not satisfied, since the PRC still remained outside the Olympics and Taiwan was not formally expelled from the IOC, just the use of the name "ROC."

Chinese gratitude was thus given grudgingly, even though Canada had made a strong commitment to the bilateral relationship and, in the process, had aggravated relations with its friends. In a later interview, the PRC ambassador said that, while Canadian efforts had been "somewhat helpful," Taiwan was still a member of the IOC. It continued to call itself China, so "Canada had essentially failed." His words rankled those Canadians who had done their best to uphold the one-China policy under trying circumstances. Was there a lesson for Canadians that foreshadowed future problems in the relationship with Beijing? The Department knew well enough that, on August 2, the day after the Games were over, PRC watchdogs would again be waiting at the doors of the Pearson Building in Ottawa, bearing complaints about a Taiwan group that had just arrived somewhere in Canada calling itself "ROC" and waving its flag.

Taiwan – The Republic of China

Taiwan lacked official status in the negotiations, but it was a central player. Canada could communicate indirectly from time to time with Taiwanese officials through meetings in a third country, although such meetings happened rarely. The contents of Mitchell Sharp's letter of May 28, 1976, to Lord Killanin were passed on to Taipei through American auspices in Washington in early June. The Taiwanese realized that Canada intended to apply "the normal regulations governing entry to Canada for persons from Taiwan who intended to participate in the Olympics and related meetings." Canada probably was not going to budge, and it was clear that the Taiwanese could not call themselves "China" when they were in Canada.

Taiwan's strength lay in its alliance with the Americans and the support it had from the international sports movement, including from inside the IOC. While the pro-Taiwan lobby in the United States had lost some of the influence that it had in the 1950s and 1960s, it still had enough power to maintain a profile of Taiwan as a loyal anti-communist ally of the Americans. A second image was that of a small, defenceless nation trying to compete in international sport. The pro-Taiwan lobby had persuaded Ronald Reagan to support Taiwan in his campaign for the 1976 Republican presidential nomination, which had forced President Gerald Ford also to become a strong advocate for Taiwan's participation in the Montreal Games.

Taiwan's support in the international sports movement was based on the fact that the island was a member of the majority of the twenty-six international sports federations and a member of the Olympic Committee. It had an exceptionally strong connection with American sports institutions and organizations. Taiwanese athletes were familiar names and faces to Americans. Many had competed in America while attending university, and they often remained in the United States afterwards to continue their training and engage in competition. C.K. Yang, the Taiwanese decathlon star, was as well-known as any American athlete for his achievements in the late 1950s and early 1960s. It was Yang, a Taiwanese team coach in 1976, who pleaded unsuccessfully with his government to allow his athletes to compete in Montreal.

Despite being advised by American sports and administration officials to compete in Montreal using the modified Rome formula, the Taiwanese athletes were nevertheless ordered to return home by their government in Taipei. Was Taiwan's withdrawal the best tactic? When fighting for one's sovereignty, a name can mean everything. The island was in a difficult situation. It was awaiting the outcome of talks between the United States and China that would determine its future autonomy, which finally occurred in 1979 when the Americans also agreed there was only one China, while continuing to guarantee Taiwan's autonomy and security.

Logical and Consistent

The crisis faded quickly. The PRC acquired IOC membership in 1979. Both the PRC and Taiwan participated in the Los Angeles Games in 1984. The modified Rome formula had found a permanent solution for Taiwan to compete as China (Taipei), a designation that would be used not only in future Olympiads, but also for dual PRC and Taiwan membership in other multilateral organizations. By the 1990s, few Canadians would remember that there had been an Olympic crisis in 1976, and that the issue had created so much trouble for Canada.

One can say that Canada's strategy was a success because the government stuck to its position and ultimately prevailed. As Trudeau said, "our policy was logical and consistent." That was also my reaction at the time, first as a participant in the decision-making process in Peking and later from an academic perspective.

Some of my former colleagues in the Department felt Canada may have been too logical and too insistent on driving its "one-China policy" to a rational conclusion. Canada lost a significant amount of prestige internationally, and it was criticized for being too close to Peking. Did some critics really believe Canada took this stand just so it could sell China more wheat? What appeared to many Canadians as a sign of independence was perceived elsewhere as embracing China too closely, and once more sacrificing Taiwan.

In the end, Canada experienced the rigidity of China's policies and a taste of the Chinese perception of "friendship." The PRC let us know that it was dissatisfied with Canada. We had also alienated our allies, in particular the American protector of Taiwan. It was an awkward decision, "logical" to use Trudeau's assessment, and also "consistent," in that Canada reinforced its "one-China" policy. The outcome was not very satisfying, and Canada was roundly criticized for its defence of that policy.

What did it say about the Canadian foreign policymaking process? The Department did its job, was well prepared, and supplied the appropriate information and briefing material. It also provided the rationale that made the decision "logical." This consistent application of policy echoed the thinking of the prime minister. There were no surprises here. This position was Trudeau's policy, and everyone fell in line, including those members of the government who felt we were too rigid and that Ottawa might have made an exception for the Olympics. Canada had constructed a new bilateral relationship with the PRC, but when this relationship became tangled up with the interests of so many other countries, Canada was not well prepared to deal with the ensuing criticism. We may have waited too long to act, thinking that others would support us. When Canada did act, it relied upon the intervention of a strong prime minister playing the national card, with the rationale of "logic and consistency," to see us through. Not a smooth ending, but perhaps the best that Canada could have hoped for under those challenging circumstances.

chapter four

Development Assistance for China

After ten years, the Cultural Revolution finally ended. Mao Zedong and Zhou Enlai had died, and China was slowly restoring order. In 1976, Ambassador Arthur Menzies recommended organizing more ministerial visits, promoting exports, and widening educational exchanges and technology transfer with China. In 1979, the two sides negotiated an agreement to send 500 Chinese to Canada for training in science and technology. This initiative was the beginning of Canada's aid program with China, although at the time it was not called "development assistance."

China needed assistance. At least 80 per cent of China's population lived below the official UN poverty line, and its annual per capita income was still under $US300. In the wake of Beijing's split with Moscow, Soviet aid had evaporated, leaving China stuck with unfinished projects. During the Cold War, communist countries normally did not take aid from the capitalist world, but the Maoist period was over, the Cold War was waning, and Beijing could now explore that option. China approached the United Nations Development Program (UNDP) for help, and it also started development assistance initiatives with Australia, Japan, and Belgium.

It took Canada several years to establish an aid program with China. While the polls supported extending Canadian aid to China, no "new money" was available to finance such a program, and there were conflicting views as to what type of assistance Canada might offer. Should Canada even be giving aid to communists? Should it focus on large infrastructure projects such as dams and bridges, or should it emphasize smaller projects, such as human resource development and technology transfer? How much funding should go to support trade related projects, and how much for basic aid? Was the Canadian International Development Agency (CIDA) prepared to work with China?

The PRC signalled to Canada that it was interested. Now it was up to the Department and CIDA to consult with the various stakeholders and produce a draft proposal for Cabinet's approval. After nearly two years of discussion, the Department proposed a five-year budget of $100 million, and "new money" was found to fund the program. Ottawa informed Ambassador Michel Gauvin of the decision, and he immediately cabled back his strong opposition. "Why are we giving aid to communists? Why don't the Chinese spend their money on helping their own people, instead of on nuclear weapons and space exploration?" He asked Ottawa to suspend approval or at least to substantially cut the budget. Cabinet reduced the amount by $20 million, and it was approved with almost no opposition. Everyone knew that Prime Minister Pierre Trudeau supported this initiative.

The two sides agreed to establish the program during Foreign Minister Mark MacGuigan's visit to China in 1981. The focus of the program was on aid and not trade. No big projects – "no dams, no bridges." The goal was "to train the trainers." Marcel Massé, the president of CIDA, called this program "the multiplication of contacts at the thinking level," with "human resource development as a principal activity." Initial areas of emphasis were agriculture, forestry, energy, and management. It would begin with university linkages and commercial activity, and then spread to other partnerships with China.

The program became one of the most innovative and influential parts of the bilateral relationship. For almost three decades, CIDA provided training to thousands of Chinese in the PRC and in Canada. The program ended in 2013, when PRC per capita income rose beyond the level that allowed China to remain eligible for Canadian development assistance. CIDA-funded university cooperation led to the development of canola, now an annual multibillion dollar export to the PRC. In management, Canada became a leading trainer of Chinese managers, establishing the first MBA program in China. In agriculture, Canadian assistance helped China to double its pork production. For both sides, the opportunity to spend time in each other's country was invaluable for reducing cultural and ideological barriers.

In the 1990s, CIDA widened its China programming to include governance, human rights, gender equity, and the environment. Canada was training judges, organizing legal aid clinics, supporting grassroots civil society projects, and helping women in rural communities. It was training members of China's National People's Congress (NPC) in legislative practices, and it was working with the Central Party School on issues of environmental management. CIDA had moved into the realm of long-term social and political change. Some have criticized Canada for trying to bring Western value change to a country determined to resist such efforts, and the jury is still out whether these politically focused initiatives will produce the desired outcomes.

In our China aid program we will not be building dams and bridges. We will train the trainers and focus on human resource development. We will do this in both countries. I call it the multiplication of contacts at the thinking level.

– Marcel Massé, president of CIDA, 1982

After the Cultural Revolution

By 1976, the Cultural Revolution was over, and the cost to China was substantial, with careers disrupted, families split apart, purges of China's top leaders, and the loss of over a million lives. Mao's name was on everyone's lips: on wall posters plastered all over China; in 800 million Little Red Books, the Bibles of Revolution that one had to read every day; and in the political struggle sessions that determined whether you were a "class enemy." A decade of revolution had passed, and China was still poor. The majority of the population was living in poverty in a weakened economy, with a revolutionary ideology that was taking its toll on social relations. Over a million people had perished, and an atmosphere of distrust, if not fear, pervaded China. Politically, it wasn't at all certain that the Communist Party could maintain its grip on power. Factionalism had laid bare the myth of Party unity, and the Sino-Soviet split was challenging the cohesion of a waning international communist movement.

China sorely needed to restore momentum, to give direction to its place in an evolving international order, and to focus on the urgent tasks of modernization. The thrice-purged Deng Xiaoping had returned to power after Mao's death, becoming China's "paramount leader." He was taking China on a new path that was opening it up to capitalist markets, experiments with privatization, decollectivization, and closer relations with the outside world. At a key Party meeting in 1978, Deng said that China had to *"kaifang* (open up)" and *"xia hai* (jump into the sea)." It was time to enter the global marketplace. This decision was startling – a Communist Party-state ready to engage with the capitalist world on the latter's turf.[1]

Ottawa cautiously welcomed this opening. Ambassador Menzies reported that China's isolation was apparently ending and that Canada should start organizing more ministerial missions with China:

> The Chinese attach importance to such exchanges, and they can be used to move bilateral relations forward. It was also time to expand the dialogue on multilateral issues. Canadian efforts to engage the Chinese in such a dialogue have not so far been successful. Today Canada has the capability of systematic political, economic, and military reporting on China with ten officers, six of whom have spent two years or more studying Chinese. The Canadian government is well within the top six or seven best informed on China.

The Department proposed an exchange of visits by the foreign ministers of both countries to expand the bilateral economic links. "The Chinese have intimated their interest in a more open trade policy, and the time has come to renew our invitation to the Chinese foreign minister to visit Ottawa." In doing so, Canada thought to steal a march on Western countries, which had not sent high-level visitors to Beijing[2] since Mao's death. The Americans, Japanese, and the major European countries were surpassing Canada in their growing trade with China, and Menzies urged Ottawa to be proactive, because it was "an opportune time for a Canadian initiative, when the Americans and others are still feeling their way in their relations with Beijing."

In early 1978, Foreign Minister Don Jamieson visited the PRC. Huang Hua, his Chinese counterpart, had been in Ottawa a few months earlier, the first visit ever to Canada by a PRC foreign minister.[3] In the next three years, over a dozen ministers from both countries made trips to Ottawa and Beijing, including Vice Premier Bo Yibo, one of China's most senior officials. A high-level group of representatives from top Canadian companies, including Power Corporation, Bombardier, Royal Bank, Cyrus Anvil Corporation, and the British Columbia Council of Forest Industries, accompanied Jamieson. The delegation soon realized that without concessional financing – granting China soft loans with low interest rates to purchase Canadian goods – exporters would have a hard time making a dent in the China market. Jamieson returned to Canada with three observations: Canada already had a large trade surplus because of the wheat sales, and it would be a challenge to sell even more to China; Canadian business needed government help to be competitive in the China market; and Canada had to extend some type of cheaper credit for China to buy other Canadian goods and commodities besides wheat.

In 1979, Canada announced it was establishing a $2 billion line of credit from the Canadian Export Development Corporation (EDC) to finance trade with the PRC. The EDC said that this line of credit was the most significant agreement it had made since its inception in 1944, and Ottawa thought it was now possible for Canadian power, telecommunications, and mining companies to win large contracts in China. The EDC normally would not offer such a large amount to one national trading partner, but "the Canadian government is convinced this is the right time to give its exporters all the possible support in their efforts to penetrate the Chinese market." Unfortunately, the line of credit remained largely unused because it was offered at standard consensus interest rates. The PRC wanted long-term financing at much lower concessional rates, with little or even no interest – and they were getting it from other foreign governments. It would take another seven years, until Prime Minister Brian Mulroney visited Beijing in 1986, before the EDC was allowed to offer competitive concessional interest loans for financing trade with China.

Should Canada Extend Aid to China?

The Canadian government wanted to keep pace with its competitors, notably the Japanese, who were lending China $6 billion and granting concessional financing for large-scale projects. Moreover, Japan was willing to use development assistance funds to win Chinese customers. In Beijing, Canadian Embassy officials reported that the precedent set by Japan in extending aid to China for trade purposes meant that Canada needed to review its policy. Paul Desmarais, head of the Quebec-based Power Corporation, had been developing economic and political links with the PRC since the end of the Cultural Revolution in 1976, and he urged the Canadian government to step in and support trade through technical assistance and long-term low-interest loans under the rubric of aid. According to Desmarais, China had become a "spoiled market" in which foreign sellers were forced to ignore internationally agreed upon standard consensus financing rates. Instead, they were offering financing at lower, concessional interest rates in order to clinch deals.[4]

Was Beijing ready to accept aid? The PRC had taken substantial assistance from the Soviet Union in the 1950s and 1960s, but in the wake of the Sino-Soviet split, this aid had disappeared, leaving China stuck with a large number of unfinished projects. The Soviet experience made China wary of dependence on foreigners. During the Cold War, communists did not take help from the capitalist world, and the policy of *ziligengsheng* (self-reliance), which emphasized Chinese self-sufficiency, also made it difficult for China to accept outside assistance. However, the Maoist period was now over, Soviet assistance had ended, the Cold War was changing, and China was exploring new options. It needed large amounts of capital, advanced technology, and expertise that it could not get from its own resources or from its former friends in the communist world.[5]

In the late 1970s, China began testing the development aid waters, and it became a member of the World Bank and the International Monetary Fund, as well as the UNDP. The latter agreed to fund several programs in China, and it opened an office in Beijing. In 1979, China accepted $19 million in direct aid from the United Nations High Commissioner for Refugees (UNHCR) to help resettle Indochinese refugees to China. Aid programs involving China were soon established by the World Bank, several United Nations agencies, Japan, Germany, the United Kingdom, Belgium, and Australia.

Canadian unofficial development assistance with China started soon after recognition. The two countries began scientific and technical exchanges in 1972. The government organized over sixty exchanges with China during the 1970s – in geology, oceanography, remote sensing, health care, permafrost construction, metallurgy, coal mining, railways, ports, agriculture, forestry, and fisheries. PRC missions came to Canada to learn about the Canadian experience and to establish potential commercial and research contacts. Canadian groups had a lesser agenda – a chance to visit China and discuss potential future cooperation. They were invariably struck by China's low level of technological expertise, and they wondered how long it would take to develop research partnerships and obtain commercial benefits for Canada. These exchanges were an early form of development assistance to China, which was now portraying itself as a third world country in need of substantial technical aid, eager to catch up with the outside world.

I was responsible for overseeing many of those early programs. Both sides talked about reciprocity, although Canada was giving China far more than it was receiving. Two anecdotes speak to this point. In 1974, a Canadian forestry delegation came to northeast China to see how it was dealing with a plague of spruce budworms that were threatening its forests. Canada had a similar infestation, and we wanted to see what kind of pesticide China was using and how often it was employing chemical sprays. What we saw were large numbers of Chinese up in the trees using hand labour to eliminate the budworms. No machines or any pesticides. Our Chinese hosts said that hand labour was their best option and that Western chemicals and technology were not cost effective for them.

The PRC then sent their foresters to Canada. When they came back three weeks later, their team leader said: "We learned a lot in Canada – especially that we are far behind you. We need machines and chemicals. We thank you for this opportunity." The Canadian side agreed: "We saw what they were doing in China, and there's nothing much for us to learn there. It's all about what China can learn from us."

The PRC wanted to send a group to Canada to talk about construction on permafrost, the frozen ground on which Canada constructs roads and buildings in the Canadian north. But why was China interested in this technology? It only had a bit of permafrost in its north, bordering Siberia, and on the sparsely populated Tibetan Plateau. We brought them to Canada to see permafrost construction, and to talk with our government and university specialists. Thanking us for organizing their visit, the group returned to Beijing without telling us anything more. Thirty years later, China built a 1,000-kilometre railroad over the permafrost on the Tibetan Plateau to connect Tibet with the rest of China. The lessons we learned were that China always has a long-term view, that there is a national purpose in everything China does, and that is very good at keeping its secrets.

In 1975, the Department sent a senior officer to Beijing to evaluate the Embassy's performance, and he asked us whether Canada should continue to support these scientific and technical exchanges. We said that the Chinese really liked the program, but that the cost was substantial and Canada was getting almost no benefit. He made the following observations:

> Are we really helping the Chinese? So far we have not seen any positive trade results, and Ottawa is wondering whether we are going too far, too fast, just to please the Chinese. There are those in Ottawa who want to stop this infatuation with China until we have a better sense of where that country is going. Can we in any way say these programs are having a positive impact?

That was in 1975, just a year before the end of the Cultural Revolution. By 1979, the situation had changed. The two countries negotiated an arrangement for up to 500 Chinese to be trained in Canada in science and technology in our universities, laboratories, and government organizations. Over the next ten to fifteen years, Canada trained several thousand Chinese in Canada and in the PRC. According to Ambassador Menzies, this training was the real start of Canadian development assistance to China: "It may have been the most important thing Canada did while I was Ambassador. To have so many Chinese come to our universities and government organizations to work with us, to see what we are doing. That was the beginning of our aid program with China, even though we did not actually call it official development assistance."

Menzies also set the stage for transferring technology to China. He promoted a fledgling partnership with Canada's International Development Research Council (IDRC). Ivan Head, the former foreign policy advisor to Prime Minister Pierre Trudeau, had become the president of the IDRC. He was committed to improving North-South relations, and was especially interested in working with China. In 1979, the PRC wanted a software package that belonged to IDRC, and it approached Head, whom China considered "a friend" because of his close connection to Prime Minister Trudeau. Head viewed China's interest in IDRC's technology as an opportunity. "We now had a lever. I wanted to get an agreement with China that could link it together with our third world projects in other countries." The initial IDRC agreement was modest, just $3 million, but according to Head, it was one of the first official bilateral development assistance agreements made between China and a foreign government.[6]

By 1980, Beijing was signaling that it was ready to accept foreign aid. The Department initiated an internal discussion on an aid program for China, with the observation that Canada had never discussed aid for China seriously because of the PRC's past policy of self-reliance and China's belief that accepting foreign aid was humiliating, especially when given by capitalists. If the PRC was ready to receive foreign assistance, Canada could think about creating a program that provided aid while also helping Canadian business. The EDC's mandate had made it impossible to provide the low-interest financing that China wanted, but the Canadian International Development Agency (CIDA), which was responsible for administering official Canadian development assistance to other countries, could offer low-interest concessional financing. So why not give aid to China under CIDA's direction, since it could provide the low-cost financing that was required for big development projects?

A well-run aid program could advance Canada's relations with China. The PRC was always complaining about the huge trade deficit it had with Canada because of the wheat sales. Canada's offer to fund development assistance in China could offset China's large trade deficit and end those complaints. Giving development assistance was an important political gesture that could enhance relations with China in all spheres, and if Canada could set up an aid program that focused on technical or economic cooperation, "it would not offend Chinese sensitivities on aid receptivity." Any aid program had to avoid an excessive emphasis on export credits and concessional financing, and it also had to be broad enough to encompass a wide range of Canadian needs, keeping in mind that support for trade should not be at the expense of direct aid. The government had to develop "a basic Departmental position" on how much of the aid would belong to the traders, and how much was for the giving of development assistance.

Within three weeks, a debate developed within the Department. One officer said: "China has not yet formally requested assistance. We do not offer help to a country that has not asked us for it." More to the point, from where would the money come to fund a program with China "that could be so substantial as to make any regular bilateral aid initiative unthinkable in the present economic climate?" China had a huge population, over 700,000,000 people, with the majority at or below the poverty line. No country could even begin to provide the scale of necessary assistance. Other countries also needed help, and a case still had to be made for making China a priority recipient instead of India or Pakistan. As for linking aid and trade by using CIDA's concessional facility in an aid program, why should Canadian development assistance be so attached to trade goals? "We should debate the developmental, political, and budgetary aspects of Canadian aid to China before deciding whether a portion of that assistance is linked to our capital goods exports." That was a compelling argument within CIDA, where most of the staff and officers favoured supporting "aid over trade" and opposed using CIDA funds for large-scale trade projects that in their view "were being masked as development assistance."

In February 1980, CIDA and Department officials met to decide how to proceed. Relations between these two government bodies had been awkward. The Department and its political elite often undervalued CIDA, which had been established in 1968 and was a relative newcomer in the Ottawa bureaucracy. As one Department member put it, "rejects from Foreign Affairs often wind up in CIDA." Officials in CIDA were concerned about the potential distorting effect of a large China aid program. With its current funding commitments, CIDA was already within 5 per cent of its 1979–80 spending limit, and it had been told by Treasury Board that it could not make any additional financial commitments until 1982–83. There was talk of increasing its real resources by 5 per cent in 1980–81, but this increase was a small amount, not enough for a new program with China, and a downturn in the Canadian economy was squeezing existing government budgets. If CIDA were to set up a China program the size of India's without receiving any new money, it would have to be at the expense of either India or Pakistan.[7]

The Department put forth three options. The first, and least likely because of CIDA's budgetary constraints, was "supporting large-scale capital projects in China on concessional terms, say, three percent interest, 30-year term, of the sort EDC could not provide." The second would be "to blend CIDA's concessional financing with consensus or commercially generated funds." This option, called "crédit mixte," would bring down the interest rate for specific projects. The third option would be limited, well-conceived technical assistance, developmental in nature, possibly arising from the 1979 arrangement for training the 500 Chinese in Canada. Technical assistance would have to be generally supportive of commercial initiatives, have access to a minimum of $1 million per year for each project, and could not take resources from Canadian aid programs in other countries.

CIDA was asked to prepare a report on the policy issues involved in extending assistance, including China's eligibility, the type and terms of aid, and the institutional mechanisms, domestic or international, that were needed to establish a program. In October, the CIDA report still had not been written, so the Department stepped in and finished it. The Department's report recommended "modest, well-directed technical assistance, with a three-year budget of $12 to 15 million, beginning in the 1981–82 fiscal year."

CIDA then proposed a much larger China aid program in the amount of $200 million, divided into $40 million per year, for the five-year period 1982–87. The Department said that the amount was too high and that CIDA had overestimated the cost. Australia was providing development assistance to China with a more realistic annual expenditure of only $14 to 17 million, and the Department commented that, "in order to combat what appears to be a view, in some CIDA circles at least, that China is a 'bottomless pit,' we urge our government to create a more modest program, like the Australians."

Ottawa was anxious to reach a decision, since PRC Foreign Minister Huang Hua had invited Foreign Minister Mark MacGuigan to visit Beijing in the summer of 1981, potentially offering a convenient opportunity for signing an agreement with China: "Therefore, decisions about our aid policy toward the PRC will have to be pursued with some dispatch." The Department and CIDA finalized a policy discussion paper on the potential granting of Canadian aid to China, asking five questions: (1) Could Canada make a significant contribution, given its budgetary limitations and the huge scale of China's development needs? (2) What kind of policy was most consistent with current Canadian relations with China? (3) Was China able to manage such an aid program? (4) Did CIDA have adequate resources to administer it? (5) Did Canadian public opinion support the giving of aid to a communist country, especially one that was a nuclear power and had a military force of over two million soldiers?

CIDA also had a number of additional concerns. China was scaling back its economic reforms and retrenching. The residue of Soviet-style planning and management was still evident, which could hamper the implementation of any proposed development assistance initiative. CIDA pointed out that "China has not yet become a liberal Western economy, and we will need to deal with it as a centralized socialist state." Providing China with aid would mean adding additional staff, and it was vital "to start at the right point in the Chinese governmental structure, for example, finding the best Chinese partner for administering Canadian aid." Given these comments, CIDA added, somewhat hesitantly: *"Now is perhaps the time for a cautious Canadian decision to move forward, although we still have many questions about China's capacity to administer this program"* (emphasis added).

From Beijing, the Canadian Embassy weighed in, observing that "the PRC is likely to become a major receiving country of funds from international aid institutions, and this could bring substantial benefits to Canadian firms that are looking to secure new business." It was referring to the United Nations aid programming and World Bank financing that had become available to China, and it said that Canadian business was missing the boat. The Canadian ambassador urged Canadian representatives in those multilateral institutions to help Canadian companies take advantage of these new sources of funding. He repeated that same message to members of the Canadian business community in Beijing: "There are multilateral sources of funding for exporters to China. If EDC financing isn't helpful, try the World Bank and the United Nations."

Fourteen months had now passed since the Department began its discussion of a possible aid program for China, and what was opaque in 1979 had become clearer. Canada was willing to give development assistance to China, subject to budgetary limitations; the PRC was ready to receive aid from foreign capitalist countries; and the principal rationale for providing China with development assistance was to advance Canadian trade, using CIDA's concessional facility. By early 1981, the Canadian government was committed to an expanded North-South initiative to assist third world countries, a project that Prime Minister Pierre Trudeau was actively leading. The Department knew that he wanted to extend development assistance to China as soon as possible: "We heard it from Ivan Head, who told us that Trudeau fully supported a China aid program. The Chinese MFA told us they were ready to go ahead and that it would raise Sino-Canadian relations to the next level."

Ottawa commissioned a survey on Canadian attitudes towards aid giving. It revealed that Canadians supported granting aid, a legacy from Canada's missionary past and from its work with poor

Commonwealth countries after post–Second World War decoloni-
zation. In 1980, two-thirds of Canadians said that Canada should
help less developed countries, and informed Canadians took
pride in Ottawa's promise to raise official development assistance
to one of the highest levels in the West – close to 0.7 per cent of
GDP – although fiscal problems emerging in Canada in the late
1970s raised doubts whether Canada could reach that target.

The Cold War was ongoing, so why was Canada helping its
enemies? Yet, once it became known that Canada was considering
a China aid program, few anti-China or anti-communist groups
emerged to lobby Ottawa. It was acceptable to engage with China
in development assistance if it brought back dollars in trade. The
PRC was changing for the better, looking to modernize, and was
ready to collaborate with the non-communist world. These were
positive indicators, and Canadian assistance could help the PRC
open up more quickly.

According to one survey, while granting aid was relatively popular, CIDA was not. The Canadian media were replete with tales
of failing Canadian aid initiatives, with CIDA the main culprit.
It was frequently criticized for poor planning, weak administration, and expensive projects. Any new CIDA-administered initiative would have to deal with these concerns, along with the real
or imagined difficulties of working with a very large communist
country. Thus, the Department noted: "When the two sides finally
meet, we will not make public the dollar amounts involved to avoid
any public backlash in Canada." In retrospect, Ottawa may have
been overly cautious, since the Canadian media later welcomed
the new China aid initiative and accepted that it would be administered by CIDA. Hardly anyone complained when a substantial
figure of $80 million over five years was leaked by the media.

The Ambassador Objects

On March 9, 1981, the Department cabled Ambassador Michel
Gauvin in Beijing with the summary of its submission to Cabinet.
It recommended that Canada should establish a five-year program

with China in the range of $75 to $100 million "to begin possibly as early as 1981–82, with the bulk of the funding concentrated towards the end of the five-year period." The rationale was twofold:

The establishment of an aid program represents a logical progression in the development of Canadian and PRC relations, particularly in the economic/commercial sphere, and also from a general bilateral and strategic perspective. This is responsive to genuine development needs in the PRC, particularly in the realm of technology transfer.

Given China's recent period of retrenchment, which at that time is restricting foreign capital investment in China, and CIDA's limited capacity to take on a large programme, the aid will likely concentrate on more affordable technology transfer, rather than on large-scale development loans or capital project assistance.

Aid was divided into three sectors: agriculture, energy, and industry. It utilized a range of channels, from a small budget for local projects to be administered directly by the Embassy; to technical cooperation, training, and institutional arrangements; establishing demonstration and research centres; and the transfer of equipment. Concessional lines of credit, "provided they pursue a development rationale," were available for the purchase of Canadian high-tech products and services in telecommunications, oil and gas, and electric power and mining equipment. Industrial cooperation grants would be available to Canadian firms exploring potential business in the PRC. However, no funding would be given for large-scale infrastructure, such as dams, bridges, or roads.

Ottawa wanted to make sure that everyone understood that this money was not a handout, but rather a chance for Canada to expand economic cooperation for both countries' benefit. A well-conceived program would provide political and strategic advantages to Canada, and it was consistent with Western attempts to assist in China's modernization. Given the modest initial funding that was projected – an average of $20 million a year for five years – "traditional clients of Canadian aid will not be neglected." Opinion polls had shown that a majority of Canadians were favourably disposed towards helping China, and they would support the type of aid described in the cable that Gauvin had just received.

Michel Gauvin was the first Canadian ambassador to China who was not the son of Canadian missionary parents in China. His predecessor Arthur Menzies had been a model career diplomat who understood China well, spoke Mandarin, and was committed to bringing China out of isolation and into the world community. It was widely known that Menzies was a strong supporter of expanded exchanges in science and technology, education, and the training of Chinese in Canada.

Gauvin, however, was different from Menzies. He had a deep loathing of the Chinese communist system: "Although I grew very fond of the Chinese people, I opposed the PRC government system, and I was against such a huge aid program. It was premature. They were communists after all." Gauvin had an image of himself as "shooting from the hip." He had made his diplomatic career serving in tough situations, most prominently in Indochina. "I think I was sent to Beijing because someone thought it was time for a change from those mish kids. I was available. I am an old soldier, cool and reliable. I was the obedient public servant who could stand his ground."

Ottawa's cable caught Gauvin unawares. He had earlier made known his opposition to giving development assistance to China, and he now complained that Ottawa had not consulted him when drafting the discussion paper. That was true: his subordinates at the Embassy, and those to whom they reported in Ottawa, knew his critical views, and they had deliberately kept him out of the loop as long as possible. They later told me: "We had to contain him. Aid to China was going to happen. The Prime Minister fully supported it."

According to Gauvin, his objections were well known in Ottawa, and he was not impressed that others were already giving aid to China. "Why should Canada rush to copy what some other countries were doing? Take Australia, for example. It has different needs than Canada, being closer to Asia, and it is unwise to view Australia as a model or a competitor." Gauvin argued that "China does not satisfy the criteria which are normally associated with aid. It is too literate, with vast unexploited resources, and has generally well-trained cadres. Furthermore, Deng Xiaoping and his associates are old, and they cannot offer any real guarantees that the present limited liberal tendency will bear the fruits they have hoped for." In Gauvin's view, Canada should have waited to see how other countries were faring in their China aid programs "before launching into a sea of uncertainty." Gauvin later said:

As the senior Canadian responsible for our interests, I had to register my strong reservations on the principle and the timing of extending aid to China. Maybe the Chinese would buy more from Canada if we had a program in place, but maybe not. The Chinese only buy from us what they need and what they cannot obtain elsewhere at a better price. Many Canadians are caught up in a "China fever," seeing only the tip of an iceberg. That euphoria is already dying down, and it is better to be realistic.

He reminded Ottawa that the Chinese had only used $8 million of the EDC line of credit:

If Canada does decide to give aid to China, it should be for the promotion of trade, with perhaps a small mission-administered fund to cope with any unforeseen opportunities for gestures of good will. The time frame for implementing the program is too short, and the PRC lacks the skilled administrative personnel to carry it out. The Minister is scheduled to come to Beijing in August, and we don't have enough time for consultations with Chinese officials in advance of his trip and for in-depth discussions between CIDA and the Post's political and trade officers.

Gauvin acknowledged that his subordinates did not share his views on China. "In fact they disagreed with me." He then summarized their arguments "in fairness to them, and to you." Gauvin talked about "a mentality in Ottawa that favours China. Before helping the communists, and don't forget that they are communists, why not first help our friends?" As for the general concept of aid, Gauvin supported it. When he had served in Ethiopia, he had convinced Ottawa to grant aid to that country, but as soon as its elite abused the aid, Gauvin had opposed its continuation. "You also have to remember that our aid people have their vested interests. We have professionals of aid, people who make their living from it. There's nothing better than to show kindness, especially when you are also preserving your own jobs."

Ottawa was not surprised by Gauvin's strong reaction.

> He had a reputation as a loose cannon. We knew the general tenor of his views. Yes, he was the Ambassador, but arrayed against him on this issue was almost everyone else at the Post. We knew from our officers in Beijing that he would oppose giving aid to China. They had been quietly working with us on the proposal. We managed to keep him out of the loop until the last part of the process, when we thought it would be too late for him to object. We were surprised that he objected so vigorously, and it created problems, but he wasn't the only person in Ottawa who had strong anti-PRC or anti-communist views.

One of the ambassador's allies was the Canadian commissioner in Hong Kong, Bill Warden, who expressed "his full concurrence" with Gauvin's reservations. Warden argued that there was "turmoil, real and potential, just under the surface in China, and it made more sense to wait for the political situation to settle down." He was not convinced that Canadian aid would make an impact, and he predicted that many of China's Asian neighbours would be upset with Canada's decision to render aid to a communist regime. He agreed with Gauvin that China lacked the proper infrastructure to administer an aid program, and he was certain that there would be a negative Canadian public reaction to this initiative. According to Warden, China's human rights record was abysmal, and the prospects for political liberalization were dim. China was building up an arsenal of nuclear weapons, so why should Canada give aid to a country that was using its scarce resources to build weapons of destruction instead of alleviating the poverty of its people? He ended by saying that, if Canada planned on giving aid to China, it should be narrow and concentrate on specific Canadian interests, such as economic and commercial relations.

In replying to Gauvin, Ottawa pointed out that "China satisfies the criteria for Official Development Assistance (ODA) in almost every respect." In 1981, China was a poor country, at the level of

Pakistan and Tanzania. Most Western observers said that China's policy of modernization was continuing: "China's approach of self-reliance suggests it would stand high on any list of countries able to define their own priorities. It has a large and literate bureaucracy – a positive feature for administering development assistance – although it lacks management skills, and its level of technology is backward. This is precisely where a well-crafted aid program can be effective."

The Department reminded Gauvin:

> While China is to a considerable extent responsible for its own isolation between 1949 and 1970, and although history and geography have always made it inward looking, and it will continue to do so, China has followed more outgoing policies since 1970. Selection of the development assistance option is no more than the adaptation of policy instruments in response to the evolution of the Chinese environment. Indeed, it would be inconsistent with the fundamental and successful elements of Canada's China policy to rebuff Beijing or fail to provide encouragement.

Ottawa told Gauvin that "no one expects a bonanza" and that there was "no China fever" behind the decision to grant aid to the PRC. Aid would start slowly with small disbursements in the period up to 1983–84. Very little was going to happen in 1981 and 1982, giving both sides time to prepare the framework of the program. Regarding Gauvin's comment that the Chinese had not asked for aid, Ottawa reminded him that Vice Premier Bo Yibo had raised the matter with Foreign Minister MacGuigan during Bo's recent visit to Canada, and Beijing's readiness to proceed had been noted at least three times in recent meetings with senior Chinese officials in Ottawa and in Beijing, just before Gauvin had presented his credentials.

Gauvin sent one last message to Ottawa, arguing that "aid to China at this time and in the scope proposed appears to me unwise." He asked a number of tough questions:

> Should we grant aid to a country which restricts the movements of our diplomats in order to control them? Is it proper to give aid to a country that constantly spies on our diplomats? How do we reconcile our human

rights policy with the non-existence of human rights in China and the sentencing of Wei Jingsheng to up to fifteen years in prison? How do we reconcile giving aid to a country that gives priority to the development of nuclear weapons over economic development and the raising of the standard of living of its citizens? Why should we assume that China will not revert to hard Marxism-Leninism and abandon the course of reform?[8]

Having posed these questions, Gauvin argued for prudence, with a plea to "wait a bit more until changes have taken place." He had made his case, and he expected his reservations to be included in the Cabinet submission, along with the critical comments made by the commissioner in Hong Kong, and by others who had similar views. Gauvin observed: "I did not have a popular position. Everybody was on the China bandwagon. I wanted to wait for a while, sensing that it was premature. In the end, I only managed to slow it down a little. They wanted a five-year budget of $100 million, and it was reduced to $80 million."

Was Prime Minister Trudeau aware of Gauvin's objections? While Trudeau stayed in the background, Ottawa knew that he fully supported the China aid initiative. As for his thoughts about Gauvin, Trudeau later said:

I knew him from a long time ago. He was some sort of military hero. I can't even remember appointing him. He was a stubborn man. I would have thought our China policy was secure enough to endure him. There may have been some others who thought giving aid to a communist country was a bad idea, but I don't recall their names.

In early 1981, I wrote in my diary:

Am in Ottawa. The talk in the Department is about giving aid to Beijing. Ambassador Menzies favoured that. Heard that the new Ambassador is tough on China. Some may object to giving aid to a nuclear power with a huge army and expensive space program. And China is communist. The Minister will be going to Beijing soon. If that happens, it's a big step forward from the science and technology exchanges that we were doing with China in the mid-1970s.

A Decision Is Made

The Department took the draft document, which reflected the views of middle- and upper-level officials in the Department and at CIDA, and convened working-level meetings with "officials in the other concerned departments." After that, the proposal was discussed at the deputy minister level, and the final document, including Gauvin's objections, was delivered to Cabinet in mid-May, laying the groundwork for Cabinet approval before the minister's forthcoming trip in August. The Department, CIDA, Agriculture Canada, and ITC all supported the proposal, but the Department of Finance and the Treasury Board were still expressing reservations about the cost, so it was decided that the new program should be phased in gradually for administrative and financial reasons.

In the Cabinet submission, the new dollar figure was tentatively set at $80 million for five years. This amount was a small reduction from the original figure of $100 million, and it appeared to acknowledge Gauvin's criticism, although members of the Department later said that his opposition had little impact on the final budget figures: "It most likely would have been reduced by $20 million dollars anyway, with or without the Ambassador's intervention." Objections that aid to China would be at the expense of other poor countries also needing assistance were put to rest when it was confirmed that the program would be "fully funded from new money." It was said that Trudeau himself directly intervened to loosen the purse strings. The Department pointed out: "A decision to embark on a China program now, moreover, coincides with a period of expansion in our overall ODA, including increased disbursements for virtually every recipient of Canadian aid in Asia, thus serving to lessen fears of 'diversion' away from our traditional clients."

The submission to Cabinet made the following recommendations: (1) China is designated as an eligible recipient of Canadian development assistance with disbursements to begin as early as 1981–82, with a five-year allocation of $80 million for 1982–87; (2) CIDA officials are authorized, in consultation with the Department,

ITC, and the Canadian Embassy in Beijing, to engage in preliminary discussions with Chinese officials to determine the shape and scope of Canadian aid to China; (3) two additional person years for program development and planning purposes will be allocated for the program.

According to the submission, China's commitment to market reform was strong:

> While retaining a statist orientation to economic management, China ascribes a substantial role to the capitalist West in its development prospects, and therein lies the opportunity and the need for the West, including Canada, to respond affirmatively. Prospects for political stability within the Chinese leadership over the medium term, ten to fifteen years, appear to be good. Despite many abuses, China's human rights practices are not unlike those in a great number of less developed countries.
>
> Programmatically, a balanced program, phrased in terms of "economic cooperation," combining elements of both altruism and "mutual benefit" will in the longer run be a more effective agent in promoting Canada's overall interests in the PRC.

Roads, dams, and bridges were rejected as aid targets, in favour of highly selective areas such as managerial systems, engineering administration, and specialized equipment. The Canadian government was reluctant to target integrated rural development projects and other activities that were aimed at meeting "basic human needs" in areas where China already had a demonstrated capability. While technical cooperation was a priority, successful implementation of technology transfer would require great skills and creativity, requiring an emphasis on human resource development:

> Human resource development is gaining wider acceptance in development circles ... Canada may be in a strong position to respond in this area, having achieved a high level of educational excellence and possessing an under-utilized education network. At the same time, China is suffering from a critical gap in trained human resources as a result of the breakdown in their education system during the Cultural Revolution.

Giving aid to a large communist country was a challenging concept, and the Chinese side was still hesitant about getting too closely involved with foreigners. Chinese "at junior levels" had expressed general interest in CIDA aid programs that could promote bilateral cooperation. At the senior level, however, the PRC remained focused on trade and concessional financing. Canada had not yet received an official Chinese request for aid, only "positive indications," and until the PRC actually said it wanted to establish a development assistance program, many in Ottawa thought it would be better if Canada did not volunteer to offer it. The two future partners were about to initiate a ritual diplomatic mating dance, but neither seemed ready to take the next step.

What about Canadian public opinion? The business and financial community, the universities and colleges, individuals and groups with long-standing institutional or personal interest in China, and most Canadian media were likely to be largely supportive. Some segments of the Canadian public would criticize giving aid to China because it was communist and because of its poor human rights record, asking why China should even be eligible for development assistance – the Gauvin argument – and pointing out that building a China aid program would be at the expense of Canada's current relations with other "friendly" third world nations, especially in Asia.

On July 13, Cabinet approved the proposed program without opposition. Everyone knew that the prime minister supported the initiative. MacGuigan, his foreign minister, said that he never had to consult with the prime minister on giving aid to China. Ivan Head recalled that Trudeau "had created a positive climate for Canada to extend aid. He was chairing the North-South Summit in Cancun, he wanted Canada to help the third world countries to develop, and China was one of those countries." The dollar figures remained the same, $80 million for five years, and the emphasis was on aid, although "the aid can also be supportive of trade, in view of the coincidence of Chinese development priorities and Canadian supply capabilities."

The Cabinet did not want the decision to be made public, since the minister intended to announce it in Beijing during his visit, as a major Canadian "deliverable." Canadian officers met with their Chinese counterparts before MacGuigan's visit to inform them of Ottawa's decision and to avoid any surprises. Officials in the Department and in CIDA breathed a sigh of relief. After almost two years of discussion, Canada had finally approved the aid program, and now Canada could formally approach the PRC to set it in motion.

The Minister Arrives in Beijing

MacGuigan said: "I was ready to go to Beijing. This was an opportunity for Canada. China wasn't my first priority, but I knew it was important, even if we were giving aid to a communist country." He was a strong advocate for human rights, but he did not feel that rights criteria should be applied to aid policy. In his view, "aid should be given almost without regard to politics." He saw the advantage to Canada of giving aid in support of trade. He recalled: "In the past year, the Minister of State for Trade and I have broken down the barriers between trade and aid in general, and now we want to work with China."[9] The Department had prepared its brief well, and MacGuigan was on board. Ambassador Gauvin's intervention was brushed aside. Gauvin later said that, once the funding was approved, "I had given my objections to Ottawa and then, as Ambassador, it was my duty faithfully to carry out my government's instructions." There would be no conflict between the ambassador and his foreign minister when the latter arrived in Beijing.

As the visit drew closer, Canada made last-minute plans to ensure that the announcement of the new program went smoothly. The Embassy said it was making arrangements for MacGuigan to meet with Vice Foreign Minister Zhang Wenjin, the former ambassador to Canada:

He can tell Zhang that he wants to discuss the matter in more detail with Foreign Minister Huang Hua. We want to know whether such an initiative on our part would be agreeable to the PRC. We will refrain from referring to any monetary figures of the aid program, and leave that to the Minister. Once PRC agreement is given in principle, Ottawa will inform PRC Ambassador Wang Dong of the talks. Canada can tell Wang that during his visit to Beijing the Foreign Minister will make a public announcement of the CIDA agreement, and both sides can simultaneously issue a press release in Ottawa and Beijing. If they think it is necessary, a Memorandum of Understanding on the principle of bilateral development assistance cooperation can also be signed during the visit.

Ottawa agreed with the Embassy's scenario, although it stated that development assistance "should not become the exclusive focus of the visit." Aside from the aid program, the meetings included a review of key bilateral and multilateral issues, with a discussion of East/West concerns, the impending North-South Summit, consular relations, claims negotiations, and trade. Mac-Guigan intended to tell his hosts that the Canadian government had "approved in principle the funding of aid cooperation with China" and if he received a positive response from Foreign Minister Huang Hua, he was ready to discuss the matter "with a leading official from the responsible Chinese government department concerned."

The MFA requested an estimate of the precise sums involved. Not yet wanting to reveal any dollar figures, Canada said the funding depended on the number, size, and type of aid projects. The MFA asked if the aid was in the form of capital grants or loans, at what interest rates, and whether it would be for trade, food aid, or for technical cooperation and human resources. The Canadian side replied that technical cooperation and human resource development were the principal objectives, but that such details would be better explored later. Canada mentioned that CIDA's concessional facility was available for special trade-related projects.

China announced that the State Import and Export Commission (SIEC) would be CIDA's partner. This was a surprise, since Australia's bilateral aid partner was the Ministry of Foreign Economic Relations and Trade (MOFERT), and the World Bank and the Japanese were working with two other PRC units. The MFA invited the president of CIDA, Marcel Massé, who was accompanying MacGuigan, to meet with SIEC to talk about future cooperation.[10]

Foreign Minister Huang praised Canada's role in promoting efforts to close the gap between the rich and poor countries. He said that "China appreciated Canada's positive approach" in the North-South Dialogue, "whose goal is to help developing countries." At dinner, Deng Xiaoping asked MacGuigan to give his regards to Prime Minister Trudeau, adding that "one of my sons went to Canada for medical treatment, and I am very grateful to the Prime Minister and to other Canadians."[11] Deng also commented on the EDC line of credit, saying: "Canada is giving us $2 billion to spend, but we are not clear on how to use it." In discussing China's economic reforms and the broad area of development assistance, Deng said: "Equipment, management, and technology are neither capitalist nor socialist." MacGuigan replied that Canada wanted to promote development as a priority, rather than investment and trade, and that this focus would benefit both sides: "Canada intends to emphasize the human element and the transfer of technology, and this has greater value than dams over the long term, although a portion of the aid will support commercial projects."

Marcel Massé met with the vice chairman of SIEC, and it was evident that it had little understanding of the nature and size of the proposed CIDA initiative. SIEC was primarily interested in large concessional loans and big capital projects, although it did say its role was changing and that it could become a Chinese coordinating channel for technical assistance by delegating project implementation to technical ministries, who would have direct working-level contact with CIDA. The encounter with SIEC was not positive. The CIDA representatives on the mission said afterwards: "It did not give us the impression of an organization that had much experience of, or interest in, the comparatively small technical cooperation projects with which Canada planned to start."

After meeting with SIEC, MacGuigan met again with Huang. MacGuigan pointed out that CIDA's primary focus was on aid, rather than trade, although the latter would also be part of the

CIDA program. In the early stages of the program, the Canadian government was proposing to begin with the following initiatives:

- Exchange of experts for technical cooperation;
- Training of Chinese experts and managers in Canada;
- Twinning of institutions (for example, universities, agricultural colleges);
- Adaptation to China of Canadian technology (wheat growing, soil testing for potash, forestry, pulp and paper, electric transmission lines, transport, telecommunications, and health);
- Industrial cooperation (pre-feasibility studies and testing of markets by Canadian firms); and
- Pre-feasibility studies and feasibility studies by Canadian firms with advanced technology.

Huang now understood that Canada was prioritizing aid over trade, and he welcomed CIDA's proposal to send a working delegation to China later in the year to discuss specific areas of cooperation. The Canadian media focused on the aid-trade link, and the *Globe and Mail* commented:

> The aid program is ... clearly meant to let Canada mesh into the Chinese trade market. MacGuigan would not admit that in so many words. "We don't give our aid with an ulterior motive," he said with a smile. "Canada is unusual in the purity of its motives."

The *Globe and Mail* reported that MacGuigan had said the program would be "somewhere under five million dollars a year, for an indefinite period." It concluded that "it was apparent yesterday that the Canadian side had little idea what kind of aid the Chinese want." According to the Canadian Press, Massé had referred to "a national amount of eighty million dollars over five years. This is not a firm spending figure, and it was not relayed to the Chinese." The *Windsor Star* was critical of the small amount that was officially announced, with the headline "Canada's Aid to China Little More Than an Insult." The paper said $5 million was insignificant for a country like China. It reported that MacGuigan had denied rumours the total could rise to $80 million in the first five years. It was also critical of the omission of large projects such as port facilities, railroads, and dams in the Canadian aid package. "Apparently large-scale infrastructure projects are no longer in fashion as gifts. Nobody is giving away dams anymore."

Canadian media coverage was generally favourable, although sparse, and after a flurry of articles focusing on the minister's trip and a few reports by Canadian journalists accompanying the delegation, the issue disappeared from public view. The program was still a concept that had to be fleshed out, and Canadians apparently had no strong feelings for or against investing a small sum of $5 million in China, either for developmental reasons or to enhance trade.

After close to two years, the focus had shifted to a program focused on technical training, human resource development, and small-scale projects, rather than dams and large infrastructure projects. There was no public outcry against giving aid to a communist country, one that was a nuclear power and suppressed basic individual freedoms. Most Canadians seemed either supportive or indifferent. China was viewed as a country in need, and part of Canada's mission was providing development assistance. The next step was to put this program in place, a task that would take another two years.

Implementation

CIDA now moved to the centre of a process that the Department had previously dominated. The latter had provided the political and strategic thinking that brought the discussion to a concrete resolution, although, in the final stages, CIDA began to acquire more responsibility as it took over the operation of the program. Marcel Massé, CIDA's president, had a clear and workable vision of how Canada should proceed, and he cooperated closely with key Department officials. One Embassy officer said: "Massé's commitment was absolutely vital for shepherding the aid program through all its stages. Everyone knew he had Trudeau's confidence."

CIDA took stock of the situation. Back in Ottawa, Massé held discussions with the Department and with multilateral aid agencies, to get a sense of recent developments in China. The PRC was slowly emerging from its period of retrenchment, and it was in the midst of compiling a new five-year plan, scheduled for 1982. It had acquired a reputation for financial reliability, and CIDA felt confident that once China made an agreement it would abide by it. In conversation with other foreign donors, both multilateral and bilateral, CIDA had learned that Chinese priorities for foreign aid were in human resources, management, energy, transportation, agriculture, and industry. Conditions for foreign experts working in China were relatively primitive and restricted, so on-the-ground implementation by Canada was going to pose problems, and developing a cohesive aid program would take considerable time and effort on both sides.

A "pre-planning" CIDA mission went to Beijing in December 1981 to explain how CIDA functioned, and to establish working arrangements with its new Chinese partner. After the mission arrived, it discovered that SIEC had been replaced by MOFERT, the same partner that was assigned to administer Australian aid. CIDA was pleased, since MOFERT had a better understanding of development assistance and of what Canada intended to do. One mission member had been pushing for large-scale infrastructure projects, rather than for smaller training initiatives, but after meeting with MOFERT, he realized that big projects were inappropriate. Another thought CIDA should be dealing with the more powerful State Planning Commission (SPC), but after learning about the large sums of money involved in SPC projects, he understood that CIDA was moving in a different direction, with smaller, less capital-intensive projects that were better suited for a partner like MOFERT, and more closely fit CIDA's objectives.

Information obtained during the pre-planning delegation enabled CIDA to prepare for a major programming mission to China, scheduled for April 1982. Back in Ottawa, CIDA put together an "Interim Strategy Paper," with recommendations for the upcoming mission. Concerns were raised that Canada might be giving a "traditional" response to what was a rather unique situation. Was China "different" because of its size, centrally directed economy, and communist system, or could it just be treated as a typical third world country? Some questions were raised: Could China manage a development assistance program at the local level? Would the granting of aid to China be similar to what Canada was doing with other countries, such as India or Pakistan?

CIDA senior management approved the Interim Strategy on March 31. Massé had presented a creative and visionary statement that matched Canadian capabilities and objectives with China's long-term needs. From later discussions with CIDA and Department officials, as well as with several Cabinet ministers, we know that Massé had decisively shaped the Canadian strategy. His key contributions are embodied in two phrases: *"multiplication of contacts at the thinking level"* and *"human resource development as a principal activity."* Massé elaborated:

> Multiplication of contacts, that is how we should spend not only our money but also our administrative resources, multiplying them in a large number of fields, high technology preferably, but also methods of doing things, training trainers. We should help to multiply contacts in the universities, certainly, but also maybe a number of small projects.

Massé talked about Canadian neurosurgeons who had developed a new technique for spinal injuries and had gone to China to perform an operation demonstrating this technique. He continued: "It cost us about a hundred thousand dollars, but the possibility of transferring information of that type, and the capacity of that type of action to influence development – this is so much more important than the amount of money we spend." The trouble, he observed, was that, if you do a hundred of these, you've already spent $10 million. "But to me, ten projects of that type are more important than one hundred and fifty million dollars put into a hydro dam, in terms of our long-term objectives."

The key objective was "to train their trainers in how to develop new technologies." Massé stated with confidence:

> We can do that. We can create the contacts, the understanding. We can create the contacts in terms of training trainers at a level where you

have to deal with attitudes and values, and where our people who are training will gain as much as they are giving.

Our pay-off will be small in the commercial area, but it will be extremely high in facilitating cooperation and in the discovery of new technologies, or on a social and cultural level in changes of attitudes or understanding of attitudes, and learning by our own people. That may be better for our own economy than large- scale contracts.

CIDA emphasized the potential for a substantial multiplier effect: "A major tactical objective is to upgrade the human resource capabilities. The sectors designated for training and development are agriculture/forestry, management, and energy. Long-term CIDA objectives are geopolitical and strategic, societal and cultural, rather than commercial. The most fruitful cooperation is from the multiplication of contacts between people, contacts in which both parties have something to learn and something to impart."

The Department's reaction was positive, although "it was probably too early to assess the chances of 'trickle down' working in China." It agreed with the emphasis on agriculture/forestry, management, and energy, but some officers also suggested targeting transportation, communications, mining, and social infrastructure "when worthy development opportunities present themselves. This would contribute more flexibility to the CIDA program and give some additional support to the CIDA exporting interests. That comment does not, however, imply any disagreement with the principle that the majority of these training resources should flow into the top three sectoral areas."

Some officers in the Department complained that "we have now accepted a position of virtual impotence in trying to influence CIDA policies." They insisted that the broad outlines of CIDA planning had to be decided by the Department, not CIDA, since development assistance was an instrument of Canadian foreign policy. It should not be allowed to drift into the hands of others. "Just as war is too important to be left solely to the care of generals, we consider that aid is too important to be left solely to the care of aid administrators." They argued that the minister had to establish a more effective consultation process between CIDA and the Department. This discussion produced a statement from the minister that the Department's mandate was not to direct Canadian aid policy, although aid was an instrument of foreign policy and a key element in bilateral relations. What was needed was better consultation between CIDA and the Department to ensure that development assistance initiatives were in accord with Canadian foreign policy objectives.

The CIDA mission in April 1982 under the direction of Nobel Power, vice president for Bilateral Relations, was comprised of four groups: human resources/management, agriculture, forestry, and energy. It was hosted by MOFERT, and the four groups held separate meetings with Chinese government departments, enterprises, and institutions. They were investigating potential projects in several sectors to ascertain which ones should take precedence, which were financially viable, and whether the PRC had the capability to manage them. Members of the mission were becoming comfortable with MOFERT, their new partner, and they were encouraged by the initial results. "After waiting so long, we were finally able to talk about concrete projects, and we could establish working relations with Chinese counterparts." When the mission returned to Canada, the human resources/ management group moved quickly to set up a program for management training in China, and human resource development would become a cornerstone of aid to China after final approval in October 1983.

Almost four years had passed since the Department had started internal discussions for a development assistance program with China. The rationale had changed from support of trade, to a focus on aid and human resource development. The pro-aid group in CIDA had prevailed over those who wanted a strong focus on trade. What Canada was creating had the potential to be innovative, yet unspectacular, with no big dams and no investment in large-scale infrastructure. The program's hallmark was Massé's statement prioritizing human resource development – "the training of trainers" and "the multiplication of contacts at the thinking level." The Department had taken the government on a long journey, and now it was up to CIDA to do its job. The program that they had created would become one of the key instruments in the bilateral relationship for the next thirty years.

A Success Story

The CIDA China program is a success story and one of the most innovative and influential parts of the bilateral relationship. For almost three decades, Canada provided cost-effective training to thousands of Chinese in the PRC and in Canada. It ended in 2013, when per capita income in China rose beyond the level at which the PRC was still eligible to receive official development assistance. At one point, the annual CIDA China budget reached $100 million, of which $60 million went to support aid to China carried out by multilateral agencies, such as the United Nations, the World Bank, and the Asian Development Bank. The remainder – up to $40 million – was for the annual bilateral Canada-China program. Between 12 and 15 per cent of the $40 million in bilateral funding was reserved for projects that focused directly on trade. During a research trip to one Chinese province in the late 1990s, when my hosts discovered that I was a Canadian, they excitedly said that a CIDA agricultural training initiative had helped them to double their pork production. They told me: "CIDA is as big a hero here as Norman Bethune. We won't forget Canada."

Canadian universities and colleges established partnerships with counterparts in Chinese universities in engineering, medicine and health, agriculture, language training, environment, and education. Joint collaboration between Canadian and Chinese educational institutions led to the development of canola, which became one of Canada's largest exports to the PRC. Canada became a leading trainer of managers, developing the first MBA programs in China and setting up a major management training centre in the inland city of Chengdu. One MOFERT official told me: "First you introduced us to the new scientific and technical skills that China needed, and then you showed us how to manage what we learned."[12]

In the 1990s, CIDA widened its in-China programming to include governance, human rights, and equity for women. These were controversial topics for foreigners working in China; yet Canada was able to carry out modest initiatives – training judges, organizing legal aid clinics, collaborating on environmental issues, and funding projects for women in rural communities. It also began supporting civil society initiatives at the local level. At the national level, Canada had two politically sensitive projects, with the Central Party School in environmental management and with the National People's Congress, China's Parliament, for training in legislation. Canadians had high hopes that these projects, which emphasized social and political change rather than the acquisition of scientific and technical knowledge or increased trade, would provide an opening for the emergence of democracy in China, and bring greater attention to human rights.

Beginning in the late 1990s, I was a participant in those CIDA projects with the National People's Congress and the Central Party School. We were engaging top-level officials in central level institutions, what we called "institution building." We were learning more about what the PRC government and the Party did, while showing them what we were doing in Canada, thinking that our voice might lead to better governance and improvements in human rights in China. That wasn't yet happening, but we had initiated a process that we hoped might bring those changes in the future.

The projection of values is replete with cultural and political roadblocks. Unlike the doubling of pork production or the invention of canola, social and political change is a "soft" process evolving over a long period of time, without immediate tangible outcomes. Some have criticized CIDA for trying to promote Western democratic value change in a country determined to resist such efforts. They have suggested that it would have been better to spend Canadian money on "hard" projects with clearer outcomes. Yet, when Massé in 1982 provided the rationale for providing development assistance to China, he clearly articulated the objectives of "the multiplication of contacts" and "human resource development." What began as aid, trade, and technical training also carried our Canadian values to China.

During its thirty-year life span, development assistance brought Canada and the PRC closer together, training thousands of Chinese in both countries. It had taken almost four years to create the program, and it then served as one of the cornerstones of the bilateral relationship. The Chinese turned out to be capable managers of Canadian aid, and they met their financial obligations. CIDA rose to the occasion, and its management of the China program received international praise. It gained status in Ottawa, attracting some of the best qualified staff specializing on China. While some Canadians have complained that Canada should not have been giving aid to a nuclear power, or to an emerging superpower that was also communist, others felt that this program was where Canada was making a difference. Massé said in conversation: "Keep the projects small and train their trainers. It will take time, but this way you can change attitudes and values, and that brings success in the long run."

chapter five

A Canadian Trade Strategy

Trade is the bottom line in Canada-PRC relations. This chapter outlines the Canadian government's strategy for expanding economic links with the PRC. The 1987 document, fifty pages in length and called the China Strategy, created guidelines for how the Canadian government and the private sector could work together to take advantage of the China market. Those guidelines still govern trade with China, more than thirty years later. The document also provides a checklist of almost every aspect of the Canada-China bilateral relationship during the first seventeen years.

In the mid-1980s, China had opened up, and the changes were striking. Foreigners were welcome, and China was testing the waters of capitalist markets. The Cold War was fading, and political liberalization was in the air. Relations between Canada and China were at their highest level since recognition in 1970, with both sides talking about a "special relationship." A large China market beckoned, and Canadian business wanted to take advantage of this opportunity.

In 1984, after twenty-one years of Liberal rule, barely interrupted by Joe Clark's brief government in 1979, the Conservatives, led by Brian Mulroney, took power. While the foreign policy focus was on relations with Washington, the government also turned its attention to Beijing. The Canadian economy was struggling, and Ottawa was looking for new markets. Prime Minister Mulroney travelled to Beijing in 1986, and he increased the five-year CIDA budget for China to $200 million. To win contracts, Canada made available $350 million in low-interest concessional financing to supplement the unused $2 billion Export and Development Canada (EDC) line of credit.

Following the prime minister's trip, the PMO instructed the Department to prepare a submission to Cabinet on trade with China. A drafting team consulted with the sixteen government ministries involved in China relations, the Embassy in Beijing, the business community, and other China policy stakeholders. In 1987, the Cabinet approved the China Strategy.

While Mulroney's visit was the catalyst, preparation for the Strategy had already begun in 1983. John Hadwen, director general of the East Asia Bureau, assembled a document recommending the creation of a Canadian trade strategy for China. He set up a China Working Group (CWG) in the Department, went to China with the EDC to meet with the key PRC financial and economic organizations, and consulted widely with the Canadian business community. The Chinese reaction was positive. State Councillor Yao Guang said: "Our relationship is excellent, and the transition from Trudeau to Mulroney has been almost seamless. Trade is growing rapidly, and we want Canadian business to expand its presence in China. We welcome this initiative."

The China Strategy contained fourteen recommendations, covering almost every aspect of Canada-China relations, from training foreign service officers in Mandarin, to elevating the dialogue on multilateral security issues, with trade as the principal objective. To capture a larger share of the China market, the government and the private sector had to work together more efficiently. Canada was too dependent on grain sales and other natural resources (rocks, logs, and agriculture). It needed to increase its exports of value-added goods. Ministries and departments had to make the most of limited government resources, since everyone now wanted to engage with China. The Strategy's success would depend on whether China could continue its current modernization, and whether Ottawa would provide enough financial and political support to the business community. While the time frame was too short to claim immediate success, two-way trade rose sharply a year later.

Bilateral relations in the late 1980s were as promising as the two sides had hoped they could be. Both said that this period was the best since recognition, and that they were creating "a special relationship." Unfortunately, the 1989 Tiananmen crisis abruptly ended talk about developing closer relations with China, and the Strategy lost its immediacy. As a guideline for trade relations with China, however, its analysis and

*recommendations have stood the test of time, and they deserve our full
attention.*

Our relationship is, generally speaking, excellent, not just good. We have a
special relationship, and we see a beautiful (*meihao*) future.
> – Yao Guang, state councillor and former
> PRC ambassador to Canada, 1987

China Opens Up

In the latter half of the 1980s,[1] most eyes were on the Soviet Union,
where Mikhail Gorbachev had emerged as the architect of major
economic and political reforms, and also on Eastern Europe,
where political opposition was challenging existing communist
governments. The Soviet Bloc was in disarray, with its economies
struggling and its human rights policies under attack. The two
superpowers were discussing disarmament and closer cooperation. Was it possible that the Cold War was about to end? Change
was in the air as authoritarian governments suddenly became vulnerable to political liberalization and vibrant capitalist markets
were threatening sluggish planned economies.

While our main attention was trained on the political changes
that were taking place in the Soviet Union and Eastern Europe,
China was also caught up in transformation. It was emerging from
self-imposed darkness into the outside world, with an awakening
of its economy and its people. I experienced this change in the 1980s
as a visiting professor at Peking University; followed by research
in Wuhan; and then, throughout the decade, conducting research
on Sino-Soviet relations in Moscow, Beijing, and Shanghai. I began
a six-year stint as director of the Province of Ontario's newly created educational exchange program with Jiangsu Province in 1986
and travelled widely in China over the next few years. The contrast with the China where I had lived in the 1970s was striking.
Places previously closed to foreigners had opened up, and we
could talk with ordinary Chinese people on the streets. Shops were
filling with consumer goods. Foreign scholars were establishing

tentative research links with their Chinese counterparts; the number of Canadian researchers and students in China was increasing; and more Chinese were arriving every day on Canadian university campuses.

I wrote in my diary:

> It's 1986. A fundamental change is occurring, one that goes to the roots of life and into one's soul. You see it in people's faces. The tension is gone and the smiles are genuine. Music is coming from within people's hearts. Laughter, singing, relaxed body language, and lovers in public places. They are shedding the suffocation of the Cultural Revolution. You see colours everywhere. No more proletarian blue. Cars are starting to compete with bicycles, and commercial advertising is beginning to replace political propaganda.
>
> They are laughing at the struggling Gorbachev reforms. "We used to learn from our Soviet Elder Brother. Now he should learn from us." Will the Deng Xiaoping reforms succeed? Can this Chinese mix of command and market economy work? What you see in China is a small market sector full of vitality, challenging a still dominant but sluggish state economy. Will the state sector yield? What are the consequences for China, and will the Party be able to adapt? Does economic marketization create political markets? Will this bring forth political parties and advocacy groups to challenge the Party's monopoly on power?

Previously inaccessible for interviews, Chinese officials were now talking about formerly forbidden subjects, such as political change and human rights. They spoke warmly of bilateral relations, pointing out that Canada was one of China's best friends, following in the footsteps of the sainted Dr. Norman Bethune. One Ministry of Foreign Affairs official, my nemesis when I had served in our Embassy in Beijing in the waning days of the Cultural Revolution, now greeted me as an old friend (*lao pengyou*). He said: "Look at what our two countries have accomplished together in less than two decades. It's a new world today." Old adversaries invited each other to dinner when they were in Canada, and they returned the favour in Beijing. I was asked to lecture at the Central Party School, marvelling that it was possible to communicate directly with Party officials who previously had carefully avoided me. We talk about political liberalization, the rule of law, and elections in the West and discuss how the Party could thrive in a more open Chinese political system.

More than fifteen years had passed since recognition, and Canada had fulfilled its pledge to support China's admission to the United Nations, as well as helping it join the World Bank and the International Monetary Fund (IMF). We had maintained our commitment to a one-China policy, and we were extending development assistance to China. Hundreds of Chinese were being trained in Canadian universities and government organizations. Party Secretary Zhao Ziyang had recently paid a visit to Canada, and a steady parade of senior officials was travelling both ways, to Beijing and to Ottawa, including Li Xiannian, China's president. In its "1984 Survey of Relations with the People's Republic of China," the Department wrote:

> While it is impossible to determine the exact measure of Canada's contribution to China's decision to become a major and responsible actor in international affairs, our role can be considered a distinctive and important accomplishment of contemporary Canadian foreign policy. A remarkable degree of confidence has been established between the two countries, given the limits that history, geography, and differing political viewpoints impose.

Not all Canadians were that positive. The business community complained that China had imposed too many unnecessary obstacles that limited their success in the China market. Human rights activists felt that Canada should be doing more in China, and that the government should be actively condemning Chinese rights abuses, just like we were doing with the Soviet Union. The Conservatives, led by Prime Minister Brian Mulroney, who took power in the fall of 1984 after almost fifteen years of unbroken Liberal China policy, said it was time for some changes. Their supporters were saying that Canada should pay more attention to Taiwan, should remember that the PRC is a Communist Party-state, and be more vigilant on human rights. Many Canadians remained suspicious of this new China, questioning whether Beijing's present openness was sustainable, whether the Party leadership could be trusted, and aside from trade, what actual benefit Canada was receiving from its relations with China.

Ambassador Gorham Arrives

Ambassador Richard Gorham arrived in Beijing in the fall of 1984, replacing Michel Gauvin. In 1972, Gorham had visited China, along with Foreign Minister Mitchell Sharp, and he had witnessed a bleak, ultra-politicized landscape:

> My main recollections of that visit back then are of a country of drabness and people all dressed in blue unisex garbs, ever present political slogans, and a suspicious hostility on the part of all passers-by ... It became abundantly clear later that what had been created in the Cultural Revolution was nothing more than mass obedience to a political dogma, based on the fear of guaranteed brutal social, mental, and physical punishment for any and all who strayed from the officially sanctioned path.

Twelve years later, Gorham, now the Canadian ambassador to Beijing, experienced a changed China:

> A remarkably different and rapidly changing China – with new leaders who themselves are personal survivors of punishment, imprisonment, and ostracism. The suspicious hostility toward foreigners, so palpable in 1972, is virtually non-existent in 1984. Premier Zhao Ziyang is ostentatiously appearing everywhere in Western suits. China has burst out of its semi-isolation. China's foreign policy has become more pragmatic and less doctrinaire; capitalist nations, once the sworn enemy of the Communist State, are now cultivated and coddled. The Sino-Soviet Bloc, which appeared so fearsome in the 1950s and 1960s, is now only a footnote in history. Party dogma now admits that Mao Zedong made serious mistakes and that even Marx and Lenin, as prescient and farseeing as they may have been, could not possibly have anticipated the situation of the world and of China in the 1980s.

Gorham's principal mandate was trade. He questioned why, if bilateral relations were developing so well, Canadian companies were not doing more business there. Canada was falling behind its competitors, especially the Americans and the Japanese. Gorham said that Canada had established "footholds," which should have increased trade. For example, Premier Zhou Enlai had told Prime Minister Pierre Trudeau in 1973 that China would always look to Canada first for buying grain. The two countries had signed a formal trade agreement as a measure of confidence, and they had established a joint trade committee that since then had held eight meetings to discuss bilateral trade issues. The EDC's $2 billion line of credit and the new CIDA development assistance program provided additional funding for large export-related projects. According to Gorham, "over the past few years, the complementarity of China's modernization priorities with Canada's areas of experience, in energy, communications, agriculture, transportation, have enabled Canadian companies to establish some strong footholds in China."

Gorham said that Canada's market share was improving, although difficulties remained:

> We have increased our exports of semi-processed and manufactured products to China, while still retaining substantial sales of wheat and other grains, potash and other natural resources. But these footholds have not come cheaply. While Canadian companies and the government of Canada have made a very significant investment in time, effort, and money over the past few years to achieve the market share we have already attained, our total sales do not yet equate with the resources we expended.

Gorham said that Canada's efforts would eventually bear fruit. "Not all Canadian businessmen may share my sense of optimism because of the difficulties they are having in doing business in China." He felt that Canadians did not always have the patience, time, and money to overcome language and cultural barriers. The Chinese bureaucracy could, at any moment, step in and change the terms of trade or impose extra costs. Often there was no follow through. For example, Northern Telecom, at the time one of the world's top five telecommunications giants, was left out of the final bidding for a major Chinese contract. "We cannot understand this. It is one of the most advanced companies in its field." He then gave another example. Challenger was making parts of its water bomber in the city of Xi'an, even though it was too costly for Canada to produce the parts there. However, it was deemed a politically effective strategy for winning another big contract, and it had the PRC's support. Gorham complained that the Chinese were now telling Canada that what Challenger did in Xi'an was irrelevant and that it might not win the new contract. He added:

> Then there is forest firefighting. Canada is one of the world's specialists in this area. There was a major forest fire in Heilongjiang. We gave them a Hercules plane worth five hundred thousand dollars to help, and the PRC media never acknowledged this. We are training them in various CIDA programs and are positioned to sell them a lot of useful equipment. We can provide the expertise they need, but they did not respond.
>
> Here's one more example of the problems we face, also in the northeast. The CIDA project located there had to set up a station, and it needed topographical maps. Canada could get the correct satellite surveys from NASA. Anyone can get these surveys, but the Chinese side would not agree. We were caught between two bureaucracies. There's no crossover here; it's a silo mentality that blocks us. Trade was easier in the old days, when it was centralized and it was like one-stop shopping.

Despite this litany of complaints, Gorham was confident that Canadian exporters could expand their presence in China. Sales of manufactured goods had risen 30 per cent, and the Embassy was overwhelmed by businesspeople arriving in Beijing to explore market opportunities. Gorham added: "In fact, there's too much business banqueting going on. According to senior Chinese officials, both governments need to step in and provide guidance to their exporters. President Li Xiannian, during his recent visit to Canada, made a point of this, and our Department of External Affairs has been working on better ways to assist Canadian companies."

Gorham was optimistic that a new Conservative government had made the expansion of Canadian exports a major objective. The Conservative strategy was to organize more high-level visits, provide

increased aid for Canadian business, appoint additional trade offi-
cers in the Embassy in Beijing, and engage in more discussion with
Chinese counterparts. "That's what's happening now with Brian
Mulroney. We are going to raise the bar for trade."

Brian Mulroney Goes to China

Public expectation was that Prime Minister Mulroney would move
quickly to distance himself from Liberal foreign policy. That was
the case with his shift to more positive relations with the United
States. The Shamrock Summits he held with Ronald Reagan in
the 1980s, and the decision he made to conduct free trade negotiations with the Americans, sharply contrasted with the pricklier
Canada-US relationship that had existed during the Trudeau era.
With respect to China, however, Conservative policy remained
almost the same, with three exceptions: Taiwan, trade, and human
rights. In 1986, the Canadian government, following the Australian model, opened a trade office under the auspices of the Canadian Chamber of Commerce in Taipei, without incurring strong
PRC objections. Canada now had a prime minister with extensive
business experience, who was prepared to use trade with China as
an instrument for revitalizing a flagging Canadian economy. As for
human rights, the Conservatives planned to increase government
pressure on China, since Canadian criticism of the Soviet Union
and South Africa was having an impact.

   Mulroney met with his Ottawa mandarins, and he pointedly
asked them: "What makes you think I should take your advice?"
He told his public servants that they needed to shed fifteen years
of Liberal values, and if they did not, "he would just give them
pink slips and running shoes."[2] The mandarins fell in line, and
the Conservatives then signalled that they could continue working with them. Mulroney rose in the House to announce that his
government's China policy would focus on continuity, rather than
change, and there would be no major departure from the Liberals.
He said: "*I have indicated to the Premier and to the President of China
that the intention of our Government is to pursue the policy set out by my*

predecessor, Mr. Trudeau, with which I agree. We have honored that in all circumstances" (emphasis added).[3] After meeting with Prime Minister Mulroney in Ottawa in 1985, President Li Xiannian reassured his Chinese colleagues back home that Mulroney's Conservative China policy was not that much different from Trudeau's Liberals, with no abandonment of the one-China policy, even if the Conservatives intended to offer more Canadian support to Taiwan.

The Canadian economy was struggling, and the government's mantra was "jobs, jobs, jobs." Mulroney recalled, after reading his briefing binders: "A simple truth became more apparent with each passing page. Canada was broke. There were many nights during that transition period when I couldn't sleep."[4] The net public debt had reached 46 per cent of GDP and was projected to rise still higher. Interest rates were soaring, workers needed jobs, and Canada's biggest export market, the United States, had turned protectionist. Aside from the usual remedies – tax reform, reduction in government spending, and the restructuring of federal transfer payments – Mulroney concentrated on trade. He had two targets. The first was the negotiation of a free trade agreement with the United States to protect Canada's vital access to the American market which received over 75 per cent of Canada's exports. The second was to create a National Trade Strategy, with additional funding for trade and investment promotion, to coordinate Canadian government and private sector initiatives, and to increase trade with the United States, Japan, and China.[5]

In January 1985, James Kelleher, the incoming minister for international trade, in a speech to the Canada China Trade Council (CCTC, later renamed the Canada China Business Council, CCBC), outlined the new government's preliminary thinking on trade and investment. The government intended to "revitalize" Canada's economic links with world markets. China was one of the main targets:

> Revitalizing Canada's trade performance is one of the highest priorities of the Conservative government. The Prime Minister has spoken about it often. We intend to examine, in consultation with the private sector and the provincial governments, various avenues of securing and enhancing access for our exports to world markets.

So much for the big picture. My purpose today is to zero in on the "small" picture – China. Some small pictures are bigger than others.

Kelleher spoke of a potential market of more than a billion people. "But *caveat emptor*, let the seller [*sic*] beware. China is by far the toughest market Canadian business has to crack." Cultural difference, red tape, trade financing barriers, unrealistic expectations, Chinese protectionism, price competitiveness, and the small size of Canadian companies – these were all conspiring to impose limitations on Canada. Kelleher reminded his audience of "the uncertainty factor." While there was stability in China at the moment, "what guarantee is there that this period of warming business relations will last? None, of course. Nobody can predict the future, yet there is a great swelling of consumerism that will be difficult to reverse. China will need things it never had before, and it will have to get them from abroad." According to Kelleher, Canadian business had to detach itself from its dependence on the American market, and the Canadian government would help. It could beef up the trade staff in the Embassy in Beijing and in Ottawa, establish a Consulate in Shanghai to focus on trade, provide more attractive export incentives, fund trade fairs, and take a hard look at export financing to see whether Canada had to extend China further concessional credits to buy Canadian technology and commodities. "We will be increasing resources, both for our Post in Beijing, and in Hong Kong, to cover China. We will also be considering ways and means of establishing a Canadian presence in Shanghai." The government also encouraged China to expand its economic activities in the Canadian market:

China is seriously considering investing in Canada to secure sources of supply in the food products and potash sectors ... The government is looking for ways to help China increase its exports to Canada. We are repeatedly reminded by our PRC counterparts that our exports will increase if we reduce the large trade surplus that Canada currently has with China.

Finally, Canada needed to organize more high-level visits to China in order to strengthen economic relations. The best way to get the big deals in China was to establish contacts at the top decision-making level. Kelleher said that Power Corporation, a founding member of the CCTC, had been doing this since 1978. He added that the Conservative government would be sending more ministers to China in search of trade: "I and many of my fellow ministers hope to lead trade missions to the PRC in the coming year." To cement the government's imprint on China policy, a prime ministerial visit was in the offing, and to no one's surprise, after a luncheon meeting in Ottawa with President Li Xiannian, Prime Minister Mulroney announced that he would soon visit Beijing.[6]

In 1986, Mulroney went to China, the first prime ministerial visit since Trudeau's celebrated trip in 1973. It was Mulroney's chance to set his agenda for Canadian China policy. He had been there in 1979 as a private citizen when China was emerging from the Cultural Revolution, and for Mulroney, the contrast seven years later was remarkable:

> I was struck by the tremendous changes in the last six or seven years, tremendous progress that we can see visibly on the streets ... There is a greater sense of well-being, a greater consumer reality that is there, that seems to be shared by the Chinese population. As Chairman Deng said the other day, the Chinese are trying to be realistic. They have an enormous problem, unique in the world, in terms of inherent difficulties that arise because of [the size of] the population itself.

During Mulroney's visit, Canada announced that the EDC was adding $350 million in concessional financing to blend with the $2 billion EDC line of credit that it had previously extended to China. This interest-free financing could be combined with financing from EDC's regular rate to permit Canada to provide a lower interest rate for financing exports. Development assistance was doubled to $200 million over the next five years, and surprised officials at CIDA wondered if they had the capacity to administer this expanded mandate. Potash fertilizer was developing into a major export, and Canada presented China with a bulk fertilizer blending plant worth $300 million to promote potash sales. Mulroney also won assurance from China's leaders that Canada would remain a favoured supplier of wheat. The PRC encouraged Canadian business to invest in the

$250 million Three Gorges hydroelectric project, giving a positive signal to the Canadian power industry consortium that was seeking to win a part of that contract. In a meeting with Canadian business-people in Beijing, Mulroney promised to cooperate with business, and with the Chinese government, "to make the next century 'the age of the Pacific.'"

Mulroney received assurances from Deng Xiaoping and Party Secretary Zhao Ziyang that China was committed to an "open door policy" and that it was following international best practice for protecting commercial rights and intellectual property. Speaking in Beijing at the CCTC's annual meeting, the prime minister told the hundred business representatives in attendance that, while Canadian companies should take the "lead role" in doing business, "my government will do all it can do to help. But the burden is primarily on you, the private sector."

While the focal point was on trade, Mulroney and Zhao also discussed other issues: Sino-Soviet relations, the Middle East, American attitudes and policies towards China, and the status of Taiwan. In the last of his four meetings with Premier Zhao, Prime Minister Mulroney talked about human rights. "This was important to me. The Chinese had to know we were taking rights more seriously. I wasn't just on a trade mission." He recalled:

> My (fourth) meeting with Premier Zhao was entirely devoted, by and large, to the human rights issue. No one can challenge the right of a duly elected government to raise any issue with a friend, even though I recognize the traditional Chinese position that this is an internal matter. I didn't raise it in a spirit of hostility. I raised it as the kind of subject that can be discussed between friends whose friendship is maturing and open to that kind of discussion.

In his *Memoirs*, Mulroney reflected on his trip, saying that his meetings with China's top leaders had been positive and that Canada had developed strong links with Beijing's top leaders:

> We had a very successful visit to China. Much remains to be done in expanding the relationship. Persistent work by successive Canadian

Prime Ministers, principally Pierre Trudeau, is clearly paying off. I think the extent and the ability, and the quality of my meetings with Chairman Deng, the Premier, President, and General Secretary, clearly indicate the value of this highly advantageous relationship.[7]

Chinese Perspectives

In 1987, I participated in several days of interviews with Chinese officials in Beijing, arranged by the Chinese Ministry of Foreign Affairs and the Canadian Embassy. Two former PRC ambassadors to Canada, Yu Zhan and Yao Guang, met with York University professor Jack Granatstein and myself to talk about the state of Canada-China relations.[8] We covered a wide range of topics, from Trudeau and recognition to the Mulroney period. These were frank and open discussions, in good part focusing on the transition from Pierre Trudeau and the Liberals to Brian Mulroney and the Conservatives. As the two of us asking questions were academics with China knowledge, we steered away from the more rigid political discourse that diplomats and visiting ministers usually employed. The conversation was divided into three sections: the current state of Canada-PRC relations, Prime Minister Mulroney's first two years in office, and the expansion of trade between the two countries.

> QUESTION: Let's start with your views of Canada-PRC relations today. After seventeen years, what have we achieved?
>
> CHINESE REPLY: The relationship is, generally speaking, excellent – not just good. The three major Canadian political parties generally have the same policy and attitudes towards China. We see a very beautiful (*meihao*) future. The top leaders visit each other regularly. The Canadian leaders, including the Prime Minister, Cabinet Ministers, Members of Parliament, your head of state – they all have paid visits to China, and we have sent similar people to Canada.
>
> QUESTION: What are some examples aside from high-level visits?
>
> CHINESE REPLY: Extensive consultations on international issues, talking about Sino-Soviet issues, about Sino-American relations, trade and

economic links. If we have a problem, we can talk with you and settle it quickly. There is a big difference between PRC-Canada relations and Sino-American relations. There are always obstacles with the Americans. They don't want to stop interfering in Chinese internal affairs.

Even though we have differing social and ideological systems, we have a close political relationship. China is socialist, and Canada is capitalist. We respect each other's systems. We don't want to change yours, and you don't want to change ours. We are very careful on this issue. We don't want to export revolution or change your social system.

QUESTION: You have witnessed the transition from Trudeau to Mulroney, from the Liberals to the Conservatives. What can you tell us about that?

CHINESE REPLY: We can say that Canadian policy towards China is constant. You have had a succession of governments, not just Trudeau. There was the Clark government and now Prime Minister Mulroney. The NDP has supported us right from the start, especially Mr. Douglas, and the present leader of the NDP is also very supportive.

During his first official visit to China last year, Prime Minister Mulroney said Canada is a friend in whom China can believe. Mulroney told us that when Canada signed a grain trade agreement with China in the early 1960s, your former Agricultural Minister Alvin Hamilton was a key person in the negotiations, and Mulroney was working with Hamilton at the time. So he was already interested in China twenty-five years ago.

Mulroney visited China in 1986. He did two important things. First, he increased the CIDA aid program to $200 million over five years. Second, he provided us with a $350 million loan at no interest. This shows a good understanding of how to do business in China.

QUESTION: What can you tell us about bilateral trade? This is of special interest for Canada today.

CHINESE REPLY: Both of our countries have adopted positive policies that will develop economic relations between them. Trade has grown rapidly. Between 1970 and 1986, the volume of two-way trade increased 8.5 times, from US$155 million to $1.3 billion, at an annual rate of 50 per cent. In the 1980s, especially in the past four years, various forms of economic cooperation between the two countries have developed, not just in trade, but also joint ventures and foreign investment.

Canada and China signed several agreements to promote economic cooperation. This laid a good foundation. The most important was the Canada-China Trade Agreement that our countries signed during Prime Minister Trudeau's visit in 1973. Now we don't need to renew it. It will last forever.

QUESTION: How can we help Canadian companies do more business in China? Ambassador Gorham just told us that Canadian companies are having difficulties in the China market.

CHINESE REPLY: We have talked with Canadian businessmen. We told them they could make a profit in China and send the profits back home. If you buy more of our products, we will buy more of yours. We want to reassure Canadian businessmen that they can safely invest in China.

Government and business should cooperate more closely, too. Just for one side it is not enough. Your government should help your businessmen do their business in China.

QUESTION: Where should we focus?

CHINESE REPLY: Today the main emphases in China's development are, first, energy, then communications, raw materials, and agriculture. In all these fields, Canada has an advantage. You can do a lot here. There is far more potential for economic and trade development than the actual arrangements that now exist.

QUESTION: What are the biggest problems limiting bilateral trade?

CHINESE REPLY: Here are some examples. The trade deficit between our two countries is still substantial. Of course, we do not want to reduce the deficit by reducing Canada's exports to China. The deficit has been slightly declining. Imports and exports are two legs of a mutual economic relationship. One leg doesn't get you very far. You need both legs.

Both sides should facilitate imports and exports for each other. Both sides need to make their products more competitive because both our markets are open to all countries, and therefore each of us has to be more competitive in our markets. The businessmen and economists of both countries should promote a better understanding of each other's economy, society, and culture. Also, as I mentioned earlier, government and business have to cooperate more closely with each other.

We had a problem with our textile exports. They are under quota restrictions in many world markets. Because of our large trade deficit, we asked Canada to give China a bigger quota. In our recent Textiles Agreement negotiations you did that.

QUESTION: Do you have any final comments?

CHINESE REPLY: Yes. We can say that relations are excellent. In his visit to Canada in 1985, President Li Xiannian said there were three obstacles or conflicts in China's relationship with the Soviet Union; one obstacle with the United States – that's Taiwan; and no obstacles in Canada-China relations.

Very recently, on April 9, Foreign Minister, Mr. Clark, the Minister for International Trade, Ms. Carney, and the Minister for External Trade, Mrs. Landry, announced the recent adoption of a Canadian Strategy towards China for Canada to develop a strong working relationship with China, especially in trade and investment.

We think this Canadian Strategy is a good thing. Your officials have already talked with us about it. We welcome your efforts to raise the level of our bilateral relations.

Preparing the China Strategy

The Department wanted to create a comprehensive strategy that would set forth in detail how Canada could best deploy its resources for working with China. In the immediate post-recognition period, a detailed framework to govern the new relationship did not seem necessary since both sides were still feeling their way around each other. Early Canadian policy had focused on two things – learning more about China and helping it to enter the world community.

In my diary I wrote:

> China is opening up and we want to consolidate relations, especially in trade. Lots of activity now. We are in the midst of a "China fever," when everyone wants to go there, just to see China. The Post is overloaded, all those visits are costly, and we aren't getting the results Canada wanted. We need a better China strategy. Look at what the Japanese and the Australians are doing.

Following Prime Minister Mulroney's trip in 1986, the government's main objective was to develop trade. China had opened up, yet trade lagged behind Canadian expectations. The PRC, still learning how to attract capitalist trade and investment, was hesitating to provide foreign companies with the legal and intellectual property protection that was standard international business practice. Canadian companies were lobbying for greater government participation to secure deals, and the PRC remained reluctant to use the EDC concessional financing fund. Canada still retained a trade surplus with China, although the gap was narrowing due to the rise of low-cost Chinese exports. Canada remained heavily dependent on resource-based exports, primarily wheat. This trend bothered Canadian government officials, who said: "It's still rocks and logs. Always rocks and logs – and agriculture. We can't seem to break through. We need to find a way to help our companies sell value-added goods to China."

In the fall of 1986, the government instructed the Department to develop a strategic plan for China. While the goal was to increase trade, the "China Strategy," as set out in a memorandum to Cabinet in 1987, also was designed to fulfil additional objectives. It consolidated the Canadian instrumentalities focused on China that had grown up over the first seventeen years of relations, and as a follow-up from Prime Minister Mulroney's visit, the Strategy would put his imprint on Canadian China policy. One officer later observed: "We were ready to do this. The PMO told us right after Mulroney's trip that he needed a key deliverable to establish his China credentials and implement the initiatives Canada announced in Beijing during his visit. We were already working on the components of an economic action plan when we received official notice to put the Strategy together."

The proposed China Strategy brought together sixteen ministries and departments under the aegis of an expanded Department, focused on foreign relations, now headed by three ministers: foreign affairs, international trade, and development assistance. It would provide an opportunity for the "political" mandarins to preserve their leadership and stave off challenges to their pre-eminence in the foreign policy arena from other parts of the bureaucracy. According to one officer, "it was a chance to retain our leading role in the coordination and implementation of foreign policy. Putting together a China strategy for the new government was a test of the Department's abilities."

The China Strategy emphasized the importance of the bilateral relationship. While trade relations with the United States were the principal foreign policy objectives of the Mulroney government, the China market was emerging as another priority, contending strongly with Japan. Implementing the Strategy also meant that Canada was optimistic about the long-term stability of China's economic and political transformation, even as factional struggles over Chinese economic reform persisted within the highest echelons of the Chinese party-state.

John Hadwen's Role

Organizations have their formal and informal histories, and the Department was no exception. While the official nod from the politicians to draft a China Strategy occurred in the fall of 1986, informally the process had already begun earlier, in the waning days of the Trudeau era. In 1983, John Hadwen put together a paper proposing that Canada should develop a China trade strategy to build on what it had achieved and provide guidelines for the future:

> There's a key document you won't find in the files. I wrote it in 1983. It was entitled "Why Canada Should Now Make a Major Effort in China." I sent it up, and no one ever sent me a reply. After a while, I just went ahead and did it. And that was that. How to get it organized? I circulated it to everyone in the Department and consulted widely, with a heavy emphasis on trade.

Hadwen had served as ambassador to seven Asian countries, most recently India. When he returned to Ottawa, he was asked to take charge of the East Asia Bureau, and he recalled:

> India wasn't part of East Asia, but they thought it was close enough to have given me enough Asia experience. Twice, I was almost chosen to be Ambassador to Beijing but it did not work out. Once it was during Gauvin's time when he threatened to resign because of the CIDA

episode, and I was put on the alert to go. The second was when Gorham was selected. It was a close call, and I almost went. I would have liked it.

From mid-1983, I worked on it full bore. Sought out the key people in the EDC. I saw that the $2 billion line of credit was hardly being used. Went to China in the fall. Met with their banks and planning commission. Wanted to show them that we could use EDC funding to develop commerce. These were government organizations, and the Chinese certainly understood government-to-government relations. So it was natural for them to work with Canadian government organizations.

Hadwen was convinced that Canada could get the Chinese on board, but the problem, he said, was in Ottawa. Too many parts of the government wanted to get involved in China without proper coordination. CIDA was off doing things on its own, and so were other government ministries. The Department and higher levels of government needed to step in and pull Canadian China policy together.

I knew this was going to be a challenge. The new Department was having problems merging its trade and political bureaucracies, and the Post in Beijing needed better direction to cope with so many initiatives, programs, and visits. Could we take charge? I realized that, in the first instance, it had to be the Department. If we could not manage and coordinate these new China relationships, they wouldn't get done.

In January 1984, Hadwen set up the China Working Group (CWG) in the Department. He later said that "it was a mechanism for coordinating the various strands of Canadian China policy. If we had not done this, there probably wouldn't have been a China Strategy." Trade was the main focus, although discussions also centred on evaluating China's political stability, linking aid and trade, coordinating high-level visits, and bringing in perspectives from academics and non-governmental organizations. "The CWG used to meet at night under my direction. We gathered at 7:00 in the evening at the Pearson Building. I ordered in sandwiches, wine, and beer. Sometimes we met two or three times a month. We took notes and circulated them to all the ministries and departments that were working with China."

In 1985 and 1986, I participated in several of these CWG meetings. Up to a dozen individuals from different government ministries reported on what they were doing with China, and at one meeting, we heard from the Wheat Board, CIDA, EDC, Energy, Mines and Resources, the PMO, and other stakeholders. Hadwen was in charge of the sessions, and he provided the Department's perspective on the issues we were discussing. Occasionally, assistant deputy ministers and other senior officials dropped in and raised the level of discourse. At one meeting, there was a "broad consensus" that China's modernization presented Canada with great opportunities and that the government had to step in and coordinate a sudden surge in China-related activities. The challenge was how to maximize Canada's trade potential, while keeping a cautious perspective.

In early 1985, Hadwen organized the "Beansprout Summit" to exchange views on China with twenty academics and journalists. The Summit was an unusual initiative, since the Canadian government rarely organized such internal meetings with outsiders. Hadwen said that, if Canada was going to develop a new and deeper relationship with China, the government needed a broader consensus to proceed. Along with insights from the business community, the government wanted to hear from China specialists. The Summit report covered the entire gamut of policy and relations. It predicted that China's opening would continue in the short term (three to five years), that China would remain open in the medium and long term (five to ten years), and that Canada had the resources to benefit from this opportunity:

China plays an important part in Canada's foreign policy considerations. There are immediate and growing commercial prospects for Canadian interests in its huge market that is now opening to exports, foreign investment, joint ventures, and technology transfer. In this context, Canada possesses both the commercial tools and non-commercial means, in particular high-level political consultations, aid programs, limited military exchanges, and cultural and academic programs, which might be utilized to influence events in China to Canada's advantage.

At a 1986 CWG meeting, we received an extensive debriefing on Prime Minister Mulroney's trip to China, and were told that his visit had significantly raised the level of relations with China. We received updates on concessional financing from CIDA and EDC, on agricultural cooperation from Agriculture Canada, and on thermal and hydroelectric power projects from a special government task force on the hydroelectric power sector. We were processing a great deal of information within the constraints of time and available resources. One official commented: "It's like herding cats. Too many independent-minded departments, egged on by business and political interests. Too many egos. It's a big challenge. Mulroney's visit has made China a priority, and we have to get organized."

Since 1983, Hadwen had dedicated almost three years to this effort, in his words "beginning pretty much on my own." Some members of the Department later questioned what he had actually done on his own. One officer said: "I was there the whole time, and we hardly paid attention to what he was doing." Another pointed out: "You can't do these things without authorization and help from the higher levels. No one in the Department is ever alone." Hadwen did acknowledge that, without higher level encouragement, he could not have set the stage for creating the 1987 China Strategy. "Once they learned what I had been doing, I had quiet support behind the scenes from two assistant deputy ministers, several key people at EDC, and also from other ministries and departments. When the Conservatives decided to go ahead on China, I knew they were ok with what I was doing, especially with the Department back in the middle of the game as a major player."

I wrote in my diary:

Have been attending Department meetings in the past few months. The government is developing a China trade strategy. Am learning a lot about how to make policy. How difficult it is to get everyone to agree. Hadwen and his group are working hard. Then it has to go to the upper-level mandarins to approve their recommendations. All this is taking time. A lesson in decision-making for sure.

Submission to Cabinet

After a series of interdepartmental discussions, the drafting process for submitting a memorandum to Cabinet was launched at a CWG meeting in January 1987. The drafting team worked with the sixteen government ministries and departments, the CWG, the Embassy in Beijing, and selected members of the China policy community. Copies of the draft were sent in March to the three ministers involved and then forwarded to the Cabinet Committee on Foreign Affairs and Defence Policy at the end of the month. Cabinet approved the China Strategy in early April 1987. The entire drafting and submission process had taken less than five months.

The basic issue was how to capitalize on Canada's growing fascination with China. Ottawa was hoping to seize the commercial and trade opportunities created by China's modernization and position Canada for the year 2000, when it was expected that China would have the world's third largest GDP after the United States and Japan. The drafting team recommended that all ministerial visits henceforth had to meet concrete federal government guidelines to stanch the excessive flow of officials who were making questionable journeys to China. Those government trips were putting an undue strain on government resources. Hadwen said: "We have to get over this sudden China craze. Everyone in every ministry and department wants to go there now. It's new and exciting, and we are curious, but we are getting in each other's way, and Ottawa cannot afford it."

The Department's drafting team made fourteen recommendations, covering almost every aspect of the bilateral relationship. Decades later, these recommendations have stood the test of time. They outlined a strategic framework that has governed future trade relations with China:

- Elevate the China dialogue on key Asian strategic concerns and global arms-control issues to the ministerial level. *Initiatives below the ministerial level will have a lesser impact.* (author's comments are in italics)
- Develop a cadre of Chinese-speaking officials and specialists to deliver programs in China. *The Canadian Foreign Service needs more officers with Chinese language expertise.*

- Promote better partnership between government and the private sector in order to promote long-term objectives. *The Chinese prefer government-to-government encounters, and second, the Canadian government should cooperate more closely with private business.*
- Have high-level visits target economic objectives. *Major trade deals with China are best made at the highest levels.*
- Establish *ad hoc* federal, provincial, and private sector working committees under the authority of the China Working Group to prepare action plans to match Canadian and Chinese sectoral capabilities and priorities. *Build on the experience of the CWG. Develop interdepartmental and federal-provincial cooperation.*
- Convene periodic meetings of leading business, academic, and other China specialists to ensure that Canadian strategy is based on national consensus. *Continue to hold meetings like the Beansprout Summit. Provide public support for government investment in trade and other initiatives.*
- Establish working committees that can link federal, provincial, and private-sector groups to promote trade objectives. Use the Department to organize this. Provincial trade initiatives are expanding. *The Canada China Trade Council can be a valuable partner. Promote twinning with Chinese provinces and large cities.*
- Promote shared developmental and economic interests in China. CIDA can work with the private sector on large projects. *A portion of the CIDA budget should be reserved for commercial projects.*
- The Minister of Foreign Affairs and the Minister of International Trade should approve a negotiating strategy for China's entry into the GATT (General Agreement on Tariffs and Trade) to bring greater discipline to Chinese trading practices and to meet Canadian access objectives. *The Canadian government supports China's entry into the GATT (later the World Trade Organization) as the best way to regularize and promote China's trade practices.*
- Increase Canada's use of the "China connection" through Hong Kong. A large percentage of China trade passes through Hong Kong. Work with the Post in Hong Kong. *Canadian companies should use the colony as a base for trading with the PRC.*
- Pursue co-financing arrangements with international financial institutions to leverage greater procurement opportunities for

Canadian companies. *Canada can partner with the World Bank, and other institutions, to bid on large projects in China.*

- Simplify visa requirements, and renegotiate consular instruments, to provide better protection for Canadians in China. *The business community wants better Canadian governmental assistance and protection.*
- Extend academic, cultural, professional, sports, media, and other exchanges in order to increase the number of Chinese students in Canada, to promote people-to-people contacts, to enrich Canada's multicultural heritage, and to project Canada's image as a highly developed and open society. *Strong people-to-people links enhance trade and other forms of cooperation. Education breaks down ideological and cultural barriers.*
- Implement an expanded program of defence relations with China, including naval visits, consultations on security issues at the level of military staff, and the promotion of defence-related equipment. *China is ready to purchase Canadian military equipment. China wants to develop modest defence-related relations with Canada, including peacekeeping.*

The China Strategy highlighted China's growing political, economic, and strategic importance to Canada. According to the document, "China is a dominant Asia power. Canada has a stake in China's stability. Canada's recognition of the Asia-Pacific region as key to Canadian security and economic interests requires that our political dialogue be strengthened." Canada must position itself "to meet increasingly fierce competition" in the China market, and a careful approach to China is "vital to commercial success." In an accompanying press release, the government said it was creating "a focused, orchestrated and aggressive strategy, to cope with our fascination about China, which often is undertaken without a sufficient assessment of real potential benefits to Canada." Ottawa added that there was "an urgent need for more timely and incisive knowledge of developments in China so that we can do a better job in managing Canada-China relations."

Ambassador Gorham, who had been in Beijing since 1984, commented: "It has taken three years to get to this point, and we've learned a lot about how to work with China." In his view, foreign observers should not be deluded into thinking that China would emerge as some sort of mirror image of Western democracy, with full freedom of political expression, a free press, and respect for individual rights and liberties. Nonetheless, the current reforms "appear to have legs," and "the excellent state of Canada-China relations puts Canada in a favoured position to take advantage of China's opening up and modernization." However, he told Ottawa to proceed with caution and to approach China trade with a dose of realism:

> A hardnosed look would lead us to conclude that the returns on our investment (over and above Chinese expressions and sentiments of friendship and goodwill) have not been impressive, other than a sustained market for our wheat (which the Chinese buy because they need it) and recent encouraging sales of high-tech end products. We can cite no evidence that the lustre of the Maple Leaf or the memory of Norman Bethune, despite all our efforts and our investment of human and financial resources, have persuaded Chinese negotiators to opt for sourcing their requirements in Canada.

Gorham "welcomed the general thrust" of the China Strategy, "especially the mandate to organize the new interests of the various government departments and agencies that previously were not involved with China." He was critical, however, of several parts of the draft. Targeting ministerial visits to sectoral trade priorities was a good idea, but it was almost impossible to achieve. "Dialogue will not produce Chinese recognition of Canada as a world power. If we want to improve our knowledge of China and train more Chinese-language speakers, we need to provide substantially more resources and move out of the quill pen era." The China Strategy draft included a recommendation that Canada should promote Chinese exports to Canada to reduce the large Canadian trade surplus, as a goodwill gesture to China. However, Gorham felt that Ottawa would be building up China as a trade competitor. He also thought that the enthusiastic comments about China's rapid economic development were oversimplified. China's absorption of Western technology and management principles required substantial social and political liberalization, and China was going to encounter many difficulties in disengaging from its authoritarian past and present. He added: "The principles which have governed Canada's relationship to China remain valid, and the Strategy will build on what has already been achieved." However, he also cautioned Ottawa: "Don't be mesmerized by the sheer size of China and this current shift in PRC policy."

Selections from the Text

The fifty-page China Strategy was a summary of Canadian thinking about China at the time, with a convincing set of assumptions and policy recommendations. The following are a few highlights from the document.

On China's Commitment to Reform

China's modern history has been marked by a realization that it cannot become a major power without accepting foreign technology and management techniques, and also by a deeply xenophobic reaction to the penetration of Western ideas and philosophy ... The long-term durability of the reform program is not to be taken for granted ... China is unlikely to waver from its objective to become a modern industrial power in the shortest possible time ... To achieve this status is a matter of urgency and pride for all Chinese, "reformers" and "conservatives" alike.

On China's Key Political and Strategic Role

A nuclear weapon state, China is a major military power, a key player in the Asia-Pacific region, which is increasingly vital to Canada's long-term security and economic prosperity. China's relations with the United States have become increasingly warm, although United States policy towards Taiwan, including arms sales, hinders Sino-American cooperation. The situation in Asia remains volatile. The Soviet Union, perceived by China as its main threat, occupies Afghanistan, subsidizes an expansionist Vietnam, arms Filipino rebels, and is increasingly close to a dangerously unpredictable North Korea. Annual ministerial-level consultations on security issues are essential to promote a growing convergence of security interests with China.

On Canada's Relations with Taiwan

The one-China policy has been the cornerstone of Canada's mutually beneficial relationship with the PRC since 1970. Canada does not maintain official relations with Taiwan, but the government encourages people-to-people contacts. The recent establishment by the Canadian Chamber of Commerce of an office in Taipei should result in better access to a potentially lucrative market.

On Canadian Development Assistance

CIDA's involvement in China was a logical step in the construction of Canada's bilateral relationship. Development assistance responds to real needs in China, particularly in the area of technology transfer and human resources. Canada's program is now one of the largest in China, ranking second only to Japan's. CIDA's philosophy is to build upon China's open-door policy, designed to acquire Western technologies and skills, in jointly identified sectors where Canadian expertise meets Chinese priorities, for example, agriculture, energy, and forestry, as well as telecommunications and transportation. CIDA also provides pre-project studies through its Industrial Cooperation Division. These provide substantial opportunities for Canadian companies with commercial interests.

On Trade Issues

The composition of Canada-China trade has undergone major changes. Over the past two decades Canada has enjoyed a large surplus in our bilateral trade, largely as a result of strong grain and resource exports. The gap has shrunk in recent years. Large rapid gains in the sales of Chinese clothing and textiles account for the declining deficit with Canada. Negotiations to renew the clothing restraint schedules ended without an agreement this January. Chinese textile exporters still have room to maneuver, moving "up market" or into unrestrained categories. Grain sales have been the core of Canada's exporting success in China ... As China's wheat production increased in the early 1980s, Canadian sales declined ... The dramatic recent drop in world wheat prices slashed receipts to Canada by almost one half. New suppliers have entered the fray, and competition is felt from expanding Chinese production capacities.

Overall conditions for doing business in China are becoming increasingly complex (decentralization of decision-making, financial reform, and the evolving regulatory environment, are examples of this trend). To launch joint ventures in a complicated and unfamiliar environment, where foreign exchange is scarce, Canadians must be well-informed, persistent, and adaptive. Hence, government support should be directed in a selective fashion to those Canadian companies that have the products, technology, and expertise that respond to China's priority requirements, as well as the "staying power" to weather both economic ups and downs and the slow approval process. We are seeing encouraging progress in our capital goods sector. For example, Babcock & Wilcox have sold steam generators worth 203 million dollars, and are in close pursuit of similar contracts. Oil and gas equipment sales were [worth] almost 120 million dollars in 1986. Super heavy mining vehicles represented some 70 million dollars of exports.

On Competition in the China Market

China is a fiercely competitive market. Japan, the United States, Hong Kong, and Germany are the most important exporters to China, with Canada ranking a distant fifth. Japan's remarkable success in China is based on a corporate culture which recognizes the need for long-term commitment, the presence of many trade offices throughout China, and an industrial and trading house capability that can deal with Chinese requirements for countertrade and commodity trade purchases for export sales.

The Americans sell fewer consumer durables than the Japanese, but successfully compete in China in the heavy industry, oil and gas, mining, and transportation sectors, a result of the proven quality of American technology and the staying power of the multinationals. The Australians have adopted a successful trade strategy that targets limited public and private resources to sectors where Australian companies are internationally competitive, for example, iron and steel, wool, textiles, non-ferrous metals, transportation, communications, and coal. This targeted and pragmatic approach is more relevant to the Canadian situation.

On Canadian Government Activities in China

Various federal departments and agencies have been active in China for several years. While the Program for Export Market Development and the Promotional Projects Program are the prime programs for export promotion, the federal government has recently provided funding for new tools specifically targeted to China. These include the 350-million-dollar concessional financing facility administered by EDC. The CIDA Technical Cooperation Program is designed to provide funding for feasibility studies. The Canadian National Trade Strategy, which was adopted in the fall of 1985, supported the opening of the Shanghai Consulate and the resources to create two new trade officer positions in Beijing.

While appreciative of government assistance, business groups are concerned about the lack of focus of government efforts and the potential duplication of federal, provincial, and municipal programs. Business groups have also voiced a need for more in-depth analysis and identification of commercial opportunities. Federal government financial assistance should be channelled into sectors where it can make the greatest difference, i.e., energy, agriculture, communications, transportation, and resource development.

On Academic, Community, and Non-Government Organizations

Many leading Canadian academics are actively involved in the promotion of exchange programs with China, often as advisers to provincial or municipal governments. Several have served in our Embassy in Beijing and have maintained close ties with the federal government. Their advice is regularly sought. Several NGOs (i.e., Amnesty International) are increasingly active in pursuing human rights and other questions in China. Continued consultations are under way with them to ascertain the appropriate means to conduct a useful dialogue on such sensitive issues with the Chinese government.

Applying the Strategy

Human rights were only mentioned in those last two sentences of the document. Prime Minister Mulroney had raised this issue with Zhao Ziyang during their meetings in Beijing, and the Canadian government had signalled that it intended to elevate human rights to a more prominent place in the bilateral relationship. In the China Strategy's communications plan, the government said that Chinese human rights abuses were not yet "a major problem" for most Canadians: "Although China's record on human and civil rights is a relatively poor one, Canadians seem prepared to overlook this area of concern. Exceptions include Catholic church groups and Amnesty International."

In the first of two annexes, the Department focused on the government's links with the private sector. Separate meetings were held with executives of the Canadian Export Association, the Canadian Chamber of Commerce, the Canada China Trade Council, and eleven companies trading with China. The business associations flagged the following concerns: "an urgent need for better control over the growing number of visits to China; insufficient knowledge of the China market; the need for long-term corporate and financial commitment; learning how to set up joint ventures [and] how to utilize government programs." They also reaffirmed "the value of carefully selected and timed visits to China by federal ministers attuned to trade objectives." They recommended better, more competitive financing arrangements, and they asked for a "Canada Inc." approach to China, following the example of the successful Japanese model, which linked government and big business closely together.[9]

In a second annex, the Department attached its communications plan, drawing upon speeches by government officials and the Canadian media. The objective was to deliver a positive and also realistic message to China stakeholders and to the Canadian public:

It was a challenge for the government to channel Canadians' general and sometimes romanticized notions about China along more realistic and constructive lines. Public opinion would support a government initiative to make our relations with China more productive, particularly one directly linked to furthering Canadian economic interests and generating jobs for Canadians.

The document also stated:

Communications tools of choice include speeches by ministers and senior officials to prestige audiences, tailored information materials, such as a booklet on the relationship and detailed background briefings of the specialized national media. Mass audience tools, such as national television, would be appropriate only with target audiences in mind. Educational television will be a more effective tool than national network television.

Leaders representing the Canadian ethnic Chinese communities said that they "would support the new government initiatives with respect to China." Canadian ethnic Chinese had been politically quiescent for the first fifteen years of relations, but that was starting to change now that China had opened up and it was possible to do business there, study at PRC universities, and visit with relatives. In carrying out the China Strategy, the government intended to deliver the following message to all Canadians: "It is in the interest of Canadians that relations with China be concluded in the context of a national strategy that gives coherence to exchanges taking place at all levels of government, by NGOs, and by the private sector. A successful further development of relations with China means potential prosperity and jobs for all Canadians."

Senior officials in the Embassy were expected to return home and go on comprehensive tours across every region of Canada to talk about Canada-China relations. "A slide show, emphasizing and standardizing our message, will be developed for use by government speakers at service clubs, trade organizations, and other targeted audiences." The government would also provide briefings about the China Strategy to the Canadian media to enlist their support.

> The government will conduct seminars and background sessions for Canadian journalists. Some elements of the Canadian media may seek to criticize the cost of extensive ministerial travel to the PRC, as envisaged in the work plan. One way to attenuate such criticism is to ensure that visas are linked to specific and identified goals, and cast as part of a coherent approach to China.

In April, the government introduced the China Strategy to the public with a press release announcing future visits to China by Pat Carney, then minister of international trade, and Joe Clark, the minister for foreign affairs. Clark and Carney were directed to speak at various venues in support of the China Strategy, before and after their planned trips to the PRC. The press release stated: "Members of Parliament and Senators are to be briefed on the Strategy, and information suitable for use in their constituencies shall be made available to them. Minister Clark will send a letter to the Chairman of the Parliamentary Standing Committee on External Affairs and International Trade, and to the Foreign Affairs Committee of the Caucus, outlining the elements of this strategic approach to relations with China."

Historical Perspectives

The China Strategy aptly summarized the state of relations at a key point in time, when China was opening up, the Cold War was fading, and the opportunity to engage with China on a closer level was beckoning. First and foremost, it was an action plan designed to take advantage of China's opening to maximize Canadian trade potential. To do this, it had to examine the whole bilateral relationship. It was a "whole of government" enterprise, cutting a swath through the Ottawa bureaucracy, strengthening government-to-government links, and solidifying the Department's position as policy coordinator and implementer, if not also on the cusp of making China policy.

Ambassador Gorham completed his posting and returned to Canada in the fall of 1987. In the ambassador's customary farewell report to his foreign minister, Gorham gave Clark a positive appraisal of relations during the past three years:

> The general relationship between Canada and China is excellent, and there are no serious problems between the two countries. I believe that during the three years of my assignment we have achieved much progress in the enhancement and further development of our relations with China, to the extent that, to quote the Chinese Vice Minister of Foreign Affairs at a farewell banquet he hosted for me, "More has been accomplished in the past three years, than in any similar period since diplomatic relations were established."

The Kelleher and Mulroney visits had opened doors, but would the China Strategy open them wider? Gorham had been optimistic in his report to Clark, although in conversation he was more cautious. While he had taken on a role as an advocate for improved economic and political relations with China, he was also a realist, aware that, even when both sides foresaw a congenial environment for closer economic relations, rapid advances might not occur. However, signed contracts for larger sales of wheat, other grains, and potash were positive indicators, along with an increase in value-added exports – high-tech items such as aircraft, thermal power boilers, telecommunications equipment, and oil drilling equipment. Canadians were still learning how to do business in China; too many other countries were competing for China market share; and Canada remained overly dependent on exports of resource-based goods. Nevertheless, Hadwen was optimistic about what had been accomplished and stated: "We've created a context, like building a four-lane highway to get to China. The asphalt has been laid down, and we are ready to hit the road."

The trade figures were positive. Between 1985 and 1988, exports to China doubled to $2.6 billion, and imports from the PRC also doubled. 1988 was a banner year, with total two-way trade rising to $3.5 billion, a figure not reached again until the mid-1990s. By 1991, PRC exports to Canada were five times greater than in 1989, and the balance of trade had permanently shifted in China's favour. How much of this development can be attributed to the events of 1986 and 1987 is debatable, since the time frame was too short. A drop in Canadian exports occurred in 1989, due to the disruption caused by the Tiananmen crisis and a short-term reduction in Canadian wheat sales. The great surge in Chinese exports to Canada that later began in the 1990s reflected the PRC's emergence as the world's largest producer of low-cost manufactured goods, a development that would forever transform economic links with the PRC.

Relations in the late 1980s were as good as both countries had hoped they could be, not just because of the growth in trade but also because of the elevation of all aspects of what many were calling "a special relationship." At the beginning of 1989, both Canadian and Chinese officials agreed that they were in the midst of the best period since recognition. Canadian public opinion was supporting closer relations with China, and it was widening its opening to Canada. For Canadian scholars, it was an unusually open time for conducting research in China, and we were able to engage in frank meetings with senior officials and gain access to archives that had been closed to foreigners.

The Tiananmen crisis cut short this "Golden Age." After Chinese soldiers killed their own citizens by the Square on June 4, 1989, the gold turned to brass. Imposing sanctions on the PRC took centre stage in Ottawa. It took four years for relations fully to resume, and when they did there would never again be a "special relationship." As for the China Strategy, it lost its immediacy when the Canadian government imposed sanctions on China after Tiananmen. The Strategy is a reminder of how well our relations were unfolding in the 1980s, when China was opening up and Canada was expanding links with its bilateral partner. Thirty years later, two-way trade was twenty-five times greater than it was in 1989. As a guideline for carrying out economic relations with China, the China Strategy stood the test of time and it is a document that deserves our attention.

chapter six

Tiananmen Crisis

*In this chapter, we see how Ottawa responded to the killings at Tianan-
men Square on June 4, 1989, and the effect that this event had on bilateral
relations. Tiananmen marked the end of the period of "special relations"
between Canada and China, and brought a rethinking of Canadian China
policy.*

*Warning signs of a crisis were emerging in China in the latter part of
the 1980s, with close to 20 per cent inflation, increased unemployment,
and extensive official corruption. The Party was split between conservative hardliners, who opposed any dismantling of the Marxist party-state,
and moderate reformers, who argued that Chinese socialism had to adapt
to new conditions. One of the reform-minded Party leaders, Hu Yaobang,
who had strong support from university students, lost his position in
January 1987. His death in April 1989 precipitated a series of demonstrations against the top leadership, culminating in the June 4 "Tiananmen
massacre," when many hundreds were killed in Beijing. A group mainly
comprised of students had occupied Tiananmen Square for over fifty days,
and the images of their unsuccessful confrontation with China's leaders riveted international observers. At that precise moment, communist
regimes in the Soviet Union and Eastern Europe were perilously close to
collapsing. Was China also a candidate for regime change?*

*In Beijing, the Embassy was carefully monitoring these events.
Tiananmen was the focal point, but demonstrations were also taking
place in many other Chinese cities. Ottawa was concerned for the safety
of the estimated 700 Canadians living and working in China. Within a
week, almost every Canadian was evacuated, leaving a rump Embassy*

in Beijing. In the House, Prime Minister Mulroney and Foreign Minister Clark condemned the killings at the Square, and Ottawa imposed a preliminary set of sanctions on China. The Canadian public reacted with outrage, urging Ottawa to take further action. Premier Li Peng, who allegedly gave the order for the troops to clear the Square, was labelled the "Butcher of Beijing" by his many critics.

Ottawa formed a three-person crisis management group, headed by Howard Balloch, to assess the unfolding situation in China and organize the evacuation of Canadians. The group turned to preparing an official Canadian response to the June 4 killings. It consulted widely with the government ministries and departments involved in the bilateral relationship, the Canadian business community, representatives from the Canadian ethnic Chinese communities, human rights activists, the media, and the academic community. On June 22, it organized a National Roundtable with forty hand-picked individuals to advise the government on sanctioning China for the killings at Tiananmen. The group discussed various scenarios and recommended options to Foreign Minister Clark. Should Canada suspend or cancel programs with China? How could Canada take action critical of China without jeopardizing trade? What could be done about Chinese violations of basic human rights? How should Canada deal with China's political and military leaders who were responsible for what happened at Tiananmen? Finally, what were other "like-minded countries" doing, and was Canada in step with their efforts to sanction China?

In the government's June 30 Statement, Foreign Minister Clark said it could not be "business as usual." Canada suspended or cancelled programs with China and deferred high-level visits indefinitely. Restrictions were imposed upon the financing of large Canadian infrastructure projects in China. As many as 10,000 students from the PRC who were already studying in Canada were eventually allowed to gain permanent residence status in Canada. The government said it would be a mistake to push China towards isolation, and it recommended that the focus should be on maintaining "people-to-people" links and on developing a human rights strategy that could change China's behaviour.

As we shall see in the next chapter, after four years these measures failed to move China. Its leaders ignored criticism from Canada, as well as from the international community as a whole. The Canadian public, which initially had pressed Ottawa to "show blood," had mostly lost interest.

China did not change, and Canada turned to other matters. The two countries re-engaged, but the damage from Tiananmen would be permanent.

I say to those young heroes: "Do not despair, victory must eventually be yours because liberty cannot be denied" ... Indiscriminate shootings have snuffed out human lives, but they can never snuff out the fundamental urge of human beings for freedom and democracy.

– Prime Minister Brian Mulroney, June 1989

Prelude

In the late 1980s,[1] Canada was enjoying a trade surplus, and the government had just approved its China Strategy to further develop economic links with the PRC. Innovative programs were providing development assistance to China and supporting reunification in Canada for Chinese families separated by the Cold War. Following Prime Minister Mulroney's visit in 1986, over thirty ministers and deputy ministers from Canada and China headed delegations to both countries to solidify links. Personal ties between the top leaders reinforced the perception that the two countries had a "special relationship" and that Canada was "mentoring" China's emergence into the international world order. At a Ministerial Roundtable in Vancouver in 1988, Foreign Minister Clark told a group of China specialists: "The Government is presiding over a significant growth in our relations with China, and this augurs well for Canada's emergence as a Pacific nation."

Clark added a caveat. Relations could continue to grow "provided that China remains committed to the current course of reform and opening up for the longer term." In the early 1980s, China had entered a world of capitalist markets that brought new challenges. Uncertain about the direction and depth of economic reform, its Party leadership was divided between reformers and hardliners. Party conservatives worried about the erosion of Marxism and the political consequences of engaging in capitalist markets, while reformers were ready to test the global waters, with some even experimenting with political change. However, the sudden removal of the reform-minded Hu Yaobang in 1987 as head of the Communist Party raised questions about the sustainability of China's reforms. The Thirteenth Party Congress in 1987 had approved the limited establishment of capitalist markets within Chinese socialism, yet it was not certain that Deng Xiaoping and his supporters could sustain this major ideological change, even though the Chinese economy was beginning to grow as it opened up to the outside world.

In the latter half of the 1980s, the world was riveted on the Soviet Union, where Mikhail Gorbachev was opening up the Soviet party-state to experiments with capitalism and Western democracy. The Americans and the Russians were discussing disarmament and better cooperation. Political opposition forces in Eastern Europe and the Soviet Union were challenging the rule of existing communist regimes. Was it possible that the Cold War was about to end? Change was in the air, authoritarian governments were vulnerable to political liberalization and democracy, and planned economies were threatened by resurgent capitalism. Would China also become a target for possible regime change?

The Soviet Union was receiving intense criticism for its treatment of dissidents and Soviet Jews, but the Chinese dissident community was small in comparison, poorly organized, and well contained by the party-state. There were no Chinese Solzhenitsyns or Sakharovs to mobilize support for political change. Canadians were withholding major criticism of China's repeated campaigns against "bourgeois liberalization," "spiritual pollution," and "peaceful evolution," all representing the potential danger to Beijing of Western influence. Canadians had an image of China as a slowly liberalizing communist state, where prospects for the emergence of political liberalization and an improving rights regime appeared hopeful, if not on the immediate horizon. For the moment, most Canadians, including myself, had exempted China from our general critique of communist regimes, anticipating a better future for Chinese political change than the Soviet experience.

In May 1989, Vice Premier Tian Jiyun, a senior PRC leader, visited Canada. Bilateral relations were at an all-time high. The Canadian government wanted to expand high-level consultations with the Chinese leadership to demonstrate Canadian industrial strength in areas of pertinence for China's modernization and to underline Canada's economic potential for China, especially in the hydroelectric sector. Since 1961, Canada had profited from its large wheat sales to China, selling billions of dollars of grain, and Ottawa wanted to ensure that Canada remained China's first choice for these purchases. It urged Tian to take advantage of the $2 billion dollar line of credit that Canada had made available in 1979, together with the $350 million dollars of EDC concessional financing offered to China during the prime minister's visit in 1986. The government reaffirmed its commitment to supporting China's re-entry into the GATT (General Agreement on Tariffs and Trade, forerunner to the World Trade Organization), and it assured Tian that the free trade agreement that Canada was negotiating with the United States would not penalize Chinese exports to Canada.

Also on the agenda was a string of issues linked to China's emergence into the international arena. After the collapse of Sino-Soviet relations, China had been searching for new allies to strengthen its strategic position. The PRC had played its "America card" in the 1970s by normalizing relations with the United States and by starting to define itself as the principal regional power in East and Southeast Asia. By the late 1970s, China had given up its commitment to world revolution, and it was ready to assert itself as a responsible member of international organizations, including the United Nations, the World Bank, the Asian Development Bank, the International Monetary Fund, and the GATT. For the moment, the Taiwan issue was relatively quiescent, and China and the United Kingdom were negotiating acceptable terms for Hong Kong's return to Chinese sovereignty in 1997 with the "one country, two systems formula" (*yi guo liang zhi*). To be sure, China still had a few "bad habits," such as pursuing hard-line policies in Tibet that continually drew international condemnation, an unwillingness to halt nuclear testing, and supplying nuclear technology to countries such as Iran, Pakistan, and Algeria. While China's relations with the United States had "normalized" after 1979, they remained tense and uncertain, especially over continuing American support for Taiwan.

Canada was also changing. Beginning with Pierre Trudeau in the 1970s, Canadian foreign policy had departed from its previous emphasis on Pearsonian internationalism, and it was shifting to a stronger focus on Canadian national interest, a change later described by one ambassador as "moving from romanticism to realism."[2] A Department official characterized the shift with these words: "We were Boy Scouts in world affairs, helping others to settle disputes and build international institutions. That's how the world saw us. Now we are just like them, mainly focusing on what's good for ourselves. That's realism. The days of Canadian Boy Scouts have, regrettably, passed." Except for peacekeeping, development assistance, and support to the United Nations, Canada was occupying an increasingly marginal place in international affairs, while at the same time a more self-confident China had less need of Canadian support.

Yao Guang, the former PRC ambassador to Canada, remarked in 1987: "For the first dozen years or so, we turned to Canada to help us understand American policy. Now that we have established relations with the Americans and are members of international organizations ourselves, we don't have to do that anymore." The relationship with the United States was China's top priority, followed by settling the PRC's more than two-decades-long conflict with the Soviet Union. The Cold War was winding down, and issues such as disarmament, nuclear proliferation, test bans, Taiwan, and Afghanistan were being played out among the Americans, Russians, Japanese, and Europeans, now joined by the PRC, while Canada was often watching from the sidelines.

For Canadians concerned about high inflation, unemployment, the nagging threat of Quebec separation, and an impending free trade agreement with the United States, relations with China were not at the top of their list, although the polls showed that in 1988, most Canadians held positive views of China. A majority expected China to play a bigger role in world politics in the coming decade and supported closer engagement with China. The recent reforms in China were bringing real change, especially the rapid rise in the standard of living and increased Chinese literacy – although there was almost no progress in human rights.

I was doing field research in Moscow and Beijing, and the changes taking place were startling. Despite twenty years of experience as a political scientist, I dared not predict the outcome of either the Soviet or the Chinese reform initiatives. In my mind, any transition from a command economy to a market economy was fraught with peril and likely to precipitate major convulsions. I had doubts about the sustainability of China's economic reforms. The newly formed partnership between the Chinese public and private sectors was still tentative, and the Party leadership remained split over marketization and revisions to Marxism.

In my diary I wrote:

> Want to be optimistic about China because so much has changed since the Cultural Revolution – for the good. Not all my Chinese friends are that enthusiastic. G. says not to set hopes too high, since the political system is still the same. Behind the scenes, leaders are fighting with each other. There's even more corruption now, and the state has all the power. Look at what happened to Wei Jingsheng. Maybe China will not follow Gorbachev's lead. The Soviet template may not fit the Chinese.

Ambassador Earl Drake took up his post in Beijing at the end of 1987. In his Letter of Instruction from Foreign Minister Clark, he was asked to implement the China Strategy that Cabinet had just passed, to oversee Canadian economic interests in China, and to monitor the rapid changes that were taking place there.

> As our Ambassador, your fundamental objective is the protection and promotion of the complex of Canadian interests in China. This is particularly necessary given the wide range of Canadian activities that have developed in response to the ambitious Chinese "open door" and modernization policies. It will be your task to oversee the implementation of the China Strategy, to broaden our mutual understanding of common interests in the Asia-Pacific region, which is increasingly key to Canadian security and economic interests.

Drake wrote that, prior to arriving in Beijing, "China had beguiled him in a perverse way." Once at the Embassy, however, he was concerned about what he called "the rose-coloured views of China held by Canadians." While China's reforms were impressive, "layers upon layers are hidden from the view of most foreigners." He soon realized that Canada was not that important strategically or economically to China and that foreigners, especially diplomats, were deliberately kept isolated from normal contact with the Chinese people. "It was the only time in my long career that I was unable to mix freely and make friends with local residents."[3]

The Crisis Unfolds

The unexpected death of former Party secretary Hu Yaobang on April 15, 1989, set in motion an extraordinary fifty days that ended with the Tiananmen killings of June 4. Two years earlier, conservative Party elements had purged Hu, ostensibly for permitting too much Western-style liberalization. He had been one of the first post–Cultural Revolution leaders to wear Western dress in public instead of the iconic blue revolutionary Mao suit, and he had supported student protests. The students in Beijing used the occasion of his funeral to ask for better living conditions for themselves, for an end to growing corruption, and for changes in how jobs were allocated after graduation, a system that openly favoured the children of Party officials. They wanted an end to restrictions on their freedom of speech and assembly, and they asked for the right to form an independent student organization.

The students were unsuccessful in arranging a suitable meeting with top Party leaders to plead their case. None of their demands were met. On April 20, the night before Hu's funeral, over 100,000 people gathered in Tiananmen Square to join the large group of students mourning him. Teachers, workers, and even Party members participated, and protests against the government quickly spread to other cities. On April 26, the Party, worried about the sudden escalation of these protests, accused the students in a *People's Daily* editorial of plotting to overthrow the PRC's socialist system of government by creating "counter-revolutionary turmoil."

The students insisted that their goals were "patriotic," and not "counter-revolutionary," and that they only wanted to initiate a dialogue to bring their complaints to the attention of the Party leadership. They refused to acknowledge that they were creating any kind of "turmoil" and asked for an official retraction. But China's leaders rejected their demands. Buoyed by the surprising support they were receiving from the Beijing public, the students extended their demonstrations to May 4, a date that traditionally marks the revolutionary role of China's youth. On May 4, 1919, Chinese students had demonstrated against the weak response by the Chinese government over the decision made at the Versailles Peace Conference to award a part of Shandong Province to Japan, instead of returning it to China. Thereafter, students had been at the centre of key political moments in China throughout the twentieth century. Young Red Guards had played a critical role in the Cultural Revolution, and now, twenty years later, students once again were challenging their government. Rebuffed by China's leaders, they escalated their protests to demand democratic reform. They criticized the Party and the government by placing small broken bottles on the Square. These bottles, called *xiao ping* (little bottles), were a homonym for Deng Xiaoping, China's paramount leader. At the end of May, they erected the "Goddess of Democracy," a ten-metre-high white statue, a duplicate of the American Statue of Liberty, on the Square directly facing Mao's famous portrait.

Soviet leader Mikhail Gorbachev visited Beijing in mid-May. After almost thirty years of poor relations, his meeting with Deng Xiaoping marked the end of conflict between China and the Soviet Union – a major political achievement for both leaders and of great international significance. Over 1,000 representatives from the foreign media had arrived in Beijing to report on his visit, with full television coverage from CNN, NBC, CBC, and other foreign networks. Taking advantage of this unexpected gift of international media attention, on May 13 the students began a hunger strike in Tiananmen Square, vowing that they would not eat until the leaders retracted the April 26 editorial.

When Gorbachev arrived, the stage was set for a showdown. About 250,000 protestors joined the band of hunger strikers at

Tiananmen, preventing any official meeting there between Gorbachev and China's leaders. It was a major embarrassment for Deng, for whom the restoration of links with the Soviet Union was intended to be a personal triumph. The crowd rapidly grew larger, eventually reaching more than one million people. Those who assembled in support of the demonstrators now included newly organized workers' groups, officials from the Ministry of Foreign Affairs, members of the People's Liberation Army (PLA), faculty and students from China's top universities, representatives of various government ministries, the PRC media, the Central Party School, as well as protestors from other parts of China.

Gorbachev's visit was supposed to herald the end of almost thirty years of bitter relations between China and the Soviet Union. Instead, the huge demonstrations blockading Tiananmen Square had forced China's leaders to hold the formal welcoming ceremony for Gorbachev at the Beijing airport. Later, his tour of the Forbidden City was cancelled. It was a humiliating experience, and the international television cameras gleefully recorded the event, China's leaders smarted from their loss of face, and the demonstrators had made their case to the outside world.

On May 18, Premier Li Peng, emerging as the leader of the Party's hard-line faction, agreed to talk with the student leaders, but the meeting ended badly without any resolution. A day later, Party Secretary Zhao Ziyang, who headed the Party's liberal faction supporting the students, came to the Square to meet with them. He tearfully said that he could not help them anymore: "Classmates, we've come too late. You have good intentions. You want our country to become better." On May 19, the Chinese government imposed martial law and ordered the end of live foreign television coverage of the demonstrations. The international media henceforth had to rely on telephones, video cameras, faxes, and other means, sending their footage out via Hong Kong to show what was happening in Beijing. Zhao was relieved of his duties and disappeared from view, stripped of his official positions and confined to house arrest for the remainder of his life. The leadership ordered military units to enter Beijing, but its residents, who were determined to keep the PLA out of the centre of the city, barricaded the major intersections to stop the troops from reaching the Square.

At the Post

The Canadian Embassy was monitoring these events with alarm. For several months, it had been reporting to Ottawa about the weakening Chinese economy, rising corruption, and mounting criticism of the Party inside China. The escalation of the student protests and the imposition of martial law had raised concerns in Ottawa that the confrontation at Tiananmen Square might not be settled peacefully. The students were receiving support from other Beijing residents, the split within the top leadership was becoming more obvious, and the summoning of the army was an ominous step. Demonstrations against the government, some of them violent, were now breaking out in other parts of China, and they would eventually spread to several hundred cities.

Historically, foreigners are a convenient target in China, and the Canadian government was right to be worried about the safety of its citizens. Diplomats remembered the sacking of the British Legation in 1967 during the Cultural Revolution, and the twenty-seven months that British journalist Anthony Grey had spent as a hostage in Beijing between 1967 and 1969 under cruel conditions. The Embassy was responsible for protecting Canadian nationals, and it was worried about the possibility of civil war. On May 20, Foreign Minister Clark, expressing concern for the safety of Canadians in China, called in Ambassador Zhang Wenpu to urge his government not to use force against the demonstrators.

Ironically, during the calm before the storm in May, the Embassy held a major event, Canada-China Friendship Month, to raise Canada's cultural and trade profile in China. The program, for which planning had begun a year earlier in 1988, included an Emily Carr art exhibition and performances by synchronized swimmers Carolyn Waldo and Michelle Cameron, as well as by classical pianist Angela Cheng. Chinese Minister of Culture Wang Meng and twenty-two Chinese officials of vice ministerial rank attended the opening banquet. Prime Minister Mulroney's video greeting to China was shown multiple times on national Chinese television to an audience of 600 million people, and the CCTC organized several popular events highlighting Canadian products in several cities. Friendship Month was a success. It showcased the positive relations that had developed between the two countries and was intended to be a prelude for a more comprehensive celebration scheduled for October 1990, when the two countries would commemorate the twentieth anniversary of the establishment of diplomatic relations. However, as it turned out, the events of June 4 squelched later thoughts of any official celebration, and the twentieth anniversary was marked quietly without fanfare in the fall of 1990.

Ambassador Drake recalls:

> We were fascinated by the crisis as it was unfolding. The turning point came on April 26 when the students were accused of causing "turmoil." The sons and daughters of the Chinese political elite who were involved in the protests understood the coded language to mean "Get off the Square right now, or else."
>
> We said to ourselves and to Ottawa, the party's over. This is serious. Ottawa at first did not believe us. It waited until May 13 to set up a crisis management group in the Department. From our perspective, the crisis had arrived more than two weeks earlier. Ottawa finally moved when the international television cameras began to pay attention, and that had to do with the Gorbachev visit on May 15.

The Embassy was monitoring events, in constant contact with Ottawa, and it was keeping in close touch with friends in the American, British, Australian, and German embassies. With a major crisis looming, Drake sent his officers to Hong Kong to purchase walkie-talkies, without requesting permission from Ottawa. The Post distributed these walkie-talkies to Canada's allies, setting up an informal Beijing communications network to monitor what was happening on the university campuses and to keep track of military movements. After martial law was declared, contacts with the Chinese Ministry of Foreign Affairs, Canada's principal

Chinese interlocutor, diminished. The MFA either did not know what to tell the foreign diplomats in Beijing to do, or it was afraid of engaging in conflict with its own military and security organizations. It was in a difficult situation because many of its officials were more sympathetic to the students than members of the other Chinese government bureaucracies, and a number of its younger officials had joined in the protests.

The Embassy was not prepared for a full-scale evacuation of Canadians. The Department's crisis manual badly needed updating – the last emergency that the Post had dealt with was a Beijing earthquake in 1976, which only involved moving Canadians out of buildings into nearby tents. Aside from the eighty Embassy officials, staff, and dependents, the government estimated that at least 700 Canadians were living, studying, working, and travelling in China. If there was a sudden emergency, could the Embassy find them all? It was becoming difficult just to get around Beijing. Canadians were scattered throughout the city and also living in other parts of China, and most of them did not want to leave.

Escalation

Now fully aware of the seriousness of the situation, the Canadian government established a crisis management group on May 13 to coordinate the response to what was happening in China. Ambassador Drake recalls: "At first we were concerned that Ottawa wasn't able to deal with these fast moving events in Beijing, but we soon realized that the three members of the Ottawa crisis group had a good understanding of the situation, and we could work smoothly together." The Department proposed sending in special satellite equipment to help maintain communications, but the Embassy had enough equipment. The walkie-talkies they had just purchased in Hong Kong were proving effective. "In any case," said Drake, "we knew we could rely upon the British and the Americans in a communications emergency."

The crisis management group was housed in the Department, under the direction of the assistant deputy minister for Asia-Pacific affairs. It reported daily to Foreign Minister Joe Clark and his staff. While Prime Minister Mulroney and the PMO were kept fully informed of the unfolding crisis, Clark was responsible for day-to-day decisions on China policy. He and the crisis management group took charge of preparing the Canadian response to China's actions. It organized and regularly briefed a special task force of key government ministries and departments, including Agriculture, CIDA, Finance, and Immigration, which met weekly to make policy recommendations. The group also maintained close consultations with friendly governments to gain as much information as possible about what was happening in Beijing in order to coordinate Canada's response with that of its allies.

Howard Balloch, the head of the North Asia Relations Division, was in charge of the day-to-day activities of the group, and he was assisted by Bruce Jutzi and Gordon Houlden, two officers with substantial China experience. They operated out of the Branch on the fifth floor of the Pearson Building, instead of the larger Operations Centre on the second floor.

> We should have been in the Operations Centre on the second floor and consolidated everything there, instead of staying upstairs. It would have been more efficient. They had all the facilities, including 100 telephone lines, television screens, computers, faxes, a kitchenette to nuke food and brew coffee, and cots for sleeping. After martial law was declared, everything speeded up. We had to move fast and do things not always according to procedure. We often bypassed our Director General and the Assistant Deputy Minister, with their consent, and went straight to the Minister. We had good relations with the PMO. It was essential to maintain connections with the Prime Minister. When we approached June 4 we went into a 24-hour mode. We were consulting with our allies, especially the American and Australian task forces. We briefed the various Canadian ministries and departments, Members of Parliament, and the media.

Events in China in late May were remarkable. Anti-government demonstrations were taking place in close to 300 cities. Seven Chinese generals protested the imposition of martial law, and forty members of China's national legislature, the National People's Congress (NPC), petitioned to overturn that decision. Its chairman, Wan Li, visited Canada in early May and then rushed back to China from Boston on May 24, ostensibly to support the protestors. He was detained in Shanghai and not allowed to return to Beijing until he agreed to side with the hardliners. The commander of the 38th Group Army, feigning illness, disobeyed orders to move his troops into Beijing, saying he did not want to end his career turning Chinese troops against the Chinese people. Protestors presented soldiers with food and drink, and told them: "The PLA is our army. You are our brothers and sisters. You are Chinese. We believe you have a conscience. You must not crush the movement."

It appeared that martial law was working, since the students were abandoning their hunger strike, their numbers were dwindling, and they considered leaving the Square. Then, at the end of May, they erected the "Goddess of Democracy" statue on the Square. It immediately became a symbol of the Chinese people's fight for democracy, although many saw it as the last gasp of the Tiananmen demonstrations. One account described the situation:

> By the end of May, the Square had become a smelly squatters' camp. Heaps of garbage baked in the hot sun. Makeshift latrines in municipal buses with their seats removed stank terribly. Most Beijing students had already drifted back to campus. The only new faces were students arriving from the provinces. For a week, the student leaders debated whether to stay or go. Chai Ling, their most radical leader, was against retreating, but even she finally agreed to leave.[4]

Until the government shut down international television coverage on May 19, the outside world had an unparalleled view of an authoritarian party-state openly challenged by its citizens. Canadians reacted positively to the images of young, idealistic students confronting an aging Party leadership. After Chinese censorship was imposed, it was still possible for foreigners to receive inspired coverage from intrepid foreign journalists, who each day continued to send out dramatic images. Soon, less information was seeping out, as the regime authorities were playing a cat and mouse game with the foreign and domestic media, trying to stop the Tiananmen images from circulating. Canadians were caught up in the *zeitgeist* of the moment. Was China on the precipice of regime change, and would this be the point in history when authoritarian communist regimes were going to fall to capitalism and democracy? If so, what better instrument of change than young, idealistic students?

One wanted to be optimistic that political reform was going to happen as a result of the student protests, yet the reality was that the troops surrounding Beijing were slowly tightening their grip, the students had no weapons, and in all likelihood there would be bloodshed. The demonstrators had put up signs in the Square asking: "Where is China's Gorbachev?" And the people realized that he was nowhere to be found. The situation remained tense, even as the number of protesters was declining. Would there be civil war? Could the party-state survive?

On May 27, I wrote in the *Globe and Mail*:

> The events of the past six weeks in Beijing have been so astounding it may take years for China and the rest of the world properly to digest them. At last report the number of student demonstrators on Tiananmen Square was slowly diminishing, fresh troops have surrounded Beijing, and hardline elements appear to have taken charge of the Party and the government. Whether this means the end of the current uprising or not, one thing is certain: China will never be the same again. From now, on every May 4, the anniversary of the first great student uprising in 1919, whoever is in power will anxiously scan the horizon to see whether the students are mobilizing. They are the bearers of what is left of Marxist revolutionary values, and also of Confucian ethics. Who can say that any other group of young people in any other country has acted with more bravery, self-discipline, or patriotism?

In Toronto, most of my students from China supported the protests. It was the beginning of June, the Canadian university term had ended, and their families told them to stay in Canada until the situation in China had improved. The Chinese Embassy in Ottawa and the Consulate in Toronto were urging them to return home.

They said that events in Beijing were "normalizing" and that the PRC students in Canada would not be punished for supporting the demonstrations. In private, however, those same officials were telling a different story. They were worried about the threat of military action and even civil war. "Maybe the students should stay in Canada until the situation in China has improved."

Over the next few days, one of those rare moments occurred when Chinese diplomats briefly let down their guard and criticized their own government. Later, eleven PRC government officials working in Canada defected and received political asylum. As for my students, they took advantage of the Canadian amnesty that allowed them to stay in Canada, and they all applied for visa extensions and then permanent residency in Canada.

June 4, 1989

After June 2, events spun out of control. PLA troops were turned back by Beijingers on the streets. But the army kept coming, and on June 3, amidst growing violence, tanks and armoured personnel carriers surrounded the Square, entering it early in the morning of June 4. By then, almost all the students had left. In the next twenty-four hours, army units took over the Square, and an estimated 700 people were killed, mostly in the Wuxidi area just west of Tiananmen Square. The army fired indiscriminately at people standing on nearby streets or watching from buildings, including at the nearby residences housing foreign diplomats and their families. Beijingers were shocked by this outcome, with many in tears, not believing what their own army and their political leaders had done.[5]

The effect on Canadians was profound; in fact, it was unprecedented. Televised images of the army's takeover of Tiananmen evoked expressions of outrage, anger, and dismay. On the night of June 4, I was a commentator on Canadian national television, together with Patrick Brown, the CBC's Beijing correspondent, the China historian Diana Lary, and Paul Lin, the historian and pro-China activist who had been closely connected to the Chinese regime since the late 1950s. His teachings had produced a group of radicalized Canadian students who had enthusiastically praised the policies of Mao Zedong and the Communist Party, including the Cultural Revolution. I sat in that CBC studio in stunned silence when, in a shaking voice, Lin angrily castigated China's leaders for ordering the army to shoot its own people. He later said: "The Chinese government had committed a crime against the people. The regime had made a qualitative change, and I had to speak out in condemnation. I also felt it was my duty to 'speak truth to power' on behalf of friends and colleagues in China who had been silenced by the government's violence."[6]

The CBC's Beijing correspondent could hardly speak, choking back tears. Images of the Chinese army shooting unarmed citizens were later played and replayed on Canadian television. China had been transformed before our eyes from a benignly modernizing communist state into a brutal dictatorship.

I wrote in the *Globe and Mail*:

> After the June 4 massacre, those Canadians who believed that China had changed fundamentally in the Deng Xiaoping decade recoiled in anger at what they had seen. Many demanded major economic sanctions, and even the withdrawal of diplomatic relations. The urge to punish China for its open brutality and failure to conform to our expectations was strong. Others, from the beginning more skeptical about the real depths of Deng's liberalization, saw an authoritarian system reverting to type, and while dismayed by what had happened, were less willing to "punish" a system that in their view would have been expected to respond to the demonstrations with violence.

The Canadian Reaction

During a prolonged emergency debate the next day in Parliament, Clark said Canadians shared "a deeply felt sense of horror and outrage as they were watching unarmed students and citizens gunned down by tanks." There was "fighting between various factions of the military" and "military chaos." He lamented the silencing of "cries for greater democracy, for the establishment of basic rights and freedoms." He reminded members of Parliament: "In 1970, we were among the earliest of Western countries to establish diplomatic relations with the People's Republic after almost two decades of isolation. We are not going to become 'anti-China.' Our condemnation and outrage should be focused on the violent and aggressive actions that we cannot and will never condone, and on those who initiated and condoned those actions." Clark said that the government was in constant contact with Ambassador Drake in Beijing, and it had put contingency plans in place for the evacuation from China of all students, Embassy staff, and all other Canadians living and working in the PRC. Aircraft were available on short notice to take them back to Canada immediately.

Abruptly, in mid-speech, Clark announced: "In fact, Mr. Speaker, we have just decided to advise Canadians to leave China now."

The day before, Clark had called in Zhang Wenpu, the Chinese ambassador, for a second time, "to underline the seriousness with which we view the situation, and to ensure that he passes to his authorities our call for a stop to the killing, and to convey the depth of our outrage." Clark stated: "Canada is not alone in calling on the Chinese leadership to stop the carnage and return to peaceful methods. Most Western governments, governments from around the world, even communist parties in other countries, have joined in condemning the brutality of the methods used to clear Tiananmen Square."

Balloch, the head of the Department's crisis management group, said: "The government had to make an immediate statement condemning China, so Clark announced a few measures we could quickly put into place while we were deciding what to do." Canada was deferring or cancelling all bilateral events planned for the immediate future. The signing of a series of memoranda of understanding on proposed CIDA development assistance projects was postponed, as were nuclear cooperation consultations. High-level visits were "deflected until a more appropriate time." The Canadian ambassador to the United Nations was instructed to meet with other UN members, and with the secretary general, to utilize "the moral suasion of the United Nations." Clark assured the estimated 5,000 Chinese students then studying in Canada that "we will be sympathetic to any requests for extending your stay until calm returns to your homeland." The modest program of defence relations between the Canadian Armed Forces and the PLA was suspended immediately, as were sales of military equipment to China. Balloch said: "These were the government's first measures. After three weeks of consultations, including the June 22 National Roundtable, we issued the June 30 Statement, with a full list of sanctions."

Troops were firing at the residences of foreign diplomats in Beijing, creating panic among the foreign community. Fifteen years later, one could still see the bullet holes scarring the walls of the building in the Beijing diplomatic quarter where our family had lived. The smell of imminent civil war floated in the air, and evacuation was the immediate priority. The crisis management group and the Embassy hurried to locate all the Canadians still in China, chartering aircraft and making arrangements for a quick and orderly removal. Telephone lines between Ottawa and Beijing were kept open for days, and Balloch recalls: "As long as someone was talking on the phone the Chinese operators would not shut us down, so we had our people reading novels and calling out hockey scores, eating pizza, and drinking lots of coffee." While it was vital to keep the telephone lines open between Ottawa and Beijing, the Embassy was hard pressed to find enough people to keep staffing the phones.

Ambassador Drake remembers:

We kept the phone lines to Canada open, non-stop for two days. It served an important purpose to the Canadian public, showing that the government cared and was in constant touch with Canadian officials in China. It was a real nuisance to keep the lines open. We were busy with the evacuation and trying to keep tabs on what was going on in Beijing. I could not spare an officer or staff member so we eventually conscripted some of the evacuees to sit at the phone. It was just like those filibusters that you read about in the US Senate.

Most Canadians were in China's big cities, studying at the universities. Drake said it was a struggle to collect them all. "The

Embassy sent convoys draped in Canadian flags through the army lines to rescue our students and bring them to Embassy homes for shelter. We felt relieved after we had accomplished that risky task, and then we learned that several students had returned to campus on their own because they had left their favourite rock music behind." Many of the Canadian students and faculty on the Province of Ontario's exchange program in Jiangsu Province, which I was administering, resisted leaving, saying they were better judges of their own safety. Compared to Beijing, they felt that the situation in Jiangsu was less threatening. We told them that they had no choice, demonstrations were escalating in Jiangsu, and the government of Ontario insisted they had to leave. We promised to send them back to Jiangsu when it was safe to do so.

The ambassador described the situation:

> We were one of the first of the Western countries to get everyone out and had the most calm and orderly crowd at the airport. We gathered most of our people at nearby hotels and were the only Embassy to house some evacuees in tents on our grounds. We arranged our own bus convoys from the Embassy to the airport in order to provide protection and save scarce fuel.
>
> We breathed a sigh of relief when the last evacuation flight departed. Only then did we realize that there were just twenty of us left to run the Embassy in a hostile environment. It felt a bit eerie to be alone in a city virtually denuded of foreigners and inhabited by a frightened local populace controlled at every intersection by young, nervous, gun-wielding soldiers.

A visiting Canadian described a somewhat different Canadian evacuation scene in her diary:

> Scenes of mass chaos at airport, so many people leaving on special flights. Some went on and on about their cats – pets had to be left behind temporarily. Instant expertise at its very worst. All the pushing and shoving of people trying to check in at the airport. These people were safe. They just had to wait a few more minutes before they got on the plane, yet all they could think about was themselves. Very scary moment just before

we took off, when the border police came on the plane and did a check of passports to make sure we had no Chinese on board.

By June 9, over 500 Canadians had left China. A week later, the government announced that the evacuation program was complete, although the Embassy had been unable to find every last Canadian, and "at least one hundred were probably still in China." On June 4, Solidarity roundly defeated the Polish Communist Party in a national election, sending a frightening message to the Chinese Party leadership that communist regimes elsewhere were hanging on for dear life. The Canadian media abruptly changed course from its previous qualified support of Chinese "soft" political reform to angry denunciation of an authoritarian communist regime. The *Ottawa Citizen* called for an immediate embargo on all flights to China, urging the government to let all the PRC students stay in Canada as long as necessary, demanding that foreign aid must be linked to human rights performance, and that Canada should immediately terminate technology transfers to China. The *Financial Post* insisted that Canada should end EDC financing for trade with China and should no longer support PRC accession to the GATT.

On June 5, Prime Minister Mulroney announced that he was "appalled by the tragedy that's been visited upon young people in China seeking greater democratic freedoms." Later he said: "I thought back sadly to my visit to China and my talks with the Chinese leadership in 1986, before I braced myself to speak to the press in the aftermath of the massacre. What do you say in such circumstances? I tried my best ... I said it's a calamity for them and it's a calamity for the breath of fresh air that was a democratic impulse running through China."[7]

In the House, John Turner, leader of the opposition, spoke forcefully:

The Chinese Government, the leaders in China, must be made to understand that all the goodwill built up over the last several years, all the international friendships, all the increase in commerce, all of the increasing influence of China over world affairs can be shattered by the ferocity and brutality of the past few days.

In the course of human history, governments all too often have taken decisions which come from the dark side of human nature. The decision of the Chinese Government to use tanks against young students comes from that dark side of human nature. Such a decision taken by a single human being would be madness. Such a decision taken by a group of human beings is collective madness.

Balloch reported:

Our group was doing things that did not follow established procedures. We ran close to the flames. I was chartering planes without approval, talking directly with the PMO. Prime Minister Mulroney was basically out of this loop, having delegated responsibility on the China file to Joe Clark. We met all the time, at least once or twice a day. It was a 24-hour mode.

The evacuation was carried out relatively smoothly, and foreign diplomats in Beijing commented on the efficiency of the Canadian departure. One Italian diplomat observed: "The Canadians? One day they were here, and three days later it seemed they had all disappeared, while we, being Italians, were still trying to get organized."

The government was deciding how it would respond to demands by Canadians to impose strong sanctions on China, whether it could find a course of action to satisfy those who wanted to "punish" China for killing its citizens but did not want to permanently damage relations that had been carefully built over twenty years. How could Canada produce a policy statement that would be in step with the statements condemning China being made by "like-minded" countries such as the United States, Australia, New Zealand, Britain, France, and Germany?

Balloch recalls:

The crisis management group circulated internal "backgrounders" providing up-to-date information to the government about the situation in China, contingency planning, the key issues, and measures taken. There was no internet, so we were using the telephone, faxes, and special messengers to keep everyone informed of the latest events. We kept track of public opinion and consulted with our allies. We were on the edge of policymaking, acting as liaison between the PMO, the Minister, and the bureaucrats, raising issues which, in effect, became policy.

June 4 shocked and mobilized a large number of Canadians, not just the small group that had previously comprised the informed public and stakeholders involved in Canada-China relations. Chinese community organizations across Canada were holding candlelight vigils, demonstrating in front of the Chinese Embassy in Ottawa and outside the Chinese Consulates in Vancouver and Toronto. Canadian television screens were full of powerful images of troops confronting unarmed Beijingers, for example, the young "tankman" with his briefcase, who courageously had halted the parade of tanks going through Tiananmen. The *Globe and Mail* columnist, John Fraser, who had stood together with Wei Jingsheng and other Chinese rights activists at the Democracy Wall in Beijing in 1978, welcoming the emerging "sprouts of Chinese democracy," now wrote: "For 12 years the world has turned a blind eye to the dark and evil side of the Beijing regime as it embraced the notion that a brutal, totalitarian oligarchy was capable of dwindling into benign quietude. The terror that has descended on China is neither new, nor unpredictable."[8]

The Tiananmen crisis widened the size of the China policy community, opening it up to participation from groups and individuals who wanted action from Ottawa. Rights advocacy groups, previously accustomed to playing a marginal role in Canada's relations with China, found themselves courted by ministers and policymakers. The government brought these groups into the consultation process as it framed its formal response to June 4. Before Tiananmen, I had rarely seen an ethnic Chinese Canadian face, or a human rights advocate, sitting at the table in government-organized meetings discussing bilateral issues. After June 4, it became *de rigueur* for Ottawa to be sure to have consulted with ethnic Chinese community organizers and human rights advocacy groups. Even representatives from the media, *bêtes noires* of policymakers everywhere, were invited to join in these consultations.

Between June 7 and June 22, Prime Minister Mulroney, Foreign Minister Clark, and members of Cabinet met with ethnic Chinese community groups across Canada at least eight times. Younger Chinese Canadians, who wanted a strong response to the events of June 4, had energized the traditionally apolitical Canadian ethnic Chinese communities. They urged the government to extend the stay of the thousands of PRC students stranded in Canada who were reluctant to return home. Their agenda also included the suspension of development assistance programs, recalling Ambassador Drake in protest, and halting government financial support for trade with China.

The crisis management group had a challenging task to perform:

> We were under a tight time constraint. We had to take into account the views of the Minister and his colleagues, Members of Parliament, the business community, Canadian Chinese, Canadian China experts, the bureaucrats, provincial leaders, the media. We also had to coordinate with the Embassy in Beijing, and with our "like-minded" allies. We were doing this behind the scenes, like an impresario organizing a performance. The situation in China was unclear, and we had to make sure we were not out of step with the other countries, in particular, the Americans.

Everyone was waiting for the American response. If the United States decided not to impose meaningful measures, then sanctions imposed by the other like-minded countries would have little impact. President George Bush had served as the first head of the American Liaison Office in Beijing in 1974 and 1975, and he had maintained warm personal relations with China's top leaders, in particular with Deng Xiaoping. While Bush was visibly upset by the events at Tiananmen Square, he did not want to break relations with China, despite strong American pressure to impose sanctions by the Republican right and the Democratic left. Bush argued that America had to make "a measured response" to preserve the links between the two countries, keeping open a dialogue on strategic issues requiring big-power consultation, while at the same time conveying American outrage over Tiananmen and serving as a model for other countries. Bush recalled:

> I didn't want to punish the Chinese people for the acts of their government ... We had to remain involved, engaged with the Chinese government,

if we were to have any influence or leverage to work for restraint and cooperation, let alone human rights and democracy. We discussed appropriate language for a statement and decided on a list of retaliatory measures. They included suspension of all government-to-government sales and commercial exports of weapons, suspension of visits between US and Chinese military leaders, and sympathetic review of requests by Chinese students in the United States to extend their stays.[9]

The Canadian government kept in close contact with the Americans to see how they were responding:

We were in communication with officials in the United States, and we knew that Bush wanted a moderate response, while Congress and many Americans wanted a lot more. The American government could not suspend high-level talks because it had to resolve important international issues in discussion with China, such as Cambodia and the Gulf War – places where Canada wasn't a major player. We wanted to know how far the Americans were willing to go without stopping key links with the PRC.

At the end of June, the Americans dispatched two secret emissaries to meet with Deng Xiaoping and Li Peng to discuss international security concerns, even as the United States announced sanctions that forbade any such meetings with the PRC's top leaders from taking place in the foreseeable future.

China Responds

Between June 4 and June 30, the Chinese government expanded the military occupation in Beijing, hunted down the student demonstrators, executed several dozen people in Beijing and Shanghai, set up a hotline to encourage citizens to turn in "wanted criminals," refused to apologize for its actions, enforced martial law, and forcefully told Western governments to stop interfering in China's internal affairs. For Deng Xiaoping, the issue was regime survival, not democracy or human rights. Communist party-states were collapsing everywhere. Gorbachev's hold on power in Moscow was weakening with each passing day. It was a dangerous moment for a Party leadership struggling to maintain legitimacy and control while it dealt with internal factionalism, corruption, and economic crisis. The Chinese Communist Party had dug in to defend itself.

In the lead-up to June 4, it had been apparent that several elements in the military had not supported the action in Tiananmen. Would the PLA continue to listen to the Party, and would the crisis spread to other cities in China where there had been demonstrations and violence? The Party knew that the majority of the people who had confronted the army on the streets of Beijing had not been students, but ordinary Beijingers who supported the student-led demonstration against the regime. China's leaders moved quickly to defuse the situation, singling out key individuals for punishment, focusing on "the criminal elements and unemployed workers," and accusing them of responsibility for the deaths of up to 150 soldiers. Beijing announced that it might extend leniency to those "misguided" students who had demonstrated peacefully. Government spokesman Yuan Mu gave a press conference, where he pronounced: "First we are not afraid. Second, we hope that international opinion and foreign governments will take a long-term view." The mayor of Beijing congratulated the army "for its initial victory against the rebellion," and he warned of "a long and complicated struggle."

On June 8, Premier Li Peng and a subdued Wan Li, chairman of the National People's Congress (NPC), who earlier had given the impression that he was sympathizing with the students, appeared together on Chinese television in a show of Party unity. The next day the top Party and military leaders, minus former Party secretary Zhao Ziyang, were shown together on national television in a special group appearance. Confronting conservative elements in the Party, Deng Xiaoping gave a spirited defence of market-oriented economic reform. According to Deng, the problem was "poor political practice." The Party "had failed to educate the people, educate the students, and educate all the cadres and Party members." He thanked the generals for "quelling the turmoil. This was a test that we passed." On June 16, he defended the existing regime, saying that "only socialism can save China."

On June 21, Foreign Minister Clark called in Ambassador Zhang for the fourth time to tell him that the Chinese Embassy and Consulates had to stop harassing PRC students studying in Canada. The students were complaining that PRC officials were trying to force them to return home. Shortly afterwards, Ambassador Zhang asked me to tell my PRC graduate students that they could return at any time without suffering any penalties, but they had no intention of going back until the situation in China stabilized.

PRC diplomats posted in Canada were struggling to cope with what had happened. The unexpected shooting of their own citizens by the Chinese army, and the wave of strong criticism of China by the international community, had thrown many of them off balance. Was Tiananmen a prelude to regime change in China, and if so, what would happen to these Chinese officials and their families? For most of the next few weeks, because of the long amount of time I had spent in both the Soviet Union and China, PRC officials regularly sought me out to talk about developments in Moscow and the communist world, and how these events could affect Beijing. Dropping their guard, these officials, all of them Party members, wanted to know if China was bound by what was happening in the Soviet Union, and if so, whether I thought the Chinese party-state could survive. I could not answer their questions, although I felt the Chinese regime was in a precarious survival mode.

I wrote in my diary:

> Had dinner again in the Chinese Embassy, just me and the Ambassador. We always begin with generalities, then quickly get down to serious talk. Not much on foreign sanctions or human rights, or the PRC students. Always about whether the Chinese party-state can avoid the fate of "Soviet Elder Brother." Of course I have no answers to give.

The Canadian Ambassador Is Recalled to Ottawa

On June 15, Canada recalled its ambassador, the only country to do so. This was a politically significant act, although Ottawa carefully noted that Drake had only returned "for consultations," and his departure from Beijing was not considered an official protest.

Ottawa emphasized that he would return in ten days. In conversation afterwards, Drake said he had been reluctant to leave Beijing, but his government had insisted. He later said:

> No, I did not want to go back to Canada. I felt I should stay at the Post, that I was needed more there than in Ottawa. We just had a skeleton staff after Tiananmen. I thought it was bad for morale. Also there were issues that an ambassador could solve more easily than a chargé d'affaires, for example, securing landing rights for the Canadian planes evacuating Canadians. Before I left, we held a session at the residence, ambassadors from other countries were there, and they said my recall was a terrible precedent.

The crisis management group thought recalling Drake was a questionable decision, but the PMO and Foreign Minister Clark wanted him to return because his presence in Canada could serve as a valuable focal point for consultations with the minister, Cabinet members, members of Parliament, and the broader political community. Drake was scheduled to meet with the Cabinet Committee on Foreign and Defence Relations, the Standing Committee of External Affairs and International Relations of the House of Commons, the leaders of the three major political parties, the media, business community, provincial officials, and other China stakeholders.

When Drake had arrived, he was quoted in the press saying that Canadians had been "naïve" about China. Many interpreted his words as blaming the Canadian government for having ignored the realities of the Chinese authoritarian party-state and inferring that the Canadian government, rather than the Canadian people, had been "naïve" about China. As a result, his visit got off to a bad start. Later, in conversation, he clarified his remarks:

> I never said that "the government was naïve about China." I did say, off the record, that "some Canadians were naïve about China." This made a big splash. If you keep talking to the media all the time, eventually you fall into a situation like this. That is one of the dangers ... I was being used a lot with the press. You really have to walk a tightrope. The Department wanted me to return for public relations. They told me to talk with the media, but not to say anything.

Appearing in the House on June 20, Drake provided a detailed summary of the events leading up to the June 4 crisis and of the current situation in China. He supported the demonstrations on the Square, although, in his opinion, "the demonstrators got carried away by their success, and the Chinese government dithered." The students' fatal mistakes came when they publicly humiliated Deng Xiaoping during Gorbachev's visit, and when they tried to establish an independent student union. When the Beijing workers who were supporting them said they also intended to form a union, it was too much for Deng and Party leaders, who feared the emergence of a workers' organization separate from Party control. One PRC official said: "Can you imagine what might happen if the Party of the proletariat is challenged by the very proletariat class that it represents?"

Drake complimented Canadians for speaking out early and forcefully, and for the non-partisan nature of the debate in Parliament. However, he opposed economic sanctions because, in his opinion, they were not workable: "The Chinese economy is largely independent of the world economy. It is one of the world's most self-sufficient economies, and if all investors stopped investing it would slow up China's economic development, but it would not have an immediate effect on this leadership."

Jean McCloskey, the assistant deputy minister for Asia-Pacific affairs, used the occasion to remind Canadians what the government had done between June 4 and June 20:

> Mr. Clark was the first foreign minister to make a public statement. The Chinese Ambassador was called in less than 24 hours after the massacre. The emergency debate, the unanimous resolution, a variety of measures announced, some to assist Chinese students in Canada, some to make our views known to the Chinese government; and as recently as last Friday a process was established to assist the Chinese students in a very particular way with information, counselling, job referrals, and financial assistance.

Canadians applauded the decision to allow the PRC students to stay indefinitely, perhaps permanently, although this decision clearly upset the PRC. Canadian ethnic Chinese community organizations were pleased, and the media were fully supportive. The government said it would help financially, finding them jobs if necessary. Later it announced that they could apply for visa extensions and landed immigrant status if they did not want to return home. This program continued until October 1990, sixteen months after Tiananmen, and no other country had such a generous policy. The original group, estimated on June 4 to be about 5,000, eventually doubled in size to 10,000, adding individuals who had arrived in Canada well after June 4 and, nevertheless, could also apply for permanent residence.

Trade became a contentious issue. Could it be "business as usual," or should Canada impose more stringent economic sanctions? In the wake of Tiananmen, most Canadians doing business in China had left Beijing, yet barely two weeks later, some were already returning. The idea of businesspeople acting as if nothing had happened on June 4 was offensive to many Canadians, who demanded that the government stop providing loans to help finance exports to the PRC. They wanted Canada to link trade directly with improvements in Chinese human rights practices. The business community countered with claims that trade helped the Chinese people, since it promoted economic reform, opened up China to the outside world, and introduced values of rule of law and democratic practice.

Prime Minister Mulroney was committed to maintaining economic ties with China, as were his key ministers, including Finance Minister Michael Wilson, International Trade Minister John Crosbie, and President of the Treasury Board Pat Carney. However, Minister of Citizenship and Immigration Barbara McDougall was critical of China and wanted strong sanctions. Keeping in mind that there was a split in Cabinet, the crisis management group considered a range of possible trade-related sanctions. They asked whether there should be an embargo on grain sales, since grain comprised almost 70 per cent of Canadian exports to China. On June 14, the prime minister emphatically said "no." Ottawa also ruled out restricting PRC access to Canadian markets, in particular, banning the large textile imports that were an important source of hard currency for China. "Some of the other options that we considered were withdrawing trade officers from the Canadian

Embassy, stopping financial support for PRC-hosted trade shows, halting the transfer of Canadian technology to China, and suspending soft loans and concessional financing to PRC companies."

The National Roundtable

The crisis management group had been preparing the government's official response to the killings. Now it was setting the stage for the official Canadian imposition of sanctions on June 30, and it organized a National Roundtable on June 22 to canvass opinions from forty members of the Canadian China policy community on how Canada should respond. Most of the participants had already talked with the crisis management group and with other government officials. We were expecting a strong Canadian response, and welcomed the government's decision to provide a forum to state our views about what Canada should do.

The crisis management group provided a concise rationale for holding the roundtable:

> We understood that the principal purpose of sanctions was political, not economic. Clark's statement of June 5 had focused on political issues. These weren't exactly sanctions, but expressions of anger and dismay. When the Chinese leaders continued the repression of their citizens after June 4, despite our protests, we had to elevate our response and coordinate with our like-minded allies. We didn't want to disrupt trade, yet it could not be "business as usual." In formulating the Government's statement of June 30, we consulted widely. We decided to hold the special National Roundtable on June 22 to canvass opinion from the business sector, sinologists, ethnic Chinese Canadians, and key members of the China policy community.

Foreign Minister Clark convened the roundtable, together with Jean McCloskey, Earl Drake, and Howard Balloch. The forty participants included the heads of the top corporations trading with China, leaders of national and regional Canadian ethnic Chinese community organizations, prominent human rights activists, and many of Canada's China specialists. Each participant was allotted four minutes to state his or her views and make recommendations. Members of the business community spoke with one voice, saying that economic sanctions would be harmful to Canadians and to the Chinese people. They would have no tangible impact on China's leaders, and one company executive argued: "Why punish our farmers and the common Chinese who will be eating our grain?"

Participants representing the 500,000 ethnic Chinese then living in Canada were the strongest advocates for punishing the PRC. They were embarrassed and appalled at what had happened, and they demanded strong action. The dozen China specialists were a mixed lot. Some were scarred by having actually witnessed the killings in Beijing. They were visibly upset. Others had friends in China whose fate was unknown, or they had participated in the evacuation of Canadians from Beijing. A larger group, some of whom were sinologists who had previously served as diplomats in the Embassy, recommended the continuation of economic, cultural, and educational linkages to preserve "people-to-people" relations, while also supporting the suspension of high-level visits and the cancellation of a few development assistance projects.

The sense of the roundtable was that Canada had to convey "outrage," although not at the expense of economic links or of the ties it had built with the PRC over twenty years. Canada was doing the best it could in a difficult situation. The lessons of history said that hard sanctions were unlikely to force China's leaders to change their behaviour, although the Canadian public was demanding strong action.

In my allotted four minutes, I said:

> Agree that sanctions should not threaten the links that we built up with China. Encourage the moderate forces that can bring about political reform and don't isolate China. If we want to do more, let's give refuge to their students and target a few high-profile projects for temporary suspension or cancellation. Stopping high-level visits is a short-term option, but isn't sustainable policy. To be blunt, I don't think we have that many options.

Most of us assumed that the government had already decided upon its course of action before our meeting and that the roundtable was a public relations device to secure approval for actions that the government had already prepared and was about to announce. The crisis management group had hand-picked the participants, and there were not likely to be any surprises or complaints that important voices were left unheard. Were we "co-opted" by a government that wanted to show that it had the full support of its China policy community? Balloch didn't think so, saying it was clear that everyone at the roundtable favoured Ottawa's decision to make a strong statement that imposed limited sanctions. If there were any differences, they were going to be about tactics, rather than strategy. He recalls: "After the Roundtable, we submitted our proposal to Cabinet for final approval on June 29, and on the next day Foreign Minister Clark announced Canada's official response to Tiananmen. This was done quickly because we wanted to get Canada's response out there ahead of the other countries, before the G8 meeting in Paris in July."

On June 30, Ottawa gave its official response to China's actions. Foreign Minister Clark announced that Canada was framing its post-Tiananmen policy in the context of four basic parameters and three criteria – "ground rules" that constituted the principles that would frame Canada's relations with the PRC "in the months ahead." It could not be "business as usual," but it also could not be "anti-China." The government was suspending or cancelling projects that gave support to the military and to those leaders who were responsible for the killings. There would be no high-level visits with PRC leaders, and Ottawa intended to tell China forcefully that it had violated basic international principles of human rights.

An Evaluation

Relations would never be the same afterwards. Canadians abandoned their romanticized views of China, along with any thoughts that a special link existed between the two countries or that Canada could continue as a self-appointed mentor for China's emergence into the international community. June 4 had left a lasting impression on a Canadian public, which had previously paid limited attention to events inside China. After Tiananmen, the China policy community expanded in size, in particular with the addition of a large number of Canadians of ethnic Chinese origin and human rights activists. Canada's ethnic Chinese communities were concerned about the upcoming retrocession of Hong Kong in 1997, and they were worried that China's reversion to overt authoritarianism could negatively affect the lives of the 100,000 Canadian citizens then living there, almost all of them ethnic Chinese.

When the Canadian government had responded to what was happening in Beijing, it did not have an "on-the-shelf" manual to guide it during the crisis. One official recalls: "Until Tiananmen, we never had a need for such a manual. A few natural disasters in another country, or maybe watching on the sidelines when there were problems in some other country – those were easily manageable. Tiananmen was different because we were evacuating hundreds of people and organizing policy discussions back home." Balloch commented:

> Much of what the crisis management group did was by the seat of its pants. We had never evacuated that many people so quickly anywhere else. We had to move fast, and we were charting new territory. Afterwards, based on our Tiananmen experience, we compiled a crisis management handbook, which was later used with success during the collapse of Yugoslavia and in the Gulf War.

In the world of diplomacy, an embassy defers to headquarters, but sometimes the latter may be too busy with other matters to pay close attention to what is going on in the field. Ambassador Drake complained that, before matters escalated in mid-May, it had been hard to get Ottawa to focus on what was happening in China. Since early 1989, the Embassy had been sending back reports of internal Party struggles, a worsening economy, large-scale official corruption, and a loss of popular support for the Party. From the Embassy's perspective, Ottawa was too involved with Canadian domestic issues, and it lacked sufficient China expertise to be on top of what was happening in China. Yet, when the crisis broke, Ottawa at first blamed the Embassy for not having made it aware earlier of the serious nature of the situation in China. When Drake later came to Ottawa for ten days to brief Canadians on what was happening, officials in Ottawa were worried that his publicly expressed opinions might differ from those held by the Department. When he was misquoted in the press that the Canadian government, rather than the Canadian public, was "naïve" about China, many privately said it had been a mistake to recall him and that it was best to send him back to Beijing as soon as possible.

Canada's response to June 4 was multipartisan. Tiananmen was a national issue, calling for a strong and united statement by all the major Canadian political parties. Parliament had unanimously approved the June 5 Resolution condemning the June 4 events at Tiananmen. The Liberal opposition leader, John Turner, supported the Conservative agenda, and the New Democratic Party (NDP) was also on board. By the third week in June, however, when the direction of the Canadian response seemed clear, the opposition began raising questions about a number of issues, for example, the recall of Drake, visa extensions for students, and the linkage of trade with human rights. These were matters of tactics, timing, and political positioning, rather than criticism of overall government strategy, which was not disputed. All the political parties supported some type of sanctions, although not at the expense of trade. None wanted to disrupt trade or to link it to improvements in human rights practices. All supported ending military sales and freezing high-level visits.

The reaction to Tiananmen reflected the continuing transition from a Canadian foreign policy that, in the past, had emphasized a commitment to internationalism, to one with a greater emphasis on Canadian national interest. The need to punish China was rooted in domestic politics, and the sanctions were designed as much, if not more, to appease Canadian public opinion, rather than expecting to change the PRC's behaviour. In the first instance, trade had to continue because it was in Canada's national interest to sell China our grain and gain the electoral support of western farmers. Canada's China policy was no longer the preserve of a small elite seeking "to bring China into the world community." Canadian internationalism was passé – did Canada have to continue to be good Boy Scouts, helping other countries when Canadians needed jobs and money was scarce? Other interests now had seats at the China policy table, for example, Canadians of ethnic Chinese origin, human rights advocates, and even the media. China's leaders weren't listening to Canada, and international institutions such as the United Nations, where Canada in the past had a major role, were ineffective in influencing the PRC's behaviour. After a month of effort by Canada and other countries, the United Nations had been unable to pass a single resolution condemning China for the Tiananmen killings.

Prior to June 4, Canadians thought we were teaching China about the modern world, showing China how it could adapt to the way we live and think. We were the teachers, and the Chinese were our students. Our ideology reinforced this "secular missionary impulse." For some Canadians, our "mission" was to wean that Chinese regime from communism and push it in the direction of Western democracy. In the first twenty years, we thought engagement would encourage the development of the rule of law, democracy, and human rights and that China would eventually become more like us. Once Deng Xiaoping embraced capitalist markets, we expected this change would bring political liberalization. That did not happen.

We were guilty of overestimating our ability to influence China's leaders, and Tiananmen rudely brought Canadians back down to earth. We had to punish China, and Ottawa obliged with the June 30 Statement that imposed sanctions on Beijing. However, China continued to abuse human rights, and it never apologized for Tiananmen. In the next chapter, we look at how Canada applied these sanctions, and why they failed to change China's behaviour.

chapter seven

Applying Sanctions

The Canadian government had to take action. The images of PLA soldiers shooting their own citizens had a profound effect on Canadians, who expected a strong response from Ottawa. But would Canadian sanctions have any impact on China's behaviour?

Official high-level visits were halted indefinitely. Several development assistance projects were cancelled or suspended. Students from the PRC currently in Canada were allowed to apply for visa extensions. Export financing that benefitted China was placed under review. Projects providing support to the Chinese military and its propaganda apparatus were cancelled. Canadian criticism of the PRC's human rights practices escalated. Trade and people-to-people exchange became the principal link between the two countries.

Relations with China markedly cooled. In Beijing, Ambassador Drake complained that he had nothing to do, and the business community said that it was losing market share. The Chinese leaders did not apologize, nor did they modify their position on human rights. Premier Li Peng angrily told Ambassador Drake: "We don't need you." By the end of 1990, the sanctions had failed to produce the desired impact. Attempts to loosen them ran into opposition from members of Cabinet, hard-line officials in the Prime Minister's Office (PMO) and the Privy Council Office (PCO), human rights activists, and the Canadian media. Barbara McDougall, the new foreign minister, strongly resisted efforts to re-engage with China. In the fall of 1991, more than two years after the Tiananmen crisis, Canada resumed official high-level visits, sending Bill McKnight, the minister of agriculture, to Beijing.

In 1992, three members of Parliament arrived in Beijing to protest the human rights situation in China. After they had visited the
families of dissidents, without asking for Chinese permission, PRC
security forces abruptly ended their visit, drove them to the airport,
and put them on a plane to Hong Kong. This incident precipitated a
diplomatic crisis, but soon afterwards relations began to improve. In
1993, Michael Wilson, the minister of international trade, travelled
to China with a group of Canadian business executives in search of
expanded trade. The Embassy found itself inundated with Canadian
business visitors, and it was also hard pressed to accommodate a surge
in visa applications from Chinese delegations wanting to travel to
Canada. At the Embassy, governance activities expanded to include
projects on Chinese institutional reform, the training of judges,
and even a joint project on democratic development championed by
Ambassador Fred Bild.

Joe Clark visited China in early 1993 – almost four years after
Tiananmen. He said that, while China was too important to isolate,
Canada was still not ready to end the sanctions. However, for China's
leaders, the visit by Clark, architect of the 1989 sanctions, was per-
suasive. In their view, it was now just a matter of time before relations
would be normalized. Soon afterwards, Prime Minister Mulroney
invited rising star Vice Premier Zhu Rongji to visit Canada. Zhu
came in mid-1993 and was warmly received. He dazzled Canadians
with his energy and openness. He was "the anti-Li Peng," not saddled
with the responsibility for Tiananmen, and he was ready to work with
Canada. A few years later, he would proclaim that "Canada is China's
best friend."

Zhu's visit marked the waning days of the Canadian sanctions. They
had lasted over four years, longer than those of almost any other country,
and China's behaviour had not changed. In late 1993, a Liberal government took power in Ottawa. Prime Minister Jean Chrétien made trade
the main link with China, and he reduced the government's emphasis
on human rights. By the end of 1994, he led the largest trade mission in
Canadian history to Beijing. Canada and the PRC had re-engaged, and
both sides now had a more realistic understanding of what was possible
after Tiananmen.

We will continue to sanction China for what it did on June 4. There is no drift and no softening of our position. Canada has a clear policy line, and we are executing it.

– Foreign Minister Barbara McDougall, September 1991

The June 30 Statement

After three weeks of consultations, highlighted by the National Roundtable on June 22, the Canadian government issued its official response to Tiananmen:[1]

> We had to do something significant. We actually didn't want to use the term "sanctions." That was too strong. We preferred "measures," although everyone immediately called them sanctions. We were afraid that if we made them too strong it would set back the relations we had cultivated for twenty years. Yet, if they were not tough enough, we wouldn't get the Canadian message across to China, nor satisfy those Canadians who expected the government to deliver a strong response. We also wanted to be among the first countries with a comprehensive set of measures, ahead of the Americans.[2]

In addressing Parliament, Foreign Minister Joe Clark said: "We cannot determine how events are going to unfold with the kind of precision that allows us to set in stone the parameters and mileposts that should govern our relations with China over the next few years." In making adjustments to the initial response that Canada had made on June 5, he announced that Canada was framing its post-Tiananmen policy in the form of *four basic parameters and three criteria* to govern relations with China "in the months ahead," and he provided the following details:

> On the basis of the recommendations we heard during the National Roundtable, we are framing our policy in the context of *four parameters.* First, Tiananmen Square and the subsequent campaign [to hunt down the demonstrators] have changed the relationship between Canada and China. The Chinese authorities have called for "business as usual." This

cannot be accepted. Second, we value the friendship between our two peoples. We have not become, and will not become "anti-China." Third, we must try to avoid measures that would push China towards isolation. Fourth, we should try to maximize the impact of whatever measures we adopt, via a relatively coordinated approach of likeminded countries.

The following *three criteria* will be applied to all future bilateral links: First, the existing links forged by government, industry, and academics over the past decade should be preserved to the extent possible. Second, new initiatives in the relationship should focus on people-to-people exchanges. Third, programs which benefit or lend prestige to the current hardline policies of the Chinese will be cancelled. (emphasis added)

The government had already stopped all high-level official visits to the PRC, and it continued to support a joint resolution at the United Nations that condemned China's actions. Ottawa intended "to stay in touch with our friends and allies" to ensure that Canadian policy resonated with that of the other like-minded countries. "If we are not all united, these measures will not succeed." The government reduced Canada's trade representation in Beijing by one-third "in response to the changed circumstances in China and in anticipation of an expected downturn in trade activity, and also added an officer in the Embassy in Beijing to monitor human rights in China." The international students from the PRC, now numbering more than 7,000, were told that they could stay indefinitely until they were ready to return home. They were granted visa extensions, and Canada was providing work permits, job counselling services, and financial support for those who needed it. Clark added:

We are not pressuring them into definitively cutting their ties to China. If in the end they choose not to return to China, then we will look at individual cases sympathetically, but we continue to hope that the situation in China will encourage them to decide, at the end of their academic programs, to return to China, bringing with them Canadian concepts, Canadian ways of doing things, and a healthy commitment to truth and the rule of law.

Canada withdrew from three additional CIDA development assistance projects – state auditor training, an oil refinery centre, and police training in urban management – because Ottawa decided that these three projects benefitted the PRC military and propaganda apparatus. One of the five CIDA projects that had been previously postponed, a community college linkage, was permitted to go ahead.

Funding for PRC-hosted trade shows and exhibitions was "halted for the rest of the year." A project to develop a television transmission facility in Shanghai was cancelled, because it was deemed "clearly supportive of China's state propaganda apparatus."[3] Commercial projects that provided soft loans and financing for Canadian projects in China were to be closely scrutinized. Deals that drew on the EDC $2 billion line of credit, and the $350 million concessional finance package that was extended in 1986, now had to meet the test of the four parameters and the three criteria before any were approved.

The sanctions reinforced Canada's criticism of China's actions without jeopardizing the basic links Canada had established for the past two decades. Some Canadians, however, complained that the Statement was not tough enough, and that Canada was not tying future trade and development assistance to improvements in human rights.

In Ottawa, the Chinese Embassy expressed "its deep regret" over Clark's announcement, and it issued the following statement: "Any attempt by any foreign government to bring pressure to bear on the Chinese government, and to interfere in China's internal affairs in this or that manner, is unwise and futile, and can only result in harming themselves." I was summoned to a meeting with the Chinese ambassador. He said that the June 30 Statement had seriously damaged relations, and he urged me, "as an old China hand, to help end this unwarranted criticism of the PRC. Give China's leaders a chance to restore order." I said this was impossible. We had seen it happen on our television screens, Chinese troops shooting at and killing their own citizens. The Canadian public, like people in many other countries, was demanding action, and the Statement served that purpose. China needed to understand what it had done. I would debate this issue with the ambassador, and with other members of the Chinese Embassy, for the rest of the year.

Prime Minister Mulroney congratulated his foreign minister, who, in turn, praised Balloch's crisis management group for how well it had prepared Canada's response. A senior Department official, displaying Canadian hubris, declared that the Statement was "a major achievement, putting Canada ahead of the other Western governments, with its nicely crafted sanctions." The president of the Chinese Canadian National Council said: "Mr. Clark's announcement did not contain all the guarantees we were looking for, but, in practice, it is outstanding." The business community was relieved that the economic sanctions were limited to measures that would not appreciably disrupt commercial links, although the Canada China Trade Council complained that "big business connections are made during high-level visits. That's when we get the top-level approvals we need to seal major deals. Canada will be handicapped by this ban on high-level visits."

Canada had to make a strong response, but one had to be sceptical whether the sanctions would change the PRC's behaviour, since this was not the first time that China was faced with sanctions. It had survived a far tougher twenty-year American-inspired blockade after 1949, and there were always ways to beat an embargo, especially when the foreign business community was anxious to expand trade. The Japanese were the first to break unity, as its businesspeople returned under the radar to China right after Tiananmen, disguised as tourists, and Canadian companies soon joined them.

In early July, Prime Minister Mulroney and Foreign Minister Clark attended the G8 summit in Paris, along with Fred Bild, the Canadian assistant deputy minister for international political affairs, who would replace Earl Drake as ambassador in Beijing in the fall of 1990. Bild recalls:

While some of the other G8 members voiced intentions similar to ours regarding future relations with the PRC regime, and the curtailment of certain programs, there were exceptions. An interesting distinction appeared between the Canadian and American approaches. The

Americans did not want any cessation in military links: they had established military intelligence surveillance facilities in western China aimed at the Soviet Union, and both sides did not want to shut them down.

Unlike Canada, the United States had urgent international security issues that required consultation with Beijing's top leaders. As we will see, those issues forced Washington to break the sanctions within a year, while Canada continued to observe them well into 1993.

I wrote in my diary:

> Waiting to see how these measures will affect relations with China. Have now spoken with officials in the Chinese Foreign Ministry. It's like walking on eggs. You can tell they are shaken up. Still, they say the regime had no choice after waiting over 50 days for the Square to empty. They say foreigners have no business telling China what to do – its leaders don't have to apologize for anything.
>
> Trying to get back on track with China. While fancying myself a "realist," am wondering if, like many others, I have romanticized China, thinking it will turn out better than the Soviet Union, and believing that Canada had a "special relationship" with the PRC. Wrong on both counts it seems. Need to collect my thoughts about where China is going, and where the bilateral relationship is heading. Maybe Ambassador Drake was right in saying we were "naïve." Have I misread China?

Ambassador Drake Returns to Beijing

At the end of June, Drake returned to Beijing. A bleak landscape of empty streets awaited him, with soldiers everywhere and residents avoiding each other. Only a handful of Canadians were left in Beijing. It was hard to find any Chinese officials who wanted to talk, and it was too early to see if the sanctions were working.

> It seemed as if the whole city was dead. No foreigners. A few diplomats. The city was barely functioning. Heavily armed units at all intersections, not just at the Square. Young and nervous soldiers dropping their guns, which occasionally went off. It took a year before things thawed out. A

few Canadians wandered out of the back woods. I remember several dinosaur bone hunters showed up. Their main concern was how to get their bones out. Lots of Chinese were trying to leave. We tried to do what we could to help them. Some managed to get to Hong Kong via a Chinese "underground railway." We could also give some help with visas.

American Ambassador James Lilley painted an equally sombre picture of a city under siege:

In the first few weeks after the massacre, a gloom hung over Beijing. The overcast weather was the silenced population's funeral dirge. Residents of Beijing stayed home, and largely mourned in solitude. In the face of a countrywide campaign to arrest opponents of the government, and a numbing, relentless propaganda campaign, a palpable fear ripped Chinese cities. In July 1989, with the embassy compounds surrounded by three rings of armed guards with AK 47s, and our own strong reaction to what had happened exactly a month earlier, we reduced the size of our annual July 4 celebration, and had no reception for our Chinese hosts, or for the Beijing diplomatic corps. Minus the evacuated American dependents, there was a rump group of about thirty to forty Americans in the main embassy compound. Each of us felt a palpable sense of standing against the guns, misinformation and thuggery that had enveloped Beijing in the past months.[4]

The city was still in shock. Canada and China were now trying to come to terms with the sanctions. How to deal with Chinese anger at Canada for giving sanctuary to thousands of their international students, for restricting export financing, and for suspending and cancelling development programs? Could we conduct "normal" business with China without upsetting Canadians back home, who were deeply affected by the killings on June 4 and wanted Canada "to show blood?"

In conversation, Drake provided more details:

QUESTION: Some foreign diplomats said that the Canadian Embassy simply shut down, and all of the officers had gone. They were surprised that Canada was abandoning its Post in Beijing. Was this true?

AMBASSADOR DRAKE: No, not at all. We did send five trade people home, but the rest of our officers remained in Beijing. We evacuated their families. It was a functioning embassy. Maybe they were referring to the trade officers. We had some unanticipated problems. If we had to burn our files in a hurry, how to do it? There were tons of files. How to destroy them without attracting attention? So we conducted experiments using the trade files. We quickly found out from our experiments that we could never get rid of our files if conditions warranted a quick evacuation.

What to do with all the pets once their owners had flown out? Animals were not allowed in the evacuation. We were responsible for feeding this left-behind menagerie until we could send them out later. "All the makings of a real Hunan feast!" said one Chinese to a Canadian diplomat, who was not amused.

QUESTION: What was the Chinese reaction to the June 30 Statement, and how did it affect your work at the Post?

AMBASSADOR DRAKE: I first talked with officials from the Ministry who were responsible for our development assistance program. They were upset over the CIDA and EDC sanctions. They bristled, and became very officious. They said cooperation was bilateral, but we had decided to act unilaterally. Everything became formal with them. At the end of July, I was summoned to the Ministry of Foreign Affairs, and to the State Council, to talk about the PRC students, to whom we were giving asylum. The Chinese wanted them back, in particular the ones funded by the Chinese government. At one point they accused us of kidnapping them.

QUESTION: Did you feel that the Chinese government was angry at Canada more than at some of the other Western countries? Did this make it difficult for the Embassy to carry out its duties?

AMBASSADOR DRAKE: Yes. It was not easy to maintain contact. The MFA was actually the most civilized of the bunch. The Director General of the Americas and Oceania Department was Zhang Yijun. In 1994 Zhang became Ambassador to Canada, and we later had a good relationship with him.

It was a discouraging period. There were no high-level visits in any direction. There was nothing to do. It was hard to find Chinese officials willing to meet with us. Not much to communicate back to headquarters in Ottawa. Canadian politicians, the general public, and the media seemed totally alienated by the sudden discovery that China's leaders did not respect Western definitions of human rights. We were still getting used to the sanctions. Tiananmen provided a large dose of realism, yet I had little success in bringing objectivity and national interest to bear on the relationship, except with Foreign Minister Joe Clark.

So I decided to leave Beijing and visit parts of China that had long-standing connections with Canada to keep the doors open for when relations would again normalize. In most places, my visit was welcomed, but I had a very different reception in the large industrial city of Wuhan.

None of the usual contacts would see me. I was shuffled off to see minor flunkies, or snubbed entirely. We tried to return to Beijing, but things got worse. No one would confirm a return flight for me, my wife, my sister, or my accompanying local staff member. Finally my wife and sister were allowed to leave, but only after spending hours at the airport. At last, an official who had long contacts with Canada took us aside, and he whispered that everyone was embarrassed to treat me this way, but orders had come from the very top that I was to be snubbed in reprisal for the Canadian criticism of the events at Tiananmen Square. Just before I was finally allowed to take my return flight, the same friend admitted that the orders had come directly from the President of China.

The Embassy's political section was monitoring the situation in China, sharing information with colleagues from other embassies. Drake emphasized that "we were never instructed not to be friendly to the Chinese. We were following Foreign Minister Clark's four 'parameters,' to maintain positive relations and not become 'anti-China,' in effect, letting the sanctions speak for themselves." Despite what had happened to the ambassador in Wuhan, the Embassy's cultural counsellor felt that her relations with Chinese counterparts "were fairly cordial, although there was definitely a reserve, and a lingering criticism of Canadian policy, for example, the State Education Committee continually complained that 'Canada had plundered Chinese talent' by giving the PRC students permanent residency."

The Embassy took the first and second criteria in the June 30 Statement seriously and kept open contacts with the intellectual and artistic community, went to university campuses, arranged meetings in quiet places, and helped to secure visas for them. According to Drake, "it was important for us to maintain human contact. Bilateral programs may have stalled and official relations had soured, but at the lower levels of the system we were still working together." With trade at a low ebb, and with no traction in human rights, people-to-people ties were the link that was keeping the Embassy busy.

George Bush Hesitates

At the end of June, when the international community was imposing its sanctions, US President George Bush sent a secret mission to Beijing to talk directly with its top leaders because the US-China relationship was too important to be frozen. Only a few people knew that National Security Advisor Brent Scowcroft and Deputy Secretary of State Lawrence Eagleburger had flown to Beijing for urgent talks with Deng Xiaoping, Li Peng, and Foreign Minister Qian Qichen, and the visit remained a secret for over six months. Bush later explained why it had been necessary for the United States to ignore the post-Tiananmen ban on high-level visits, and meet directly with China's leaders: "China is getting back on track a little with the Soviets, and they could indeed come back to the Russians much stronger if we move unilaterally against China and cut them off from the West. Deng still worries about 'encirclement,' and so do I. Am determined to try and preserve this relationship, to cool the rhetoric."[5]

Deng told Scowcroft and Eagleburger: "The various aspects of United States foreign policy have actually cornered China. With regard to how to resolve the issue, a Chinese proverb says: 'It is up to the person who tied the knot to untie it.' Our hope is that in its future course of action the United States will seek to untie the knot." Li added: "It is also an old saying in China that emotion is no substitute for policy."

China's leaders knew that, three days prior to the trip, the United States House of Representatives had voted 418 to 0 to impose strong sanctions, and it was also clear to the two American emissaries that China's leaders were not about to apologize for their actions. "With a wave of his hand, Li said that both sides understood each other's position, so 'let us talk of something else.'" Putting Tiananmen aside, they turned to discuss relations with the Soviet Union, the situation in Cambodia, Taiwan, arms control, Iraq, the Persian Gulf, and nuclear disarmament. It was also important to preserve the American-run military intelligence surveillance station located in western China that was monitoring Soviet behaviour. According to Scowcroft, "it was essential to keep China engaged in a strategic dialogue regarding world affairs, and the visit was a welcome opportunity to do so."

There was too much at stake for the United States to stop talking with China's leaders, especially when it involved American strategic concerns. Sanctions are a two-level game, put in place to satisfy domestic desires to condemn and isolate an adversary, yet loose enough to allow strategic collaboration with that adversary when one's national interest is at stake. When a great power is concerned about its national interest, it sets aside its multilateral commitments and acts unilaterally. America had not hesitated in the past to depart from its multilateral commitments, so this meeting was not unexpected behaviour. Also, despite having imposed sanctions on China, after a short interval other Western leaders also started to meet again with their Beijing counterparts to discuss important bilateral and international strategic issues, doing it quietly, even secretly.

Following a second Scowcroft and Eagleburger visit in the late fall, the Americans continued talking with their Chinese counterparts at multilateral meetings in the United Nations and in other multilateral venues, and the major Western countries followed suit. Foreign Minister Qian Qichen met with counterparts from the United States, Britain, and France to talk about threats to Cambodian independence from Vietnam and the Soviet Union. This issue was of strategic importance to China. Qian also met with Western foreign ministers at the United Nations to discuss whether China intended to support the invasion of Iraq by UN forces. The PRC then abstained during the UN vote, legitimizing the Gulf War and reinforcing the importance of keeping open the links with China's leaders.

Meetings on the margins at international summits continued in 1990. Official high-level contacts with Chinese government counterparts were proscribed, but visits to Beijing by prominent former public figures were acceptable. For example, Richard Nixon and Henry Kissinger, carrying messages from the Bush administration about international security issues, met with Chinese leaders in Beijing in late 1989 to talk about relations with the Soviet Union, Cambodia, and the situation in the Gulf.

Applying the Sanctions

Several months had now passed, and members of the Department were asking themselves whether Canada had altered Beijing's behaviour in any way. Hardliners said it was too early to make a judgement, and Canada had to continue enforcing the sanctions. But some members of the Department felt that the sanctions had served their purpose: "A shot across China's bow, to remind them of who we are and of what normal states do. We delivered a message. Maybe now we can begin to loosen them." Others said the sanctions were not enforceable: "Our traders are finding all sorts of ways to evade them, and our senior officials are again meeting with their PRC counterparts. We need to rethink our strategy."

Official visits became an issue when Tang Fuqian, the PRC consul general in Toronto, pointed out that Foreign Minister Clark had met with Foreign Minister Qian in July at the 1989 Paris conference on Cambodia. Tang claimed that this meeting proved that Canada was ready to restore relations; however, Clark's office hastily replied that he had only talked with Qian "to discuss China's position in Cambodia because China is a power in the region – not because Canada has changed its ban on high-level contacts." The Department took pains to differentiate bilateral high-level official visits from working meetings with Chinese officials at international conferences, saying: "They are not the same thing. Canada remains committed to banning all contacts above the director level, and that includes deputy ministers and ministers. There's no question this has an impact on both countries. Interaction at the highest level is how you get things done in China."

In September 1989, a Canadian official attended a conference in Beijing that was organized by the Chinese government. The Department immediately announced that he was only a middle-level official and that the meeting had not involved any contact with senior Chinese officials. It stated that "Canada has interests to defend at this conference. The venue happens to be in China, but it's a United Nations event. China is the host and co-sponsor, but it is under the auspices of a UN agency. Other countries, including the United States, Australia, and West Germany, are also attending the conference."

In February 1990, Jean McCloskey, the assistant deputy minister for Asia-Pacific affairs, made a quick visit to Beijing "to talk about Cambodia and other geopolitical issues, such as the crisis of Soviet communism and the future return to China of Hong Kong, with its 100,000 Canadian citizens." Hardly anyone in Canada was aware that this visit had happened. The Department later said that she had discussed matters too important to be left to junior officers and that it had required face-to-face interaction between McCloskey and her senior Chinese counterparts. Joe Clark talked with Qian Qichen at the United Nations in 1989 and 1990, and several PRC vice ministers quietly came to Ottawa to talk with their Canadian counterparts, including Liu Huaqiu, the vice minister for foreign affairs. One Department official commented: "Maybe they might encounter each other on the margins at international meetings, but when these people come to Ottawa to talk with our officials, we make sure they don't see any higher level officials. Of course, accidents may happen."

It was apparent that the sanctions applied by other countries were having little or no impact on PRC behaviour, and their governments were already beginning to explore re-engagement. The Department discussed possible adjustments to the Canadian sanctions, proposing that Canada should hold another National

Roundtable, similar to the one that was held on June 22. The proposed roundtable could discuss whether Canada should resume new project funding by CIDA, terminate the PRC student amnesty, restore full trade promotion support, and send a government minister on a visit to Beijing. However, after discussion at senior levels in Ottawa, it was decided that Canada was not ready to reduce the sanctions, although it approved the new CIDA community college project and resumed government support for trade promotion programs.

A few months later, the Department asked again whether it was time to hold a set of roundtables to discuss reducing the sanctions and, if not, should it "just continue to follow the June 30 Statement with some refinements?" It recommended ending the amnesty for the PRC students who had stayed in Canada after June 4: "The amnesty has been in place for too long. Other countries have ended them, and we should do the same." That proposal had support in Cabinet, with the notable exception of Barbara McDougall, the minister of employment and immigration, who steadfastly opposed its termination. After much discussion, the government concluded that "neither the pace of change in China, nor Canadian public opinion, is ready to support a fundamental shift in our China policy at this time."

In April 1990, almost one year after Tiananmen, most like-minded nations, including Germany, France, Japan, and the United States, had started to restore their links with China, especially in trade, and they were ending their student amnesties. Supporting a softening of the sanctions, the Department pointed out that the PRC was more important to Canada as a trading partner than it was to most of the other Western nations, whose commercial ties with China made up a smaller percentage of their total foreign trade. Ending the ban on high-level visits and restoring full EDC funding would enhance Canadian access to Chinese markets.

A proposal to have a prominent Canadian official make the first post-Tiananmen visit to China in late spring of 1990 was shelved due to Cabinet's hesitation, and because of three upcoming controversial Chinese anniversaries: the May 4 celebration of the 1919 student demonstrations against the Chinese government; the May

19 imposition of martial law in Beijing in 1989; and the June 4 military action against the Tiananmen demonstrators. Police with rifles were blocking the roads to Beijing's university area, and heavy security elsewhere in the city was stifling any organized attempt to protest what had happened a year ago at Tiananmen. The number of PRC students in Canada had swollen to nearly 10,000, and the Department announced that "a letter has been forwarded for Mr. Clark's signature to Minister McDougall, recommending the elimination of the special programs which make it particularly easy for Chinese nationals to immigrate to Canada, or remain in Canada." However, McDougall decided to continue the student amnesty, and it would last another six months before it was finally terminated.

Later in the year, at a CIDA conference in Canada, Ambassador Drake spoke about the state of Canada-PRC relations:

> Canada is in a holding pattern, in need of a long-term policy. We are unwilling to think in terms of a new relationship. China is a bad news story, and our politicians do not want any bad news right now – they have their domestic concerns.
>
> The media are still emotionally scarred, and we need to have more objective reporting. We cannot change China the way we want to. It's time to de-emotionalize China. The Chinese won't listen to me. They need to hear it from our very top leaders. The high-level visits are a key. They are more than symbolism. Remember, China is a top-down society. We are losing a chance to influence China by excluding high-level visits. It is time to be realistic.
>
> The best way to succeed is to open up communications, both officially and through people-to-people contacts. Help them to modernize their economy. Move ahead with CIDA projects, promote trade expansion, get out from Beijing and develop more links with Shanghai, Guangzhou, and Sichuan.

This frank assessment by a serving ambassador was bound to rattle a few government officials. Had the June 30 sanctions locked Canada into a "holding pattern" with China, and was it time to acknowledge that China was not going to behave the way Canada wanted, and that we had to "stop trying to change China"?

Echoing the ambassador's call for Canada to move forward, in June 1990 the CCTC, whose members included the most powerful Canadian companies trading with China, released the *Special Report: Assessing Canada's China Policy: Is It Time for a Change?* The report contained informal interviews with two dozen business executives, government officials, and academics, and it asked three questions: Should the policy be modified now, or in the near future? If not, what conditions would you see as requisite before a case can be made for modification? If so, when should it be modified, how far should the adjustments go, and what aspects in particular should be changed?[6]

Human rights activists and members of Canada's ethnic Chinese communities said that post-Tiananmen China had not changed, and that Canada had to keep the sanctions. The business executives said increased engagement with China was a better force for democratization and political reform than a policy that isolated China. One said: "The Japanese are not waiting. We cannot withdraw and leave the market to the Americans, the Japanese, and the Europeans. Canadian business is losing out to other countries that are dismantling their sanctions." A Vancouver manufacturing company executive observed: "Leave well enough alone. Why shouldn't everything be the way it was before? China needs help, not hindrance." A banker claimed that he did not care how the policy went, one way or another. "Banks mostly ignore governments anyway, Chinese or Canadian, and politicians don't do things for economic reasons."

In the summer, I met with Chinese officials in Beijing to talk about relations. I had just come from meetings in Moscow with Soviet Party officials, who were desperately clinging to power. It looked grim for those Russians, and my hosts talked about the effect that Soviet regime collapse would have on China. "We think that the worst is over for China. We restored order after Tiananmen, and your sanctions don't bother us." Then they turned to discuss relations between China and Canada. First, they said it was time to end the ban on high-level visits since, in their opinion, Canada had already broken that sanction. Second, Canada had to stop "kidnapping" China's international students by offering them permanent resident status. Canada was one of the few remaining countries still doing this. Third, even if current relations were constrained, it was essential to maintain economic links and halt any restrictions on financing trade and development projects with China.

I wrote in my diary,

> Just returned from China. The sanctions are making life difficult for the Post, and for visiting Canadians. Relations with Chinese officials are at half-speed. Keeping up with "people-to-people" links, but there's a cooler reception for Canadians. Several of my research meetings have been cancelled. The MFA told me: "You know why."

Back in Canada, I conducted a survey of eighty Canadian China scholars, asking the question, "Did our government respond correctly during, and immediately after Tiananmen?" Half of the respondents said Canada was acting as best as it could, under difficult circumstances. Others criticized the slow process of "normalization," noting that Canada was lagging behind other nations in restoring relations after Tiananmen:

> The sanctions are unfortunate. There is no good time to lift them. Unlike the Australians whose sanctions have an expiry date, we have been stuck with them for too long. We fell behind most of the major countries. Sanctions are a crude and blunt instrument of statecraft.
>
> Fortunately, ambiguity, fudging, and waffling are the essence of the nuanced Canadian soul. As a result, our government has managed to avoid a major foreign policy disaster over Tiananmen. It responded as it should have, and the sanctions are appropriate.
>
> The government listens in the first instance to the corporations. Then it has to deal with the human rights activists, the media, and the Chinese communities. Have we succeeded in persuading China to stop those rights abuses? We don't know if the policy will work or not. We're in the same boat as the Americans.

The Americans Normalize

It was the United States that first "normalized" relations. Relations with America had become the principal relationship for China, and their leaders had to talk with each other: how could they not reconnect? After Scowcroft and Eagleburger's secret visit, Washington struggled to reshape relations and overcome several domestic obstacles, for example, the split between President Bush, who favoured a measured response, and the US Congress, which wanted tough sanctions. The United States was also hampered by its decision to offer sanctuary in its Beijing Embassy to the Chinese dissident Fang Lizhi[7], and constrained by its military support to Taiwan, which was an enduring sore spot in relations. The Americans had to deal with China over important strategic considerations: Cambodia, the Gulf crisis, and restructuring relations with Russia and the collapsing Soviet Bloc. Finally, unlike Canada, each year America had to approve most favoured nation trade status (MFN) for China. That was holding its president hostage to Congress, and it was perpetuating uncertainty in US-China economic relations.

After the Scowcroft and Eagleburger visit, the Americans broke the sanctions in piecemeal, zigzag fashion. In early July 1989, Bush approved the sale of four Boeing aircraft to China, even though their cockpit navigational systems had been banned by the American sanctions. According to Ambassador Lilley, "to sidestep violating the sanctions, we removed the black boxes from the cockpits and had them stored, first in Hong Kong and only later in Beijing." In the fall of 1989, Chinese military officers were allowed to return to America to resume the upgrading of Chinese F-8 fighters. Between July and September, Bush and Deng exchanged several letters in which they sought to ease tensions. Secretary of State James Baker discussed the state of US-China relations with Foreign Minister Qian in September at the United Nations, and he concluded that the PRC was not ready to take any steps to allay American Congressional and public anger with Beijing. In November, when Henry Kissinger visited Beijing, he and Deng discussed a package deal that would allow Fang to leave China, remove several economic sanctions, and implement one or two major joint projects. It took another six months, however, before Fang finally received permission to leave China.

In December 1989, Scowcroft and Eagleburger made their second visit to Beijing. This time, the trip was publicly announced. Scowcroft said to his Chinese interlocutors:

Speaking as a friend, I would not be honest if we did not have profound areas of disagreement – on the events at Tiananmen, on the sweeping changes in Eastern Europe. We see your complaints about us in the pages of *People's Daily*. In both our societies there are voices of those who seek to redirect or frustrate our cooperation. We both must take bold measures to overcome these negative forces.[8]

The two sides focused on their positive links and agreed on a "road map" of mutual concessions and reciprocal gestures. Immediately following the meeting, Bush approved export licences for three American communication satellites to be launched in China. He also waived the ban on export-import bank loans to US companies conducting business there. In response, following the lifting of martial law in Beijing in January 1990, the PRC accredited an American correspondent, accepted Peace Corps workers, and freed a large number of dissidents.

The main issue in US-China relations was China's MFN status. Could the president withstand pressure from Congress to tie trade to improvements in human rights? To win American approval of its MFN renewal, in early spring the PRC released 211 dissidents and lifted martial law in Tibet. In May, President Bush decided to renew China's MFN for another year without imposing any conditions. The PRC let Fang and his wife leave China, released more dissidents, and announced that it intended to purchase Boeing jetliners for several billion dollars. The US House of Representatives still voted against granting MFN, but the Senate decided not to deal with the issue. Bush's renewal had held the day. American public opinion, however, remained split on improving relations with China, with nearly half of those surveyed wanting stronger criticism of Beijing's human rights practices and the continuation of the sanctions.

Progress was made on geopolitical issues. When Scowcroft and Eagleburger made their second visit, they had briefed Deng on Bush's recent meeting with Gorbachev, addressing Beijing's concerns that Washington and Moscow might decide to ally against China. Foreign Minister Qian met with President Bush in Washington later in the year to talk further about international security issues, and to reassure the PRC that America and Russia were not entering into an alliance against China.

By December 1990, relations between Washington and Beijing were essentially repaired, yet it was a fragile restoration. Strong anti-China feelings would continue to persist in the United States, and the PRC's leaders would remain suspicious of American power and motives. The two countries had reached an accommodation, although the path to full normalization would remain uncertain. The MFN issue was an obstacle, US attempts to link trade with human rights would continue, and the two countries would maintain a long-term deadlock over the future status of Taiwan.[9]

At the Post

Prior to completing his posting, Drake and several other departing ambassadors met with Li Peng in Beijing. The premier asked when Canada intended to "normalize" relations with China. Drake counselled "patience." He said to Li: "The wounds of recent events will take more time to heal." Then, to Drake's surprise, "Li flushed, turned on his heel and snarled at me: 'You take all the time you want. We don't need you.'"

Taken aback by Li Peng's riposte that China did not need Canada, Drake tried to make the best of his remarks: "At that moment, I realized that none of us was as emotionally detached as we thought ourselves to be. Even the aloof and haughty Li Peng was clearly emotional about Canada. The Canada-China relationship had more depth to it than I had realized. It would eventually recover from this latest crisis and be a positive factor for both countries." In retrospect, this incident was a defining moment. Despite Li's cold rebuke, Drake, the professional diplomat, saw a positive future for the bilateral relationship. But Li's words contained a warning that Canada was not as important to China as Canadians may have thought, and China was ready to say this openly at the highest levels.[10]

Fred Bild succeeded Earl Drake as ambassador in the fall of 1990. He arrived in time for the celebration of the twentieth anniversary of the establishment of diplomatic relations. Canada had placed a ban on celebratory events with China, so it was a disappointingly low-key affair. The ambassador wrote:

> The Canadian festivities in Beijing included the Chinese premiere of the film "Bethune, the Making of a Hero," the first joint Sino-Canadian film production. No Chinese minister attends, as no Canadian at that level would be attending the reception given that same day at the Chinese Embassy in Ottawa.
>
> What an awkward time to start a new relationship. It would have been nice, though, to have some sort of blueprint around which to plan the architecture of our redefined programs. Clark's June 30 Declaration will have to do. Reorient our programs to favour people-to-people relations, reorient the trade and CIDA programs in such a way as not to favour the coercive arms of the Chinese government. Keep senior official contacts to a minimum.[11]

Despite the coolness in official bilateral relations, trade and development assistance projects were beginning to move ahead. Bild wrote:

> As we move into 1991, trade figures look up after the disastrous lows of 1989–90. The overall objective, however, remains a conundrum: how to continue a cooperative relationship without reverting to business as usual? The trials of dissidents are proceeding apace, with not the slightest sign that foreign representations have had an effect.

Bild saw that China's political system was stabilizing. Beijing was keeping its commitment to economic reform and was intent on restoring external relations to pre-Tiananmen levels. Regarding the latter, Bild wrote:

> Starting with its own neighbours, the PRC normalizes its relations with Indonesia and Singapore, establishes diplomatic relations with Brunei, the last ASEAN member with whom it had no official relations. In the same period, China manoeuvres North Korea into accepting the two Koreas solution for UN membership, resumes boundary talks with

India, makes peace with Vietnam on its own terms, recognizes South Korea, increases cross-border trading posts on its northern border and, as they come into being, with its three newly sovereign neighbours in the west, Kazakhstan, Kyrgyzstan, and Tajikistan. Foreign Minister Qian Qichen confidently declares, "China's policy of good-neighbourliness has created harmony throughout Asia – we are welcomed as friends in all the countries we visit."

China was mending fences in its neighbourhood, and it had fashioned a re-engagement with the Americans. Was Ottawa also ready to move forward? Bild was not convinced it was happening. He wrote: "Canadian policy remained unmoving, not to say stagnant. Instructions from Ottawa became less and less clear. Rumours reached us of a division within Cabinet, with the ministers bearing economic portfolios calling, though not loudly, for a reprise of high-level visits for the benefit of the business community."

There was not enough money to support the people-to-people initiatives that Ottawa had prioritized in its June 30 Statement. Without funds, the Post had to rely on its ingenuity. The cultural counsellor visited the twenty Canadian studies centres located in China's universities, carrying a shopping bag full of US dollars to help them buy a few books about Canada. When visiting in the provinces, officers were required to give short talks on Canada to local audiences. Bild wrote: "The Embassy scrapes together whatever it can find in the way of not too outdated film and video material, gets it translated into Mandarin and/or Cantonese, and peddles it directly to local TV stations. The motto for the interim is: update the image of Canada by whatever information is at hand."

Ottawa was aware of the Post's complaints. Embassies always seemed to be short of funds and invariably complained that Ottawa was ignoring their needs. The Department gave a number of reasons for the inadequate funding:

Given the sanctions, and the continuing public criticism of China, Beijing remains near the bottom of Ottawa's list for funding. Historically, Departmental cultural programs are always underfunded. Part of the problem also is the current division in Cabinet over our China policy, between hardliners and those who want to end the sanctions.

Foreign Minister McDougall Holds Firm

It was mid-1991, and the government was now ready to hold roundtables in Toronto and Vancouver to explore possible changes in its relations with China. Two years of sanctions had passed, and China had not responded as Ottawa had hoped. Ottawa was committed to a policy that was more honoured in the breach than in the observance. Other countries were re-engaging with China, and if Canada was ready to follow their lead, how should it proceed? I wrote in my diary:

Attended the Toronto Roundtable. It was different than the June 22 Roundtable in Ottawa which was held to win support for sanctioning China after Tiananmen. In 1989 we just approved the government's agenda. This 1991 Roundtable is not the same. I think Ottawa wants to loosen sanctions on trade and high-level visits, but it is worried about public reaction, and there is opposition from government "hard-liners." Other countries are re-engaging with China. Ottawa doesn't seem to have a clear plan. Maybe this time we can have a real input into policy.

Representatives from business, ethnic Chinese community organizations, academics, human rights advocacy groups, the media, and the government attended the roundtable. Most participants supported the renewal of high-level visits and contacts as part of a process of gradual normalization. The business community wanted to remove all the obstacles to trade imposed by the June 30 measures, and it urged Canada to restore full EDC export financing for trade with China. The following comments expressed the views of the business executives:

Many other countries are fully back in the China trade, providing the PRC with soft loans, for example, Germany and Japan. And the

Americans have also found ways to restore trade. We are being out-competed. If we do not resume economic ties, we are only isolating ourselves.

I am on the business bandwagon. Limiting trade is not an answer. I support the re-opening of high-level contacts as soon as possible. That's where the big deals are made.

In my experience doing business, the more contacts you have with China, the more you open it up to democracy.

Participants from the Canadian ethnic Chinese communities, human rights organizations, and the media wanted Canada to continue the sanctions because China was still abusing human rights, using torture, arbitrarily detaining individuals, and ignoring due process – all with no sign of improvement. They argued that Canadians should remember that foreign policy was about more than trade, and there was little evidence that expanded economic links were going to bring about democracy or improvements in human rights in China.

Despite those reservations, the Department recommended that Canada should change its tactics and that "Canada should adopt a policy of gradual normalization. Ministerial visits should recommence in an area of substantive Canadian interest, beginning with the Minister of Agriculture this summer, possibly later; Canada must continue to keep after the PRC on human rights, in bilateral and international relations. Annual arms control and nuclear discussions between Canada and China could be officially resumed" (emphasis added).

In April 1991, Barbara McDougall became foreign minister, and Michael Wilson was appointed minister for international trade. Loosening of the sanctions and re-engagement were not an issue for Wilson, who was committed to trade and saw opportunities in China. This was not the case with McDougall. Previously, as minister of employment and immigration, she had stalled on ending the prolonged student amnesty program, even after being asked by then foreign minister Clark to shut it down. She had a visceral dislike of the current PRC regime, and the next few months would see ongoing tension between members of her Department who advocated loosening the sanctions, and the minister and her supporters in Cabinet, who were reluctant to do so.

Ten of us were invited to meet with McDougall for a September 1991 briefing session at the Pearson Building in Ottawa. She was listening to a group of Canadians with China expertise who were asking the government to resume high-level visits and open the doors wider for renewed relations with China. Even the representative from Amnesty International was in favour. I presented a short brief, recommending that we should step back from the sanctions because our current policy lacked credibility and leverage. Over two years had passed, and where were we? Beijing's behaviour had not changed. Other countries were loosening their sanctions and re-engaging with China in search of trade, and I was struck by the lack of focus and the drift in our China policy. The minister glared at me and responded: *"Drift? There is no drift. We have a clear policy line, and we are following it."* The minister was brusque and unyielding, her message was unsettling, those in the room were embarrassed, and the dialogue petered out.

One can speculate what might have happened if Joe Clark had continued as minister of foreign affairs. While remaining committed to the sanctions, Clark was more open to re-engaging with China than his successor. McDougall in that moment had the prime minister's backing, even if she did not have the support of several members of his Cabinet. One minister later said: "It was ok for Barbara to hold fast on rights, that was our signature policy, but not at the expense of trade. She didn't understand trade, and she certainly didn't like China. When the Prime Minister asked her later to visit China, she refused."

Those in the Department responsible for China policy felt that their minister was working at cross-purposes with them. Whatever they suggested, she would initially oppose. One Department official said: "In good part, that was the lingering Conservative suspicion of bureaucrats, since in her mind we were all Liberals. She also did not like China, and we had to find a way to get around her. Not an easy task." Another recalled: "She also had a very political reason for her hard line on China. Many voters in her riding were ethnic Chinese. She assumed they were anti-Beijing and likely to support a strong anti-China stance from a Conservative government. It turned out later that this was a mistaken assumption on her part."

Former prime minister Kim Campbell took umbrage at the criticism of McDougall. She reminded me that MacDougall was "a woman in the testosterone-loaded corridors of Ottawa power. They don't take kindly to a woman minister." There is substance to this view when one recalls the tribulations of such prominent female ministers as former foreign minister Flora McDonald, former minister of international trade Pat Carney, and former deputy prime minister Sheila Copps. Whatever the reason, when chronicling the history of Canada-PRC relations after Tiananmen, it is McDougall, perhaps somewhat unfairly, who is criticized in the first instance for Canada dragging its feet and falling behind the other major Western countries.

Minister McKnight's Visit

At the end of October, McDougall relented. She agreed to send Minister of Agriculture Bill McKnight on an official visit to China. Canada chose him because he was not a high-profile minister. The Department said: "We wanted a modest outcome, nothing dramatic. It had been several years since a minister had gone to China. The last had been Pat Carney, President of the Treasury Board. We drafted the following letter to be sent from the Foreign Minister to the Prime Minister":

> As part of a balanced strategy for our bilateral relations with China, it would be timely for a Minister to visit China. I view the Minister of Agriculture, the Honourable Bill McKnight, as an appropriate minister to initiate contact with China. Canada, in particular western Canada, has substantial economic interests in China. The PRC remains the largest buyer of Canadian wheat – indeed, 1991 represents the 30th anniversary of grain sales to China.

While cooperation in agriculture was the stated purposed of this trip, the PMO reminded the Department and the Post that

McKnight was bringing two main messages with him: trade and human rights. Other bilateral issues could also be discussed, but they were of secondary concern. The minister's advisors told the Post: "We will have to contain your desire to make up for several years of ministerial absence in one trip."

The visit met its objectives. It identified encouraging prospects for increased trade in agriculture, transportation, oil and gas, and energy. McKnight also forcefully stated the Canadian position on human rights. Bilateral relations were not back to where they were before Tiananmen – that was going to take time – but the visit was a positive step.

Ambassador Bild made these comments:

QUESTION: After the McKnight visit, would you characterize the current state of Canada-China relations as "normalized"?

AMBASSADOR BILD: I don't like the expression "normalized," because it's mainly used for political purposes, and I believe that where trade and economics are concerned, our relations with China have not been affected to the same degree. We readjusted some of our programs to make sure that they were more geared towards people-to-people relations.

QUESTION: Can you comment on the significance of ministerial visits?

AMBASSADOR BILD: Ministerial visits are a good thing when there are reasons for them. We had a very good reason for the visit by the Minister of Agriculture. It is still the most important part of the Chinese economy.

QUESTION: Is the lack of a well-defined Canadian policy on China still negatively affecting business relations?

AMBASSADOR BILD: We have continued to make strenuous efforts to maintain normal relations in the trade and economic areas. Obviously relations as a whole are not as cozy as they should be.

QUESTION: What are some of the current highlights in the bilateral relationship?

AMBASSADOR BILD: We've got a number of interesting projects in communications, hydropower, and as I said, agriculture. CIDA's development program is going well. It is people-to-people oriented now, and fits in well with China's Eighth Five-Year Plan.

QUESTION: Could you comment on prospects for Canada-China trade?

AMBASSADOR BILD: Whatever you say or do, China's going to be there.
Whatever ups and downs China goes through, you have to take the
long-term view.

McKnight's trip marked a slight turn in relations, moving the
two sides forward from the doldrums of post-June 30. The traders
were placated, but not those Canadians who still wanted to punish
China for Tiananmen. However, after two years, the images of the
killings in Beijing were beginning to fade from memory, and the
Canadian public was thinking about other matters, in particular,
the state of the Canadian economy, free trade and relations with
the United States, and the threat of Quebec separatism. Prime Minister Mulroney spoke about linking trade and development with
improvements in human rights, but his government did not apply
that linkage to China. Not to be forgotten in this mix were the Chinese interlocutors from the MFA, who had toed the party-state line
after Tiananmen. They were looking for ways to cooperate with
their Canadian counterparts. In my meetings in Beijing, I found
that these MFA officials were embarrassed by what had happened,
generally understanding of what Canada had done, and quietly
working to help restore relations.

Three Members of Parliament Arrive in Beijing

A bizarre event occurred in January 1992. Three members of Parliament arrived in Beijing as guests of the Chinese government
to investigate human rights. Prior to their departure, they had
openly announced that, once in Beijing, they intended to depart
from their official itinerary by meeting with the families of Chinese
dissidents, laying a wreath in protest of PRC government policy,
and visiting a prison. The MPs fully expected this announcement
would provoke a strong PRC reaction, and in the words of their
leader, Svend Robinson, they declared: "Torpedoes be damned, full
speed ahead!" They said that they were "determined to offend and
embarrass the Chinese government in a good cause, the cause of
democracy and human rights." In the midst of their visit, however,

the three MPs were abruptly picked up by Chinese security forces, taken to a police compound against their will, forced onto a bus, driven to the Beijing airport, and put on a flight to Hong Kong, with their belongings stuffed into green garbage bags. An official of the Canadian Embassy accompanying the group was denied access to them, and Ambassador Bild was prevented from talking with them before they were expelled.[12]

Bild recalls "spending most of the daylight hours at the Foreign Ministry, pounding the table about the ungracious treatment meted out to our three-party parliamentary delegation." In a Hong Kong press conference, the MPs said they were "demanding a full and comprehensive review of Canada's relations with China as a result of their expulsion. Aid and trade should be tied to human rights." They said that what had happened to them in Beijing had seriously disrupted the normalization process, certainly halting the ministerial-level visits that had just been resurrected. Robinson said that this incident would stop any plans the foreign minister had for improving ties with China. "She will not be travelling to Beijing in the near future."

Parliament rallied in support of its three members, although many felt the MPs had behaved inappropriately. Before they had left for Beijing, the Department objected to their plan to contact dissidents' families and lay a wreath at Tiananmen Square without first securing official Chinese permission. "We sensed trouble with this group," said one Department official. "Since they were members of Parliament, we could not stop them, and they had support from our hardliners. They had been invited by the Chinese Foreign Ministry on the initiative of the Chinese ambassador in Ottawa, who thought their trip would improve relations." The ambassador later told Bild that he had realized his mistake and "his superiors in Beijing had punished him" for inviting the MPs.[13]

Five weeks later, Canada convened a meeting of the Parliamentary Standing Committee on External Affairs and International Trade to examine China policy.[14] The rough treatment meted out to the three MPs, and the PRC's violation of diplomatic protocol, provided the focus for a serious examination of relations, in particular, whether Canada should stop any further loosening of the sanctions. Howard Balloch, the newly appointed assistant deputy minister for Asia and Pacific affairs, reminded the committee of the various measures that Canada had taken since the June 30 Statement. Then he asked: "Where are we now?" Replying to his own question, he answered: "We are on track. Some adjustments have been made. Ministerial visits and meetings have taken place here in Canada, in China, and at international events. *China is simply too important internationally.*" He continued:

Having led the way on our China policy among the G7, along with a couple of other major players, we are clearly trailing on the way out ... Only one other G7 country has not had its foreign minister visit China.

We are not uncomfortable with that position by the way. We believe there are some real prospects for engaging Chinese institutions in substantive dialogue on human rights, and related issues and processes of change.

Mrs. McDougall made this very clear a week or two ago. The PRC Foreign Minister is not being invited to Canada for the time being, and she has absolutely no intention of going to China for the time being.

Balloch was making the case that the MP's fiasco had not halted Canada's measured re-engagement with China. Neither their forcible expulsion from Beijing nor the reluctance of the Canadian foreign minister to keep up with the other G7 countries that were easing up on the sanctions would stop re-engagement. In one breath, he was criticizing his own foreign minister for letting Canada fall behind, while at the same time he was saying that what had happened to the three MPs would not derail the re-engagement process.

A large part of the hearing was devoted to trade. Svend Robinson complained that Canada was rewarding China with bargain-basement export financing, instead of adhering to the June 30 sanctions policy.

ROBINSON: Concessional financing is apparently offered to China at a rate of interest of zero percent, with a ten-year grace period, and forty years allowed for repayment. That is very concessional, Mr. Chairman.

BALLOCH: We believe it is the nature of the Chinese market today that this kind of activity is required to support our exporters. This is not something we view as aid, or as concessional, to reward China for its performance, economically or politically. It is part of the marketing of Canadian products and services in that market, given the activities of other countries, and is simply part of the price of being involved in those markets.

ROBINSON: What kind of signal is this sending to China, to say here is $175 million to buy stuff from Canada at zero percent interest, with a ten-year grace period and repayment over forty years? It seems to me that this does not really square with the Prime Minister's suggestion that we are going to link aid, and presumably concessional financing, to respect for human rights.

EDC Vice President Robert Van Adel replied that this type of soft loan financing was common practice in international export financing:

Sixteen OECD countries have financing facilities that parallel those offered by EDC. Compare it to what Canada's EDC has done – Italy US$493 million, Japan $463 million, the UK $168 million, Spain $143 million, Germany $417 million, Finland $112 million, Australia $56 million, and Canada approximately $143 million. It is a well-established fact that if we were not matching these financing facilities from other countries, there would be no significant sale of capital goods and services from Canada to China.

Robinson said that the current sanctions policy had not changed China's practices, and the government should rethink its tactics, certainly not by loosening the sanctions or by focusing on trade at the expense of human rights. Ontario Human Rights Commission official, Dora Nipp, and Lloyd Axworthy, the Liberal MP for Winnipeg and later Canada's foreign minister from 1996 to 2000, criticized the government for mishandling the situation:

NIPP: Three MPs recently returned from China. I'm really disappointed by the lack of support the three parties have given these individuals. Had

Canada taken the initiative to send these MPs over to investigate the human rights situation, community organizations wouldn't have had to organize their trip.

AXWORTHY: Well, one of the consequences of the visit is this meeting, where we are using the opportunity to come to grips with some of these issues, so that we might be able to present recommendations to the government, to our parliamentary colleagues.

NIPP: Let me just add this one last comment. Had the three Members of Parliament not gone to China, would this meeting have occurred? Would we be talking today? Probably not.

Despite renewed calls from Canadian media, and by members of Parliament, to condemn China, the government weathered a storm. It had voiced its concern about the rough treatment of the Canadian MPs, and then it moved on to other matters. The prime minister again floated the idea of tying trade and aid to improvements in human rights, but Ottawa did not follow through with any linkage. Practitioners like Balloch and Bild, who were at odds with the current policy of minimal engagement with China, defended that policy in Parliament, while at the same time looking for ways to work around it. A few weeks later, Michael Wilson, the minister of international trade and a senior Cabinet minister, made a visit to Beijing that widened the opening for re-engagement.

Michael Wilson Visits China

In early 1992, Deng Xiaoping made his famous "southern trip," the *nanxun*, to Guangdong and Fujian, where he proclaimed his strong support for a socialist market economy. By the end of the year, he had seemingly vanquished his opponents. The market was there to stay, and China was embarking on over twenty-five years of sustained economic growth. In the aftermath of Tiananmen, a more confident China was emerging after three years of relative isolation, and it was taking on a major role in international affairs. Sanctions had failed to stop China, and Canada had fallen behind its trading competitors.[15]

A month later, Minister Michael Wilson led a delegation of corporate executives on a five-day visit, with the aim of expanding trade. "Our objective," he said, "is not to isolate China – the objective is to try to build bridges." Summing up his first day of talks in Beijing with Foreign Trade Minister Li Lanqing and Vice Premier Wu Xueqian, Wilson pointed out that Canada still had disagreements with China:

We were looking for action on their part ... They said our view was different from theirs. They put a higher value on the collective human rights of better food, better living conditions. We were not trying to say, "We are only trying to trade with you if you abide by the same level of human rights as we do." If we did that there would be a number of countries we couldn't trade with.

Wilson said that prospects for better relations with China were encouraging. Canada had restored high-level visits, and the business community had confidence in the sustainability of the expanding Chinese market. He later made the following observations:

QUESTION: What kind of follow-up to this mission is the government considering?

MINISTER WILSON: Governments can help move contracts along, they can help open doors, and they can facilitate, but they can't close deals. That is really the work of the private sector.

QUESTION: Are there any plans to invite senior level Chinese to Canada, perhaps a Vice Premier?

MINISTER WILSON: The Minister for Communications has invited the PRC Minister of Posts and Telecommunications to Canada, and that is a standing invitation. I discussed this with the PRC Minister when I met with him in Beijing, although he was not at that time in a position to say one way or the other.

QUESTION: China is undergoing another wave of reform initiated by Deng Xiaoping. Could you comment on the opportunities that you see this reform wave presenting to Canadian companies?

MINISTER WILSON: I asked a number of people whether they saw this as a surge before an easing back. Almost invariably, I got the response from Chinese people, and from Canadians who have been in China for a number of years, that this was a surge forward. They do not see any likelihood of a withdrawal from the movement towards a market economy. With this movement will come more economic freedom. More political freedom must flow from that in due course – which obviously will be of benefit to human rights concerns.

According to the Department, "after almost three years we were moving forward. This was a clear signal to Beijing, and to those in Ottawa who still wanted to punish China for Tiananmen. Focus on trade and downplay the rhetoric, because we have to work with the Chinese." Although the polls showed that a majority of Canadians now favoured restoration of relations, not every Canadian was that positive. The media criticized the cost of the minister's trip and reported that rights groups were complaining there was too much emphasis on trade and too little on rights. The *Ottawa Citizen* wrote: "The abysmal state of human rights in China hasn't stopped the Canadian government from organizing a trade mission of high-powered executives to the People's Republic." One senior official in the Department expressed disappointment over the small number of announced trade deals during the Wilson visit. "Of the hundred million dollars, only two or three are real deals. The others are memoranda of understanding. Maybe they will lead to completed contracts, or maybe not."

The Post was suddenly busy. Deng Xiaoping's *nanxun* remarks had opened the door for foreign traders, and Wilson's visit led to a surge in Canadian commercial activity. Ambassador Bild, who had been complaining about not having much to do in Beijing, found that the increase in visitors was straining the Post's resources:

Ever since May I've been involved almost full-time in commercial matters ... [T]he number of Canadian business visitors seems to be doubling by the week. Is this how trends affect policy? What was the impetus that brought the Canadian business community back to this side of the Pacific? It was the 88-year-old Deng Xiaoping's *nanxun* that did it. Not only did business start up immediately, but his visit south also set

things moving for the Party to promote a slew of reform-minded officials at the Party Congress planned for the fall.

Re-engagement was in the wind. The visa section at the Embassy
had to reorganize its services to accommodate the surge in applications. People-to-people links were expanding. The Embassy's
governance activities accelerated to include joint research projects
on institutional reform, the training of Chinese judges, and even
a project that brought Chinese and Canadian scholars together to
discuss democratic development. The ambassador complained
that he needed more officers to handle this explosion of activity.
"If only we could contract long-term loans of personnel from other
missions. I sure could use some of the thirty-five people in our
Hong Kong office, who do nothing but issue visas."

The PRC's ambassador to Canada, Wen Yezhan, announced,
rather prematurely, that the Wilson visit represented "the full
normalization" of Canada-PRC relations. He said that Canada
should withdraw the June 30 Statement "because conditions have
changed. China is ready to resume relations, and Canada needs to
keep pace with the other countries. The Wilson visit is bringing to
a close three years of poor relations."

In my diary I wrote:

> Had dinner with Ambassador Wen. His last post was North Korea, and
> he's an old Cold War warrior. He thinks foreigners should stop trying
> to punish China. He says that the sanctions are a failure, and Canada
> should cancel them. Told him that the Wilson trip was a step forward,
> but Canadians are still waiting for PRC behaviour to improve.

The End of Sanctions

In March 1993, Joe Clark, now president of the Privy Council
Office, arrived in Beijing. Before leaving Canada, he was briefed
that his trip should not represent "a dramatic break" in policy.
Rather, it was "a step forward," and he was instructed to say: "We
have not closed the book on Tiananmen." Clark had meetings with

Premier Li Peng, Vice Premier Zhu Rongji, and Foreign Minister Qian Qichen, and he told Qian that Foreign Minister McDougall was inviting him to visit Canada "at a mutually convenient time." Clark also reminded his hosts that Wilson had extended an invitation to Vice Premier Zhu Rongji to come to Canada when it was convenient.

Clark discussed a range of issues with his hosts: economic and trade relations, Canadian support for the PRC's entry into the GATT, the status of Canadian citizens in Hong Kong after retrocession in 1997, human rights, international strategic issues, nuclear proliferation, defusing tension on the Korean peninsula, India-Pakistan relations, and the evolving US-Russia-China triangle. Qian said economic relations with Canada were progressing, although he complained that Canada "had to shed its unforthcoming approach to normalization." Vice Premier Zhu impressed Clark with his understanding of economic and trade issues, and his desire to repair relations, and he asked Clark to let him know when he could pay a visit to Canada.

Clark's meeting with Premier Li Peng was the highest-level dialogue between Canada and the PRC in over four years. Li did not mince his words: "Canada is a country of peace; relations used to be very good, but you joined others in imposing sanctions. We should, however, look ahead, not back. The resumption of visits is essential to rebuild PRC-Canada relations. Your Prime Minister will be welcome in China, and also the Governor General."

Clark said his conversation with Li was challenging:

> I will not pretend there was a meeting of minds. For Li, the purpose was more to restate his position, than to listen to mine. Now I know what a hard line is. I did not persuade him, but what was interesting was that for the first time, to my knowledge, he not only repeated the argument that we come from different systems, he also acknowledged it is important for people who come from different systems to meet together and discuss these issues.

At a press conference in Hong Kong, when Clark was asked about the state of Canada-PRC relations, he replied:

After Tiananmen we took a position that had two strong parts. One was that we expressed our profound disapproval of those events and sharply reduced several of our programs. Stopped high-level contacts, stopped military cooperation – stopped a lot of things. But the other principle was that we were not going to cut off or isolate a nation that powerful and that large. We don't think that isolation is the way to establish constructive relations. We did not make MFN conditional, but we stuck to our guns, and we have gradually increased the level of ministerial contacts.

Both our Trade Minister and our Agricultural Minister have been in China in the last 18 months on specific portfolio-related matters. I am the most senior Minister to go, to discuss political questions and other general matters, and I have made it clear we were doing this as just another step in our relations.

The Chinese have made it clear that they want us to declare that the sanctions have ended, and I made it clear they would not be receiving such a declaration.

Despite Clark's assertion that the sanctions had not been lifted, the Chinese were suggesting otherwise. Ambassador Zhang Yijun said that, by sending Clark, the architect of the June 30 sanctions, to Beijing, Canada had signalled that bilateral relations had approached normalization; Vice Minister Liu Huaqiu stated: "Clark is giving a clear signal. Four years is long enough, and we have to restore full relations. That's basically done now. Minister Clark and I had a good conversation when he was here." The Post reported that Clark's discussions with China's leaders went well, even the meeting with Li Peng. In Ottawa, the Department expressed its satisfaction: "China is still China and it hasn't changed much, but we have to re-engage with each other. Minister Clark said what had to be said. So did our Chinese counterparts."

In Ottawa, an important event occurred behind the scenes. Prime Minister Mulroney met with Ambassador Zhang and Paul Desmarais, the founder of CCBC, to talk about resetting the bilateral relationship and possibly inviting Vice Premier Zhu Rongji to visit Canada. The Department organized the meeting with Mulroney, but it did so without the knowledge or approval of Foreign Minister McDougall. The Department viewed the meeting as a key turning point, because it brought the prime minister on board in support of re-engagement. However, Mulroney did not wish to raise the matter in Cabinet, where McDougall was not alone in her resistance to a policy shift towards re-engagement with China. In discussion between Department officials and the PMO, it was agreed that, while there would be no formal invitation extended to Vice Premier Zhu, and the visit was not an "official visit," should the Vice Premier agree to come to Canada, the prime minister would host an "unofficial dinner" for him.

How to get Zhu to Canada without an internal Cabinet discussion, or without precipitating a parliamentary furor, especially since a federal election was not far away? The solution was found by arranging a private invitation to an event in Toronto, the "Annual Goodman Forum," which in fact was not really an annual event at all, having been held only once previously. Eddie Goodman, a leading Canadian lawyer, was supportive of re-engagement, and when Balloch and Desmarais approached him, he was happy to cooperate. Business leaders across the country were thrilled, and Zhu was naturally the draw. The vice premier was visiting Canada at exactly the right time, and in his speech to the business community, given almost entirely without notes, he dazzled those in attendance with his energy, openness, and his readiness to work with Canada. Portrayed as the "anti-Li Peng" in the eyes of many Canadians, Zhu represented the "good China" that Canada thought it knew before Tiananmen.

The PMO agreed that, once Zhu was in Canada, he could be invited to Ottawa for a "private dinner," which the prime minister would host at 24 Sussex Drive, his official residence. Beijing predictably interpreted this event as a message that relations had "almost normalized." In his *Memoirs*, Mulroney elaborated on this decision:

> I knew that another signal had to be sent. Paul Desmarais was one of the leaders of the Canadian business community who saw that China would be the key economic player on the world stage in the coming quarter century. At his suggestion, I hosted a dinner at 24 Sussex for

Chinese Vice Premier (and later Premier) Zhu Rongji. Attended by Paul and André Desmarais, the dinner was intended to demonstrate that Canada would be prepared to fully engage with China in the years ahead – cautiously, of course, in light of our appropriate human rights concerns. During a subsequent visit to China, after leaving office, I was told that my family and I would forever be welcome in China, because of the positive signal I had sent with that invitation.[16]

The "informal dinner" with Zhu was a relaxed affair and a terrific success in the eyes of the Canadians and the Chinese who attended. It was followed the next day by a private lunch in Montreal, hosted by Paul Desmarais, with a dozen business leaders from across the country. Zhu then made a short visit to Vancouver. While the Canadian government again stated this was not an official trip, Beijing characterized it as a successful four-city official visit in Canada, an outcome that the Department had anticipated.

By mid-1993, the Conservative government was fading badly in the polls. Mulroney stepped aside in June and passed the leadership mantle to Kim Campbell, but the Conservative government was on life support, and Campbell and the Conservatives were doomed to a crushing defeat in the late fall. It was a perfect time for Canada to complete the change in direction of its China policy. Waiting in the wings were the Liberals, led by Prime Minister Jean Chrétien, who had no interest in trying to punish China.

At the end of 1993, just weeks after taking power, Chrétien had an extensive bilateral meeting with President Jiang Zemin at the first Asia-Pacific Economic Cooperation (APEC) Summit in Seattle. That encounter with President Jiang was extremely positive. Jiang was gracious in praising Canada's historic role in China, from Norman Bethune's legacy to the wheat shipments in 1961, and Canada's decision to establish diplomatic relations with the PRC in 1970. In his capacity as CCBC chairman, André Desmarais, Chrétien's son-in-law, also attended the meeting. While his attendance was not publicly mentioned, the Chinese interpreted it as an indication of the prime minister's emphasis on expanding bilateral economic ties.

The issue of human rights never arose, even though Chrétien had been well briefed on the matter and had agreed to raise Canadian concerns with Jiang. Following the meeting, Howard Balloch asked Liu Huaqiu, the Chinese vice minister of foreign affairs, who was accompanying Jiang on his visit, "to ensure that the official record of the meeting would record that human rights had been raised in an open and friendly fashion." In this way, Chrétien was not leaving himself open to domestic criticism for ignoring human rights. The vice minister reluctantly agreed, and when Chrétien later said to the press that he had raised human rights issues with President Jiang, the Chinese did not contradict him.

The most lasting result of the Seattle meeting was the warm personal relationship that developed between Chrétien and Jiang, a relationship that blossomed over the remaining nine years of Jiang's presidency. They had more than a dozen further meetings during state visits and in bilateral encounters at multilateral events. Following the meeting with Jiang, Vice Premier Zou Jiahua visited Canada in early 1994 to begin a quiet dialogue that would lead to nuclear cooperation between the two countries with the sale of two CANDU nuclear reactors to China. The crowning event took place in November 1994 when Chrétien went to China, leading the largest trade mission ever sent abroad by Canada, called the "Team Canada" mission.

By the end of 1994, newly elected Liberal Prime Minister Jean Chrétien was ushering in a period in which human rights no longer occupied centre stage, and economic relations held sway. Looking back at the more than four years of sanctions, had Canada changed China's behaviour? The likely verdict was "barely, if at all." Canada hung onto the sanctions, while other countries were abandoning them, and then it scrambled to catch up. Did enforcing the June 30 Statement set back bilateral relations? Yes and no. Yes, because Canada never recovered the "special relationship" it had lost on June 4. No, because Canada re-engaged with China, although with a more realistic, more subdued appraisal of its bilateral partnership with China. From the latter's perspective, once Clark came to Beijing in 1993, the sanctions were on life support. A few months later, Prime Minister Mulroney's dinner in Ottawa with Zhu Rongji settled the issue.

In late 1993, I talked with Department officials and asked them if the June 30 Statement had changed anything. The following transcript of that conversation provides a Departmental overview of the issues that had confronted the government during those four years:

QUESTION: Do we still have any sanctions in place against China?

THE DEPARTMENT: We tried not to refer to them as sanctions. Called them "first signals" or "limits on policy." Sanctions are only effective if everybody imposes them, and there was quite a bit of slippage from others.

In China's mind they were sanctions. They always referred to them in that way, especially for high-level visits and concessional financing in trade. Mention of other measures, such as CIDA project freezes, reductions, or cancellations, and suspension of military exchanges, drew minimal reaction. The latter were not seen as significant. Cancellation of celebratory exchanges did not bother anyone. Sanctions did not have the hoped-for impact on China. We knew that would happen.

The public perception is hard to gauge. The press talked of sanctions for quite a while. Those angriest at China wanted us to withdraw our Ambassador, or link human rights to Canadian aid.

QUESTION: What is absent now in our relationship in late-1993 that was present in May 1989? If something is still missing, can it be restored?

THE DEPARTMENT: No longer giving China the benefit of the doubt. We are pragmatic now, more realistic. It's a more mature relationship. There has been a "loss of innocence." The fever is gone. We've abandoned our romantic notions about China. We are more critical.

QUESTION: Has our China policy process changed in any way since Tiananmen?

THE DEPARTMENT: We have more consultations and more Roundtables. The Roundtables are a success. We think they are a good idea, and it is likely we will have another one soon. The China policy community has changed. Tiananmen created a public that had previously been dormant, not just in the human rights area but also in the way it had activated the Canadian ethnic Chinese communities.

QUESTION: What was the impact on the Department?

THE DEPARTMENT: The restructuring of the Department, combining trade –
Industry Trade and Commerce (the ITC) with the former Department
of External Affairs (the DEA) – was a key change, not exactly due to
Tiananmen, but it greatly helped during the crisis. Our China policy is
better coordinated now, especially since trade became the key link after
June 4.

We had a great Minister in Clark, but then had to deal with a
Minister who created obstacles, until she was instructed by the Prime
Minister to move forward on China. We had a strong Trade Minister in
Wilson, and that helped us.

QUESTION: What are the key items on the China policy agenda for 1993,
and beyond?

THE DEPARTMENT: We restored high-level visits with Clark's recent trip.
Zhu Rongji's visit was another step forward. What is left? We have to
keep working on human rights. It's a big political issue domestically.

We also have to get CIDA back on track. Its programs of institution
building are a success. Trade is going to be a priority. How to catch up
to the other countries? Future relations will still be a concern. Plenty of
challenges lie ahead for Canada.

Had Ottawa wasted four years trying to apply sanctions, mis-
takenly thinking that Canada possessed enough leverage to hold
China to account over Tiananmen? Other countries soon abandoned their sanctions, yet we kept ours far too long, and it became
a half-hearted enterprise, performance art to please our domestic
audience and ourselves. The compulsion to trade and to re-engage
with China undermined the sanctions. They had no impact on
China, and we had to adjust our policies and expectations. The
balance in the relationship was also shifting in Beijing's favour:
Canada would have to learn how to live with a different PRC, one
that was less inclined in the future to listen to what Canada had to
say, unwilling to apologize, and ready to use its powerful economy
to steer bilateral relations in a different direction.

chapter eight

Team Canada Goes to China

The 1994 Team Canada mission marked the official end of the Canadian sanctions. It was the largest trade delegation Canada had ever sent abroad, and it was headed by Prime Minister Jean Chrétien. Nine of the ten provincial premiers joined him, as well as over 400 representatives from Canada's business community. They concluded more than $8.5 billion in contracts – the biggest amount ever signed by a visiting trade mission to China.

After Chrétien took office in late 1993, he told Senator Jack Austin, a long-time Liberal, a member of caucus, and president of CCBC, that he wanted to rebuild commercial relations with China. Chrétien said to Austin: "Let's go to China to lead a trade mission." It took eight months to organize this unprecedented mission, which they called "Team Canada." It was the first time that a Canadian prime minister and the provincial premiers decided to join together in an international trade delegation. Could they put aside their political differences and strong personalities, and function as a team? The CCBC was responsible for organizing the business part of the mission, while the Department took care of the diplomatic agenda. Could the government and this trade organization work together effectively, and was the Chinese side ready to give the mission a positive reception? If so, would this mark the resumption of full relations?

The Department was responsible for day-to-day mission planning, under close supervision from the Prime Minister's Office (PMO) and the Privy Council Office (PCO). As the mission took shape, the organizers had to deal with a number of special issues, for example, arranging a secret visit to the Darlington nuclear facility for Vice Minister Zou Jiahua, as the PRC was closing in on a deal to buy two CANDU nuclear reactors during the Team Canada visit. Zhang Yijun, the PRC ambassador to Canada, and senior Ministry of Foreign Affairs officials offered their strong support. It was soon clear that China wanted the mission to be a success. In mid-year, Austin flew to Beijing to find a venue that could accommodate 1,600 people – officials, businesspeople, Chinese guests, and the media – for the grand banquet to be hosted by Premier Li Peng. The Chinese government agreed, for the first time, to let foreigners use the Great Hall of the People at Tiananmen Square for such an event.

The government in Ottawa pushed hard to get early commitments from the provincial premiers. The premier of Quebec did not intend to join the group. Instead, he wanted to send his minister of trade. Chrétien's team said: "No. Only premiers can come. We are not ordering pizza here; you cannot ask for substitutes." Later, in Beijing, Premier Li Peng asked Chrétien why there was no premier from Quebec in the group. Chrétien replied that he represented the federal riding of St. Maurice in Quebec, to which Li replied in French: "Bonjour monsieur."

Prime Minister Chrétien stated that Team Canada was a trade mission, and not a forum for discussing human rights. In his view, increased trade and re-engagement – not passionate statements – would improve the human rights situation in China. This stand produced a chorus of criticism from the media, opposition parties, and NGO activists. During the visit, members of the mission studiously avoided mentioning human rights.

When Team Canada arrived in Beijing, the prime minister's car was followed by nine purple vans, one for each provincial premier and his or her staff, arranged by the order in which the provinces had joined Confederation. During the visit, the premiers emphasized national unity and teamwork. Alberta's Ralph Klein famously said: "The Prime Minister is the door-opener, and we are the ushers." The highlight was the signing of fifty-four commercial contracts worth $8.5 billion dollars, including the sale of the two CANDU nuclear reactors. The CCBC reaped a financial bonanza by sponsoring the banquet in the Great Hall, and the business community gained access to top-level political and commercial contacts. Most important, the leaders on both sides had re-established personal relations.

After the visit, Chrétien basked in the team's achievements. Canadians reacted positively, although some criticized the $8.5 billion figure, *pointing out that half were letters of intent and memoranda of agreement, incomplete deals that still required months of future negotiation. Others said Team Canada had sacrificed Canadian values and principles on the altar of material gain, and still others questioned why Canada intended to sell nuclear reactors to a communist country.*

The prime minister led three more Team Canada visits to China. The mission in 2001 was the largest, and also the last. The cost had escalated, and the government could not sustain seconding officials from their regular work to spend months organizing these missions. It was also unlikely that so many provincial premiers would again join in such an event. Members of the business community felt that they were acquiring enough access in China to make large business deals on their own. What had been a spectacular event marking the restoration of bilateral relations in 1994 became a distant memory only a few years later.

From the moment I was elected, I made China a priority. My first international meeting as prime minister was the APEC Summit in Seattle in 1993; my first Team Canada trip was to China a year later; and I met Chinese President Jiang Zemin so many times that he used to refer to me as his English teacher!

– Prime Minister Jean Chrétien

Jean Chrétien Takes Charge

In the fall of 1993, the Liberals took power in a landslide election. Unencumbered by previous Conservative policy, they restored relations with Beijing, making expanded trade their primary goal. The Canadian economy was struggling, and the lure of the China market was irresistible.[1] Prime Minister Jean Chrétien decided that Canada was well equipped to benefit from this situation: "We enjoyed the advantage of having British Columbia as a gateway to the Pacific, with Vancouver's busy airport, the expanded port facilities at Prince Rupert, and a network of railway connections across North America. We were ready to sell everything from subway cars to CANDU nuclear reactors in Asia's colossal markets."[2]

Canada's trade with China was languishing, even as China's economy was opening up. Canada's competitors had increased their share of China's expanding market, while Canada was falling behind. According to the CCBC, in 1993 bilateral trade between Canada and China was $4.6 billion, the same as in 1992. Canada had dropped to fourteenth in China's trade rankings, falling behind Australia, Italy, France, Singapore, and Indonesia. Exports to the PRC had declined by 29 per cent, and the trade balance with China was showing a substantial and steadily rising deficit for Canada.

Resource-based goods continued to be Canada's primary exports, although value-added exports to China were showing a moderate increase. The CCBC pointed out: "Overall bilateral trade performance has not been satisfactory. While Canada's exports to the world have increased by 14%, exports to China have fallen. In view of this, further concerted effort is necessary if Canada is not to lose more of its share in the rapidly emerging China market." The message from the business community was that opportunities in China were plentiful, but more aggressive marketing strategies and financing were required from Ottawa for Canadian business to realize them.

In late 1993, at the CCBC Annual General Meeting (AGM) in Vancouver, Roy MacLaren, the new minister for international trade, emphasized the importance that the new government was placing on trade with China. "Too often Canadians, like the frog in the old Chinese saying, 'have looked up at the sky from the bottom of a well.' We tend only to see the opportunity on our own doorstep." MacLaren went on to say:

> The China market, once a source of some frustration and disappointment, has truly arrived. How many of our French or German or Japanese competitors can boast of the in-house Chinese expertise that Canadian companies are so fortunate to have? As the Minister of International Trade, I'm committed to putting myself and the significant resources of my department at your disposal.
>
> The markets of Asia-Pacific, and of China, are full of promise, but I appreciate they are not always easy to penetrate. *We must develop a Team Canada approach* if we are going to enjoy success. This is more evident when it comes to the China market, where the competition is fierce and the field of play is not always a level one.[3] (emphasis added)

The "Team Canada" name had been popularized by Canadian success in international hockey in the 1970s in matches with the Soviet Union, although it had not been applied previously to trade policy. MacLaren said the current situation in China required a closer partnership between Ottawa and the business community in order to gain access to China's top business leaders. The government appointed Raymond Chan, its first minister of ethnic Chinese origin to serve as secretary of state for Asia-Pacific, to assist in trade promotion and to work with the Canadian ethnic Chinese communities. In furthering the idea of a team approach, MacLaren said that the public and private sectors needed to pool their resources to achieve their common objectives.

Team Canada had the prime minister's complete backing. As we saw in previous chapters, when leaders take charge, results are obtained in dramatic fashion. Prime Minister Chrétien said that trade was his priority, and he told his ministers, his public servants, and the business community to make it happen. He was determined to use his power, and that of the government, to organize the biggest trade delegation in Canadian history. According to York University political scientist Daniel Drache, Chrétien was "a perfect leader in an unheroic time, a clever tactician, and a man of shrewdness." University of Waterloo professor Andrew Cooper called Chrétien "Canada's first salesman, leading a number of high-profile Team Canada missions to putative big-market countries around the globe."[4]

The business community supported this initiative, especially the CCBC, which since 1978 was the principal Canadian organization promoting trade with China. Its founder and chairman, Paul Desmarais of Power Corporation, had developed close ties with senior Chinese leaders and had flown to China a number of times in his private airplane to conduct business there, including one trip right after Tiananmen. The Desmarais family and Power Corporation had close personal and business connections with three prime ministers: Mulroney, Chrétien, and Paul Martin Jr. Chrétien's daughter was married to Paul Desmarais's son André.

The CCBC's AGM alternated between China and Canada. It was usually attended by over 100 Canadian business representatives, along with senior officials from both countries. The CCBC intended to hold its annual meeting in Beijing as part of the proposed Team Canada visit, and its members were eager to restore the access to China's top decision-makers that had been disrupted by the Canadian embargo on high-level visits. Four members of the CCBC would assume an important role in reopening China for Canadian traders: Paul Desmarais; his son André, CCBC's chairman; Senator Jack Austin, the CCBC president, who played a central role in creation of the Team Canada mission; and former ambassador Earl Drake, who would serve as the link between the CCBC and the Department.[5]

Once they realized that the sanctions were ineffective, the Canadian China policy community, the media, and the general public had largely lost interest in punishing China. The prime minister had a wide electoral mandate to fix a struggling Canadian economy, so why not increase trade with China if it created jobs? The Germans had just returned from a China trade mission that had netted $5 billion in new business, and the Americans were preparing to do the same. This didn't mean that Canada had to abandon its criticism of China; that could continue, albeit in a less confrontational fashion. It was time to move on from prioritizing human rights. This change in thinking was evident in the Canadian media's measured reaction to Chrétien's decision to re-engage with China. While the media did not abandon their role as critics of Chinese human rights abuses, they were softening their position. The new situation required more intensive economic engagement with China. The prevailing view was that the government could manage human rights more strategically, within a broader framework that prioritized trade and restored relations. Senator Austin announced:

We are going to take the case of Canada-China business opportunities to the Canadian public. We've seen the new government show a significant increase in awareness. Mr. Chrétien, in his statement accepting the results of the election, mentioned Asia – the only part of the world that he did mention. We now have a Secretary of State for Asia-Pacific, and in our Trade Minister we have Roy MacLaren, a person who is very enthusiastic about Canada in Asia.

Senator Austin was the link between the CCBC and the government. A member of the Liberal Party caucus, he could talk with the prime minister directly at the policymaking level. In conversation, he recalled the following: "After Chrétien becomes Prime Minister, he says to me, 'I want to rebuild commercial relations with China. You are president of the CCBC. Tell me what to do. Let's go to China to lead a trade mission. When should we go?'"

Austin welcomed the prime minister's enthusiasm. "I knew that once the Prime Minister was on board, we could do something." The federal government's annual subsidy of $300,000 to the CCBC had just ended, and the trade organization was in the midst of a financial restructuring to enable it to continue its work. Ten of its largest corporate members had each agreed to contribute $250,000 over the next ten years, setting up an endowment to support the CCBC's operation. A major trade mission to China, headed by the prime minister, would be a tremendous boost to the restructured trade organization. Austin told Chrétien: "The bigger the mission, the better."

Behind the scenes, Beijing supported the idea of a Canadian mission that could highlight restored relations. The head of the PRC State Planning Commission told Austin that, if the Canadian side was serious about sending a large trade mission, China would respond favourably. Ambassador Zhang Yijun and Vice Minister Liu Huaqiu, who had waited out the long period of difficult relations between the two countries after Tiananmen, both warmly welcomed the idea. It was likely that Vice Premier Zhu Rongji, who had visited Canada six months previously, would meet with the trade mission in Beijing, as well as Premier Li Peng. According to Austin, "the Chinese I talked with saw this as a Canadian government initiative. They never believed the CCBC was autonomous from the Canadian government. That served us well, because although the CCBC is an independent organization, going to China as part of an official high-level Canadian delegation was a tremendous opportunity for our members."

With the prime minister, senior PRC officials, and most major Canadian corporations doing business with China on board, how to move forward? In the past, Canadian prime ministers had travelled to China accompanied by a number of business executives. However, those were official visits, with trade occupying only a part of a broader bilateral agenda. Regular trade missions were usually headed by a trade minister, as was the case with Michael Wilson's visit in 1992. Organizing a large delegation to China, headed by the Canadian prime minister, after almost five years of difficult relations, meant dealing with sensitive political issues, overly optimistic expectations from the business community, and a sceptical reaction from the Canadian public. Austin recalls: "We knew we had the right idea; yet we also knew we had obstacles ahead of us."

Good fortune shone on the mission's planners when Michael Harcourt, the premier of British Columbia, became involved. Harcourt had already been to China several times promoting his province, and he was a strong advocate for expanded trade with the PRC. Austin recalls that the idea of including the provincial premiers in the Team Canada mission came from a discussion that he and Harcourt had, following a tennis game in Vancouver:

> I described to him the Team Canada trade mission that would be headed by the Prime Minister. I knew he would be interested, as he had long been keen on the China market, an interest we shared. Harcourt said why not also include the provincial premiers? I suggested he take it up with the Prime Minister. I know the idea did not come from the Department, but it certainly supported it.

Harcourt said to Austin: "There's a First Ministers' Meeting coming up in December with the Prime Minister and all the provincial premiers. I definitely will suggest this to the Prime Minister, and we can raise it at the meeting."

This was a novel idea. There had never been a trade mission combining the top federal and provincial leaders. At first, some of the provincial premiers who had busy agendas hesitated, wondering about the political implications of joining a prime ministerial delegation. Still, the idea resonated at a time when the provinces needed an economic boost and Canadian national unity was under threat from Quebec separatists. Harcourt recalls: "Promoting national unity in the face of possible Quebec separation from Canada wasn't my first concern. I saw it as a great trade opportunity for Canada to get back in the game with China. As the mission evolved, I realized we were also coming together, to stand up for our country."

Setting the Stage

Team Canada took shape in the first few months of 1994. High-level visits require extensive planning, and a prime ministerial visit much more so, especially since this was the first prime ministerial trip to China since Brian Mulroney's visit in 1986. The group was going to be large, much bigger than any previous mission to China. It was now possible that a number of provincial premiers might join. Could so many political leaders, representing different political parties and interests, get along with one another, and could Canada count on support from the Chinese side?

In a speech at the University of Moncton in early 1994, Chrétien said trading with China did not mean sacrificing Canadian criticism of its human rights record--talking about China's human rights practices could still be part of an expanded trade initiative. According to Chrétien, Canada needed a fresh perspective on China:

> If I were to say to China, "We are not dealing with you anymore," they would say, "Fine." They would not be threatened by Canada strangling them.
>
> You have to measure your strength ... Sometimes you will have influence, and sometimes you won't.
>
> I'm the Prime Minister of a country of 28 million people. He [Jiang Zemin] is the President of a country with 1.2 billion. I'm not allowed to tell the Premier of Saskatchewan what to do. Am I supposed to tell the President of China what to do?[6]

In March, Foreign Minister André Ouellet said that he "did not intend to get bogged down by Tiananmen Square when dealing with China." It was time to improve relations with Beijing's leaders and "take advantage of the opportunities there." A few weeks later, he remarked that "the time has passed when Canada had to act like Boy Scouts." Serving as a model for others by doing good deeds internationally was no longer a Canadian priority. That behaviour belonged to the past, when Canadian foreign policy was less in tune with Canadian domestic priorities and Canada was still a major player in international affairs. "It's a change in tactics," he said. "The objective of promoting human rights is the same, the values that are important to us are the same, but how to go about it and achieve it – that has changed."

The media took note. The *Globe and Mail* wrote that past relations with authoritarian regimes "had contained a hidden ingredient: the subversive virus of Canadian-style democracy and human rights." Prime Minister Chrétien and Foreign Minister Ouellet were pushing too hard for trade, and "in their haste to fashion an 'independent, made-in-Canada foreign policy,' human rights was becoming an afterthought in the pursuit of commercial interests. We must have a more precise explanation from the Prime Minister and Mr. Ouellet, about how they intend to operate their post-Mulroney policy of quiet diplomacy on human rights." The *Washington Post* wrote: "Canada's trading opportunities in Asia are a key element of its economic recovery, and thus of foreign policy. Human rights violations, while still officially a Canadian concern, are unofficially bygones."

The Americans were the gold standard for confronting China on human rights violations, and Prime Minister Mulroney had more or less followed American criticism of China. Ties between the United States and China had weakened after President Bill Clinton took office in 1993 and tried to pursue a tougher US policy on human rights. In March, Secretary of State Warren Christopher went to Beijing, a visit that Henry Kissinger later called "one of the most pointedly hostile diplomatic encounters since the US-China rapprochement." Christopher demanded changes in Chinese human rights practices in exchange for the US granting most favoured nation (MFN) trade status with the United States. In response, Premier Li Peng bluntly told him that China's policies were none of his business, and the Christopher visit ended badly.

The *Washington Post* observed that Canada had taken note of the increased tension between Washington and Beijing, and it was now moving in a different direction, as part of a Liberal foreign policy agenda that sought more independence from United States influence. This strategy was seen as a return to the policies of Pierre Trudeau, when Canada wanted "to offset the disproportionate economic power of the United States." Now, in order to increase its trade with the PRC, the Canadian government appeared ready to sacrifice aggressive human rights criticism of China.

Roger Clark, general secretary of Amnesty International Canada, argued that a Canadian prime minister claiming that he could not tell the president of China what to do contributed to further human rights violations. Clark stated: "If nothing else, it is breaking obligations under UN declarations and Conventions ... [I]t is the responsibility of each country to uphold and promote rights and prevent human rights violations. It's the publicity and the public record that counts. Even the most reprehensible governments pay attention when there is a public focus."

Marian Botsford Fraser, president of PEN Canada, weighed in with an eloquent critique of Canada's new policy:

> Canadian politicians are streaming to China. They flock with the noisy single-mindedness of migrating geese, flapping and honking before the multi-billion-dollar economy they see shimmering on the horizon.
>
> "Let us trade, let us make deals, let us do business," they squawk. "Let us not get bogged down by Tiananmen Square; that's just history. Nowadays, we wouldn't dream of criticizing great big China; we're just little Canada, waddling up to the trade table. Here, here, over here..."
>
> And nary a peep, not the tiniest chirp, about that enormous albatross perched in the middle of the banquet hall, the factory, the prison and the public square – China's record of human rights abuses.
>
> By declaring Canada puny and impotent, our political leaders have undermined Canada's clout internationally, and they have significantly, negatively altered the context for all Canadians working on human rights abuses.[7]

Former Conservative foreign affairs minister Barbara McDougall attacked the Liberals for ignoring what was happening in China: "the suppression of Tibet and the massacre at Tiananmen, the arbitrary removal of farm workers from their land and workers from their livelihood, the absence of occupational health and safety standards, the lack of access to education and jobs for those deemed 'politically incorrect,' the harsh political repression of the most innocent activities, and the use of prison labour." She pointed out that Canadians "had to be true to our own fundamental values that have permitted us to live and prosper, and raise our families in this most privileged of countries. We cannot adopt a policy of parking our principles at the border, when we pick up our passport." McDougall questioned why Canada was again sending high-level missions to China, since those visits "are widely exploited by Chinese leaders within China as a blessing from Western leaders." She ended by exclaiming loudly: "Shame Mr. Chrétien!"[8]

Vice Premier Zou Jiahua arrived in Canada in April. Not many Canadians knew who he was. The agenda for his trip appeared modest, highlighting trade opportunities and improved relations. However, Zou's visit set the table for one of the most important deals in the upcoming Team Canada mission: the sale of two CANDU nuclear reactors worth $3.5 billion. During the Cold War, and continuing after Tiananmen, the idea of nuclear cooperation with China, a communist country, was unimaginable. When Zhu Rongji had visited Canada in 1993, Ambassador Zhang told Assistant Deputy Minister Balloch that the PRC was considering acquiring several Canadian heavy-water nuclear reactors. Zhang Guobao, a member of Zhu's delegation, wanted to discuss the possible acquisition of the nuclear reactors with Atomic Energy of Canada (AECL). Balloch remembers: "I called Deputy Minister Reid Morden and told him I was going to arrange a meeting for Zhang Guobao with senior AECL people on a very informal basis. Hearing no objection from Reid, I then did so."

Then, just before Zou's arrival, Ambassador Zhang Yijun told Balloch that Zou Jiahua wanted to visit a Canadian nuclear facility so that he could see a nuclear reactor in operation. The Chinese side had avoided raising this issue in the normal course of planning Zou's visit because of its sensitive nature. Balloch was pleased with Ambassador Zhang's caution, since he knew that if Zhang's request had been made officially, the Canadian government could not have kept the matter confidential, and it might have turned it down. Balloch said: "I decided to set up the visit, but to do so secretly, and not advise Foreign Affairs Minister André Ouellet." He told his deputy minister that he was planning to take Vice Premier Zou to the Darlington nuclear station "without any press or public knowing about it."

The morning after Zou's arrival in Toronto, Balloch, Vice Premier Zou, Ambassador Zhang, and three Chinese officials left the Four Seasons Hotel at 5:00 a.m. for Darlington. A fake motorcade, headed by the vice premier's empty car, left for the officially planned visit to the Nortel plant at 9:00 a.m. Meanwhile, Zou and his hosts toured the Darlington nuclear reactor site and met with AECL executives. He asked a dozen highly technical questions, and he wanted more details about the capital and operating costs. Neither the media nor the public knew about this covert visit. Behind the scenes, the government realized that China was serious about purchasing the nuclear reactors and that Zou's visit would have a large impact on the success of the upcoming Team Canada mission. The announcement later in Beijing, that Canada had sold China two CANDU nuclear reactors, turned out to be one of the highlights of the Team Canada mission.

It was the beginning of May, and the successful visits of the two vice premiers, Zhu in 1993 and now Zou, raised expectations on both sides that relations with the PRC "were almost back to normal." Canadian Governor General Ray Hnatyshyn held talks with President Jiang Zemin, and Foreign Minister Ouellet was scheduled to meet with Premier Li Peng in July. Most important was the official announcement that Prime Minister Chrétien was planning to visit China in November, leading a large trade mission.

I wrote in my diary:

Am in Beijing. Lots of things are happening. The Chinese side is relieved, almost enthusiastic. I talked with people in the MFA. They think that the Prime Minister's visit will be a huge success. Will have to find out more about it. Seems that after so much attention on human rights, suddenly it's all about trade. Wonder how this is going to be played out at home?

In Ottawa, planning for the trip was already underway. Everyone was talking trade. I had dinner with Ambassador Zhang, who reminded me that relations were now changing rapidly. Ever since he took over in Beijing as head of the North America and Oceania Division of the MFA, Zhang had worked to overcome obstacles in the bilateral relationship. He had brokered the Zhu and Zou visits, and he was quietly assisting in the organization of the Team Canada mission.

Behind the scenes, Austin was gathering support for the visit. He was talking with his contacts at the Chinese State Planning Commission, the MFA, and with Ambassador Zhang. Austin recalls: "My big connection was with Jean Chrétien. I could meet with him, and also with the Prime Minister's Office (PMO) and the Privy Council Office (PCO), both key organizers for the trip. Along with former Ambassador Earl Drake, who was a CCBC Board member, we brought the business community into the planning of the mission."

The competitive nature of the China trade brought some urgency to Austin's efforts. He continued: "I was following the model of German Chancellor Kohl's recent visit, when the corporate representatives who accompanied him had signed business deals worth $2.3 billion, just in one afternoon. Our initial target was at least $1 billion – more if we sold the CANDU reactors. Those would be actual commercial contracts, not just memoranda of understanding." As for human rights, "we were as adamant as the Americans on human rights. We knew trade would open things up. We said that, when we are doing business, we will always have certain values to proclaim about the importance of the individual."

Foreign Minister Ouellet outlined the government's new China strategy – that several realities determined Canada's future relations with the PRC. China was too important to ignore, and renewed engagement was the best way to move ahead. Canada could accomplish this new arrangement through trade, creating sorely needed jobs, and Canadian values would be reflected in every commercial transaction. The new Canadian strategy was called the Four Pillars. "Economic partnership" was the most important pillar, followed by "peace and security," "sustainable development," and then "human rights, good governance, and rule of law." Ouellet said: "This will open doors for Canadian companies, when the Prime Minister visits China in November."

In my diary I wrote:

> Just spent two weeks in Ottawa talking about the "Four Pillars." The new policy does two things. It makes economic links the top priority, and it pushes human rights into the background. This puts Canada in line with most Western nations. Even the Americans have given in and renewed China's MFN status. Big enthusiasm over Chrétien's upcoming trip. It promises to be quite an event.

Organizing Team Canada

It took the better part of 1994 to organize the mission. The size of the proposed delegation – the largest prime ministerial and trade mission in Canadian history – was going to tax government resources and place a heavy burden on Canadian staff in Ottawa and Beijing. The Department was responsible for the official part of the mission organized by the government. It deferred to the PMO and the PCO for policy guidance. While Team Canada's stated purpose was to develop trade with China, a prime minister would be heading the mission, so the PMO had to showcase Chrétien and Canada's new China policy. In May, Ottawa set up a task force comprised of several sections within the Department, plus Protocol, the PMO, and the PCO, to organize the visit. Three other groups were established to discuss policy options and to draft a month-by-month schedule to carry out mission planning: a Steering Group, a Government/ Business Coordinating Committee, and a Working Group.

These groups held discussions in Ottawa and Toronto in mid-May, and they continued to meet regularly over the next five months. The Working Group was responsible for coordinating with the Posts in Beijing, Shanghai, and Hong Kong, as well as for responding to requests from companies wanting to join the mission. It submitted a logistical plan to the Steering Group, which approved the plan and made adjustments to the mission objectives, the itinerary, and the likely scenarios for meetings in China. The Government/Business Coordinating Committee was responsible for bringing together the participants from the government and business, focusing on the collaboration between the Department and the CCBC, which was organizing the business side of the mission.

The mission was expected to last five working days: two in Beijing, a day and a half in Shanghai, and another day and a half in either Harbin in the northeast or Sichuan in west-central China. Later, both Harbin and Sichuan were cancelled. After visiting Shanghai, the delegation would finish the mission with two days in Hong Kong. Preparatory work began for the meetings between the prime minister and PRC's leaders, in particular with Jiang Zemin, Li Peng, and Zhu Rongji. Chrétien had already met Jiang in Seattle at an APEC meeting in the fall of 1993, and he had seen Zhu in Canada earlier that year but had not yet met with Li, who would prove to be an elusive target, right until Team Canada's arrival in Beijing.

While the promotion and support of Canadian commercial interests in China was the mission's main purpose, the government had several additional objectives: "to advance the bilateral relationship with an emerging superpower, to enhance Canada's profile in China, and to remind China of issues of concern to the Canadian public, for example, human rights." The prime minister also planned to talk with China's leaders about the effect of the retrocession of Hong Kong on the 100,000 Canadian citizens then living there. Other items for discussion included regional security issues, cooperation in environmental policy, Beijing's commitment for a moratorium on nuclear testing, and the expansion of Canadian development assistance programs in institution building and the fostering of civil society.

In June, Chrétien wrote to the provincial premiers, formally inviting them to participate in the mission. He also met with his advisors to discuss strategy and to identify the Team Canada "trip deliverables," for example, a nuclear cooperation agreement (NCA) to enable the sale of the two CANDU reactors, the announcement of six new CIDA projects, and the possible completion of a foreign investment protection agreement (FIPA). The prime minister talked with Austin in caucus, and he agreed to be the key speaker at the CCBC's AGM in Beijing during the mission. Chrétien was to preside over the business contract signings and then attend the CCBC's large closing banquet. Austin asked Chrétien

> to confirm the conversation we had at caucus June 22 regarding the afternoon program on Tuesday, November 8 ... You will give short remarks, and then answer no more than 8–10 questions from the audience. Also we are giving Paul Desmarais, the Honorary Chairman of the CCBC, and Rong Yiren, Vice President of the China International Trust and Investment Company (CITIC), awards of distinction during the AGM. I hope you will be able to present them with their gold medals.[9]

Cooperation between the government and the CCBC had its contentious moments. Normally, the Department organizes a prime ministerial visit, acting together with the PMO and the PCO. It was unaccustomed to sharing the planning spotlight with a non-governmental organization. The CCBC's director of operations said that she would assist the Department by providing the names of companies prepared to sign contracts in China, and the CCBC would help with the logistical arrangements for the business participants. However, government officials were suspicious of partnering with the CCBC, and complained that the two organizations had different capacities and objectives: "The CCBC people didn't realize that a major political agenda was involved. They didn't have enough staff. Their goal was to sell their products, whereas our job was to restore the bilateral relationship. This was more than just a trade mission, and we had to find an appropriate division of labour."

According to Austin, the idea of a government-CCBC partnership took some time to sink in:

> There was friction. The Department never really accepted us. Team Canada was CCBC's idea, our mission. Yes, it was a prime ministerial

mission, requiring major government planning, but we in the CCBC had recruited the Prime Minister, and it was our contacts that made this happen.

I could talk with Chrétien at any time, and knew what he wanted. CCBC also had real *guanxi* (good connections) with the top Chinese leaders because of the business links established by Paul and André Desmarais. We knew how to work with the Chinese. We had a track record.

The international trade group in the Department had trouble from the beginning trying to include the CCBC in their thinking and planning. I recognized their dismissive attitude at the outset, and tried to keep them in the business loop. There was always a struggle with the government's trade people.

Earl Drake, the former ambassador and now CCBC vice president, was the liaison person between the Department and the CCBC. He and Austin worked closely together. Drake complained that it was now difficult to work with his former Department: "I was an unpaid volunteer, had retired from the Department. Now they seemed to view me as some kind of intruder. They didn't want a bunch of businesspeople milling about. They were sceptical about us. They worried that we would stumble and mess things up." As the preparation for the mission moved further into the summer, however, the two sides managed to settle most of their differences. The Department's diplomatic expertise took over, once it got its working orders from the PMO and the PCO, and the CCBC spent most of its time preparing for its meetings in Beijing and organizing the rapidly growing group of business participants.

At the end of July, Foreign Affairs Minister Ouellet visited China, the fourth in an escalating series of high-level visits designed to set the stage for the mission. Aside from reviewing key bilateral issues, Ouellet discussed the sale of the CANDU nuclear reactors, and he told Beijing that, if it intended to purchase them, China had to sign a nuclear cooperation agreement (NCA) that required it to follow strict inspection and safeguard standards, which were meant to guard against their use for military purposes. If the two sides could reach an agreement before November, the NCA could be signed during the Team Canada mission.

Ouellet expressed his concern about Chinese trade practices, especially the PRC's non-tariff barriers that were limiting Canadian companies from doing business in China. The Hudson's Bay Company was hoping to set up operations in Beijing, but the PRC had not yet approved the establishment of foreign-owned commercial retail outlets in China. The Royal Bank of Canada wanted to open an office in Beijing, but it could not get approval, and Manulife had been trying to become the third foreign insurance company licensed in China. Nortel was waiting for the PRC to designate it as one of five foreign telecommunications companies permitted to do business in China. China was looking to gain entry into the GATT and asked for support from Canada, but Ouellet said Beijing would have to liberalize its trade policies if it wanted Canada's help. He said that a large delegation of Canadian companies would be coming to Beijing in November, ready to sign large contracts if the Chinese business climate was more favourable.

By September, planning for Team Canada had moved into high gear. The number of companies committed for the mission was nearing 300. New recruits were signing up almost daily, and the CCBC realized that it needed a larger venue for the banquet for the political leaders, the business delegation, and the Chinese guests. What had started out as an event for about 700 to 800 people, held in one of Beijing's larger hotels, had grown to twice that size, so Austin flew to Beijing to look for an appropriate venue. Chinese authorities offered him space for close to 1,600 people in several locations, but Austin had a better idea: "Why not rent us the Great Hall of the People? It is right beside Tiananmen Square in the middle of Beijing. This is your best facility. This is where you usually receive top foreign delegations, and it would be a fitting venue for this special Canadian delegation." At first, the Chinese were taken aback by his request, because foreigners apparently had never asked to use the Great Hall for a major trade event. Austin persisted, and surprisingly he managed to obtain permission from China's top leadership. The rent for the Great Hall was nominal, only $1,000. The big expense for the CCBC would be the food and service, for which the PRC was charging $110 per person. The total cost of the banquet in the Great Hall would be about $200,000, paid for by the business members who were attending the banquet.

When the number of confirmed participants passed 300, the Canadian government worried that the mission had grown too large. One Department official said: "It's too big. Not just all those businesspeople, but the Prime Minister, two federal ministers and their staff, a large number of provincial premiers with their staff, several mayors, over 40 government officials from the Department, Protocol, Defense, the RCMP, the PMO, the PCO, plus at least 35 media representatives, a large number of spouses, and special participants. When we count all the businesspeople, we will have well over four hundred going on the trip, probably closer to five hundred." Due to the mission's expanding size and complexity, the PMO asked everyone "to keep the lines of communication simple and direct during the visit planning phase" and "to keep the distribution of documents as restricted as possible."

The first advance team arrived in Beijing at the end of September. The team included officials from the PMO, the PCO, the Department, Protocol, Security (RCMP), and other government services. It needed to know whether the Chinese were prepared to handle such a large foreign delegation from both a logistical and a protocol standpoint. The Post told Ottawa to expect difficulties, because when Governor General Hnatyshyn had visited in April, the Chinese abruptly cancelled his scheduled speech without warning, and when Foreign Minister Ouellet was in Beijing, reporters were barred at the last minute from attending his meeting with Li Peng. The PRC had not allowed Ambassador Bild to ride with Ouellet in his official car after Ouellet's arrival in Beijing so that Bild could brief his own minister. The Embassy advised the advance team to be cautious, to go over the itinerary carefully with the Chinese side, and to keep in mind that political and protocol matters weighed heavily on their host's shoulders. Embassy officers stated:

We have to be flexible. The Chinese think they've invented protocol and that we Canadians are amateurs at diplomacy. We have to make sure there are no surprises. One big problem will be the provincial premiers. The Chinese consider our provinces to be like theirs, but Canadian provinces have far more power and status in our federal system. We don't want our provincial premiers being marginalized by the Chinese.

The advance team spent over a week in Beijing and Shanghai discussing security arrangements with their Chinese counterparts, meeting with the MFA, and inspecting the venues for the various Team Canada activities. Technicians from the PCO wanted to know how to set up the twenty telephone lines that would provide direct access to outside lines without going through the switchboard at the Kempinski Hotel, where most of the delegation was staying. Canadian technicians also reminded their hosts that they intended to fly in several thousand kilograms worth of equipment – office supplies, sound systems, and communications devices – a few days prior to the Team's arrival.

In meetings with the MFA, the advance team concentrated on the prime minister's agenda, confirming meetings with China's top leaders; signing the nuclear cooperation agreement and six new CIDA agreements; arranging Chrétien's appearance at Peking University, where he would be giving a speech; coordinating arrangements for the welcome dinner to be hosted by Premier Li Peng; and planning the prime minister's keynote address at the CCBC AGM. In addition, the two sides had to organize the contract signing ceremonies at the Kempinski Hotel; the CCBC banquet at the Great Hall; meetings and contract signings in Shanghai; and access for Canadian and Chinese media during the mission.

The team realized that Canada did not have enough officers in Beijing to handle such a big event. It recommended that Canada draw on its Shanghai Consulate, the Hong Kong Trade Office, and the Canadian Chamber of Commerce Office in Taiwan for additional staff and interpreters. One of the officers in Beijing at the time recalled: "After the advance team's visit, we realized that the Team Canada mission would be a real challenge. We would have to help organize the daily activities of hundreds of business executives and their spouses, and do daily diligence with the MFA and the Chinese security people."

The team wanted assurances that the provincial premiers would be properly received. The MFA had said: "During the visit, your provincial leaders and ours can meet separately." The Chinese initially had intended to pair them with lower ranking provincial-level PRC counterparts and did not want them to participate in meetings with the central-level leaders. In later conversation, Zhang Yijun said:

> We had to adjust our thinking. According to Chinese protocol and experience, we should have been matching your provinces with our provinces. But the Canadians were objecting, and I knew your provinces were substantially more important in your system of government. Higher in status than ours. So we had to try to include your provincial premiers in central-level meetings. It wasn't easy to do this.

By the end of September, almost every Canadian province had signed up for the trip. Ontario Premier Bob Rae was still trying to clear his schedule, and only Quebec Premier Jacques Parizeau did not intend to join the mission. He was playing separatist politics, saying he was too busy to go. He said: "Could someone explain to me, from a trade point of view, what importance there is in lining up the Prime Minister of Canada and all the provincial premiers like a row of onions in a photo?" Parizeau announced that Quebec would send its trade minister instead. However, the prime minister had made it clear that only premiers could participate, and a Canadian government official, speaking for Chrétien, said proxies were not permitted on the mission. "There will be no substitutes for first ministers. We are not taking deputy premiers or industry ministers or trade ministers from any province ... They are not ordering pizza here; they can't ask for substitutes." In the end, all the provincial premiers, except Parizeau, joined in the Team Canada mission.

The advance team decided that the Great Hall of the People was actually too big for the banquet, since 1,600 people would only be occupying part of the space, and it recommended making the event more intimate by spreading out the tables and adding decorations, risers, and partitions. The team also went to the Beijing airport to confirm the details for Team Canada's arrival. The prime minister would be met by a mid-level Chinese minister, and he would then lead the Canadian motorcade into Beijing in a limousine, followed by a long string of purple vans, one for each premier and accompanying staff. Back home, the advance team wondered whether the provincial premiers would be willing to trail behind the prime minister's fancy black car in their ordinary purple vans. As one official said, "there will be quite a few large provincial egos sitting in those vans."

A second advance team went to China at the end of October to deal with last minute details. Both sides were now optimistic that the mission would be a success: the Canadians because they had turned the page on Tiananmen and were hoping for a bonanza in trade; and the Chinese, who saw this event as a vindication of their post-Tiananmen policies.

I wrote in my diary:

Ambassador Zhang has been working on the Team Canada mission visit. Also Vice Minister Liu Huaqiu. Talked with both. If the Prime Minister's trip is successful, they deserve a great deal of credit. Also kudos to the political and trade people in the Department. A lot of planning on both sides, although the outcome remains somewhat uncertain.

It was now the end of October, and the government quietly predicted that there would be more than $1 billion in contract signings, especially if the Chinese agreed to buy the two CANDU reactors. When participation numbers for the provincial premiers and the business community were still tentative, Ottawa had kept the news about Team Canada under wraps. By the fall of 1994, however, as the provincial premiers and the business community were lining up to participate and it was certain that China was welcoming the arrival of the mission, the PMO said: "We changed our communications strategy. Now we were in a 'Prime-Ministerial mission mode.' Get the information out to the media and the public. Emphasize Chrétien's trade agenda, and focus on how the mission contributes to Canadian unity by including the premiers. Anticipate criticism of our human rights policy by emphasizing the link between it and trade."

The media fixated on several "stories" criticizing the Team Canada idea. One was obvious: the mission was abandoning human rights in favour of trade, despite the government's denials. The second concentrated on the inclusion of the provincial premiers, calling it a political stunt that would backfire because it contained too many politicians with inflated egos. The third pointed out that the Canadian taxpayers were subsidizing a free trip abroad for government officials and business executives under cover of seeking trade, although it was explicitly stated that the hundreds of business executives were paying their own way.

Ten days before Team Canada's departure, nineteen human rights advocacy groups sent an open letter to the prime minister protesting that the trip amounted to "Canada blessing a brutal Chinese dictatorship." They said that the PRC was continuing its crackdown on dissidents, "suppressing freedoms of expression, association, religion, and repressing calls for independence from minority groups, such as Tibet." The *Montreal Gazette* criticized the Canadian government for ignoring human rights, and it contrasted Canadian policy with that of the United States, where President Clinton had taken office in 1993 with a strong position on human rights in China: "Canada's position, in short, differs from the line taken in the United States, where human rights have been linked to trade policy, and to China's 'most-favoured-nation status' [MFN]. Still, the United States and China did more than $27 billion worth of business last year."

Chrétien responded by saying: "I will raise human rights in private, okay? You don't go out on a square and make a speech. It is all a controlled audience organized by them." And Department officials added: "Trade raises all boats – it opens up China to the values of the outside world." The *Toronto Star*, in a more balanced editorial, observed there was little to gain from the prime minister "making a public scene" in China, and it added:

> That would just invite a cold shoulder from Beijing. But Asian leaders should be warned that Canadian public opinion won't tolerate trading with regimes that flout basic human rights. That truth ought to be hammered home by Chrétien, and by *every* politician, official and businessperson, in meetings with officials at all levels.
>
> We can behave like decent guests, without parking our values at the door.

Spending so many days together, would the prime minister and the nine provincial premiers get along with each other? The premiers came from three political parties, and they had been forever clashing with the federal government over financial and constitutional issues. Many were strong leaders with national reputations, for example, Ralph Klein from Alberta; Roy Romanow from Saskatchewan; Mike Harcourt from British Columbia; and Bob Rae from Ontario. None of those four were Liberals. Except for Catherine Callbeck from Prince Edward Island, they had all been to China before on trade missions. Did they really need the cachet of Team Canada to do business in China, and would they defer to Chrétien during their time in China? Was this trip another government boondoggle, a free ride for 500 people? The mission was costing well over $1 million – although the business participants repeatedly pointed out that they were paying their own way. The Beijing correspondent for the *Globe and Mail* expressed her strong criticism of the mission: "It's going to be a lot of fanfare and photo ops. I don't think they can get anything done of substance. I think it's just one big show, a terrible logistical nightmare. It's pomp and ceremony, and not a lot of content."

Arrival in Beijing

Team Canada arrived in Beijing on November 5. During the long flight, the prime minister remarked that he probably should have gone to China much sooner, since his grandchildren had already visited China. New Brunswick Premier Frank McKenna strolled down the aisle wearing a special red-and-white Team Canada hockey sweater, with a captain's "C" on the front. Nellie Cournoyea, the government leader of the Northwest Territories, handed out Team Canada T-shirts picturing a polar bear peering over the Great Wall of China. There was little fanfare upon their arrival at the Beijing airport, since the official welcome would take place the next day. The prime minister and his wife, Aline, were whisked to their hotel in two black limousines, followed by a lengthy motorcade of nine provincial premiers, two territorial leaders, two mayors, federal politicians, and dozens of government officials crammed into the purple minivans.

The Team Canada Briefing Book provides a description of the official welcoming ceremony the next morning:

> The Prime Minister, accompanied by Premier Li Peng, will walk down the red carpet and mount the dais facing a Guard of Honour representing China's three military services. Madame Chrétien will remain standing at the head of the Canadian entourage (including Minister MacLaren, Secretary of State for Asia-Pacific Raymond Chan, and the premiers). A military band will play the Chinese and Canadian national anthems, while a 19-gun salute is fired. The Commander of the Guard of Honour will report to the Prime Minister and invite him to inspect the Guard of Honour. The Prime Minister, accompanied by Li Peng, will descend from the dais and walk along the red carpet towards the Guard of Honour. The Prime Minister and Premier Li will halt before the army flag, where the Prime Minister will give a brief bow of the head. The Prime Minister will then inspect the Guard of Honour of the three services.[10]

On the first day, they met with President Jiang Zemin and Premier Li Peng. Prime Minister Chrétien signed a number of bilateral agreements, including the nuclear cooperation agreement that would pave the way for the sale of the two CANDU nuclear reactors. He visited the Great Wall, and later attended a dinner hosted by Li. On day two, he spoke with students at Peking University, met with the business representatives at the CCBC Forum, and presided over a dramatic contract signing that totalled $8.5 billion in trade. During those two days in Beijing, the CCBC held its AGM at the Kempinski Hotel with over 400 attendees, organized the upcoming banquet at the Great Hall, and met with Zhu Rongji. Meanwhile, International Trade Minister Roy MacLaren and Secretary of State Raymond Chan held talks with senior Chinese trade officials and with Minister of Foreign Affairs Qian Qichen.

Prime Minister Chrétien's private meeting with Premier Li Peng was originally scheduled for thirty minutes; however, it lasted well over an hour, in good part due to Chrétien's relaxed and folksy manner that set Li, who was known to be awkward in meetings with foreign visitors, more at ease. At the start of his meeting with Chrétien, Li noted that Quebec leader Jacques Parizeau was not in the delegation. Chrétien quickly replied: "Yes, but I am from the federal riding of St. Maurice in Quebec." *"Bonjour, monsieur,"* said Li. *"Merci,"* replied Chrétien. Li then talked about his 1985 visit to Canada and his well-known interest in Canada's hydroelectric technology and CANDU reactors. He also accepted Chrétien's invitation to visit Canada again in 1995 to celebrate the twenty-fifth anniversary of the establishment of diplomatic relations.

Chrétien told Li that the purpose of his visit was to consolidate Canada's political and economic relationship with China by building on the "Four Pillars" policy, making economic cooperation the key for renewed engagement with China. Some obstacles needed to be resolved by both sides, for example, removing restrictions on foreign entry into certain sectors of the Chinese economy, such as telecommunications and insurance, and resuming the stalled negotiations for a foreign investment cooperation agreement. (FIPA). The prime minister hoped that China would stop its underground nuclear tests and refrain from selling nuclear weapons to other countries, and Canada was ready to invite China to take part in bilateral discussions on arms control and peacekeeping. Regarding the forthcoming retrocession of Hong Kong, Chrétien asked for assurances that the rights of the Canadian citizens residing in Hong Kong would be fully protected after 1997.

Later in the day, Chrétien and the premiers met with President Jiang Zemin in Zhongnanhai, the heavily guarded compound in central Beijing that houses China's top Party and government leaders. The *Toronto Star* gave this account of the meeting:

> Birds sang and waterfalls could be heard in the background as the meeting took place. Chrétien, who had met Jiang at a gathering of Pacific leaders in Seattle last year, greeted the president with jocular familiarity.
> Jiang responded in kind, saying he envied Chrétien governing a country the size of Canada, with a mere 28 million people. China has a population of 1.2 billion.

"So you have an easy time," he told Chrétien.

"You think so?" the Prime Minister replied. "I have eight premiers with me, and they represent three political parties. You should try it."

Jiang stiffly replied that there were eight democratic parties in China.

At that point the journalists were ushered out of the room.

In his meeting with Li, Chrétien had raised the issue of human rights, saying that Canada wished to maintain a dialogue with China, and it would not link trade and human rights. The six CIDA development cooperation projects that the two leaders were signing would strengthen women's rights, improve China's legal system by training its judges, and build new links between Canadian and Chinese universities. There was a chilly silence from Li in response to Chrétien's brief remarks, and the Chinese government spokesperson told reporters: "The issue of human rights hasn't been raised. The talks between the two prime ministers were concentrated on how to promote trade." The Canadian media reported: "Critics suggested the Prime Minister had made his case so briefly and tentatively that the Chinese could easily ignore his message. 'There was no debate,' Chrétien acknowledged, 'I said what I said, and Li then moved on to something else.'"

Premiers Rae and Romanow confirmed that they heard Chrétien's remarks about human rights. "I think it was handled correctly and properly," Romanow said. "I'm sure Bob Rae, and everyone in the room, heard it the same way." Rae agreed: "I don't think it could have been clearer. We maintain the right, and not only the right, the obligation to have an open dialogue."

The following day, Chrétien gave his speech to 500 students at Peking University. The university had a reputation for political activism, and many of its students had participated in the 1989 Tiananmen demonstrations. His speechwriters had carefully prepared a talk for him that introduced Canada to the students, together with a message of cooperation and re-engagement. "We know he's speaking to a handpicked audience. They've been thoroughly briefed by their political mentors. We're not going to change many opinions, but it's an opportunity to be heard. These students are part of China's future elite. And it plays well back home." Chrétien concluded his talk with the following statement:

> It is your generation that will change the face of China in this time of transition. You will bring an ancient culture into the 21st century in a way that respects your proud history. You will be the architects of international engagement for the next century – the century which many people believe will be called the "Pacific Century." As Prime Minister of a Pacific country, I thank you for this opportunity to speak to you of our friendship and our future together – our two countries, Canada and China.

The two-day CCBC meetings began on the evening of November 7 with a networking reception attended by a group of business representatives and federal and provincial officials, chaired by Senator James Kelleher and hosted by the CCBC Board. Kelleher had been minister of international trade in the Mulroney government, and now he was a CCBC board member. The PRC's minister of the State Economic and Trade Commission pointed out China's major economic achievements, including its high GDP growth, increased exposure in international markets, rising foreign direct investment, and the adoption of reforms to enable China to obtain entry into the GATT. However, he also said China continued to suffer from high inflation, and it still needed to undergo major financial, taxation, and enterprise reforms.

In the afternoon, the prime minister fielded questions from an audience of several hundred business representatives at the CCBC Prime Minister's Forum, moderated by Senator Austin. Issues discussed included the removal of trade barriers encountered by Canadian small and medium-sized enterprises (SMEs), the need for clarification of Chinese taxation regulations, and the lack of transparency in relations with their Chinese counterparts. Canadian business executives criticized Ottawa for failing to provide adequate export financing, pointing out that, if Canada truly wanted to be competitive in the China market, it had to make additional funding available for large projects, with better concessional financing.

Chrétien told his audience that International Trade Minister MacLaren had asked for more money for export financing, but the government's financial specialists, led by Finance Minister Paul Martin Jr., objected to the cost. Martin, who would later succeed Chrétien as prime minister, had said: "In the end, the government cannot be the banker for everybody." China already was the number two recipient of Canadian government loans in support of trade, and an expansion of export financing to China would provoke criticism back in Canada. Chrétien said that business and industry organizations should press Canadian banks to become more active in export financing, and he also encouraged the business community to make better use of existing government trade promotion programs.

Signing the Contracts

The highlight of Team Canada's visit was the contract signing ceremony in the ballroom of the Kempinski Hotel. The representatives of the Canadian companies and their Chinese partners were introduced to the prime minister and to the rest of the official Canadian delegation. Fifty-four companies participated in the one-hour session. They signed $8.5 billion in contracts, agreements, and memoranda of understanding, including the MOU for the sale of the two CANDU reactors, worth $3.5 billion. The Department provided the following instructions for the contract signing ceremony:

> On the Prime Minister's arrival at 15:30 an announcement will be made in English, French and Chinese as he enters, and then he will work his way from table to table in a clockwise direction. He will leave the room through the same door in which he entered.
>
> The Prime Minister will take one minute with each firm; to witness the signing, offer congratulations and be photographed. Depending on the province of the Canadian company, the appropriate provincial premier will also be included in the photographs.
>
> After shaking hands with the Prime Minister, and the Chinese Minister of Internal Trade, Zhang Haoruo, a commemorative photograph will be taken of each company with the Prime Minister. Returning to

the individual signing tables, each company will be presented with a bottle of British Columbia champagne in order to toast the success of their ventures.

"It was a very exciting day," the prime minister said after the completion of the signings. Asked how many jobs the deals would create in Canada, he replied: "I don't want to put a finger on it, but everyone knows it creates thousands of jobs. The figures are there. They are extremely big and extremely diverse, across our country." CCBC officials were ecstatic. Austin said: "We were hoping we would be successful, but we never expected we could sign over eight billion dollars in deals. It was remarkable." Following the PMO's instructions, the Canadian government had for weeks deliberately downplayed the expected dollar value of the signed contracts. The figure had been fixed at $1 billion, because "a billion dollars in deals" sounded very good and would not embarrass the prime minister. Anything above a billion was a public relations coup, and the Department had written: "We strongly recommend that, while the figures are very encouraging, we will continue to lowball the figure at $1 billion plus. Then we can pull a few extra rabbits out of the hat at the last minute."

Following the contract signing, Zhu Rongji met with the business delegates in the Great Hall. He reported that the total dollar value had surpassed that of the recent German trade mission and the mission was a great success. In response to questions about China's economy and future trade prospects, Zhu commented:

Yes, there was 20 per cent inflation, but China's economic development is stable, and we will not have a serious inflation problem in the future. Sectors such as energy, transportation, and raw materials will remain under state control ... Only 15 per cent of enterprises are privately owned ... China has imported from Canada an accumulated total of one hundred million tons of grain, valued at US$10 billion, and China will continue to import wheat from Canada ... China plans to allow some foreign banks to engage in RMB business. I hope the first one can be a Canadian bank, and you should make great efforts ... As for insurance, China has approved AIG of the US and Tokyo Maritime Insurance to operate in China. I hope the third one will be a Canadian company, the fourth, European. You can see that we place Canada before Europe.

Zhu then announced that Manulife had received approval to operate in China. Austin added the following comments:

CCBC had invited about forty-five business leaders to meet with Zhu Rongji. I had seated Manulife President Dominic D'Alessandro far away from the head table. Zhu asked if anyone from Manulife was present. Dominic stood up at the back of the room. Then Zhu told him that Manulife would be the third foreign insurance company to receive a joint venture licence. This was a special gift to Canada.

The Banquet

Chrétien was in an ebullient mood. As "Team Captain of the All-Star Team," he congratulated the CCBC for the mission's success, and he remarked how proud he was of "the most successful, unprecedented, largest, and highest-level trade mission to China." The visit's positive outcome prompted him to declare that the two countries could reach $20 billion in trade by the year 2000, a huge jump from the $4.5 billion in 1994. Chrétien recalls that he also took the opportunity during the banquet to tell Li Peng about democracy:

With thousands of people seated in the Great Hall, I said to him: "In a democracy, you know, you have to get elected. To get elected, you have to be nice to everybody you meet, to say hello and shake their hands. It's rough. Come with me, I'll show you how we do it.

We got up and started moving from table to table, shaking hands and making jokes. Everybody was laughing and applauding. They were so amazed. "Look how well you're doing," I said to Li. "You'd make a great street campaigner, though I guess it might be a big job if you have 700 million voters."[11]

No one had expected that Li would stay for very long. The night before, he had hosted the state dinner for the delegation, at which Chrétien said he hoped Li would attend the CCBC banquet the next night. Li said maybe he'd be there for fifteen minutes, and it was possible that Vice Premier Zhu Rongji would then take his place. In fact, Li stayed for the entire two hours. He was struck by the novelty of holding such a banquet at the Great Hall, and he was charmed by Chrétien's folksy manner. The Chinese security people were astonished when Li decided to stay. The Chinese MFA officials were pleased, since they had been trying to rehabilitate Li, who had been called the "Butcher of Beijing" by many foreigners for his actions during the Tiananmen crisis in 1989, when Li had ordered the PLA troops to clear Tiananmen Square by force.

Seating arrangements for the banquet posed a challenge for the CCBC organizers, since they had to satisfy the egos of the key participants and the requirements of diplomatic protocol. It was a difficult task, but Austin and Drake were able to work out the very complicated seating arrangements:

> The head table included the Prime Minister, Premier Li Peng, Vice Premier Zhu Rongji, State Councillor Song Ping, Minister Zhang Haoruo, Minister MacLaren, Secretary of State Raymond Chan, Senator Jack Austin, CCBC Chairman André Desmarais, and Ambassador Fred Bild.
>
> We organized ten head tables of ten persons each. One for the Prime Minister and guests, then nine for the provincial premiers, numbered from 1–9 in order of their entry into Confederation. At each table, we had a Canadian government official and a Chinese counterpart. We had a problem with the NWT leader, Nellie Cournoyea. We wanted to put the NWT and Yukon territories together at one table, because they were the smallest units in the delegation. But she refused to sit there. So in the end we had two five-person tables and eight ten-person tables, plus the Prime Minister's table.
>
> We had 150 tables in all, with 1,596 guests. We had no more seats, but Canadian businesspeople kept showing up at the last minute. One was so incensed when we said there were no more seats that he actually lifted up the CCBC person at the door and shook her, saying: "I have to be at this banquet. Get me a ticket."

We finally yielded, sold him one, and we found him a spot at a table in the back.

About two-thirds were paid seats. There were quite a few freeloaders: Canadian officials, media, and Chinese guests. We also sold corporate tables. A table of ten was $2,000 dollars. Since the Great Hall charged $110 dollars per person for the dinner, plus incidentals, the CCBC ended up making a lot of money.

The unruly behaviour of Canadian businessmen caught Chinese security people by surprise. During the banquet they kept getting up, walking around, clinking glasses, making toasts, and going right up to Li Peng to say "hi." This made the Chinese security people nervous. We had to keep reassuring them that our businessmen were having a good time, and were not a threat.

Shanghai and Hong Kong

Team Canada then travelled to Shanghai, where an additional fifteen contracts were signed, with a value of $329 million. Canada presented the mayor of Shanghai with a red cedar totem pole, carved by a famous Haida artist, to mark the twinning of the ports of Vancouver and Shanghai. At the conclusion of the ceremony, which featured three Haida dance performances and a Chinese lion dance, the prime minister observed: "Now there will always be a piece of Canada here in Shanghai." Twenty years later, however, after a careful search, the Canadian Consulate General in Shanghai was unable to find any trace of this piece of Canada in Shanghai. That evening, the delegation toured the historic Bund and admired the emerging Pudong skyline with its television tower, Shanghai's answer to the CN Tower in Toronto. Later, several of the provincial premiers took to the dance floor in the famous jazz bar at the iconic Peace Hotel, where Premier Rae delighted his audience with an upbeat piano performance.

In the more relaxed Shanghai atmosphere, without the pressure of so many Beijing high-level meetings, the provincial premiers reflected on what they had accomplished in media interviews and with plenty of photo opportunities. Rae said: "There's no reason why we can't keep doing this. The Team Canada model is an excellent way to get trade results because it maximizes Canada's trade opportunities." He added: "Canada is too small. We're only 28 million people in a great wide world, and we've got to work together." New Brunswick Premier Frank McKenna praised "the positive, congenial environment which made it possible to remove irritants between us and work together for the good of the country." PEI's Catherine Callbeck asked: "How else could someone from a small province like mine have access to the most important leaders of China?" Newfoundland's Clyde Wells observed that there was a great spirit of cooperation between the premiers and Jean Chrétien: "The Prime Minister is the spokesman for the country. Indeed, it is almost a relief that he is carrying the ball. This is a team effort, and that means we don't have to rush like lemmings to a microphone whenever anyone makes a statement." Alberta's Ralph Klein said: "Notwithstanding the absence of Quebec, we are together. We are a single country. The Prime Minister is the door-opener, and I guess we are the ushers."

The Canadians left for Hong Kong on November 10. The government wanted to "show the flag" to remind China's leaders that Canada expected a smooth transition for the retrocession of Hong Kong in 1997, one that would not jeopardize the status of the Canadian citizens living there or disrupt the significant trade that existed between Canada and Hong Kong. It was Remembrance Day, and the prime minister visited the Sai Wan War Cemetery to honour the over 2,000 Canadian troops who, in a hopeless cause, had been left to defend Hong Kong in November 1941. Altogether, 283 lay buried in that Hong Kong cemetery, 1,600 had been captured, at least 135 died in prison in Japan, and 550 never returned home.

The next day, Chrétien addressed the Canadian Chamber of Commerce. Its members sought reassurance that the Canadian citizens in Hong Kong could continue working and living there after 1997. Chrétien had raised the issue of Hong Kong in Beijing. He told the Chamber that the Chinese leaders he met in Beijing said they were committed to preserving Hong Kong's unique character and vital economic role after 1997. Li Peng had said that "we need Hong Kong as it is," and neither the PRC nor Canada wanted to jeopardize their economic links with Hong Kong. Canada's two-way trade with Hong Kong had reached almost $2 billion in 1993, nearly half as much as the Canada-PRC trade for that year, and a significant part of trade with the PRC was being carried out through Hong Kong. Li added: "The territory will continue to be a primary international centre for Asia, and for the whole world."

The people of Hong Kong were concerned about their fate after 1997, when an authoritarian government in China would rule Hong Kong. In 1994, it was still a British colony, although it had most of the trappings of a democracy: a civil society, open media, political parties, rule of law, free elections, and a merit-based bureaucracy. It only lacked a fully elected legislature based on universal suffrage, with an elected executive. Could Hong Kong's near democracy survive in an authoritarian China? In response to their concerns, the prime minister repeated his in-China mantra, that trade brings improvements in human rights:

> I am disturbed when I see that the public debate has become one of human rights versus trade. We must have both.
>
> I am convinced that the more contact China has with other nations, the more open it will become. We have seen in so many countries that dialogue with other nations, and with people from other nations, breaks down walls and inevitably promotes greater respect and tolerance for diverse views and opinions.

Before Team Canada left Hong Kong, and before its members said farewell to each other, the prime minister basked in the Team's achievements:

> This is an All-Star Team. As we say in hockey, it has a lot of depth, and even more strength on the bench. And it sure knows how to score.
>
> I know that together on this trip we have accomplished things that I, or the federal government, could never have accomplished alone.
>
> For me it has been the experience of a lifetime. My colleagues and I have worked hard, travelled far, and even had a little bit of fun together over the last few days. And I think the results have been good, very good for Canada.

After the Visit

The Canadian media mostly reacted positively. *The Globe and Mail* wrote: "The boosterism of the chatter about 'Team Canada' is to be regretted, but the collective effort really was a success." While there was "a good dollop of wishful thinking on our part, the amounts involved and the sheer diplomatic weight of these deals are nothing to be sneezed at in our usual Canuckish way. This week's humongous 'Team Canada' mission to China was, no matter how you cut it, ground-breaking big league stuff." The *Financial Post* wrote: "For Prime Minister Jean Chrétien, his first foray to the Pacific Rim has been both a political and a business coup that could pay dividends for federal foreign policy, and create a new concept for selling Canadian business abroad. [Newfoundland Premier] Clyde Wells has no regrets. He says the mission, unprecedented in size and scope, has created a welcome mat for Canadian business in China. It has signalled its importance as a trading nation to China, and has helped boost morale back home by showing that government leaders of all stripes could work together." *The Toronto Star* noted: "After years of regional rivalries, federal-provincial fights, constitutional squabbles and general crankiness, Canadians like Chrétien's notion of teamwork. It produced big gains in China. The even bigger returns, if Chrétien and the premiers can continue what they have begun, will come at home."

Less enthusiastic accounts focused on three areas. First, the $8.5 billion of signed "deals" overstated the actual trade results. Less than half were real contracts, and the rest were letters of intent and memoranda of agreement – incomplete deals that could require months of further negotiation. Also, many of the signed contracts had been in preparation for a long time prior to the trip, and critics said they would have been signed anyway, without Team Canada's help. Second, the prime minister and the delegation barely mentioned human rights, since it was clear the Chinese leaders did not intend to engage in any discussion over rights. By ignoring rights, many said Team Canada had sacrificed Canadian values and principles just for material gain. Canada was also criticized for the large low-interest loans that it was extending to China to enable it to buy the CANDU reactors, and because spent fuel could be used in the future by a communist country to make nuclear weapons.

The journalist Andrew Coyne wrote that the mission "was an embarrassment of premiers, a many-headed beast known as 'Team Canada,' in which the task of representing Canada abroad is no longer assigned to the government of Canada, but is instead a joint effort of the Prime Minister and the premiers." He added: "It would not be fair to say that the Prime Minister had abandoned principle in his dealings with China, since he does not appear to have started with any." Thomas d'Aquino, president of the Business Council on National Issues and a member of the Team Canada delegation, took issue with Coyne's remarks: "Consider the results of the mission. Would so much have been accomplished in the absence of the Team Canada juggernaut? Hardly. As to Mr. Coyne's point that the Team Canada approach is somehow subverting the federal government's role in international trade, I would not be so concerned. Nothing that I saw during the Chinese trip left any doubt in my mind that the Prime Minister was in charge."[12] The *Ottawa Citizen* suggested Team Canada could be a "one-time wonder – it might not herald the dawning of a new era in the way Canada will drum up new business." Most business leaders said the trip was a landmark, but some thought it was a unique event, possibly unlikely to be replicated in China again, or elsewhere.

On November 28, the Department prepared a list of speaking points for Cabinet on the mission's results, noting that it was unprecedented in scale and content, had achieved the highest level of business ever transacted in a government-organized mission, and was a major communications achievement:

> In terms of interesting the media in the efforts we made, and in generating the welcome positive spin, we need to build our efforts further. The demise of human rights on our foreign policy agenda has been exaggerated. Dialogue on the development of economic ties can and will continue while the human rights dialogue proceeds. We choose to avoid megaphones, but neither are we a doormat for repressive policies.
>
> We are not consigned in Asian minds as only a provider of rocks and logs. We can deal in value-added, high-tech, and enhanced service

areas. There was some scepticism over what was doing "hard business," and what might be wishful thinking. In fact, the great majority
of signings represented either firm sales contracts or a solid intent to do
business, subject only to details.

The Department recommended that in future Ottawa should
use the Team Canada model for repeat trade missions to China and
to Asia. There were many reasons for its success. It had a powerful
political impact because it was headed by the prime minister and
nine provincial premiers. The great growth and potential of the
China market, together with the complementarity of the two economies, were important starting points. The partnership between
the Canadian government and its private sector (the Department
and the CCBC) made it possible to sign billions of dollars of contracts. The PRC's centralized economic and political system gave
Canadian companies direct access to the top level of PRC economic decision-making. China had shown it was ready to embrace
the global economy and to welcome foreign companies, and it was
willing to develop a new post-Tiananmen economic partnership
with Canada.

Planning for the mission had started in early 1994, with a series
of high-level visits that set the table for Team Canada. Behind the
scenes, key individuals on both sides stepped up to make it happen, among them Jack Austin, Earl Drake, Mike Harcourt, Bob
Rae, André Desmarais, Howard Balloch, André Ouellet, Li Peng,
Zhang Yijun, Liu Huaqiu, Zhu Rongji, and Zou Jiahua. The decisive element was Prime Minister Chrétien's commitment and his
willingness to partner with the provincial premiers and the Canadian business community.

The provincial premiers were invited five to six months in
advance of the trip. The CCBC, which had a strong presence in Beijing and access to the highest levels of government in both Canada
and China, was responsible for organizing the over 400 business
representatives. The mission planners benefitted from the early
assignment of specific tasks and from the provision of the extra
personnel and resources that were needed for the mission. The Beijing Embassy, Shanghai Consulate, and Hong Kong Commission

did an excellent job with the on-site planning and execution of the mission.

There was a lot of "spin" involved. The PMO was all over the trip to ensure that the prime minister would always be the centre of every event. To secure a better vantage point for obtaining the best photo-ops, it installed risers that blocked the view of the head tables for some of the guests. Images of the prime minister talking with top Chinese leaders and greeting people at their tables were more important than proper sight lines for fifty or so of the dinner guests. Staging plenty of photo opportunities was a mission priority. During the trip, the Canadian public saw many images of the prime minister: Chrétien climbing to the top of the Great Wall; Chrétien riding a bicycle in Shanghai; Chrétien together with the provincial premiers, and so on. It was the PMO who had trumpeted the phrase "nine billion dollars in deals made," pumping up the ongoing trade negotiations into one big event and making Team Canada the presumptive model for future trade with China.

In March 1995, Earl Drake and the CCBC followed up with the business community. He asked "whether that big, flashy event was just a brief show, or was it a sustained effort?" Federal and provincial governments were continuing to show support for the idea, although at a less intense level. Could such a large-scale mission ever be repeated? Team Canada had cost a lot of money, and many thought it unlikely that the federal government would do it again on such a large scale.

Drake said that "follow-up" meant that the business community now had to sustain the momentum, apart from whatever the government intended to do. In the spring of 1995, the CCBC and the Canadian Chamber of Commerce jointly sponsored a series of day-long business meetings in six cities – Vancouver, Calgary, Winnipeg, Toronto, Montreal, and Halifax – on the theme "The China Conferences: Building Team Canada." Over 800 members of the business community attended. Drake urged them to build on the success of Team Canada, saying that the mission had provided the high-level contacts that Canadian business needed. "All the best efforts of the Canadian government have had only limited success to date. Now the initiative has to come from the business community itself." He reminded members that the CCBC was holding its fifteenth AGM in Montreal later in the year to coincide with the twenty-fifth anniversary of the establishment of diplomatic relations with China. Prime Minister Chrétien was planning to attend, as were several top Chinese leaders, including Premier Li Peng. This event would give the business community another opportunity to follow up on the important new contacts that it had established during the Team Canada visit.

Li came to Canada in the fall of 1995 to speak at the annual CCBC meeting and participate in the anniversary celebrations. He spent six hours with the prime minister, and told Chrétien that China was ready to finalize the purchase of the two CANDU reactors, the $3.5 billion deal that had been announced during the Team Canada visit. Li also said, to the delight of the assembled business audience, that there were big opportunities for Canada in telecommunications, potash, and pulp and paper. The Chinese press wrote positive accounts of Li's visit, and *Wen Hui Bao* reported that his reception in Canada "shows that Canada-China relations are entering the best period in their history."[13]

In the next seven years, the government sent three more Team Canada missions to China. The fourth one in 2001 had close to 800 participants, the biggest mission Canada would ever send abroad and the largest ever received by China. They signed $7 billion of contracts, slightly less than the 1994 mission. Zhu Rongji was the official host, and Chrétien was his guest. However, 2001 turned out to be the last of the Team Canada visits to China. Ottawa could not sustain taking government personnel away from their regular duties to spend months of their time organizing these visits, and it was unlikely that nine provincial premiers would again join with the prime minister on a trade mission.

One CEO said that times had changed:

In 1994, we needed the Prime Minister to get access to the top Chinese companies and organizations. That access will always be important, for sure, but I'm now getting more of those contracts on my own, and don't really need the Prime Minister's help. The 2001 trip was too big, too chaotic. Too much time wasted. Business with China is decentralizing, and I'll do what our competitors in other countries are now doing, that is, negotiating more contracts with regional and local clients.

According to Balloch, the sheer size of the 2001 Team Canada delegation had forced the Embassy staff to begin planning for the 2001 mission a full year in advance of the actual visit. He recalled:

> We were well aware that many business leaders were tired of being dragged around the world on missions that were so large that no real attention would be paid to their special interests, and during which they were going to spend a large proportion of their time either waiting for some event to start, or as apparent "extras" for political ceremonies that offered them no particular benefit."[14]

While the 2001 mission was a political success and yielded substantial contracts, it also was the Team's last hurrah. Future trade missions would be far smaller, without prime ministerial participation. The 1994 Team Canada visit to China had reset bilateral relations, confirming that trade would be the first "pillar" in the restored relationship. Economic links now had trumped Canada's human rights agenda, and the idea that Canadian secular missionaries of engagement and political modernization could still "mentor" China had fallen by the wayside. The new relationship would be tougher, less enthusiastic, not so path breaking, and more challenging. By the time the Conservatives, led by Stephen Harper, took power in 2006, Canada had fallen further behind its competitors in the China market, and the spectacular results of the first Team Canada mission had by then become a distant memory.

chapter nine

Challenging China on Human Rights

Trade and human rights are the two constants in Canada's relations with China. Two-way trade grew from a few hundred million dollars in 1970 to over $100 billion in 2020. However, Canadian attempts to improve China's human rights practices have foundered. Beijing continues to curtail individual freedoms, jail its dissidents, and reject outside criticism of its behaviour. In this chapter, we describe how Canada tried to develop an effective rights dialogue with China following the killings at Tiananmen, and why those efforts failed.

Before Tiananmen, Canadian efforts were modest. The government raised Canadian concerns during official visits, and it protested whenever China clamped down on dissidents. Prime Minister Mulroney acquired an international reputation for his criticism of apartheid in South Africa, although in relations with China he focused on trade, while mostly standing back on rights.

Tiananmen changed the discourse. Canadian government criticism escalated, and China barely responded. Ottawa kept rethinking its strategy, employing an array of tactics that had little impact on China's behaviour. It tried strong public statements from Canadian leaders, made démarches to senior Chinese officials, asked about imprisoned dissidents, and co-sponsored resolutions at the United Nations condemning PRC practices. After Ambassador Earl Drake had returned to Beijing, he was unable to meet with China's leaders. The best the Canadian Embassy could do was to improve links in education and develop people-to-people relations at the local level. Searching for an effective human rights strategy, Canada then turned to legal training, institution building, and governance programs that might bring long-term value change.

Meanwhile, China was clarifying its position on rights – that they were universal and granted by sovereign states, not by God or by birth. Economic and social rights took precedence over civil and political ones. Historical, cultural, and ideological factors made China different from Western models. It was a violation of China's sovereignty for foreigners to interfere in China's domestic affairs. In 1990, Deng Xiaoping told visiting former prime minister Trudeau that adopting Western models of democracy and human rights would bring political chaos to China.

Aside from Chinese resistance, several other issues made it difficult to carry out an effective rights strategy. The Mulroney Cabinet was split between those advocating strong human rights measures and those who wanted to focus on trade. NGOs, the media, and members of the China policy community complained that they were often excluded from the policymaking process. Two Canadian ambassadors, Earl Drake and Fred Bild, felt that Ottawa was not providing enough funds to the Embassy to carry out activities in support of human rights. While the Department said that Canada "was in the lead" among Western nations in developing a post-Tiananmen human rights strategy, informed observers considered this assertion to be Canadian hubris.

When Jean Chrétien and the Liberals took power in late 1993, Canada abandoned direct confrontation with China over rights, and trade took command. Chrétien avoided public human rights rhetoric, preferring to hold private discussions with China's leaders. His foreign minister, Lloyd Axworthy, a rights activist, had to soften his criticism of PRC practices. In 1997, after seven years of failing to pass resolutions at the UN criticizing China's rights practices, Canada chose to establish an annual bilateral rights dialogue with Beijing. The dialogue would bring senior officials from both sides together "to discuss common rights issues." After nine years, that rights dialogue was deemed a failure, and it was suspended.

A decade after Tiananmen, Canada had not moved China on rights. It had an unwilling partner and was unable to deliver a strategy that could predictably change Chinese values and practices. Ottawa began with strong confrontation and ended with dialogue and collaboration. Neither strategy was successful. When the Conservatives came to power in 2006, Prime Minister Harper adopted a hard line on rights, distancing the government from previous Liberal policy. Five years later, he scrapped that agenda because it, too, had failed. The Conservatives then reverted to the same measures that the Liberals had tried before, also without success.

Could there have been a better outcome with a different strategy? Or was the attempt to change China's practices doomed from the outset, because Canada was trying to do the impossible – exporting value change to a country whose leaders flatly opposed those efforts?

If the Western states are willing to listen, then China is ready to enter into a proper dialogue on human rights. It is time for the world to get over Tiananmen.

— PRC Vice Minister of Foreign Affairs Liu Huaqiu, 1993

Before Tiananmen

Pierre Trudeau had said: "Democracy and human rights are essential, but the eradication of poverty is more important. We sent missionaries to China in the past, but that is not our role today. What we can do is to bring China into our international institutions, and wait for it to develop." Before Tiananmen, strong criticism of China's human rights practices was not a Canadian priority.[1] The primary target was Moscow and the Soviet satellite countries, where dissidents such as Andrei Sakharov, Aleksandr Solzhenitsyn, Vaclav Havel, and the Solidarity movement in Poland were fueling efforts to push for democracy and human rights behind the Iron Curtain. In comparison, the Chinese dissident community was small in number, poorly organized, and well contained by the party-state.

In 1980, I wrote in my diary:

Feel I should be more critical about human rights in China, yet hesitate to believe that China will turn out like the Russians, who are still waiting for democracy more than three generations after the Revolution. Sadly, the Democracy Wall movement in Beijing has been crushed, and what passes for Chinese reform is all economic. Nothing political.

The road to democracy and human rights is hard. It has been almost
70 years for Moscow. How long will it be for Beijing?

The appearance of the Democracy Wall in Beijing in 1978 raised
hopes for political liberalization, as thousands of citizens gathered there, putting up posters critical of the government. It was a
remarkable event, highlighted by Wei Jingsheng's extraordinary
poster, *The Fifth Modernization*, calling for democracy, freedom, and
human rights. The Wall stayed up for a year, heartening advocates
of political reform, but Wei was arrested and imprisoned, and this
brief wave of political activism came to an abrupt end. The Wall's
rise and fall, the arrests of dissidents, and statements by China's
leaders that Western-style political change was not on China's
agenda squelched talk in China of human rights. In 1982, when
I was lecturing at Peking University on the social and political
changes taking place in the Soviet Union, the audience listened in
stony silence to my description of what was happening next door,
knowing that in China the opportunity for democracy and human
rights had been postponed indefinitely.[2]

During this early period, official Canadian concerns over
human rights in China were limited to add-ons during ministerial
visits and occasional formal representations about the fate of dissidents, especially following the creation of the Democracy Wall
and Wei's subsequent arrest and imprisonment. Canadian government action was restrained, unlike what would happen after
Tiananmen. Each minister knew the ritual: when in China, do the
business you are tasked to do as your top priority; then at the end,
or at some mid-point during the visit, briefly but earnestly talk
about human rights.

I was in Moscow in 1988, just as the Soviet Bloc was on the
brink of collapse. The sudden rise of civil society was threatening
the existing political order in communist party-states. Soviet dissidents had become legitimate reformers, advocating democracy,
freedom, and human rights. In the prelude to what was about to
happen at Tiananmen on June 4, 1989, many Canadians thought
China would follow along the path of the collapsing communist
bloc – if not regime change, then at least partial liberalization and

an opening for civil and political rights. Students were asking for more individual freedom from Party control, the people in the large cities were supporting them, and China's political leaders were temporarily paralyzed and split into factions.

After June 4, 1989

June 4, 1989 put human rights into the centre of bilateral relations. The Canadian public, having witnessed televised images of PLA soldiers shooting their own citizens, was shocked, angered, and dismayed. Western governments accelerated their criticism from afar, focusing on the repression and execution of Chinese dissidents, the suppression of individual freedoms, the absence of legal standards, arbitrary arrests and detentions without trial, the use of torture, and the mistreatment of Chinese ethnic minorities.

Could Canada create a strategy to address these abuses? According to the Department official responsible for human rights policy for China, "after Tiananmen we were being pressured by the media and the public. We had to find a better way to approach China on rights." He continued:

> It was my job to maintain the bilateral file on human rights in the PRC. Keep a record of what is happening there; know what other countries were doing; communicate with our Embassy in Beijing; meet with our other government departments, and with rights NGOs, China specialists, and the media; prepare materials for the PMO, PCO, and various ministers, and for meetings with representatives of the Chinese Embassy; plus meeting regularly with my superior officers in the China section to discuss China policy.
>
> We had a patchwork of policies, a strategy that was always in process and never satisfying, and a bilateral partner who wanted to have nothing to do with "rights talk."

The Department tried a dozen ways to deal with human rights, each having some merit, none of them effective. All were framed by the idea that opening up China exposed it to the values of the developed world. Industrialization and modernization were bringing capital markets and property rights to China, creating rising expectations on our part that this shift could transform Chinese thinking and behaviour. We thought we could change China just by "being there" with our modern Western values. At the Embassy in Beijing in the 1970s, we called this "peaceful evolution." It was value change, almost by osmosis. The Chinese leadership never liked it, since it implied that Western democracy and human rights, which challenged the Party's rule, were inevitable outcomes of China's modernization.

Twenty years after recognition, and a decade after China had embraced capital markets, "peaceful evolution" had achieved little traction. Paramount Leader Deng Xiaoping made it clear that the Party would use whatever means it had to prevent the Westernization of China's political system. After June 4, strong criticisms of Beijing's human rights abuses by Prime Minister Mulroney and Foreign Minister Clark, along with other Western leaders, had failed to move the Chinese leadership. Following the suspension of high-level visits to China, official dialogue dried up, and in Beijing the Canadian ambassador found it difficult to talk with anyone. In Ottawa, the Chinese Embassy, normally a focal point for Canadian government démarches criticizing Chinese rights policies, had temporarily shut down in the wake of Tiananmen.

Ottawa's arsenal of human rights actions had to meet two criteria: first, what could Ottawa do to "show blood" to satisfy the many Canadians who wanted to punish China for the killings at Tiananmen; and second, how to get China to improve its human rights practices. "We tried our best. Punishing China meant imposing sanctions and employing angry rhetoric, what some called 'megaphone diplomacy.' It made us feel good, but it had almost no impact on China's leaders. We needed a strategy that could change people's behaviour."

We looked at our options. Strong statements by our Prime Minister and Foreign Minister made us feel better, but that just bounced off China. The same went for sponsoring resolutions at the UN condemning Beijing. Collaborating with like-minded countries was an option. We had a better idea of what others were doing, but as a united group we still had no leverage. Linking trade and development assistance to improvements in human rights was an attractive tactic, yet that turned out to be impossible to implement. CIDA programs exposed China to Canadian values, but their influence tended to be local and long term. They did not directly impact China's leaders, and Canadians were looking for immediate results. Consultations with the Canadian policy community provided us with public input, but that did not produce workable strategies.

Departmental officials were instructed to raise human rights concerns at every encounter with their PRC counterparts. The Department compiled lists of political prisoners, made démarches to the Chinese Embassy in Ottawa about missing activists, canvassed Canadian NGOs and members of the Canadian ethnic Chinese communities on how to approach China, and consulted with CIDA and Canadian universities on how rights initiatives could be incorporated into their activities in China. Efforts were made at the United Nations to co-sponsor an annual resolution criticizing China. Responding to pressure from rights advocates, the government prepared several scenarios that would link export trade financing to improvements in human rights, but that linkage never happened. According to the Department, the results were disappointing:

> We had no leverage, no way to obtain the breakthroughs that many Canadians expected. Maybe if we actually could tie trade and aid to improvements in human rights. But we did not want to hurt trade or the aid programs. In the end, it was up to the officers at the Post to continue to raise human rights concerns in their daily duties without expecting any dramatic outcomes.

At the Post

The test of a human rights strategy is how it is received in the field. According to Drake, Ottawa was struggling in its efforts to find the

right strategy and tactics, and it was up to the Post to take charge
of human rights tactics:

> Headquarters didn't have a specific strategy for pushing China on
> human rights, other than the June 30 Statement, and the Chinese
> seemed to be hiding from us. We had an officer track what was happen-
> ing. We collected the names of those arrested and secured information
> regarding their trials.
>
> We compared our findings with what other embassies were doing,
> and also with the information that the journalists were getting. It was a
> low-key exercise. We were trying to get information and also trying to
> tell the Chinese what they could do with human rights that might have
> an impact on the outside world. We helped a few dissidents get out,
> processing as many as we could.

The Post did not have a specific human rights working group.
Human rights were the responsibility of the political section,
part of one officer's job. He reported to a weekly meeting of
all Embassy sections, chaired by the ambassador. They had no
"script" to follow, no strategy mapped out besides helping dissidents, making démarches to officials, consulting with other
embassies, and sending information back to Ottawa about the
situation there. The cultural affairs counsellor focused on keeping open contacts with the intellectual and artistic communities.
In her work, she combined "people-to-people" relations with
human rights initiatives:

> The mandate for the Embassy cultural affairs section was to support
> "people-to-people" relations. It was important to distinguish our pro-
> gram from the work of the political section. We were not just an infor-
> mation gathering exercise for the political people. We talked about
> human rights issues and policies almost obsessively the first six months
> I was there.

She spent most of her time in the provinces, away from Beijing,
living on university campuses, contacting local television stations,
and organizing Canadian studies events. She recalls:

I visited all regions of China, probably two dozen universities, and most of the time lived on the university campus, usually with one or two assistants, Chinese or Canadian, from the cultural section. This also provided me with an opportunity to find out what was really happening. Sometimes Chinese faculty themselves would talk to me during these visits. At other times, Canadian students and teachers who lived on the campuses would talk freely and tell me what had happened.

I did some reporting on these things, though that was not the main purpose of my visits. I also set up a link with the Amnesty International office in London, and through the diplomatic bag sent confidential information as regularly as I could concerning particular intellectuals who had disappeared or been arrested. This was done very quietly, and not even discussed within the Embassy. It was not at all large scale, but may have contributed a bit to the information collecting being done by Amnesty.

Officers managed to talk with Chinese colleagues at the working level, in CIDA programs, and in the universities. This discussion helped the Chinese to understand why Canada had taken the action it had, the way in which policy was made in Canada, Parliament's role, interest and pressure groups, the legal system, and the Canadian media.

There was a lot of discussion with other embassies. Our educational and cultural program was fairly exemplary, in that we had many direct links to ordinary institutions and people at the local level. In the first year after Tiananmen, we actually increased the level of contact and activity in terms of sending Chinese to Canada. The Americans, however, had a kind of moratorium for at least a year, and the French stopped all their programs.

In the fall of 1990, a visiting Canadian parliamentary delegation met with the National People's Congress (NPC), China's national legislative body. The NPC officials told them that Western media had distorted the events at Tiananmen and were ignoring the fact that many PLA soldiers were killed. They said: "The events of June 4, 1989 are about regime security, not human rights. Alternatives to the crackdown would have been chaos and civil war. Canada should understand our position so that our two countries can move forward again." The parliamentary delegation took two lessons from that visit: first, that the PRC was uninterested in talking with Canada about human rights, and second, that despite what had happened at Tiananmen, both sides wanted to preserve their bilateral ties.

China Responds

China's initial reaction to Western criticism over Tiananmen was unyielding and dismissive. Its immediate priorities were preventing a Soviet-type regime collapse and maintaining Party control. Certainly not human rights. In July 1990, Deng Xiaoping met with former prime minister Pierre Trudeau, the last meeting he would have with a Western political leader. Deng told Trudeau that China was not ready for the chaos of Western human rights and democracy:

> As soon as they have seized power, the so-called fighters for democracy will start fighting with each other. And if a civil war breaks out, with blood flowing like a river, what "human rights" would there be? If civil war broke out in China, with each faction dominating a region, production declining, transportation disrupted, and not millions or tens of millions but hundreds of millions of refugees fleeing the country, it is the Asia-Pacific region, which is at present the most promising in the world, that would be the first to be affected.
>
> So China must not allow itself to descend into turmoil; we have that responsibility to ourselves and to all mankind. Even responsible foreign statesmen have to acknowledge that China must remain stable. Human rights and democratic rights are not related to this question. The only solution is peaceful coexistence and cooperation of all countries with different social systems, not interference in other countries' internal affairs and provoking disorders. China has raised this question to alert everyone to remind all countries to be careful when they decide on their policies towards China.[3]

By the fall of 1990, China began to develop a more sophisticated response to Western criticism. Some called it the emergence of a

"Chinese human rights fever," in which China initiated a wave of research on human rights by its scholars, adopted legislation to preserve some rights, and took a more active role in debates criticizing China at the United Nations. PRC scholars published articles about human rights, the rule of law, and counter-revolutionary crime, as well as commenting on proposed PRC legislation regarding the protection of minors, labour law, women's rights, and the rights of the disabled. In October 1991, China issued its first *White Paper on Human Rights*, a forty-page document that devoted attention to the Party's efforts to improve human rights in China, albeit not along Western lines.[4]

In April, Li Peng told former US president Jimmy Carter that, for China, the first human right was the right to subsistence, food, and shelter. He said that, after those primary needs are met, other rights can follow. It was a state's responsibility to grant and guarantee rights for its citizens without outside interference. "Human rights are primarily the people's right to subsistence, and the national right to independence, and if these two basic conditions are not guaranteed, then there can be no human rights at all." In June, seventy Chinese specialists and scholars participated in a discussion covering a wide range of human rights issues, as summarized by the Australian scholar Ann Kent:

> Some conference participants argued that human rights were empirical rights (*shiyou quanli*), others that they were law-based (*fading quanli*), others that they were moral rights (*daode quanli*), others that they were essential or "outright" rights (*yingyou quanli*), and still others that they comprised four aspects – essential rights, legal rights, customary rights (*xiguan quanli*), and empirical rights.
>
> Some believed that rights were the product of the commodity economy; others contested this view. There was a debate over whether human rights were class based (*jiejixing*), or universal in character (*pubianxing*), or a combination of both. There was recognition of Marxism's impact in placing pressure on the capitalist system to improve workers' rights, and the function of Marxism in developing the concept of human rights.[5]

Despite having signed the United Nations Universal Declaration of Human Rights in 1948, China's leaders insisted that the state, not God or birth, determines the rights of the people. Collective needs take precedence over individual claims. There is a hierarchy of rights, beginning with economic needs. "The right to subsistence is the foremost human right that the Chinese people long for." Political change does not proceed along Western lines, and no foreign model can provide a human rights pathway for China. History, culture, and the level of economic development shape a people's policies, so other countries should stop trying to impose their practices on China:

> A country's human rights situation should not be judged in disregard of its history and national conditions, nor can it be evaluated according to a preconceived model or the condition of another country or region.
>
> The argument that the principle of non-interference in internal affairs does not apply to the issue of human rights is, in essence, a demand that sovereign states give up their state sovereignty in the field of human rights ... Using the human rights issue for the political purpose of imposing the ideology of one country on another is no longer a question of human rights, but a manifestation of power politics in the form of interference in the internal affairs of other countries.

The Canadian government took note of China's statement that rights were culturally and historically shaped, determined by the state, and immune from foreign influence. One Department member observed: "We see that the Chinese are now discussing rights, but they are still aloof from accepted Western practice. They don't accept the principle of universal values contained in the United Nations Charter. So let's wait and see if anything really changes. Not much room yet to craft a new strategy, or to have a discussion with Beijing."

In my diary I wrote:

> Just read China's White Paper on human rights. My Canadian students aren't sure if it represents a Chinese willingness to do something about human rights, or whether it is just a more sophisticated piece of political propaganda. My Chinese friends think it is a useful step forward taken by the Party leadership. It's too early to tell what China has in mind.

Searching for Strategy at the Post

Fred Bild, the new Canadian ambassador, arrived in Beijing in the fall of 1990. He wondered how he could deal with the legacies of Tiananmen, "knowing that scores of places and people will bring back to me the haunting pictures of this decade's most successfully televised political massacre. How to re-engage with China's top leaders? How to observe the basic diplomatic protocols and procedures? What an awkward time to start a new relationship ... Countries should not interfere in each other's internal affairs, but flagrant violations against human rights standards cannot be overlooked."[6]

Bild turned to headquarters for guidance and discovered that the Post was more or less on its own:

> How to engage our Chinese counterparts in such a way that we have an impact, finding some openings, for example, going to the provinces, getting CIDA to fund legal training and institution building, developing links with Chinese human rights specialists, choosing engagement rather than punishment.
>
> We have to use our ingenuity, be creative. We can't rely on Ottawa for help. There's no money for expanded human rights initiatives, and our politicians currently are focused on pursuing hardline encounters with Chinese leaders.

After pressure from Cabinet colleagues and from members of the China policy community to loosen the sanctions and resume high-level visits, Minister McDougall approved a visit by Minister of Agriculture Bill McKnight. Prior to that visit, I was called to Ottawa by the PMO. "You are about to visit Beijing, and you will be talking with the MFA about Canada-China relations. Make sure that you focus on human rights. That's our priority now. Our relations are not normalized. When the minister arrives in China, he will be delivering a strong human rights message to the PRC."

In my diary I wrote:

> Back in Beijing. Tried to talk rights with the MFA. Said there was a strong Canadian demand for China to respond more positively to criticism

over what had happened at Tiananmen. Was China ready to do so? My interlocutors smiled, and then they turned to complain about "the close to 10,000 PRC students that Canada was holding as hostages." It was clear they were not interested in discussing human rights.

McKnight arrived in the fall of 1991, the first visit by a Canadian minister since Tiananmen. In his diary, Ambassador Bild was bemused by how McKnight's message was being conveyed to China's leaders and to the Canadian public. It gave the impression that the main purpose of his trip was to confront China's leaders over human rights:

> Barbara McDougall, who seems to have made China-slamming her favourite pastime, is delighted how the first Canadian ministerial visit since 1989 has turned out.
>
> Bill McKnight, representing our considerable agricultural exports in China, is displayed on Canadian television in only one dimension: during the first five minutes of each meeting in Beijing, he upbraided his hosts with human rights protestations. These "photo opportunities" usually came to a close before the hosts replied, thus giving the spellbound Canadian viewer the impression that a slugfest ensued; indeed, that every moment of the visit had been devoted to berating Chinese leaders.
>
> Our Chinese contacts don't watch Canadian television ... by and large they think the visit was quite successful ... [E]ven the ministers who were raked over the coals consider it a small price to pay for breaking the ban on high-level contacts. Chinese TV, of course, put an entirely different spin on all this.

Following the expulsion from Beijing of the three visiting Canadian parliamentarians in January 1992, after they had deliberately provoked a confrontation over human rights, Ottawa had several options. It could continue with a strategy of confrontation, using strong rhetoric and in-the-face criticism of China's leaders, but that tactic had proven ineffective. Canada could also keep supporting resolutions condemning China's rights practices at the United Nations; however, for three years, the PRC had managed to deflect criticism with astute politicking among UN voting members, and it repeatedly blocked any resolutions critical of China. That was not likely to change. Finally, the Department could follow up with some of the "soft rights initiatives" it was developing at the Post, for example, expanding people-to-people links in education and culture, engaging Chinese legal scholars, building liberal institutions, and using CIDA funds for collaborative projects at the grassroots level.

The Department wrote in an internal report: "The human rights situation in China still remains poor, and repression of political dissidents, arbitrary arrests, and detentions without trial are continuing ... We are developing a strategy aimed at denouncing rights abuses. We are also assisting China to reform its judicial and legal structures in order to promote democracy and the development of rule of law." Canada sponsored a visit to Canada from the Chinese Academy of Social Sciences (CASS) to study Canadian democracy. It led to a multi-year joint CASS and Royal Society of Canada initiative called "The Democracy Project." Canadian experts came to China to give lectures on democracy. This venture evoked a Chinese interest in the Canadian political system and led to the publication in China of a collection of papers on Canadian democracy and political institutions. The University of British Columbia Law School developed a project with Chinese legal scholars, and the chairman of the Canadian Bar Association's Committee on Human Rights in Developing Countries met with the Chinese Ministry of Justice, as well as with the Procuracy, to discuss further exchanges in the legal sector.[7]

The Post was carrying out a range of programs with China:

In 1992, we began using CIDA funds to promote human rights, through projects on law and institution building. We also financed a series of small local projects of approximately $25,000 each, in various provinces, from the Canada Fund based at the Embassy, which then had a yearly budget of well over $500,000. We had several of these Canada Fund projects in place in Tibet. We went there in 1993 to check on these projects, to see whether they needed further support.

"Rule of law" made the most sense. "Democracy" was really not the best approach. The Chinese simply were not ready for that. Nor was "governance," "good governance," or the direct mention of "human rights." The Chinese balked at those. But "rule of law" was something we both could work with. That's why we set up those projects in legal studies and the training of judges.

The other possibility was "civil society." I thought that eventually would be the most promising, because we could work in the local areas, and with Chinese NGOs. But CIDA had not yet made a funding commitment for civil society, and the Chinese were not very receptive. That only happened in the latter part of the nineties.

The ambassador decided to put more emphasis on public affairs and cultural activities to raise Canada's profile in China. The Post had conducted an opinion survey just before Tiananmen, which revealed that "among Chinese, the most widespread perception of Canada was one of a vast, underpopulated, agricultural land, devoid of modern technology, with pronounced racist tendencies ... a far cry from our own image of a pluralistic urban society with state-of-the-art know-how in every field." If part of delivering a human rights message in China was to project Canadian values to the PRC, the Embassy could use Canadian "propaganda" to deliver more representative images of Canada, calling this "information work" or "public affairs." Headquarters had allocated almost no funds for this type of action, so the Embassy used its ingenuity and came up with the following strategy:

> No member of the Embassy travelling outside Beijing should fail to get in touch with any of the 20 Canadian Studies Centres in the Chinese universities, and organize some sort of social or academic activity there. Canadian students and teachers in many of these out-of-the-way places are eager to assist. Each Centre is to be encouraged to specialize in a broad sector, such as Canadian literature, economics, history, law, etc. They are also to be asked to help in the dissemination of information in scholarships and research grants, available in Canada.
>
> In less than an hour's work, we've created a whole slew of mini-consulates, honorary ones, at least.
>
> The mission will scrape together whatever it can find in the way of not too outdated film or video material, get it translated into Mandarin or Cantonese, and peddle it directly to local TV stations. The motto for the interim is: update the image of Canada by whatever information is at hand.

The head of the political section heard that Zhu Rongji was in charge of the Central Party School, which was responsible for training upper-level Party leaders. Why not raise Canada's profile by having the ambassador give a speech at the school? He contacted them, saying: "I'm a Canadian. Read in the *People's Daily* that you have a new president at the Party School. I'd love to talk with you about what this means, and maybe talk with him." They reacted positively, and asked him to come to the school the next day to talk about arranging a presentation by Ambassador Bild. The event turned out to be a great success:

> We steered the proposed discussion to Canadian federalism, said that it's a form of pluralism. They said fine. So the Ambassador and I put together a talk. We avoided referring to China. Talked only about Canada and federalism, rule of law, independence of the judiciary, and social justice. The place was packed to the rafters. Even after lunch they were still discussing what he said.
>
> Who would have thought that a two-hour presentation in front of 250 Party cadres would clear the way for similar appearances at a series of other venues ... and finally on Chinese national television?

Bild added:

> Apparently I was the first Western ambassador to address them. At one point, I gave the example of one member of Cabinet whose political career was cut short after he telephoned a judge who was trying one of his constituents. My host, in thanking me for my presentation, remarked that it would be a long time before any Chinese politician would see his career cut short because of a single telephone call!

The UN Conference on Human Rights

In 1993, the PRC defended its position at the United Nations World Conference on Human Rights in Vienna. It agreed that improvements in rights were a goal for all nations, and it supported the universal principles of the 1948 United Nations Declaration of Human Rights. However, given China's economic and social development priorities, and its cultural legacies and ideological commitments, it was up to the Chinese state to decide what was "universal." According to China, rights are not the property of individuals from birth, nor are they granted by God. The Conference, attended by 5,000 delegates from 111 countries, concluded with a statement that emphasized the diversity of national approaches to human rights and the decisive role of the state in determining rights policy: "While the significance of national and regional particularities and various historical, cultural and religious backgrounds must be borne in mind, it is the duty of states, regardless of their political, economic and cultural systems, to promote and protect all rights and freedoms."[8]

For Vice Minister Liu Huaqiu, the Vienna Conference was a turning point in international human rights discourse: "By mid-1993, China had moved significantly. We were prepared to accept the principle of human rights for all, but not as a starting point in a country's development. If the Western states are willing to listen, then China is ready to enter into a proper dialogue. *It is time for the world to get over Tiananmen*" (emphasis added). He continued:

> Everyone wants to trade with China. The leaders of all the major countries are signing big trade deals with us. Canada is probably the sole exception. In international affairs, the West needed our help in the Gulf War, Cambodia, and now the DPRK. It's time to get on with our affairs. None of us want to be held hostage to confrontational human rights encounters.

According to Liu, China was following a three-pronged approach to human rights:

> First, we are focusing on getting China on a stronger economic footing with foreigners. We have been encouraging all those trading missions – the Germans, French, Americans and later the Canadians. We timed large billion-dollar purchases of aircraft, Airbus from France and Boeing from America, to whet foreign appetites. We are showing that Western economies will suffer, especially the Americans, if they try to link trade sanctions with human rights in China.
>
> Second, even right after Tiananmen, it was clear that it was impossible to isolate China because of human rights. The West needs China's

cooperation in international security issues. We have too much political and strategic weight. Trade and international strategic concerns override human rights.

Third, in the months leading up to Vienna, we realized that many other countries were sharing our perspective on human rights, especially those in Asia. They agree with our position that rights universalism is limited by developmental, cultural, and regional issues, and that the granting of political and civil rights comes last, only after a long period of development.

The PRC was making some concessions. It agreed that human rights were universal, although it emphasized that rights are realized in different ways and sequences over time. Beijing released a few dissidents, reduced prison sentences for some demonstrators, freed Wei Jingsheng, encouraged limited discussion of human rights in China, invited foreign human rights groups to visit China, allowed them to go to Tibet, and established development assistance programs that promoted Western institutions and values. Liu complained to China's critics: *"You keep wanting more, yet we have already given you a great deal"* (emphasis added).[9]

I wrote in my diary:

It's 1993 and we haven't made much progress. The Chinese are engaging us on human rights but it's too early to see any changes. Was at our Embassy, and they just completed a two-day human rights training program. First time ever. Lots of good ideas. Ottawa is trying. Am wondering if China will respond. Maybe with social and economic rights, but unlikely with civil and political rights.

A Human Rights Training Program

In mid-1993, the Department announced that Canada was considering a different strategy, "one that will find innovative means to bring about change in the Chinese system by supporting activities in areas where we believe China is susceptible to influence." Now that China was receptive to engaging in rights talk, Ottawa wanted to expand the initiatives that had been developed at the Post over the past three years. "If China is really ready to discuss human rights, let's see how we can improve our work inside China."

The Department asked its officers in the field to take a human rights sensitivity training course "to improve coordination between what is feasible in China and what Ottawa wants to do." Fifteen officers from Beijing, Shanghai, Taipei, and Hong Kong participated in a two-day course at the Post. It was not designed to replace the usual human rights training that all officers were required to take at headquarters, but rather, it would supplement that general training by addressing special rights and democracy issues in China. According to Ottawa, this course was the first country-specific course on human rights ever offered at a Canadian embassy. The participants represented all the sectors in the Embassy: political, trade, development, consular, immigration, security, and public affairs.

The Department later said: "We were taking stock to see what we had, and what we could do. The bilateral relationship was changing, and with it our human rights strategy. We were ready to explore consultation and dialogue, instead of confrontation." The course asked three questions: first, how could Ottawa's mandate be combined to tackle human rights with its other responsibilities in trade promotion, development, immigration, and the conduct of political relations? (*To coordinate human rights policy more closely with basic diplomatic activities*); second, how should officers respond when Canada is challenged on its China human rights policy by Canadian or Chinese rights specialists? (*All officers in Canadian diplomatic missions must have a basic understanding of Canadian human rights policy*); third, how could the Embassy assist in human rights promotion and reporting without interfering with other Canadian initiatives in China? (*The Embassy's human rights officer will arrange regular briefing sessions for his or her colleagues at the Post, as well as for the other diplomatic missions in Greater China*).

The training had eight parts: (1) defining human rights in general and determining the basic relationship between human rights and development; (2) assessing current Chinese human rights practices; (3) discussing what action Canada should take to promote human rights in China; (4) explaining why Canadian human rights concerns and values should apply to China; (5) examining how the PRC was adhering to international human rights instruments such as the UN's Six Conventions on human rights; (6) analysing and understanding Chinese domestic human rights propaganda; (7) discussing China's actions in international human rights institutions; and (8) ensuring that the entire Greater China network, including missions in Beijing, Shanghai, Hong Kong, and Taipei, was involved in human rights promotion and reporting.[10]

The training started with the Canadian position on human rights:

> Canada tries to reconcile the traditional (Northern and Western) and the collective economic and social views (Southern and Eastern). We promote individual liberty and equality, good governance, and the development of democratic institutions. The goal is to foster the emergence of "national democratic cultures" in developing countries, such as China.
>
> We use a dynamic concept of democracy – a snapshot of a country's current human rights situation, grading it against our checklist ... that is, respect for rule of law and an independent judiciary; the independence and liberty of the media, as well as respect for freedom of expression and association; a process of regular popular consultation, including, but not limited to elections, and responsible and representative government, involving institutional checks and balances, such as division of powers, ombudspersons, and public participation processes.
>
> The *sine qua non* is that human rights must involve the respect and protection of dissident views and of minorities. Traditional (Western) human rights emphasize civil and political liberties: freedom of opinion, speech, media, movement, religion, peaceful assembly and association; rule of law, which requires respect for integrity, impartiality and the independence of the judicial system (police, courts, lawyers), as well as the right to legal redress and to equitable and public trials; protection against arbitrary arrest and searches; the embodying of international human rights obligations in domestic law.

The section on China presented a mixed view of the current situation in the PRC:

> In the Chinese judicial system, 99% of all accused are convicted. There is no judicial independence. Most accused have no access to lawyers, or have poor lawyers. Lawyers can only see a client one week before trial. Religious freedom is guaranteed in the Constitution but proselytizing is forbidden. All churches must be regulated by the Chinese state. Minorities are granted special rights, but these guarantees are regularly broken, for example, in Tibet. Political criteria prevail and there can be torture and lack of due process.
>
> Despite these sobering observations, in reality, the private lives of most Chinese are free from overt day-to-day interference ... The 1992 law protecting women's rights guarantees complete equality before the law ... Public health is a success story, and a 1990 administrative litigation law enables citizens to bring suits against government officials for malfeasance.

I wrote in my diary:

> An impressive statement of Canada's position, and an objective, although brief assessment of China's record. Too much to absorb in two days. It's the first time I've seen a government document that gives some praise to China on human rights and its observance of the rule of law. Are the two sides inching together – or is this just an anomaly, and actually nothing has changed?

The principal goal was the creation of a program that "fostered evolutionary change." Collaboration with China was encouraged, with "soft" programs that elicited long-term cooperation. "We emphasize areas where the Chinese themselves say progress is needed, and we seek to identify ways Canada can be helpful. We think that can be a better way to get our message across in China."

Headquarters instructed the Post to continue its démarches to those PRC government organizations whose work directly affects human rights, for example, the Ministry of Justice, Public Security, the Procuracy, and the Supreme Court. Develop contacts with the All-China Lawyers Association and with individual members of the Chinese legal profession. Organize a seminar on administrative law so Canadian lawyers can show PRC lawyers how to take a government to court. Expand development work by training Chinese decision-makers in Canadian systems and principles through programs in management, education, and institution building. Use the Canada Fund at the Embassy for small programs of up to $25,000 each, focused on women and ethnic minorities. Expand academic cooperation to include more research on Canadian politics and law.

The officer in charge of human rights activities said the Embassy was already implementing many of these initiatives, but it needed more financial support from Ottawa:

> The Embassy has been working hard for more than a year to develop programs based on collaboration with the Chinese side, focusing on the grassroots, away from the centre. Ottawa finally is backing us up with these measures. For too long we were hostages of our own political propaganda. Our rights policy was based on high principles, but it lacked practicality. Now, if only headquarters can provide the funding we need to carry out these measures.

According to Bild, the training session unified thinking among the different sections in the Embassy, as well as for the other participating missions. The trade people were being sensitized to the concerns of their colleagues in the political section, and now there was better communication between the CIDA officers who ran the development programs that centred on human rights, and the rest of the Embassy. Afterwards, the Embassy sent back an assessment of the program, saying that the course had been helpful, but it was a one-time event, a "useful exercise" that could help Canada create a human rights network in China, although it was too short. The Embassy's human rights officer added:

> Canada had a narrow view of human rights. Officers had to broaden their viewpoint, so this intervention from Ottawa was timely. The Post now had the go-ahead to expand its human rights programs, and we had a closer fit with headquarters. They wanted as much feedback as

possible. The shift to collaboration with the Chinese side, and committing to longer term outcomes, made it easier to intersect with our Chinese counterparts.

This was an opportunity to build a network that reinforced our efforts in China, and it could also serve as a model for other countries. Initially, some of us had been sceptical about this training, although it turned out to be a useful exercise, even if it was a one-shot affair and was not repeated.

The ambassador applauded the idea of building a localized Canadian "human rights network," although he said that history had taught Canada that no one can change China overnight, and these initiatives, at best, represented long-term solutions: "When all is said and done, the big issues in diplomacy have to do with weighing the interests of the long term against those of the shorter term, and with the timing of those moves. Success in human rights may be a long-term goal."

Joe Clark Discusses Human Rights with China's Leaders

Joe Clark, now the president of the Queen's Privy Council for Canada, visited China in 1993. The Chinese repeated their position that human rights first meant the right to better housing, food, and living conditions – not political and civil liberties. They told Clark that, when Trade Minister Michael Wilson had visited Beijing a year earlier, he had said there could be "different levels of human rights," acknowledging the Chinese position that there were stages of rights realization. Wilson had also said: "We're not trying to say we are only going to trade with you if you abide by the same level of human rights as we do. If we did that, there would be a number of other countries with whom we couldn't trade."

Rights were at the top of Clark's agenda, followed by trade and international security issues, the future status of Hong Kong, ending nuclear testing, defusing tension on the Korean Peninsula, and the signing of a nuclear non-proliferation treaty. However, at

Clark's press conferences in Beijing and Hong Kong, rights dominated the discussion:

> I met this morning with the PRC's Foreign Minister. The first issue I
> raised was the question of human rights and political systems. I indi-
> cated that Canada believed economic freedom and political freedom
> were part of the same piece, that it was hard to argue which was the
> chicken and which was the egg, but both needed to occur together, and
> that remained very strongly our view.
>
> We are prepared to be as constructive as possible in our relations
> with China. There are Canadian legal scholars scheduled to come here
> as part of an agreement to discuss our views of democracy. Canadian
> law schools are prepared to work with the Chinese to develop the legal
> framework that we have found to work in Canada.
>
> Li Peng and I had a much longer discussion than I had anticipated
> on the human rights question, and I will not pretend there was a meet-
> ing of minds on the issue. I will not pretend that I convinced the Pre-
> mier of the position of Canada. I do think it was useful to have the
> conversation.

Clark said both countries were searching for a better way to deal
with their differences:

> QUESTION: Mr. Clark, as a result of your meetings with Li Peng and his
> shifting position, are we back to the level before Tiananmen, or are we
> still at a kind of cautionary level that is in-between?
> MINISTER CLARK: We have taken another step in the evolution of that
> arrangement. We remain very concerned about human rights and
> democratic practices in China, but are not going to stand back and say
> these things are wrong. We are going to try to take advantage of such
> small openings as they occur to try to change practice.
>
> We are a more trusted country than others, because we have never
> been a colonial power. We have never been an imperialist power. We
> don't scare people as much as some other countries, and that's always
> been an asset. Some people accuse us of being Boy Scouts in this
> regard, but this is an important role for the world and for us, and we
> are determined to play it.

The Department said that Clark's meeting was a pivotal event: "Often diplomatic encounters are formalistic, with both sides simply restating their positions without offering any middle ground. Clark and Li had talked about 'small steps' and 'not standing back,' and we thought that was an opening on human rights." After Clark's visit, Ambassador Zhang Yijun told a group of China specialists in Toronto that the situation in China was steadily improving and that both countries were acquiring a better understanding of each other's position: "It is time for the two countries to establish a more realistic partnership. The key is trade. Move on from rights. We take our lead from the business community, and we emphasize stability, dialogue, and engagement. Deng Xiaoping said stability takes precedence over all other concerns." Zhang then emphasized China's position:

> China will not, and cannot change so drastically to be like you in Canada. We have our own needs and traditions, and must develop in our own way. We will permit no confrontations. They are counterproductive and won't work with us. They just do the opposite.
>
> We are Asians and practice Asian ways. The leaders of Malaysia, Japan, even Australia and New Zealand, all have said that China practises Asian ways of doing things. This applies to human rights, and we see that Canada is now moving in that direction. This is what I meant by realism.

Five years had passed since Tiananmen, and attempts to change China's practices had not been successful. Increased trade had become the main objective, and the Team Canada mission had just returned from China with $8.5 billion in signed contracts. Prime Minister Chrétien had ended open confrontation on human rights, saying: "We can do this privately. No need for public statements condemning China."

Li Peng Visits Canada

The twentieth anniversary of the establishment of diplomatic relations had been barely acknowledged in 1990 because of Tiananmen and the imposition of Canadian sanctions on China. However, in

1995, there was a celebration. Former prime minister Trudeau and former foreign affairs minister Mitchell Sharp were honoured for the roles they had played in 1970. Prime Minister Chrétien gave a speech, but the special guest was Premier Li Peng. The irony of inviting Li was not lost on Canadians. The city of Toronto sent a formal letter to the prime minister saying that Li was not welcome because he was responsible for the killings at Tiananmen, and the Canadian media expressed strong disapproval of his presence in Canada.

Li was concerned about public criticism of his role during Tiananmen. He had previously cut short a trip in Europe after being hounded by anti-China demonstrators. His advisors told James Bartleman, Chrétien's policy advisor, that if Li saw so much as a single demonstrator, "he will cancel his official visit and return home. Canada will suffer the consequences." Bartleman and Foreign Minister Ouellet had to come up with a plan to save the visit:

We decided to enmesh the Premier in the program in Ottawa, to make it too difficult for him to turn around and leave when he eventually – and inevitably – encountered the reality of Canadian street democracy. To lure him into our trap, we moved the scheduled talks from the cabinet room in the Centre Block of Parliament – with its banks of windows open to the parliamentary lawn that was all too likely to be filled with chanting demonstrators – to rooms buried deep in the heart of the fortress-like Pearson Building on Sussex Drive.

The first rendezvous our distinguished guest had with the Canadian public was thus with an enthusiastic group of foreign service officers in the lobby of the Pearson Building, commandeered to leave their offices and to applaud. Emerging from the elevator on the ground floor, the Premier walked through the rows of clapping officers.

Their acclamations were more than offset, however, by the howls of the banner-waving crowd outside, held back by Ottawa's finest. The RCMP and Chinese security officers decided not to risk trying to leave from the front entrance, where the crowd was concentrated, and led a deeply unhappy guest to the back exit in the basement.[11]

It was touch and go whether Li would attend the anniversary celebration or return home. Upon his arrival in Montreal, he was jostled by a group of "Free Tibet" protesters, who had breached the lackadaisical Montreal police lines, forcing him to run the gauntlet from his car to the front door. Li was furious. He announced that he had had enough and was leaving. At that point, Chrétien apparently saved the day by telling Li that the crowd was demonstrating against himself, not against Li. Chrétien remembers:

> Several hundred protesters arrived on the street, screaming insults and waving enormous cardboard tanks [to remind Li of the tanks that had indiscriminately killed people at Tiananmen] that were impossible to miss. Li Peng looked angry ... "Come with me," I said, and led him over to the window, where I pretended to be able to read the writing. "Oh, they're protesting against me!" Fortunately, and against all the odds, Li found it funny. He might have been upset, but at least he didn't leave ahead of schedule.[12]

Would Li attend the formal dinner that night? Austin recalls that he was hesitating:

> We had the Chief of Protocol do the introduction. Chrétien was there, Trudeau in his white suit, and Mitchell Sharp. The Chief of Protocol announced: "And now, the Premier of China, His Excellency, Li Peng."
> Li does not appear. There's a very long three-minute delay. The 1,000 people in the room are looking around, beginning to wonder. The room falls silent. The Chief of Protocol then says he had been premature in his introduction. He makes a second introduction:
> "Now, Premier Li will be coming in."
> We wait again, looking around, wondering what was happening. Then Li finally enters to enthusiastic applause. The crisis was averted. Later I asked Liu Huaqiu about the unusual delay. Liu replied: "We wanted to be sure that Li was received with genuine applause from the audience. We saw the protesters outside, and were worried that people in the room might have wanted to demonstrate against him. That would have been unacceptable."

During his meeting with Chrétien, Li praised CIDA, saying it was the best foreign development agency operating in China, and it could carry out its programs in governance and rule of law in China – "as long as they focus on research and training, and do not interfere in our internal affairs." He never mentioned the words "human rights." Nor did the prime minister. The PRC press produced glowing accounts of the visit and of twenty-five years of bilateral relations. The Canadian media and human rights advocates, however, did not hold back their criticism of Li, nor of the special treatment that he had received from the prime minister.

While demonstrators shouted outside and the media were writing critical articles about Chinese violations of human rights, Chrétien and Li went about their business, discussing trade and international security issues. There was no mention of rights, except for Li's statement that CIDA could carry out its programs on governance and the rule of law. According to the Department, "we weren't giving up on human rights, but we were re-engaging with China's leaders, and Li had offered an opening for our programs. Sometimes diplomacy takes centre stage. His visit turned out better than expected. It could have set back relations again."

After Li's visit, the Canadian media reported that China was continuing to deny individuals their civil and political rights, and the opposition parties were criticizing the Liberals for having abandoned rights in favour of trade. Canadian rights activists were complaining that they did not have a voice in shaping policy. Amnesty International said the government always withheld information on the rights situation in China. For example, Ottawa only handed out a brief two-page summary of its human rights initiatives in China prior to the annual NGO consultations that it held each spring.

The director of policy at the International Centre for Human Rights and Democratic Development said that wasn't enough: "Ottawa didn't want us to get in their way. Much of what it did was half-hearted, and just paid lip service to human rights. We were collecting a lot of vital information, and we had a stronger commitment to human rights than the government." The Department had a rather different view. It said that the Canadian NGOs were useful for helping it to identify abuses and letting the government know what most concerned Canadians and international human rights activists. "But they also were a loose cannon. Often they were too aggressive in their criticism of China, and the PRC did not want to meet with them. Frankly, we had an uneasy working relationship with our rights NGOs."[13]

It was the beginning of 1996, and the Department took stock. It was raising rights at every meeting with Chinese officials, initiating contact with rights advocates to discuss specific cases in China, engaging in regular quarterly démarches to the PRC's Justice and Corrections Ministries, and ensuring that every Canadian minister who went to China raised human rights with his or her interlocutors. Future activities included additional small projects in Tibet, the further training of Chinese lawyers, proposing revisions to the PRC criminal procedure code, organizing university-based workshops with joint research on human rights, and preparing materials on Canadian democracy for publication in China. CIDA was concentrating on institution building and the rule of law, and it was now targeting Chinese civil society, a potentially fertile ground for developing democratic political values.[14]

Ottawa decided to organize ministerial consultations for stakeholders to discuss Canadian China policy, first with Foreign Minister André Ouellet in 1995, and then with Foreign Minister Lloyd Axworthy and Secretary of State Raymond Chan in 1996. The participants came from government, academia, the business community, Canadian ethnic Chinese communities, and the NGOs. They concluded that trade and human rights were not necessarily in conflict; however, there was scepticism about whether doing business with China would by itself improve human rights. The government proposed working with business to formulate a code of corporate conduct for Canadian companies abroad, but many felt this initiative was just a cosmetic exercise that would have a negligible impact on both the Canadian business community and the PRC.

The 1996 Ministerial Consultation concluded with the following statement:

Canadian policy on trade and human rights need not be in conflict if Canada matches increased trade along with increased pressure on the Chinese government for human rights reform. *Canada should have modest policy goals in this area.* Canada should publicly denounce new arrests, name the imprisoned, and document cases of abuse of the Chinese rule of law.

Attention should be given to providing lower levels of government with the opportunity to internally pressure the leadership in Beijing ... Blanket denouncements and sanctions will only exacerbate an exceedingly delicate situation. Increased trade, and helping China develop a more resilient civil society, should be Canada's contribution to international efforts to assist China through a difficult transition. (emphasis added)

"Modest policy goals" indeed. Most advocates saw this statement as a retreat from the previous mandate of active engagement on rights. Canada was drifting into a realm of quiet rights diplomacy, conducted mostly behind the scenes, out of public view, eclipsed by trade and by forgotten memories of Tiananmen.

I wrote in my diary:

China is still jailing dissidents, denying people their rights. We tried to change China's policies, but couldn't get very far. On the other hand, China is changing, opening up bit by bit. I saw some progress on my recent trip. Not likely to satisfy the many Canadians who still want to punish China for Tiananmen. What we are doing now may be helpful in the longer term, with programs that can build institutions and the legal system, although no short-term success. We know more today about China. Maybe China will become more like us, or maybe it won't.

By 1997, an objective appraisal of Canadian rights policy with China would show that much effort had been spent for only a few positive results. All that work in the field had not made much of an impact, and in Ottawa the government was concentrating on trade. Human rights was like an unwelcome cuckoo that had settled into the government's nest. Human rights had taken root in Canadian foreign policy, even though some of our diplomats were uncomfortable with it. One member of the Department said: "Human rights never were part of traditional diplomacy. They didn't belong. Now we are trying to do things we never did before.

We are telling other countries how to govern themselves, and then we sanction them if they don't adopt our values and institutions."

Bilateral Dialogue

In 1997, Canada and most Western nations abandoned their attempts at the United Nations to condemn Chinese rights abuses. The UN Commission on Human Rights (UNCHR) had been unable to pass binding resolutions criticizing China for seven years – the PRC could block the implementation of any initiative. Canada had co-sponsored these resolutions, and it was expected to do so again in 1997. However, in April, Ottawa announced that it would no longer be a co-sponsor, and it issued this statement: "The government has decided, in light of the significant weakening in consensus for passing a joint resolution criticizing China, that Canada will have a greater influence on the state of human rights in China if it pursued and intensified its promising bilateral measures."

Other countries had encountered similar problems. Sanctions had failed, along with attempts to change China's policies. Their attention, like Chrétien's, was now fixed upon increasing trade, with human rights following behind. China had stabilized; Deng Xiaoping was gone; and at the Fifteenth Party Congress later in the year, Jiang Zemin consolidated his leadership, restating a commitment to market principles, and to a measure of liberalization. The economy was growing, and China appeared more resilient in 1997 than at any time since the mid-1980s.

China's leaders had decided that a controlled dialogue was the safest way to engage on human rights. In an official statement, the MFA said: "It is best for China and our bilateral partners if we have a well-organized discussion among our senior officials. Each side can present its views, and we will have positive results. We don't have to be in a position where we are always fending off attacks by foreigners on China. Let's try to partner on human rights reform." Bilateral dialogue was containable and not politically disruptive, since for the most part, it could take place among trusted officials behind closed doors, out of the reach of rights activists and the foreign media. Bilateral dialogue also fit more comfortably with how the Canadian government was approaching the rights situation – less confrontation and more collaboration. One Department official said:

> It's been eight years since Tiananmen. Most Canadians have other concerns – the economy, Hong Kong retrocession, the Asian economic crisis. China is here to stay, and Ottawa has to deal with the reality of China, with trade, and how to come to terms with a future superpower. We are expanding the CIDA programs, training more Chinese, and reaching into Chinese civil society. Now we will have a bilateral dialogue between senior officials on both sides, who will meet every year. Maybe it's not that dramatic and China continues to jail dissidents.

Lloyd Axworthy became foreign minister in 1996. He was an activist minister with an approach to China that was tougher than the quiet rights diplomacy that the prime minister favoured. Those who knew Chrétien and Axworthy found it somewhat surprising that the two of them were able to work together on the China file, since the prime minister, for all intents and purposes, "owned" Canadian policy, and he set the tone on rights. Chrétien had decided against confrontation, and Axworthy, for the most part, had to retreat and pursue his activist interests elsewhere. In his five years as foreign minister, he only visited China twice on short trips, and the relationship he developed with Chinese counterparts remained awkward at best.

Axworthy opposed the withdrawal of Canadian support for the 1997 United Nations resolution criticizing China, insisting that it was important to maintain moral pressure on China. In early April, he made a quick trip to Beijing to discuss rights with China's leaders. He then travelled to Washington, where the Americans told him that they were continuing to back the United Nations resolution against China and were asking for Canada's support. Axworthy returned to Ottawa to make the case for continuing Canada's sponsorship of the UN resolution. There was talk of a row within a split Cabinet, with the prime minister choosing to end UN sponsorship and favouring the move to a bilateral rights dialogue. Cabinet approved the new dialogue, and the Department was chosen to head the Canadian side, along with representatives from the Department of Justice, the policy division of CIDA, and other China specialists. Its PRC counterpart was the Department of International Organizations and Conferences of the Ministry of Foreign Affairs.

The first dialogue meeting took place in Ottawa, *in camera*, away from media and rights activists. The Department provided a brief summary:

> On the agenda of the July 1997 meeting in Ottawa were discussions about the Six United Nations Covenants and the treatment of the accused, matters regarding the treatment of ethnic minorities, and preparation for the next meeting. On each topic both delegations gave a presentation of their respective situation. For example, on minorities, the Chinese delegates described the powers granted to the autonomous regions and government policies aimed at ensuring fair access for members of ethnic minority groups to education, social programs, and so on.
>
> In response, the Canadian delegation explained how the government dealt with discrimination, with particular reference to the role of the Canadian Human Rights Commission. The Canadian government officials followed up on lists of individual cases of political imprisonment submitted to the Chinese authorities by Foreign Minister Axworthy, and by the Canadian Ambassador, while in Tibet.

At the second meeting, in October 1997, the Canadian delegation met in Beijing with representatives from the Ministries of Foreign Affairs and Justice, the Bureau of Religious Affairs, and the All-China Women's Federation. Topics discussed were the rights of women and children, rights of the accused, the new criminal procedure law, religious issues, and civil and political rights. The group then travelled to Kunming in southwest China to study national minority issues. The third round took place in November 1998, in Winnipeg and Vancouver. New topics included the rule of law and judicial independence, women in the workplace, and the devolution of power in Canada, from the federal government to the provinces. In all, the two sides held nine rounds of meetings, alternating between each country, over an eight-year period.

Initial optimism gave way to disappointment when Chinese behaviour remained the same, especially with respect to political and civil rights. At times, it seemed that the two sides were simply talking at each other, using prepared texts without any real dialogue, and this pattern continued for almost nine years. Finally, the Canadian government commissioned a review to assess "how the dialogue may have contributed to change in China's human rights policies and practices." Brock University professor Charles Burton, who conducted the review, had participated in four of the meetings, and had spent several months interviewing participants on both sides. Burton concluded that much of the dialogue was formalistic, lacked transparency, and the results had not met expectations. He recommended major changes, and the dialogue was suspended. After extended discussion, it was never restored.[15]

At the Post

In the late 1990s, Canada had CIDA programs in place for developing the Chinese legal aid system, training Chinese judges and lawyers, and pursuing cooperative work in minority affairs issues; it also sent a Canadian church group to China to discuss religious matters. Howard Balloch, the new ambassador, continued to endorse the use of the discretionary Canada Fund to support a raft of small projects at the grassroots level. He travelled to Tibet to visit a school for poor and disabled children, medical clinics, and a local weaving factory. This visit gave the Post the opportunity to evaluate what was happening in Tibet on sensitive political issues, such as religious freedom, women's rights, the preservation of local culture, and the condition of prisons.

The ambassador sent his report of the Tibet visit back to Ottawa; and it gave a more positive picture of Chinese government practices than what Ottawa was expecting. According to Balloch, the report "reflected accurately what we had seen, and what I believed

to be the complex interplay of positive Chinese governmental policies bringing real benefit to an impoverished region. I believed that
Western history and our own liberal traditions gave us a credible
and balanced stance, from which to both praise progress and criticize opposition."[16] He was not prepared for Ottawa's reaction:

> A day or two later, we received a redraft from Axworthy's staff, sub-
> stantially changing the tone of the report to be much more critical. I
> sent back a message saying I was not willing to change the report. I was
> at one point told that the Minister himself wanted my report changed,
> or else it could not be released. Ministerial authority to prevent the
> report's release I accepted; however, as I had not classified the docu-
> ment, the *Globe and Mail* eventually sought and obtained it through a
> formal Access to Information request. The whole matter ended more
> with a whimper, than a bang. But Minister Axworthy, and certainly his
> staff, were not very happy with me.

Rights NGOs obtained a copy of the report and said that it was
cautious in the extreme and that the quality of the information it
contained was mediocre. They stated that Canada had not recognized PRC sovereignty over Tibet, although the Canadian government has never disputed the PRC's claim that Tibet is a part of
China – it has just been critical of how the PRC treats its Tibetans.
Activists reacted negatively to a controversial statement that said:
"We saw no evidence of a deliberate central government policy of
the sinification of Tibet." Later, in conversation, Balloch replied: "It
was a fair report. Remember, we were checking on the Canadian
development projects located there. Nothing contradicted Canadian policy, for which I had been responsible for a good part of a
decade. Yes, there was sinification of Tibet; however, we tried to
provide a balanced view. Not everything has a bad outcome." Was
the ambassador, with his close relationship with Prime Minister
Chrétien and his pedigree of long service on the China file, beginning to back off on human rights and look more favourably upon
China?

Foreign Minister Axworthy, who was more critical of China,
went to Beijing to discuss bilateral matters with Tang Jiaxuan, his

Chinese counterpart. According to Balloch, Tang "assured Axworthy that China valued the formal human rights dialogue that Canada had established the year before between the two countries and that China encouraged a broader bilateral engagement on such matters as legal reform." However, Axworthy's meeting with Li Peng was a different matter. After Li welcomed him to China, Axworthy immediately confronted Li. Balloch writes of this encounter:

> Axworthy told Li that Canada and Canadians were concerned about the human rights situation in China, and continued to look for an honest accounting of the 1989 Tiananmen incident.
>
> This was not how we had suggested the human rights issue should be raised with China. The frontal approach, and the reference to Tiananmen, certainly caught the Chinese leader by surprise.
>
> He immediately reddened and lashed out at Axworthy, asking him if he had discussed his plan to raise this issue with Prime Minister Chrétien before he left Ottawa. He asked, "Why do you not follow your boss's orders?"
>
> I intervened to explain that what the Minister was saying was that the entire Canadian government, including Prime Minister Chrétien, valued the human rights dialogue as part of our broader and very healthy bilateral relationship.
>
> Li then answered me, and said bluntly, "Well, you had better tell your Minister that!"
>
> Li was uninterested in further dialogue. The meeting wound up earlier than scheduled, luckily without further rancour, but the traditional post-meeting photograph did not take place.[17]

The two sides finalized the sale of the two CANDU reactors first announced during the 1994 Team Canada visit. After the ribbon cutting in Shanghai, pictures of Chrétien playfully placing one of the big bows from the celebratory ribbons on Li's head to serve as a hat unleashed a storm of criticism back home, shocking many Canadians at the prime minister's apparent fondness for the so-called "Butcher of Beijing." In 1998, the prime minister gave a speech in China, seemingly out of character for him, where he talked about human rights, the rule of law, and freedom of expression. Balloch recalls:

> The speech, which I had played a part in drafting, talked about the importance in modern societies of free expression and of balanced progress towards both a more developed economy and a society in which fundamental precepts of human rights were respected in law and practice. It was not an accusatory approach, but the message was clear, and the press grudgingly gave Chrétien credit for broaching the issues publicly. Not surprisingly, the coverage in the Chinese media, which was fulsome, did not cover the more contentious components.

Chrétien claims that he was "the first Western leader ever to speak so bluntly about the importance of democratic principles, and the rule of law, in such an important public setting, with a question-and-answer period and the Chinese media in attendance." He told his audience:

> Some say that the right to eat is more important than the right to speak, that collective needs must always have priority over individual rights ... I would be less than frank if I did not say directly to you that many Canadians are disturbed when we hear reports from your country of restrictions on the right of free expression of different political views. And particularly when we hear of people being arrested or in prison for expressing political views different from the government.[18]

Chrétien's remarks were a notable departure from the soft line he previously held on rights. However, the situation in China had suddenly worsened before his 1998 trip, with reports of police brutality in Shanghai and a tightening up on Chinese dissidents that precipitated a wave of criticism from Canadian activists. The *Globe and Mail* wrote that Chrétien's advisors "were very aware of the domestic criticism (of Chrétien) for virtually ignoring the rights issue on his previous visits, including one where he was seen affectionately patting the head of Li Peng."

Ottawa pointed out that Chrétien's statement on human rights was not a change in his quiet diplomacy, since he had discussed rights privately with Premier Zhu the day before his speech. In fact, later that day Zhu told several Chinese and Canadian senior ministers that "Canada is China's best friend." Strong words on human rights by the prime minister apparently had not damaged bilateral relations and had given him a public relations boost back home. Chrétien's advisors were pleased, pointing out that American President Clinton had debated human rights and democracy openly with Chinese leaders during his visit to Beijing earlier in the year, also without jeopardizing US-PRC relations.

It was the end of the 1990s, and I was in northeast China, lecturing on Canada-China relations. The students listened attentively. No one in Changchun knew anything about Canada. We had a good discussion, talked about education, trade, and, of course, Norman Bethune, but when I mentioned Tiananmen and human rights, they stopped talking. I had crossed a line. Later they quietly told me: "We know what happened on June 4, and we know what foreigners are saying, but this is China, not Canada, and we cannot talk about that." That encounter set me thinking: Had nothing Canada had done on rights since 1989 made an impact? All those efforts to show China how we approached human rights and political liberalization – the meetings with China's leaders, the shift from confrontation to collaboration, the innovative work done at the Post, academic partnerships, the creation of a formal dialogue – had we just been going through the motions?

An Assessment

Dissidents were still being jailed; Tibetans continued to suffer; there was no freedom of speech, no right to demonstrate or to organize against the party-state, no Western rule of law, no transparency in governance, no electoral accountability for China's leaders, no open media, and no visible improvements in the legal system. What began after June 4, 1989 as a search for a strategy to compel or influence China to change these practices had come up short. Was this a Canadian failure of will, of strategy and tactics, or was it something else?

I pondered these questions while participating in two CIDA-funded "institution building" projects. In one, a million dollar five-year project, we were showing legislators in the National People's Congress (NPC) how Canada's Parliament made laws and consulted with its citizens, and how it held public hearings. In another, we were demonstrating to the Central Party School how the Party could engage in "environmental management." Were we gaining ground on human rights? I didn't think so. After four years, it seemed that both sides had been going through the motions. The Chinese had little interest in liberalizing their political institutions, certainly not the Communist Party or the NPC. The people at CIDA, who realized this, knew that their efforts were not making an impact. One CIDA officer observed: "We're not really talking to each other. We're being carefully played by the Chinese side. It's all superficial. I don't see any changes. I used to think we could make a difference, but now I just want to complete my program assignment."

In 2005, I wrote in my diary:

> Have been "institution building" in China in two CIDA projects. Canada is spending a lot of money – several million dollars. Am not convinced we are moving forward on human rights. Are we just wasting time and money, pretending these "close encounters" will produce the hoped-for value change? Is this a step forward for Canada, or just another failed tactic?
>
> Other countries seem to be in a similar situation. Talked with the Germans who, like Canada, are helping the NPC to improve its legislative practices. They aren't very optimistic about opening up China for more democracy and human rights. Am also not encouraged by our new bilateral dialogue that is going on behind closed doors. Afraid it is falling on deaf ears.

China was more open to foreigners than in the past, but it continued to resist the introduction of Western values. The PRC had grudgingly allowed Canada to set up programs in China to train legislators, Party members, and judges, and we could also show them how democratic institutions functioned in Canada. We had given up on peaceful evolution, linkage, United Nations resolutions, and megaphone diplomacy. We tried to bypass the top levels of the Chinese government with programs at the local level that could spread our values, but success at the grassroots did not carry very far upwards. None of these measures had changed Chinese official behaviour. So why did we think this new dialogue would fare any better?[19]

It is fair to say that we had learned Canada had little leverage with China, if indeed it ever had any. Our human rights strategy had been based on questionable assumptions: that with our help China would eventually open up and become more democratic; that Canada and China had a relationship that permitted us to tell China what it should do; that the PRC would listen; that we were "in the lead" with a workable human rights strategy, steps ahead of the other "like-minded" countries. None of these assumptions were validated. In fact, our China rights strategy was domestically driven, designed to satisfy public opinion after Tiananmen, to "show blood" to Canadians as much as it was supposed to change China. According to one Department member, "much of this was performance art. China was the objective, but we always were looking to satisfy the Canadian public."

We also saw how difficult it was for the government in Ottawa to formulate and implement a rights strategy. There were splits within the Cabinet, disjuncture between headquarters and the Post, insufficient funding for new initiatives, and bureaucratic resistance to making action on rights a central part of Canadian diplomacy. Some members of the Department felt that human rights should not even be part of official diplomacy: "I have trouble with human rights. It has only recently been inserted into Canada's foreign policy statement, and we're still learning the appropriate diplomatic behaviour." Rights activists found it hard to connect with policymakers, and government initiatives often tended to be shrouded in secrecy. Restoration of the bilateral relationship after Tiananmen meant focusing on trade and international security issues, in effect, taming rights policy and reducing its urgency. Prime Minister Chrétien and the Liberals made this shift in piecemeal fashion, sometimes with public criticism of China's abuses and other times turning a softer cheek. Examples are the Chrétien-Axworthy split on China, the prime minister's solicitous treatment of the reviled Li Peng, and Ambassador Balloch's defence of China's policies in Tibet.

Balloch exemplifies how the Liberal government steadily altered its rights strategy as it moved from confrontation to closer engagement. In 1989, he was one of the main architects of the June 30 Statement, with its hard line on China. A decade later, he and the Liberals had recast that strategy, downplaying rights in favour of trade, to the disappointment of those activists who now wondered if challenging China on rights for so many years had been a fruitless enterprise. In 2006, when Harper and the Conservatives assumed power, Canada once again took to megaphone diplomacy, arguing that the Liberal Party's policy of soft rights engagement had failed, but that was a short-term shift in tactics. By 2009, the Harper government had backed off on confrontation and was reverting to the strategy and tactics of its Liberal predecessors. China continued to abuse human rights, and the lesson Canada learned was that human rights values cannot be exported. Such change comes from within a culture and society, over a long period of time, from both its people and their leaders. At best, Canada could only hope that, in the future, the PRC might liberalize and alter its civil and political rights practices, while Canada and its democratic allies watched from afar.

chapter ten

Stephen Harper Visits China

Prime Minister Stephen Harper's first trip to China in 2009 marked the resetting of relations that were disrupted in 2006 when the Conservatives took power and moved Canada-PRC relations in a different direction, becoming tougher on human rights and treating China as an adversary. Harper provoked China by meeting with the Dalai Lama and bestowing honorary Canadian citizenship upon him. He suggested that Canada might rethink its relationship with Taiwan, and he restricted high-level ministerial visits and diplomatic contacts with China.

In 2008, relations began to change. Once again, the impetus was trade. Because of the sudden American financial crisis, trade with the United States, which normally absorbed 75 per cent of Canada's exports, was threatened by declining US demand. Canada was looking for another large export market, and a logical option was to turn to the rapidly growing Chinese economy.

The Canadian business community exerted pressure on the federal government to restore Canada's access to the senior levels of Chinese economic decision-making. A parade of Canadian ministers was dispatched to China in search of trade, including Stockwell Day, the minister of international trade. Day had been one of the Conservative hardliners on China. In 2009, he spent eight days in China, holding extensive meetings with government representatives and heads of economic enterprises. Day returned home a Canadian Marco Polo. He had rediscovered China and was promoting re-engagement to his prime minister. A few months later, Harper went to China.

Was the prime minister prepared to cast aside his criticism of China, and were the Chinese ready to receive him appropriately? The visit was a success, *although Premier Wen Jiabao criticized Prime Minister Harper for waiting almost four years to visit China. The two sides prepared a Joint Statement that became a blueprint for future engagement, covering everything from relations with Taiwan to new trade initiatives, collaboration in energy, and human rights. During his six days in China, Harper met with China's top leaders, and he spoke warmly about establishing closer relations.*

Harper's 2009 visit was a benchmark for resetting relations. The PRC radiated optimism, referring to a forthcoming "Golden Age." China was poised to invest in the Canadian oil sands, the two countries were completing a foreign investment agreement, and there was serious talk about concluding a comprehensive free trade agreement. When Harper made his second visit in 2012, it seemed that relations were on a fast track to that next level.

That was not to be. The Conservatives, split between hardliners and those who wanted more engagement with Beijing, backed away from China. Public criticism of China's actions increased. Big energy purchases by China never happened. The Chinese also stepped back. The momentum of the visits faded, and both sides retreated, for differing reasons: the Canadians because they had become wary of getting too close to a more assertive and aggresive China, and the Chinese because they were losing patience with Canada and had better options to pursue elsewhere. While the 2009 visit had restored working relations, Harper's return to China in 2012 did not lead to the next level as many had hoped, and relations again soured. In 2015, Justin Trudeau took office with a promise to reset Canada's links with China, and that will be the story of the following chapter.

Canada does not intend to sell out its values in pursuit of the Almighty Dollar.
– Prime Minister Stephen Harper, 2006

Setting the Stage

In 2003, Paul Martin Jr. succeeded Jean Chrétien as prime minister. Martin had entered politics after a successful business career. He was closely connected to the Desmarais family and had visited China several times, first as a businessman and then as a Liberal minister in the 1990s. When Paul Martin Jr. became prime minister, he felt that he had a sound understanding of the state of Canada-China relations, and of what was needed to further them. In the short time that his Liberal minority government was in power, he set in motion initiatives that promised to take relations to the next level. These included promoting China's entry into the G20; establishing a strategic partnership with China that could place Canada in the top ten countries that Beijing favoured; putting together a much-needed Canadian strategy to coordinate China policy; preparing legislation to create the Pacific Gateway – a modern transportation corridor to west coast ports for expanded trade with Asia; renewing Canada's moribund bilateral human rights dialogue; and making an agreement with China for Canada to be granted an approved destination status (ADS) for PRC tourism. To this impressive list, we can add Martin's primary agenda: encouraging PRC investment in the Canadian economy, prioritizing ministerial visits focused on trade, and identifying energy as the future basis for economic links with the PRC.

Martin was proud of his efforts to create the G20, and that he had persuaded China to become a member:

When I was Finance Minister in the mid-90s, I wanted to create a Finance Ministers G20. I saw that the G7 was too small to make the key decisions, and the United Nations was simply too big. Too many other important countries were not at the table ... The big Asian countries had to be involved. It could become an international steering committee that could deal with the increasing complexities of a globalized world.

Larry Summers, the American Secretary of the Treasury, and I talked. We needed to get India and China and others at the table. I put it to the G7 with Larry's support. Then we went to various countries and said we needed a G20 and would they join. Spoke with the Chinese Foreign Minister and with the Vice Minister in charge of finance. They spoke with Wen Jiabao. I had dinner with him, and he was supportive.

The problem was that those whom we asked at the outset were positive, but those who were not consulted were less so ... All the countries agreed, except for the Americans. They would not say yes or no. George Bush never said no. He just wasn't sure that he wanted the G7 expanded.

It took some time, however, before the G20 emerged as a viable multilateral decision-making body, and it is fair to say that, despite Martin's efforts, more than a decade later the G20 had not lived up to his vision that it would become the world's future decision-making platform.

In 2005, Martin and President Hu Jintao agreed to establish a strategic partnership designed to elevate the relationship between Canada and China. At that time, China only had ten of these partnerships with other countries, and Martin recalled: "When we had that discussion, we were well on the way. We shook hands on it. We were among the first countries to make such an agreement with China." Unfortunately, five years passed before it was finally implemented. The same fate befell ADS, which would have greatly expanded Chinese tourism in Canada, providing Canada with several hundred million dollars in revenues, but the PRC withheld approval until Stephen Harper's visit in 2009.

Did trade with China improve during the Martin period? The deficit actually increased to its highest level. Imports from the PRC soared, while Canadian exports of value-added goods failed to match expectations. The Team Canada missions were scrapped, but new funding measures to assist the Canadian business community did not lead to a rise in exports. The government encouraged PRC investment in Canada as a way to develop closer economic links between the two countries, but a high profile bid of $4.7 billion by the Chinese metals giant Minmetals to acquire Noranda Inc., Canada's largest mining company, raised Canadian concerns and failed to materialize. The ambitious Pacific Gateway initiative remained stuck on the legislative order papers when the Martin government fell in early 2006. The government tried to increase its focus on trade by dividing the Department into separate foreign policy and trade units, briefly returning to the time in the early 1980s when Canada had separate Departments of External Affairs (DEA) and Industry, Trade and Commerce (ITC). However, the split proved to be unworkable and was quickly reversed.

What about human rights? By the late 1990s, Chrétien had opted for the bilateral dialogue, soft long-term development projects, and quiet diplomacy. Many Canadians felt that their government had not progressed in its human rights strategy with China, and that the focus on re-engagement and trade during the Chrétien period had eclipsed attention to rights and democracy in China. Martin continued to follow Chrétien's script – practising quiet diplomacy and talking directly to China's leaders. For Martin, human rights represented a personal legacy, based on his father's work as foreign minister in the 1960s. In his meetings with President Hu Jintao and Premier Wen Jiabao, Martin talked about how Canada could help China to develop democracy and expand human rights:

> I've always been concerned about human rights. It runs in my family. I had some pretty extensive discussions on human rights in China. Spoke with students at Tsinghua University and always with China's leaders. We worked with the Ministry of Justice, and with their universities.
>
> I stated during my discussions that economic reforms have to be coupled with respect for human rights. Canadians are sometimes bewildered that China is becoming better off economically, but has yet to make similar progress on rights issues.

Hu and Wen took the high road in their meetings with Martin by avoiding a prolonged discussion on human rights. Instead, they chose to talk about bringing new momentum to relations, raising the level of trust between the two countries, and charting new territories and areas of exchange. It was a moment of optimism on both sides. In 2005, PRC Ambassador Lu Shumin said: "Relations have entered a golden period in recent years, featuring frequent mutual visits among leaders of both countries, dynamic parliamentary exchanges, increased trade, flourishing cultural events, and close cooperation in international affairs."[1] Lu was especially enthusiastic about the decision that Martin and Hu had made to establish a strategic partnership:

> This move is of great significance ... The two sides will work to put in place a long-term and stable cooperation framework, make full use of existing mechanisms such as the bilateral Strategic Working Group, the Trade and Economic Joint Commission and the Agricultural Joint

Commission to further tap the cooperation potential and establish, if necessary, new cooperation mechanisms.[2]

Despite Lu's optimism, many of these initiatives were not implemented. Some said that the Martin government failed to act decisively, that it threw too many balls in the air, hoping to catch a few, while letting the rest fall to the ground. Others criticized Martin for "dithering," "not following through," or "wanting to be the last person in the room." These criticisms ignored the rich potential of the measures that he had initiated during his time in office. Did he simply not have enough time to carry out his agenda? We are reminded that his Liberal minority government had only twenty-six months in office, and he had to spend a large amount of that time just concentrating on staying in power.

More telling are comments from members of his government. One Department official said: "From 2004 on, we had activity masquerading as policy." David Mulroney, an assistant deputy minister at the time and later ambassador to China in the Harper period, said that China was changing too rapidly for Ottawa decision-makers to respond effectively. The blame for not following up on the Martin initiatives could be placed on an Ottawa bureaucracy that lacked the cohesive leadership and management skills required for adapting to a changing China. Mulroney explained:

> The first decade of the twenty-first century represented something of a Chinese rediscovery of Canada as an investment opportunity, an education provider, a vacation destination, and a place to shop for property as a hedge against possible unwelcome developments back home. This was happening so quickly that Canadians were essentially playing catch-up. Canada's national mood was characterized by what might be best described as ambivalence in the face of these changes.
>
> The hard truth is that we need to step up our foreign policy game to engage a rising China ... We will need to do a much better job when it comes to the actual *delivery* of foreign policy. Instead of simply assuming that the various departments and agencies will organize themselves, we need to ensure that the leadership is in place to hold people accountable for achieving clearly defined national objectives.

It was difficult to get anybody in Ottawa to think creatively about a "strategic partnership" with China. According to Mulroney, there were just too many silos, too much indifference, and no effective coordinating mechanism. He continued: "Although the idea was to bring senior officials from Canada and China together to work on a shared agenda, it was impossible to generate much enthusiasm on the Canadian side. We had to settle for a very unsatisfying teleconference in which senior Canadian officials read overlong prepared texts at their increasingly bored and frustrated Chinese counterparts."[3]

Aside from what he perceived to be lackluster management of the China file by many of those involved in the bilateral relationship, and more explicitly by his own Department, Mulroney identified yet another side of Canada's "China ambivalence." A growing body of Canadians did not like the new global China that was emerging in the twenty-first century, a country that was becoming more assertive and less responsive to Canadian concerns. Cheap Chinese imports were disrupting the Canadian economy, and China's growing presence in Canada raised alarms about increased espionage. The PRC crackdowns on Falun Gong and in Tibet upset many Canadians, and politicians were paying attention to the negative electoral implications of supporting closer engagement with the PRC. Canadians were beginning to wonder why we were currying favour with China, and in David Mulroney's words, China had become "*unlikable*," raising questions about how, or even whether we should be continuing our engagement with it.[4]

To these factors we can add a final note. The Liberals had been in power since 1993, and except for Brian Mulroney's nine years and Clark's one-year interregnum, China policy had belonged to the Liberals for over three decades. Trudeau had established the framework, and Chrétien stood in his footsteps. Martin's defeat in 2006 marked the end of thirteen long years of Liberal government, and its successor, a brash new Conservative government headed by Stephen Harper, intended to take Canada-China relations in a new direction. As such, many of Martin's initiatives were simply set aside by Harper, who wanted to put a different, tougher stamp on China policy. In the rest of this chapter, we examine how

Harper tried to change the bilateral relationship and the results of those efforts.

The Conservatives Take Charge

Stephen Harper took power in early 2006.[5] Harper's main concern was preserving his minority government while he implemented a conservative domestic agenda. The message was clear: the "new" Conservative government was differentiating itself from past Liberal policies wherever it could do so. This separation included foreign affairs in general, and China in particular. China policy had to be rethought, since the PRC was continuing to abuse human rights, trade with China was lagging behind expectations, and after more than a decade of Liberal government, relations with China had become stale and in need of an overhaul.

In the first two years, the Harper government made a number of unexpected changes, beginning with the rejection of many of Martin's China initiatives. The "strategic partnership" that had promised to put Canada among China's top ten partners was frozen; the bilateral dialogue was put on hold and later cancelled; quiet human rights diplomacy was shelved and replaced by strong public statements challenging China; and government financial support for trade with China was reduced. Most striking was a wholesale housecleaning of the China policy community, beginning with the Department and including almost anyone associated with past China policy. The prime minister's new China policy advisor was a Canadian Tibetan, prompting one senior minister to say: "It's as if our China policy is now made in Tibet."

The Department was ordered not to talk about "the strategic partnership" or about "comprehensive engagement." Senior officials and the PMO now had to approve the Department's routine meetings with members of the China policy community. Following past Conservative Party practice, Harper moved to cleanse the public service of "pro-Liberal tendencies," recalling what Brian Mulroney said when he took power in 1984: "Just give them all pink slips and running shoes." The CCBC, which included the

major Canadian companies doing business with China, was black-
listed by the Harper government for three years because of its past
Liberal connections. Canadian China specialists were no longer
consulted, having presumably been tainted by exposure to past
Liberal policies. All of this was startling. I had not seen such a turn
in Canadian China policy since recognition in 1970.

In my diary I wrote:

> What's happening in Ottawa? No one wants to talk seriously. After 20
> years I suddenly don't have access to any China files. Hard even to
> arrange a meeting just to talk with former colleagues in Foreign Affairs.
> A code of silence, *omertà*, has descended over China relations. Who are
> these new people in charge, and why are they doing this?

In November 2006, on his way to an APEC meeting in Vietnam,
Prime Minister Harper said with reference to China: "Canada will
not sell out its values in pursuit of the Almighty Dollar." He had
a grudging encounter with President Hu that barely totalled five
minutes in real time, handshakes, pleasantries, and interpretation
aside. Former prime minster Chrétien proclaimed how embarrassing it was for Canada that its prime minister had to conduct diplomacy in a hallway outside a Hanoi toilet.[6] It took eight months
before the Canadian foreign minister received the new Chinese
ambassador – unheard of in diplomatic practice. It also took eight
months before a Canadian minister visited China, and then the
government sent its minister of agriculture, a middle-ranking Conservative, rather than a more senior official.

The PRC was puzzled. Ambassador Lu Shumin, who had spent
time in Canada as a student and knew Canada well, asked why
Canada was ignoring China, and he cited a saying: "Once the pot
is on the back-burner, you can't expect the soup to bubble for too
long." Vice Foreign Minister He Yafei added: "I cannot say Canada
is squandering the relationship, but in practical terms it is lagging
behind." In Beijing, Chinese officials were unprepared for this shift
in relations. A diplomat at the Canadian Embassy said: "The Chinese immediately wanted to know when the next federal election
would be held, saying that these were not Mulroney Conservatives.

The MFA was telling us, 'If the Liberals come back things will be ok, we'll still have differences, but not like this.' They also said a lot of other things about the Harper government that I could not report back to Ottawa."

In 2007, Foreign Minister Peter MacKay went to China, the first visit by a Canadian foreign minister in four years. MacKay, who earlier had expressed his concern about increased Chinese espionage in Canada and was perceived as a China hardliner, said Canada could engage with Beijing "in terms we feel are appropriate and consistent with Canadian values. This can be done with tact, and without being confrontational." He met with Foreign Minister Yang Jiechi for four hours, but relations were not repaired. MacKay had focused on human rights, in particular, the case of Huseyin Celil, a former Chinese national who had become a Canadian citizen. Celil was seized in March 2006 by PRC security forces while he was on a visit to Uzbekistan, taken back to China, and sentenced to life imprisonment for alleged terrorist activities. Yang rejected MacKay's "interference" in China's internal affairs. He said that both sides should instead concentrate on improving economic links, revive a joint Canada-China Strategic Working Group that had promoted closer cooperation between both governments, and restore the stalled strategic partnership. Following diplomatic protocol, the PRC should have extended an invitation to Prime Minister Harper to visit China, but it chose not to do so.

China specialists in the Department were disappointed. Their political masters in the PMO had moved China relations into unfamiliar territory. One of them recalled: "We lost control over the bilateral relationship. We did not know what to expect. We thought the Foreign Minister's trip would be a step forward; instead, relations continued to drift throughout the year."

In the fall of 2007, Prime Minister Harper met with the Dalai Lama in his office, conspicuously displaying a Tibetan flag on his desk. The Chinese government was furious and abruptly cancelled a key bilateral meeting. As the year drew to a close, rumours persisted that the Cabinet and the Conservative caucus were split on how to deal with China. Opposing positions were represented by two ministers, David Emerson, the minister of international trade, and Jason Kenney, the secretary of state for multiculturalism and Canadian identity. Emerson and several other Conservatives advocated deeper engagement, especially through trade, while Kenney and his supporters continued to attack China's human rights practices. According to insiders, the prime minister, despite his public statements and actions that were quite critical of China, was not always on the "anti-China side," and by early 2008, he had taken "a modestly cautious position on China."

The year 2008 was a turning point. Even if it still did not have a viable long-term China strategy, the government was changing its tactics. Strident human rights rhetoric had proven ineffective, and Emerson even omitted "human rights" altogether from a speech, saying that he "did not want to lecture his audience." Ministers began to talk of "a solid partnership with China," "the importance of high-level relations," and "the need to increase trade." Responding to criticism by the business community that the Canadian share of the China market had fallen, the government lifted its ban on working with the CCBC. Emerson was appointed the new minister of foreign affairs, and he revitalized the atmosphere in the Pearson Building. A delighted Department officer commented: "After several years of weak ministers, we finally got Emerson and the promise of better management of our bilateral relations."

In March 2008, riots in Tibet resulted in a bloody crackdown by the PRC. This event led to strong international opposition to the Olympic Games scheduled to take place that summer in Beijing. Hosting the Olympics gave its leaders a long-awaited opportunity to showcase a new and powerful China to its people and to the world. Prime Minister Harper, as well as several other Western leaders, chose not to go to Beijing to attend the opening ceremonies, and Ottawa continued its strong criticism of China. Members of Canada's ethnic Chinese communities criticized what they perceived to be a wave of "China-bashing" by the Canadian government and were asking: "Is Harper just attacking the PRC, or is he attacking all the Chinese people?"

The Conservatives had been hoping that their hard-line anti-PRC policy would appeal to Chinese voters in key constituencies in the upcoming fall federal election, but it was having the opposite effect. The government then stepped back and softened its criticism of Beijing. When China suffered a devastating earthquake in Sichuan in May 2008, losing an estimated 80,000 people, Canada gave $75 million in assistance, the second largest contribution of any country, and the prime minister twice sent letters of condolence to China's leaders. Picking up on signals from Ottawa, relations between Embassy officials and their PRC counterparts in Beijing also began to improve. Then, during the fall election campaign, the prime minister announced he was considering an official visit to China.

In my diary I wrote:

> It is mid-2008 and relations are changing. Am in Chongqing. Our delegation just met with Bo Xilai, a rising star in the leadership. No mention of poor relations. We talked trade and educational exchanges. It's almost as if the past two years never happened. Am off to give lectures on human rights and democracy in a couple of Chinese universities, and at the Shanghai Party School.[7]

There were several reasons for this shift. Canada's "hard line" had failed to change China's human rights policies, and it was time for the government to change tactics. The business community was actively lobbying Ottawa to restore high-level access in China, and the China policy community – the media, Canadian ethnic Chinese, business leaders, academics, and NGOs – was urging Ottawa to "reset" relations with China.

The catalyst once again was trade, and the target was diversification from dependence on the American economy. Worried about possible declining American demand for Canadian exports because of the 2008 financial crisis, the Canadian government was ready to turn to the other big market, the expanding Chinese economy. Within a previously split Cabinet, trade now trumped human rights, prompting steps towards re-engagement. The China market beckoned, and ministerial visits increased. Access to top levels in China eased, and anti-China rhetoric all but disappeared.

During the fall federal election campaign, Harper said that he was ready to go to China, but would the PRC extend a formal invitation? Setting the stage, the government sent four key Canadian ministers to China within a short four-month period: Stockwell Day (International Trade), Lawrence Cannon (Foreign Affairs), Jim Flaherty (Finance), and John Baird (Transport). Day, Flaherty, and Baird had been vocal critics of Beijing. Now they were in China selling Canadian goods and re-engagement.

In April, Stockwell Day spent eight days in five Chinese cities. A Department official later commented:

> We wanted to get Day to China to promote trade. Given his position in Cabinet and his previous views, it was important he go there to get a first-hand look. He was more independent than most of the other Cabinet ministers, and he had a solid relationship with the Prime Minister. Harper said it was a good idea to send the China sceptic to China and see what happens.

Day, who was a vocal critic of China's human rights policies and a sceptic on re-engagement, met with four Chinese ministers and senior Party officials. He announced that Canada was opening trade offices in up to six Chinese cities. Canada was ready to collaborate with China in aerospace, agriculture, construction, education, oil and gas, communication technologies, and pharmaceuticals. When asked about human rights, he said that the purpose of his trip was to focus on trade: "If an official says they're going to talk about trade, then quite understandably the media will say, 'What about human rights?' If you say you are going to talk about human rights, then quite appropriately the media will say, 'What about trade?'"[8]

Day had tested the waters, and he returned home an enthusiastic supporter of re-engaging with China. The results exceeded expectations. The Department said that it was "a remarkable trip," and the media dubbed him a "Canadian Marco Polo," calling his visit a "Damascene moment" – comparing his shift on China to the dramatic biblical conversion of the Apostle Paul on the road to Damascus. A month later, Foreign Minister Lawrence Cannon met in Beijing with Foreign Minister Yang Jiechi and Vice President Xi Jinping. Cannon said he wanted relations to be "frank, friendly, and forward-looking. There are many issues upon which we can build a constructive and forward-looking *partnership*" (emphasis added). The use of the term "partnership," which had been proscribed by Harper since 2006, marked a step forward in relations. According to Cannon, both Xi and Yang said they were "looking forward to a visit from Prime Minister Harper," and "they told me the Prime Minister was welcome to come. We didn't discuss the date."

In June, Yang came to Ottawa. Prime Minister Harper received him in the prime ministerial office, unusual practice for meeting a visiting foreign minister. Harper welcomed Yang's invitation "to make an official visit when it would be convenient." Speaking to an audience that included senior government ministers, former foreign minister Joe Clark, and top business leaders, Yang proclaimed: "We need courage, we need vision, and I'm here to learn from you, dear friends from Canada. I'm also here to say to you that we cherish our relationship."

It was now just a matter of time. According to the Department, "by September we had the go-ahead that there could be a trip in late fall, but we didn't have a concrete date. It takes time to prepare a prime ministerial visit, at least three or four months, and the Chinese just weren't forthcoming." After having welcomed Harper, was the PRC now having second thoughts? A possible reason for the Chinese delay was the upcoming visit of the Dalai Lama. Beijing wanted to wait and see if the prime minister planned on seeing him again, and if the Canadian government intended to make a big fuss over Tibet independence. If Canada did so, a fall Harper visit would not happen.

The Dalai Lama was received only as a religious leader, and unlike previous visits to Canada, no major government ministers received him. It was a low-key trip without political overtones. Not surprisingly, after the Dalai Lama's departure the PRC quickly confirmed a December 1 arrival in Beijing for the prime minister. The Canadian government agreed, even though the prime minister would be attending the APEC Leaders' Summit in Singapore just two weeks before going to Beijing. Harper, averse to foreign travel, would have to fly back and forth to Asia twice, with little time to recover from jet lag.

The Prime Minister Goes to China

Prime ministerial visits are defining events in bilateral relations. Pierre Trudeau's trip in 1973 solidified the bilateral context and framework; in 1986, Brian Mulroney put a Conservative stamp on relations; in 1994, Jean Chrétien's Team Canada mission signalled that Canada had re-engaged with China; and in 2005, Paul Martin committed Canada to policies that could have elevated relations to the next level. Now it was Stephen Harper's turn. Signals were given for hesitant Conservative ministers to get on the China bandwagon. The PMO chose two ministers, Day (International Trade) and Gerry Ritz (Agriculture), to accompany him, and it instructed the Department to prepare strategic options, briefing materials, drafts of speeches, and talking points for an imminent visit. Ottawa set up a communications strategy to get the media onside and to spin a positive message to the Canadian public. That message said the time had come to re-engage, especially through joint economic links. While the projection of Canadian values continued to be important, the Harper government was now searching for a better balance between trade and human rights, and that meant reducing the focus on the latter.

A prime ministerial visit must have "deliverables" – agreements or key joint statements that raise the relationship to a higher level. Otherwise the trip will be judged a failure. Both sides wanted a positive outcome, since this occasion was the first official visit by a top leader to either Canada or China since 2005. No dramatic results, such as moving forward with the nearly forgotten strategic partnership or concluding a major trade agreement, were expected to happen, and in the words of Peter Harder, then CCBC president, "the main deliverable is the trip itself."[9]

Ottawa prepared a host of scenarios, listing "strategic outcomes," "significant issues," "concrete deliverables," "aspirations," "possible controversies," "talking points," "sensitive issues," "management of the meeting," and "context." The scenarios were managed by the PCO and compiled by the Department in collaboration with other government departments, the Post, and the PMO. Then they were given to the prime minister and his staff for approval. Over a three-month period, the scenarios continually changed, as Ottawa kept refining its policy positions as it was learning what the Chinese side had in mind and what the prime minister wanted to accomplish during the visit.

The initial focus was on what the government intended to convey to the Chinese leadership and to those Canadians who had questions about Harper's trip. Why was the prime minister going to Beijing after being so critical of China? If Prime Minister Harper planned on making trade and investment a priority, what about the human rights file? What will he say to President Hu and Premier Wen, and how should he respond to their comments?

The early scenarios included securing an agreement on canola exports to China, which were then worth over $1 billion annually. The government wanted to create a new human rights dialogue with China to replace the bilateral dialogue that Canada had suspended in 2006, and it hoped to resume negotiations that had started in 1994 for a foreign investment treaty. Although each item was discussed during the visit, no agreement was reached on those three. From the outset, however, during the various iterations of strategic outcomes and deliverables, there was always one item that stood at the top of Canada's list – the granting of approved destination status (ADS). This would give official approval for Chinese tourist groups to travel in Canada and could annually bring several hundred million dollars of new revenues. The Department recalled: "We had to get ADS, the Prime Minister's staff insisted on this, almost as a precondition for his going to China."

The real deliverable, however, was a document called the Joint Statement, which the two sides put together to reset bilateral re-engagement. The fourteen-paragraph statement outlined a wide range of areas of cooperation, including anticipated agreements and deliverables, compiled jointly, in advance of the prime minister's trip, as if the visit itself was almost a formality. One Canadian official said: "It gave us the opportunity to work together again with our PRC counterparts, writing a comprehensive joint document agreeing on almost everything before the actual event. No controversies, no surprises. Just what the Prime Minister wanted, and a good way to restart relations."

At the Post, David Mulroney met with He Yafei, vice minister of foreign affairs, to plan the visit.

> Over lunch, I floated the idea of having a joint statement, a document that the Prime Minister and China's Premier, Wen Jiabao, could sign. In addition to being a record of agreements reached during the visit, it would allow us to point the way to a more ambitious bilateral agenda for the months ahead. I saw the statement as a highly useful way of organizing thinking on both side ... Mr. He agreed to the idea before the arrival of the fruit plate that marked the end of the meal.[10]

Mulroney admitted that he should have sought prior approval from headquarters before raising the idea with Vice Minister He. "I had taken a gamble because I thought we needed to move quickly to secure agreement. And I didn't want to get held up by a risk-averse Ottawa." The reaction from Ottawa was positive – officials had been searching for the best way to approach the Chinese side. Ottawa was relying on the Post to make the initial contact with the Chinese, and the ambassador's meeting with the vice minister was a good beginning. The Department was pleased with Mulroney's initiative: "We had been discussing something similar in Ottawa, but hadn't expected the Chinese would be interested in preparing a joint statement in advance of the visit."

The Embassy did the first draft of the statement, giving Canada the opportunity to ask for key deliverables and to obtain ADS. In 2005, the two sides had discussed ADS, but China held back. Since then, nearly five years had elapsed without any movement. Foreign Minister Lawrence Cannon had told the ambassador: "Bluntly, the success of the visit will be judged by whether or not we get the tourism deal. And we are going to get it, right?" Mulroney said: "I told Cannon that I thought it was within reach."

In the first draft, Canada included a reference to China granting ADS. Would the Chinese side cross it out or leave it in? After the Chinese side had reviewed the draft, "our words were still there. The Chinese had simply put them in brackets."

Mulroney later said:

Following each exchange with its Chinese counterparts, the Post sent
the latest revisions to the Joint Statement back to Ottawa to have its relevant paragraphs reviewed by technical experts in the departments and
agencies that would play a role in its implementation – places such as
the RCMP, Environment Canada, Agriculture Canada, and the Department of Justice. Since it was a document for the Prime Minister's signature, it was also sent to the Privy Council Office, whose job was to run
the text by the Prime Minister's own Office. As the weeks went by, the
brackets came off one by one. Just days before Harper's arrival, they
finally came off the reference to ADS.

As the visit grew closer, Ottawa was becoming concerned about
the large size of the delegation. At one point, the list contained close
to sixty names, but eventually it was pared down to forty people.
The Department pointed out: "We hadn't had a prime ministerial
visit to China since Martin went. Of course we all wanted to go,
especially since we viewed this as a new beginning with China."
With two ministers and their staff, plus officials from the PMO,
PCO, RCMP, the Department, and a half-dozen parliamentarians,
Ottawa and Beijing had their hands full. The Canadian advance
team twice went to China to inspect the venues and the security
arrangements in Beijing, Shanghai, and Hong Kong, as well as to
establish working relationships with the Post and with their Chinese counterparts. The team's main task was to ensure the prime
minister's safety, especially in public places, when he and his wife
went to buy tea in a street market, tour the Great Wall and the
Forbidden City in Beijing, or meet with people in Shanghai and
Hong Kong.

The CCBC took charge of the business side of the visit. It was
holding its annual general meeting in Shanghai, and representatives from over 100 Canadian companies would be in attendance.
The CCBC and the Canadian Chamber of Commerce organized
a banquet for 500 Chinese and Canadian business executives, at
which the prime minister was giving a speech. The CCBC was back
in the good graces of the Conservative government, which had criticized the CCBC's powerful Liberal connections and had refused
to work with it for almost three years. As one CCBC official put it,

"when the Conservatives took office, we were frozen out of China policy discussions, but times had changed. Now they needed us, and we played a major role in the visit by re-establishing business links at the highest levels."

Since the government was shifting to closer engagement and was concentrating on trade, what would the prime minister say to China's leaders about rights and values? The visit's main purpose was to open doors and to emphasize collaboration, not confrontation, so strong words on rights by the prime minister could easily raise Chinese hackles and defeat the purpose of the trip. Yet Harper was not going to sacrifice his commitment to a "principled" rights policy, and he said, upon his arrival in Beijing: "I am not checking my commitment to Canadian values at the door."

Fully aware of the problem, Canadian and Chinese officials minimized the rights issue in the Joint Statement with a key paragraph that read: "Both sides acknowledge that differing histories and national conditions can create some distinct points of view on issues such as human rights," which are to be resolved "on the basis of equality and mutual respect." Harper was on board. He would raise the human rights issue quietly, in private discussion with President Hu Jintao and Premier Wen Jiabao, just as Chrétien and Martin had done during their meetings with China's leaders. When Harper had met with Hu at the APEC Summit in Singapore two weeks earlier, he had also downplayed the rights rhetoric. For this omission, Harper had been criticized within his own party. Wasn't this a return to the old Liberal ways of dealing with China? To the dismay of some of his Conservative colleagues, he was heading in that direction.

Arrival in Beijing

When Harper arrived, I was in Beijing. Usually Canada doesn't rank that highly in Chinese media reporting. We are, after all, less important to China than we think. Nevertheless, a visit by the leader of another country is always covered, maybe not on page one or at the top of the news. However, the visit commanded front-page attention, with a surprising range of comments. *Xinhua* quoted Canadian officials as saying Harper's visit was a "positive trip" that strengthened bilateral relations and that a "thaw" was taking place in China-Canada relations. An MFA spokesman told reporters that, while the two countries may not agree on some issues, for example, on human rights, they nevertheless "have a strong, deep, diverse, and mutually beneficial relationship ... The two countries will celebrate the 40th anniversary of diplomatic relations next year ... China is now Canada's second largest merchandise trading partner. People-to-people links are at an historic level."

Some Chinese media reporting was less forgiving. One editorial blamed Harper "for the deteriorating relationship" between the two countries. "His actions had stirred tremendous dissatisfaction" from both the Chinese government and the Chinese people. "He was always raising the so-called human rights issue." As a result, "Canada-China relations had dropped behind US-China relations and EU-China relations." Relations had been "more mature" when Jean Chrétien was prime minister. Now there were "considerable obstacles to a real restart of bilateral ties." However, it was hoped the visit "could be a turning point." From the PRC media's perspective, Canada, driven mainly by its business community, "was signaling a positive shift in policy."[11]

At the Embassy, officers were busy with last-minute preparations and optimistic about the likely outcome of the visit. The dark days of poor official relations were apparently ending, and if both sides could follow the script prescribed in the Joint Statement, the future looked promising. They hoped there would be "no blunders" during the prime minister's visit. The MFA echoed these views, and said: "This is the chance for both countries to turn the page and restore proper bilateral relations."

In my diary I wrote:

It's early December in Beijing, and the Prime Minister is here. We've waited a long time for this visit. Don't exactly know his agenda. Will Canada reset relations? Seems the focus is on trade – are we returning to the days of Jean Chrétien? The Chinese media have been surprisingly critical. Have been coming to China for over 40 years, and except for the period right after Tiananmen, the past three years have been the most difficult.

Wednesday, December 2

It was a cold grey afternoon in Beijing when Prime Minister Harper arrived with his wife, Laureen. He is met at the airport by a mid-level Chinese minister, the Canadian ambassador, and the Chinese security personnel. The journalists who are accompanying him exit first, out the rear doors. They line up to greet the prime minister and his wife when they descend from the plane. The journalists take several photo ops, and then the prime minister is whisked downtown in a motorcade of black cars to the St. Regis Hotel, a favourite place for visiting foreign leaders to stay because of its excellent security facilities.

The delegation includes the prime minister's advisors, the two ministers, Day and Ritz, their staff, six parliamentarians, officials from the PCO, PMO, RCMP, and the Department, security and administrative personnel, and representatives from the Canadian ethnic Chinese communities. The business leaders accompanying him on the visit have travelled separately. They would be attending the banquet on Friday evening, as well as the meetings in Beijing, Shanghai, and Hong Kong.

After his arrival, the prime minister immediately held a press conference to talk about the Canadian economy. The assembled Canadian and Chinese media are puzzled: why is the prime minister travelling halfway around the globe on a mission to improve relations with China, and the first thing he does is hold a press conference on the Canadian economy? Harper replies that Canada, not relations with China, is his main concern. "I regret it wasn't possible for me to announce this Fourth Report on our Economic Action Plan in Canada because of my travel. The economy remains our number one priority wherever we are in the world."

In my diary I wrote:

Is this unanticipated spotlight on the Canadian economy a fallback
position in case things go awry with China? Maybe it is just unfinished
business by the government. Or is it designed to turn the focus away
from human rights? Regarding the latter, the Prime Minister reminded
the journalists that he is not backing off on projecting Canadian values.
He said, "Those are the things that give us prosperity and the peaceful
and pluralistic society we enjoy."

Thursday, December 3

Headlines in the Beijing morning papers read: "Ties to Canada to
Thaw." The visit is mentioned in positive terms on national television, and his chief spokesperson is quoted as saying that Ottawa
is looking for better relations with China. At the same time, we
are reminded that Lai Changxing, who is wanted for major corruption crimes in the PRC, has not yet been returned to China. It's
been eight years, and he's still living in Vancouver.[12] One paper
reminds its readers: "Harper is the last of the G8 leaders to visit
China."

The Embassy briefs the prime minister, the two ministers,
and their staff. The deal has been struck to grant Canada ADS
– in exchange for allowing China to open a consulate in Montreal. Four agreements will be signed, for climate change, culture, mining, and agriculture. Prime Minister Harper receives
last-minute advice for his meetings with Premier Wen, President Hu, and the National People's Congress (NPC) Standing
Committee chairman, Wu Bangguo. They do a quick review of
the delegation's briefing notes – on trade, investment, energy
and environment, international issues, North Korea, and the
global recession. All is fine until an Ottawa political staff member precipitates a crisis by insisting that a sentence in the Joint
Statement had to be changed. The prime minister sets off for the
Great Wall, leaving Ambassador Mulroney behind to rewrite
the offending sentence:

As everybody else got up to join the motorcade that would take the PM to a photo opportunity at the Great Wall, I was instructed to "fix" the wording. There wasn't much time. I braced myself and called my Chinese counterpart. He was enraged and sputtered into the phone that he had already secured the Premier's approval of the document. If we tried to change a word of the text we could forget about the Joint Statement. Then he stopped taking my calls.

I sat down, feeling a bit sick, and began to deconstruct the offending sentence. I tried to do the minimum to it possible, enough to change the tone to pass muster with the PMO, but not so much as to further enrage the Chinese. The trouble was that I couldn't get through to anybody on the Chinese side. In the end, we simply texted the revised wording to them and waited. As the motorcade was returning to the hotel, the Chinese called back to say that we had a deal.[13]

The visit began with a measure of pomp and ceremony typical of such visits. Due to the cold Beijing weather, Harper is received inside the Great Hall of the People, and he and Wen stand at attention as the two national anthems are played. They walk together on red carpets to view a colourful array of military personnel, and then head to the meeting rooms where Harper will meet with China's two top leaders, Hu and Wen.

Following Chinese diplomatic practice, the Canadians are seated on one side at a long rectangular table facing their Chinese counterparts. The prime minister's personal interpreter is sitting next to him. The media and photographers are there to record Wen's welcome remarks and Harper's reply, and then they have to leave the room. The remaining Canadian media pool reporter records the following conversation:

WEN: The China-Canada relationship experienced twists and turns in recent years, which was not in the interest of both sides. The delay for your visit was too long, which is why the media call your visit long overdue.

HARPER: I agree with you that five years is a long time. It's also been almost five years since we had yourself or President Hu in our country.

WEN: I remember my trip to Canada back in 2005, when I expressed a
wish that our two countries could set an example for long-lasting
cooperation between two countries with differing systems and
development levels. I remember quoting a Chinese proverb when I
gave a speech at that time. The proverb reads, "Common visions and
common ideals can bring people together, in spite of the thousands of
miles that set them apart."

HARPER: I saw the Great Wall this morning, which is something everybody
should see before they finish passing through this life, and I look
forward to seeing many more of the treasures of your country and
meeting with the great Chinese people.

WEN: Your visit this time has a great mission and special significance.

Harper agrees that bilateral relations are entering a new phase
and that the two countries are poised to renew their partnership.
He says to Wen:

There are many complementarities between our two large Pacific
countries. We can do much together in trade and investment, energy,
the environment and health. We welcome closer cooperation in
human rights – each side should state its position clearly. We think
Canada can make a contribution to China in all these areas. We are
pleased that China has granted ADS to Canada, and that we are going
to sign a number of important agreements at the conclusion of our
meeting.

The media race to press and to broadcast, seizing on Wen's
remark that Harper had waited too long to make his visit to China.
Was this a direct rebuke or just a statement of fact? Why did Wen
choose such an undiplomatic remark, and will this put Harper on
the defensive and disrupt the rest of the visit? Harper had countered Wen's comments by replying: "Yes, it has been a long time,
but China's leaders have also not visited Canada for five years."
Chinese social media quickly point out that the last visit by a top
leader to either country was Hu's trip to Canada in 2005. Therefore, according to diplomatic protocol, the next visit had to come
from the Canadian side.

In Canada, reaction to Wen's comments ranged from "We got what we deserved" to "This was no big deal," as well as "An inappropriate and insulting comment." Officials in Ottawa brushed his remarks aside: "The Chinese Premier can be outspoken at times. Our Prime Minister took it in his stride, and we have moved on." Michael Ignatieff, the Liberal Party leader, was not so kind, saying: "The Prime Minister lost face today, and in that culture losing face is very important."[14]

Following the meeting with Wen, Harper met with President Hu, China's head of state and Party chief, for a shorter, more ceremonial visit. Hu welcomed the prime minister, whom he had met before on the margins of multilateral summit meetings. He said that Harper's trip would raise bilateral cooperation to a new level, and he did not mention the prime minister's delay in coming to China. Hu stated:

> Your visit is of great importance. China is ready to work with Canada to cement dialogues, exchanges, and cooperation in various areas, respect each other's core interests and major concerns, and properly handle sensitive issues between the two sides. Our two countries have had a good and frank relationship during almost 40 years of diplomatic relations. It is time for both sides to expand economic links and oppose protectionism in trade and investment.[15]

Harper thanked Hu for his warm remarks and said he was looking forward to closer relations. He had always dreamed of seeing China, even as a boy. He told Hu that the two sides had a "frank," "respectful," and "positive" relationship that would lead to more collaboration. He continued: "We each have our core interests, and we will treat them with respect. Next June we will host the G20 Summit, and we will welcome your second trip to Canada."

The two sides released the Joint Statement and announced that they had signed the four agreements. Along with granting ADS, China also lifted its ban on pork imports, barred for the previous year because Canada was an H1N1 virus–affected country. Those two deliverables alone promised to bring close to $300 million in additional revenues in the coming year, and Jason Kenney, the minister of citizenship, immigration and multiculturalism, crowed that, with the granting of ADS, "our government has managed to achieve what previous Liberal governments have not." Opposition politicians were quick to point out that getting ADS was not a political coup. The reason it had not been granted since 2005 was because of current Conservative policies, not past Liberal ones. In 2005, when Martin and Hu had made it a priority, only 30 countries had ADS. Now Canada was number 140, lagging behind two-thirds of the world's countries.

The Department stated: "These are tangible gains. We are back on track, even if we still have a lot of work to do in the secondary meetings with our two Ministers and with the business community in Shanghai and Hong Kong." The leaders had formally approved the Joint Statement, which set up a new framework for relations with China, and the prime minister had raised human rights with both Hu and Wen. That evening, at the banquet in the Great Hall hosted by the Chinese premier, the conversation was upbeat, spirited toasts were made, and both sides spoke of a renewed bilateral relationship.

The Joint Statement

The full transcript of what was said and agreed upon during Harper's meetings with Hu and Wen is not available. However, enough information is found in government documents, media accounts, and from interviews to highlight what was said. The Joint Statement was made public on December 3 by both governments.[16] It provides us with a summary of the main issues agreed upon by both sides and was designed to be a blueprint for future relations. As such, the statement is worth closer examination.

It begins with a number of "feel good" statements about the bilateral relationship:

> Both sides had an in-depth, candid and productive exchange of views on China-Canada relations and major international and regional issues of mutual interest, finding consensus in many areas...

Both sides gave a positive assessment of the development of Canada-China relations in the 39 years since the establishment of diplomatic relations and acknowledged that China and Canada are both influential countries in the Asia-Pacific region ... Friendly ties have long existed between China and Canada, symbolized by such figures as Doctor Norman Bethune and the fact there are now 1.3 million Chinese Canadians in Canada ... The two sides agreed to work together to further promote Canada-China cooperation in all bilateral areas and international affairs, as bilateral relations enter a significant new era.

Article Four talks about the importance of effective policy implementation and how to "operationalize" the agreements made at the leaders' level. It states:

Both sides agreed to enhance the role of the Strategic Working Group, a bilateral mechanism established in 2005 to facilitate regular high-level bilateral exchange between officials. Deputy Minister-level officials will meet early in 2010 to discuss the nature of this enhancement and likely subjects of focus, including trade and investment, energy and environment, health and governance. Both sides further agreed to make full use of the more than 40 bilateral consultation mechanisms already in existence.

Article Five assures the Chinese that Canada will maintain its one-China policy and its current "non-state" relationship with Taiwan. That put an end to the activities of a small group of Conservative MPs who, before the Conservatives gained power, had been pressing for greater Taiwanese independence. The article states:

The Chinese side emphasized that the question of Taiwan concerns China's sovereignty and territorial integrity. The Canadian side reiterated its consistent and long-standing One-China policy, established at the founding of diplomatic relations.

Article Six represents a softening of the Canadian position that human rights are universal and should follow the Western model, as represented by "Canadian values." It proposes increased dialogue, with the understanding that China may follow a different pathway. It states:

> Both sides recognized that each country and its people have the right to choose their own path, and that all countries should respect each other's choice of development model. Both sides acknowledged that differing histories and national conditions can create distinct points of view on issues such as human rights.

Article Seven focuses on bilateral trade. It covers a range of issues, from encouraging economic cooperation between the two countries, to the negotiation of a foreign investment promotion and protection agreement (FIPA), providing a list of key trade sectors, and supporting the reduction of trade barriers:

> The two sides were in agreement that strong economic and trade complementarity exists between Canada and China ... Canada welcomes investment from China ... Both sides undertake to expedite negotiations of a China-Canada Foreign Investment Promotion and Protection Agreement [FIPA] ... Both sides agreed on the need to encourage further growth of bilateral trade from its current levels, increasing trade in goods and services in all sectors, including energy and resources, infrastructure, telecommunication and transportation, advanced technology, tourism, agriculture and financial services.

Article Eight addresses educational, cultural, business, and people-to-people links. It mentions the granting of ADS and the opening of the Chinese Consulate in Montreal:

> Both sides agreed to use the 40th anniversary of diplomatic relations as the opportunity to increase interaction between all sectors of society. China and Canada welcome two new channels to increase people-to-people interaction, through the opening of a new Chinese Consulate General in Montreal, and China's announcement during the visit of Approved Destination Status for Canada, further promoting the increased flow of tourists, students and business people between the two countries.

Articles Ten, Eleven, and Twelve discuss international and regional issues, for example, the global economic and financial crisis, the promotion of peace and security, denuclearization of the Korean Peninsula, cooperation in multilateral institutions, and global health concerns. They state:

> The two sides had an in-depth exchange of views on the current global economic and financial situation, and share the assessment that the world economy has shown positive signs of stabilization and recovery, but that this recovery is fragile. The two sides agreed to ... steadily reinforce the role of the G20 in global economic governance ... The Chinese side welcomed Canada's role in 2010 as host of the G20 Summit in June...
>
> The Canadian side welcomed China's contribution to regional peace and security through its stewardship of the Six Party Talks process, and expressed the hope that this vehicle to realize the denuclearization of the Korean Peninsula would soon be revived. Both sides noted their active roles in Afghanistan ... Leaders agreed that coordination and cooperation in fora including the UN, APEC and other multilateral bodies should be enhanced in the areas of nuclear security, nuclear non-proliferation and disarmament, food security, global health threats, climate change, and other major international and regional issues.

Article Thirteen focuses on bilateral cooperation on climate change and the upcoming Copenhagen Conference on the Environment:

> The two sides acknowledged that climate change is a common challenge confronting humanity and that international cooperation is the key to meeting this challenge. All parties should ... work together toward an agreed outcome at the Copenhagen Conference consistent with the principles established by the United Nations Framework on Climate Change.

Article Fourteen describes a rosy future. The year 2010 will mark the fortieth year of diplomatic relations with a significant expansion of travel and links between Canada and China:

Looking to the year ahead, both sides welcomed what will be visible manifestations of a deep-rooted, vibrant and growing Canada-China relationship. The Chinese side noted that the Olympic torch has passed to Canada, and welcomed the approaching Vancouver 2010 Winter Olympic Games, to which China will send a large team of athletes ... Starting in May 2010, the Canada Pavilion at the Shanghai World Expo 2010 will provide large numbers of Chinese citizens the opportunity to visit and enjoy numerous Canadian arts, cultural and other public events, commemorating 40 years of diplomatic relations between the two countries.

If we set aside the rhetoric and focus on specific policy content, the Joint Statement confirms the shift towards renewed bilateral relations. After four years of a fractured engagement, the two sides had come together and had agreed upon these fourteen paragraphs in advance of the prime minister's visit. Some parts are especially noteworthy, for example, Article Six stated that countries had the right to choose their own path on human rights. This was a concession to China. So was the affirmation that Canada was committed to the observance of a one-China policy, because the Conservatives had been flirting with the idea of rethinking Canada's relationship with Taiwan. This put an end to any further talk of Canadian support for a more autonomous Taiwan.

The Joint Statement foreshadowed a number of future initiatives. In Article Seven, the two sides agreed to take advantage of the economic links between the two countries. Three years later, they produced a major Economic Complementarities Study that identified potential high growth sectors that could serve as the basis for a free trade agreement.[17] Both sides agreed to pursue negotiations for a FIPA, which was realized in 2012. Article Four announced the resumption of the Strategic Working Group (SWG), at the deputy minister working level, to improve cooperation between officials on both sides. The SWG was a stepping stone for the implementation of the long-awaited strategic partnership. A year later, during Hu's visit to Ottawa in 2010, Canada and China finally restored the strategic partnership that the Harper government had scuttled in 2006.

While the Joint Statement dealt mostly with bilateral issues, Articles Ten, Eleven, Twelve, and Thirteen touched on global, international, and regional matters (North Korea, Afghanistan, the G20, post-2008 economic recovery, global warming, the Doha Round at the World Trade Organization, and other multilateral issues). It focused on generalities, promoting peace and security, stabilization of relations, policy dialogue, and coordination. Twenty years earlier, Canada had claimed a significant place in world affairs, believing that it could "mentor" China's entry into international institutions. By 2009, China had emerged as one of the two dominant world powers, not needing Canada's help, and setting up its own multilateral institutions. Canada's role in international affairs was steadily diminishing, helped by Ottawa's decision to lessen Canada's commitment to internationalism. What both sides had in common was their relationship with the United States, the primary trading partner for both countries. The 2008 financial crisis had weakened the American economy, and both Canada and China were suddenly looking for additional export markets. Why not increase trade with each other, given the complementarity of the Canadian and Chinese economies?

Finally, Article Eight talked of fostering educational, cultural, business, and people-to-people interaction. During the four years of poor official relations, those were the links that had kept the relationship viable. Commercial ties persisted, students went abroad, and development assistance projects continued to be carried out. In my case, the training program for Chinese executives that we began in 2000 at York University was scarcely affected by the cooling of relations. The Chinese Party and government officials we were training in Canada rarely commented on the state of relations between the two countries. The political situation also did not prevent the students I was teaching at the Beijing Foreign Studies University from listening to what I had to say about the rule of law, human rights, and democracy in Canada. It was up to them, of course, how they intended to apply what they were learning about Canada to their own situation in China.

Just before the Harper visit, I had written in my diary:

People are saying things are about to change. Cool politics disrupted bilateral relations, but they have had little effect on training Chinese executives here or in China, and no effect on my teaching in Beijing. People-to-people links keep our two countries together. Gave lectures on human rights to my Chinese students at Beiwai. No one complained. Am traveling all over China and hear good things about Canada from the Party officials we trained back in Canada. What will this current improvement in official relations bring?

Friday, December 4

The prime minister and his wife tour the Forbidden City. Afterwards, he has a courtesy meeting with the NPC's Wu Bangguo, who ranked third in China's leadership hierarchy. Wu had transited through Vancouver at the end of August, on his way to Latin America, and he now thanks Prime Minister Harper for the reception that Canada had provided him, including a special preview visit to the site of the 2010 Vancouver Winter Olympics. Wu welcomes Harper to China, repeating the mantra that "we must respect each other's core interests, each other's sovereignty, territorial integrity, and choice of development." Those are the boundaries within which China is willing to talk about human rights and governance. Wu sees several opportunities for strengthening bilateral relations in 2010: the Winter Olympics, the Shanghai Expo, and the G20 meeting in Toronto. Harper replies that his trip has been "fruitful" and that he looks forward to closer ties between the two countries and with the NPC, China's national legislative body. He mentions the work of the Canada-China Legislative Association, which periodically brings members from both sides together to discuss the work of their respective legislative bodies. In November, a delegation from the Canadian Senate had visited China as guests of the NPC to study China's economy, and Wu says such exchanges are the NPC's longest lasting and most successful links with foreign counterparts. The visit ends with affirmations of friendship and the promise of renewed relations in 2010.

The *People's Daily*, *China Daily*, and *Xinhua* present almost identical stories, each saying that the two countries have "turned a new page" in their relations. There is not much difference between the Canadian and the PRC coverage of the meetings, except for the usual Chinese avoidance of any mention of human rights. The Chinese media claim that Prime Minister Harper is finally ready to hand over Lai Changxing to the authorities in China, but no one in the Canadian delegation has heard him say this, although they have assumed that it would eventually happen. *Xinhua* writes that the prime minister "had attached great importance to the Strategic Partnership with China." However, he has still not publicly uttered the words "strategic partnership," and they would not be mentioned by him until six months later, in 2010, when Hu visits Canada and the two countries announce the resumption of the Canada-China strategic partnership.

The delegation flies to Shanghai, and in the evening, its members attend the "Canada-China Business Centennial Gala Banquet." It is a big affair, celebrating the one hundredth anniversary of Canada's first Trade Commissioner's Office in China. According to one trade officer from the Shanghai Consulate:

> It was huge. We were working day and night. We had to find a venue to seat over 500 Canadian and Chinese business leaders and officials, plus all the media and security. The Grand Ballroom in the Hyatt Hotel won the competition. We had great photo ops, a spectacular view of the Bund on one side and Pudong on the left. We built a special dais for the Prime Minister's speech. The cooking was fusion: a combination of Chinese and Canadian. Not easy to find the right Canadian cuisine. We wound up with British Columbia ice wine, Manitoba wild rice, and maple syrup ice cream. Not sure the maple syrup ice cream was a good idea.

Over fifty Canadian firms were represented, including Atomic Energy of Canada, Bombardier, the Bank of Montreal, Manulife,

Power Corporation, the Royal Bank of Canada, and SNC-Lavalin. The Chinese companies included Baosteel, Minmetals, Fosun, Huawei, Sinochem, the Industrial and Commercial Bank of China (ICBC), the China International Capital Corporation (CICC), and the China Investment Corporation (CIC).

The Prime Minister's Speech

Harper's speech is crafted to show the business community that improved commercial relations are "a bilateral priority."[18] He recognizes that China is in the midst of major economic transformation, and that the two countries have a past history of positive bilateral relations. He says that now is the time to take advantage of growing opportunities in trade and investment:

> China has been witness to the greatest surge in general prosperity in the history of mankind. More than four hundred million people have been lifted out of poverty. Over one hundred cities have grown to a population of more than a million. The economy, once directed entirely by the state, has become firmly market-oriented, and private enterprise has flourished.
>
> I could go on, but the bottom line is this: there can be no mistaking the evidence. Today, ladies and gentlemen, China is truly awake – awake, and set to help shape the future of the entire world!

The audience listening to his remarks might have wondered whether this was the same prime minister who in 2006 had dismissed engagement with China as sacrificing Canadian values for the "Almighty Dollar," and who, for the following two years, had repeatedly criticized the PRC. Harper continued:

> Today, Chinese Canadians enrich all aspects of our society, our democracy and our economy ... Indeed, through a solid work ethic, a dedication to family and community and a commitment to educational achievement, Chinese Canadians are helping to secure Canada's place in the 21st century...

And a Canadian doctor, Norman Bethune, played a significant role
in the history of this country. Canadian companies like Manulife and
Sun Life pioneered economic networks throughout China more than
one hundred years ago. Home-grown enterprises like Bombardier
and SNC-Lavalin have been thriving here for decades ... [T]he strong
ties between our two countries allowed Canada to offer, following the
earthquake last year, both significant public and private aid to the people of Sichuan province...

Our total two-way trade is now valued at over 53 billion dollars.
China is Canada's second largest merchandise trading partner and our
third largest export market.

The main section of Harper's speech addressed economic and
trade issues. Canada has invested over $1 billion in the Asia-
Pacific Gateway, an integrated system of ports, airports, road and
rail connections "that link Asia deep into the North American marketplace," cutting down transportation time to and from China
by as much as three days. Harper describes Canada as a natural
destination for Chinese investment, with "falling tax rates, a low
debt-to-GDP ratio, [and] one of the most welcoming environments
for foreign investment in the world." He emphasizes that the two
sides are a natural fit in the field of energy: "China will need stable
sources of power. And Canada is an emerging energy superpower,
a major supplier of every type of energy, seventh in the world in
crude oil production, with the second largest proven reserves, third
in natural gas production, and the largest producer of uranium."

Both Canada and China have fared well during the recent economic downturn. The recent financial crisis has been, according to
Harper, "the biggest challenge facing ... all the world's economies,"
and he urges each country to follow through with "committed stim-
ulus," "to avoid inflation and asset bubbles," and to "stand firm
against protectionist pressures ... That's why fighting protectionism
and expanding trade have been top priorities of our government's
foreign policy." The prime minister welcomes China's decision to
lift its ban on Canadian pork exports, although he expresses concern about China's continuing restrictions on canola, which "can
only lead to increased pressures for retaliation and protectionism."

Harper confirms that Canada has been granted approved destination status. Canada will also open four more trade offices in China, in addition to the ones that Minister Day opened earlier in the year. "Together, they will enhance our ability to support even more commercial links in exports, investment and innovation between our two countries." An agreement has been signed to combat climate change, to work together in energy conservation and efficiency, renewable energy, carbon capture and storage, and methane recovery and utilization. Collaboration like this "can demonstrate how to balance energy development and economic growth with environmental protection and can serve as an example of cooperation for the rest of the world."

As he nears the end of his speech, it is *de rigueur* to mention human rights, and he says:

> Just as trade is a two-way street, so is dialogue ... [A] mutually beneficial economic relationship is not incompatible with a good and frank dialogue on fundamental values like freedom, human rights and the rule of law...
>
> And so, in relations between China and Canada, we will continue to raise issues of freedom and human rights, and be a vocal advocate and an effective partner for human rights reform, just as we pursue the mutually beneficial economic relationship desired by both our countries...
>
> I will conclude tonight with an invitation to all Chinese. We are anxious to return your Olympic hospitality. Come and visit Canada next year as we host the twenty-first Winter Olympic Games. Come and enjoy Vancouver, famously rated the world's most livable city.

The audience applauds Harper's call for stronger economic ties. Chinese business leaders and potential investors like what they have heard. The Canadian business community is optimistic. The CBC reports the following comments by members of the business community:

> We have been waiting to secure better access at the top in China. His trip does that. That's how the China market works.

The Prime Minister's support for trade and investment is a long time coming. We have great potential in the fields of energy and green technology.

The opening of the new trade offices is a boon to Canadian companies. Gives us on the spot contacts with Chinese companies.

Canadian opposition politicians and the media are more critical. Liberal leader Michael Ignatieff said: "While the speech was a step forward, the Prime Minister still has a lot of repair work to do on China." The *Globe and Mail*, which is closely monitoring the prime minister's trip, writes: "Stephen Harper has an unfailing ability to take a weak speech and make it even flatter through delivery, and his address to Chinese and Canadian business leaders Friday evening was no exception." The paper did acknowledge that, "despite his mauling by Premier Wen Jiabao over the Conservative government's tardy and reluctant recognition of the importance of the China-Canada relationship, the Prime Minister's trip is substantially a success."

Saturday, December 5

In the morning, the prime minister and his wife go to a Shanghai street market to buy tea for his mother. A crowd gathers to greet the cavalcade of black limos with its foreign guests. "Canada's Chairman is coming to the market!" they shout. "Harper, Harper!" Harper and Laureen walk hand in hand to the small tea shop, followed by the media and security people.[19] They sit down for a tea-tasting ceremony and are joined by Canadian Mark Rowswell, "the most famous foreigner in China." Rowswell, known as "Dashan," is a superstar in China, an actor, comedian, and absolutely fluent in Mandarin. The prime minister buys three kinds of tea: oolong, green, and black. The shop assistant says: "The Prime Minister is a very handsome guy, and his wife is very nice, very elegant. They seem like very nice people."

The Harpers step out into the large crowd for handshakes and photo ops. The Chinese know how to put on a welcome for foreigners, and Harper's wife, surveying the scene and smiling, is overheard saying: "You're popular here." The Canadian media later write: "This was an ironic remark, given the rebukes the Prime Minister had received during his two days in Beijing, when he was reminded four times by government leaders that after four years it was time to visit China."

The prime minister meets with the Shanghai Party secretary, and they are then joined by Shanghai and central government officials, the Canadian ambassador, and the Canadian consul general, before being escorted to a meeting room where they are filmed and photographed "exchanging pleasantries." The prime minister says that Canada's presence in Shanghai began in 1909, when Canada appointed its first trade commissioner in China, and adds: "Now we are entering our second century of commercial relations." He talks about developing trade between this city of over twenty million people and Canada. The Party secretary responds by inviting the prime minister to come again next year to visit the Shanghai World Expo.

At noon, Harper attends a business luncheon organized by the Canadian Chamber of Commerce and chaired by Stockwell Day, to brief a select group of twenty-five Canadian companies on the business situation in Shanghai, based on the experience there of Canadian architectural firms, banks, and companies such as Manulife and McCain Foods. According to one person who attended, it was "an excellent situation for us to learn about actual business opportunities and pitfalls in China." Short of time, the prime minister stays for thirty minutes, just enough for photo ops and a short press conference. Then he and Dashan visit Canada's pavilion at the 2010 Shanghai Expo, designed by Cirque du Soleil and under construction by SNC-Lavalin. The prime minister is impressed: "The Canada Pavilion will be stunning. I invite everyone to come and discover this destination at Expo 2010." He adds:

It will present Canada as the modern, democratic, bilingual, diversified, and environmentally responsive country that it is. A country with successful, sustainable cities that are innovative, creative and prosperous places. It will provide an exceptional showcase for our country in this growing city, illustrating the dynamic nature of our arts and culture, as well as highlighting our Canadian values.

Saturday and Sunday, December 5 and 6

The delegation leaves for Hong Kong. There was nothing especially controversial in Hong Kong-Canada relations at the time, and this part of Harper's China trip is somewhat of an anti-climax. He is there to wave the flag for the close to 200,000 Hongkongers holding a Canadian passport. By 2009, 100,000 Hong Kong residents had been educated in Canada, and 500,000 individuals of Hong Kong descent were living in Canada. The 160 Canadian firms doing business in Hong Kong included major corporations such as Manulife, Sun Life, and Research in Motion. The one-thousand-member Canadian Chamber of Commerce in Hong Kong was Canada's largest and most powerful overseas chamber.

Since 1997, the Canadian government had been keeping a watchful eye on the political situation in Hong Kong. Ottawa was concerned about the possible erosion of the "one country, two systems" formula that could reduce political and economic freedom in Hong Kong. Accompanied by Canada's consul general, Harper met with Donald Tsang, Hong Kong's Chief Executive. Harper was hopeful that the individual freedoms, rule of law, and protection of human rights that he saw in Hong Kong would become a model for China. The business community turns out for a Chamber of Commerce event to hear the prime minister talk about his successful meetings in Beijing. Historically, Hong Kong has been a stepping stone into China for Canadian business, and Harper is bringing the good news that relations with the PRC are improving. He lays a wreath at the Sai Wan cemetery, commemorating the courageous band of Canadian soldiers who lost their lives when Japan invaded Hong Kong in the Second World War. After a day and a half, his trip is over, and Harper and most of his delegation leave Hong Kong.

The majority of the Canadian media echo the *Globe and Mail* – that Harper's visit to China was a success and that relations have been restored. However, the *Toronto Star* believes Ottawa has exaggerated the significance of the one big deliverable, the ADS tourism deal, as well as the expanded trade opportunities. "We get so caught up in the mystique of the Middle Kingdom, and the allure of its marketplace, that we lose sight of the fundamentals. Here's one. No prime minister can single-handedly open doors for Canadian industry. For all the times that Jean Chrétien waved the flag in China, he barely moved the dial on bilateral trade."

The business community sees new opportunities emerging in the China market because of the restoration of links at the top. The Canadian academic community, critical of the Harper government's China policy since 2006, applauds the shift in tone and relations. Public reaction in Canada is generally positive, although democracy advocates believe that the government has sacrificed human rights in its haste to improve the political climate for trade and investment. Amnesty Canada asks: "Has Harper bought these advantages at the price of abandoning the high moral ground on rights? We hope not, and we trust not."

Shortly afterwards, in an upbeat address to CCBC members, Ambassador Mulroney comments on the results of the Harper visit:

> The visit had many direct and immediate results, and also set our forward agenda ... China is the largest, fastest developing country in the world. It aims now to regain the political and economic position it occupied till the 1830s. This reawakening has an inevitable impact on Canada's economic, political, environmental, and security interests. We are entering a new era in the Canada-China relationship. It is time to set new goals for our ongoing, strategic engagement, our cooperation on multilateral files of common interest, our efforts to develop increased trade and investment, and the benefit citizens in both countries derive from the promotion of human rights and good governance.

Still in Beijing, I wrote in my diary:

> Went to the Embassy again today. They are exhausted from the PM's visit. Said it went well – a turning point after so many years waiting. Did not reveal all the details, but we did get ADS and pork. We are

setting up new trade offices, and there's hope we can revive the strategic partnership. As for human rights, that seems lost in the shuffle. The
Prime Minister talked with Wen and Hu about rights, but nothing was
made public. Let's see what happens.

After the Visit

From the perspective of both governments, the visit was a step
forward. Committing Harper to an official meeting with China's
top leaders, after more than three years of essentially shunning
them, was an achievement. The two sides worked out a temporary
balance between trade and human rights, and both made obliga-
tory concessions. The Joint Statement identified the main points of
agreement, clarified disputed bilateral issues, and provided a text-
book framework for future cooperation. Chinese officials radiated
optimism, with talk of a forthcoming "Golden Age" in Canada-
China relations. Organizing the visit also brought the disparate
parts of the Canadian government more closely together again,
especially the public servants and their political masters, to restore
the unified China policy structure that had been lacking for some
time.

While the post-2009 relationship offered the promise of a return
to positive relations, significant obstacles remained. Were the previously split Cabinet and the Conservative caucus fully on board?
Canadians were still uncomfortable about human rights in China
and remained wary of this more assertive China. It was going to
take time to follow up on the positive statements that their leaders
made and to implement some of these new initiatives.

In mid-2010, Hu attended the G20 Summit in Toronto, using the
occasion to pay a visit to Ottawa, and he said all the right things:
"China wishes to join Canada in a concerted effort to treat and
develop our relations from a strategic and long-term perspective,
strengthen our friendly exchanges, expand win-win cooperation,
and further advance our strategic partnership from a new starting point"
(emphasis added). Harper replied that Canada had indeed rein-
stated its strategic partnership with China: "This visit by President

Hu confirms that the Canada-China strategic partnership is gaining momentum as we mark 40 years of diplomatic relations and chart a course for the future." The two leaders signed several agreements to expand economic links, including a foreign investment agreement, and they also established a joint study to develop complementarities between the two economies as a prelude to an eventual free trade agreement.

In October 2010, the two countries celebrated the fortieth anniversary of the establishment of diplomatic relations in Ottawa. Harper reminisced about his 2009 trip, the positive changes that he saw were taking place in relations with China, and the long history of cooperation between the two countries:

> I have many unforgettable memories of my visit last year. I was struck by the contrast between the traditional and the super modern. It is one of the many signs of China's richness, its magnificent cultural heritage and its vast future potential ... Today's anniversary commemorates our heritage and our common potential. It is an opportunity to celebrate not only forty years of diplomatic relations, but also *a burgeoning partnership* and a brilliant future for our two countries. (emphasis added)

Harper told his audience that China was Canada's second largest trading partner and its third largest export market after the United States and the European Union: "And ladies and gentlemen, our total Canada-China two-way trade is now valued at more than $51 billion. Who would have guessed that forty years ago? This summer in Ottawa, President Hu and I signed agreements on tourism (ADS), environmental protection, energy conservation and law enforcement. We also have agreed to increase our bilateral trade to $60 billion by 2015."

In my diary I wrote:

> Was at the 40th anniversary in Ottawa. What a difference from meetings we had a few years ago. As if the poor relations after 2005 never happened. Foreign Minister Baird, who has been so critical of China, spoke with sugar in his mouth, and the Prime Minister was born again as a believer in close friendship with his Chinese counterparts. Even

after allowing for the usual diplomatic double-speak, this was quite an event. Will this honeymoon last? Have we managed to repair the damage of the past few years?

Seven months later, the Conservatives were re-elected, this time gaining the security of a parliamentary majority. John Baird, the new Canadian foreign minister, told a Toronto business audience: "With respect to China, my government gets it, and I as Foreign Minister get it. China is a clear priority for this government and for our economy." Less than a month later, Baird went first to Beijing, instead of making the traditional inaugural visit to Washington by a new Canadian foreign minister. Baird pulled out all the stops, saying China was "a strategic partner," "a friend," and even "an ally." He was quickly criticized for referring to China as "an ally." Wasn't this too much, too soon? After only two years of improved relations, storm clouds were already hovering over what Harper in his speech had called a "burgeoning partnership." While a majority of Canadians still supported increased trade with China, more than two-thirds were objecting to allowing Chinese state-owned enterprises (SOEs) to invest in Canada, and a growing number expressed concern about more aggressive Chinese activities in Canada.[20]

Richard Fadden, director of the Canadian Security Intelligence Service (CSIS), said that Canada was steadily being penetrated by PRC intelligence operations, including "a couple of cases of politicians and a couple of cases of public servants who we think are just a little bit too close to that foreign government." His remarks were immediately denied by both governments, but nevertheless they fed into growing Canadian concern over the PRC's covert activities in Canada. The Canadian media, after a first flush of support for post-2009 re-engagement, had returned to reporting critically about China's abuses of individual rights and freedoms, and on the hidden attempts by China to assert its influence within Canada's ethnic Chinese communities.[21]

When Harper made his second trip to China in early 2012, many saw that visit as the high tide of renewed relations. The PRC was about to clinch its $15 billion Nexen investment in the Canadian oil sands, and a definitive FIPA was in the final stages of completion. "It's About Pandas and Pipelines," read one headline. China was ready to grant Canada the much sought-after loan of pandas, and both sides were pursuing ways to deliver Canadian oil to China. Even a free trade agreement was on the table, although Harper said such an agreement was premature: "What we have committed to do is move our economic relationship to the next level. So this is a serious discussion we will be having with the Chinese over fhe next few months, and then we will decide on our next steps."

It took two years to ratify the FIPA. Big energy sales to China never happened. Talk about the strategic partnership vanished. The momentum of the 2012 visit faded. There has not been another Chinese acquisition like Nexen. There still was no free trade agreement, and both sides retreated for differing reasons: the Canadians because they were backing off from embracing a more formidable China, and the Chinese because they were losing patience with Canada and had better options to pursue elsewhere. Ambassador Mulroney said it well when he compared the prime minister's visit in 2012 to the retreat of the Mongols:

> In 1241, a Mongol army reached the gates of Vienna. But instead of pressing their advantage, the hitherto all-conquering horde mysteriously turned their horses around and rode back to Asia. For some reason this scene comes to mind when I think about the prime minister's 2012 visit. It represented something of a high-water mark in our multi-year re-engagement with China. But instead of boldly carrying on through gates that were opening before us, we turned around and left the field.[22]

According to Mulroney, "Ottawa's enthusiasm for the relationship had decreased dramatically. My guess – and a guess it remains – is that the politicians in Ottawa felt that our effort to engage China was taking us beyond the comfort zones of many Canadians. China's eagerness to push toward free trade spooked people." He added: "For every Canadian who visited China and felt he or she had seen a golden future, there were many more at home who already worried about the implications of China's rise and had no desire to see Canada more closely linked to the PRC."

The government was split on China. Fadden's criticism of Chinese intelligence work had widened concern over PRC espionage in Canada. There was also concern over possible PRC takeovers of Canadian resources, in particular, in the Alberta oil sands, as well as over China's unrelenting rights abuses. According to one Conservative member, the deep anti-China feelings that had previously motivated many of the Conservative Party's members were resurfacing. "They became more critical, saying there was no evidence that China had changed. For example, take Alberta, where hardliners who opposed closer links with China are now at odds with those Conservatives who want to sell them our oil."

In 2014, I wrote in my diary:

> Was just in Ottawa at Foreign Affairs. After the excitement of 2012, things have bogged down. Better than back in 2007, but not delivering on the promises of Harper's second visit. The Department seems to have stepped back from closer relations with China. This may be the end of Harper's shift to better relations – to what I don't know.

From his vantage points in Beijing and Ottawa, former ambassador Mulroney believed that the PRC had lost patience with Canada. He stated: "They duly noted our cold shoulder on free trade and our decision, made in the context of the Nexen takeover, to limit future investments in Canada from their state-owned enterprises. They waited patiently while the FIPA languished in legislative limbo in Canada." In Beijing, MFA officials said that China had lost confidence in Canada, times had changed, and so had both countries. "A bilateral relationship is like a marriage between two people. It can be a love affair, or it is an arranged marriage where love may or may not bloom. Today the love has gone from the relationship."

Many China observers put the blame for the end of the romance with China on the Harper government, but this was already happening under Martin, and even earlier, after Tiananmen. Harper had exposed the fault lines when he confronted China in 2006. When the two countries finally re-engaged after 2009, they had stabilized relations, but then they were unable or unwilling to go much further. Expectations had changed on both sides as China's government gradually became more authoritarian and repressive under President Xi Jinping. Canadians had become wary of China, and China had less need of a closer relationship with Canada.

Perhaps the best Canada could expect was a more modest future partnership with an emerging superpower that held to different values and goals. One Department officer said: "We tend to dramatize what we do with China. Our relations with them are not as good today as we thought they were back in the mid-1990s, but are they as bad as we now say they have become 20 years later?" In the next chapter, we will see what happened when Harper's successor, Justin Trudeau, sought to reset bilateral relations after the Liberals returned to power in 2015.

chapter eleven

Resetting Relations

Could a second Trudeau repair relations that were struggling during the Harper period? The answer was "no." Several events conspired to worsen relations, and by the end of 2020, they were at their lowest level since recognition.

The Liberals were re-elected in 2015. New Prime Minister Justin Trudeau met with President Xi Jinping at a G20 meeting. He told Xi that "Canada was looking for a comprehensive relationship" and that he was interested in concluding a free trade agreement. In 2016, he made an official visit to China and was warmly welcomed. Chinese social media called him the "Little Potato" – his father, Pierre, was the "Old Potato." In Chinese, the word for "Trudeau" (teluduo) sounds somewhat like "potato" (tudou). Hopes were high that he could follow in his father's footsteps and restore positive relations between Canada and China.

Canada joined the PRC's Asian Infrastructure Investment Bank (AIIB), a minor coup for China. The two countries signed over fifty new commercial contracts, and Canada announced that it was opening seven additional visa application offices in China to handle the growing number of Chinese tourists expected to visit Canada. Trudeau talked of creating a "progressive agenda" with China for gender equity, labour standards, the environment, and human rights. Three weeks later, Premier Li Keqiang came to Ottawa and asked Canada to sign an extradition treaty. As an apparent quid pro quo, China released a Canadian hostage, Kevin Garratt, whom they had detained for two years.

However, free trade was a long way off. The recently concluded Australian agreement had taken ten years. The extradition treaty discussion with China was shelved because of Canadian reservations about sending individuals back to countries that had a death penalty. Wariness and suspicion of China's motives continued to grow, and more Canadians were questioning the urgency of closer relations. In 2017, Trudeau again travelled to Beijing, hoping to salvage the stalled trade discussions. However, after four days, he returned home empty-handed, as the Chinese had no interest in including his "progressive agenda" in any agreement.

Meanwhile, relations with the United States were souring. Canada's largest export market had turned protectionist, and the Americans insisted on renegotiating the North American Free Trade Agreement (NAFTA). The new Trump administration called Justin Trudeau "Canada's worst president [sic]." The United States became embroiled in a trade war with China, and as the conflict between the two superpowers intensified, Canada-China relations were trapped in the middle. Pierre Trudeau once said that having a relationship with America was like sleeping with an elephant: "You have to be aware of every twitch and grunt of the beast." Now Canada was stuck between two very large elephants.

In December 2018, Canada detained Meng Wanzhou, chief financial officer (CFO) of the PRC telecommunications giant Huawei, at the US government's request. The Americans wanted Meng extradited to the United States, where she faced charges of bank and wire fraud. The PRC reacted by accusing Canada of "arrogance," "white supremacy," and of acting as a "lapdog" for the Americans. It took two Canadians hostage, sentenced another to death, and banned the import of Canadian canola, pork, and beef.

Over the next three years, relations with China continued to deteriorate. The Canadian hostages were not released, and Meng remained in detention in Vancouver, awaiting the results of the legal process that could send her to America for prosecution. Then, in September, 2021, she returned to China in an exchange that was brokered by Washington, and the two Canadians were released by China. Now both sides could start resetting relations. That would take time – in 2021 less than 15 per cent of Canadians had a favourable image of China, and the PRC's media was portraying Canada as a weak, small country, doing the bidding of the Americans.

In 2021, the Department stated that it was preparing a new strategic framework to reset relations with Beijing – strengthening the positive links in trade and people-to-people relations, while more forcibly resisting China's aggressive behavior and its hostage diplomacy. In the future, Canada's relations with China are most likely to be pragmatic and challenging: middle power to big power, democracy to one-party state, without any illusions that they will be particularly "special."

I will strive for a closer, more balanced relationship between Canada and China, one that unlocks the untapped potential of our two countries' commercial ties and advances important issues like good governance, the rule of law, and the environment.

– Prime Minister Justin Trudeau, August 2016

Two Potatoes

In 2014, when Stephen Harper made his third trip to China, relations were stumbling. The decision to allow the PRC to buy Nexen Inc., the Canadian oil and gas corporation, for $15 billion had come with a caveat: that future large foreign investments in Canadian natural resources had to show "net benefit" to Canada. After much debate in Cabinet, the message was that any large investment by a foreign state-owned enterprise was not likely to be approved again. Free trade with China also wasn't happening. Harper opposed an agreement with China, saying that Canada would be giving away too much and getting back too little.[1]

Canadians were growing more suspicious of the PRC's covert activities in the Canadian ethnic Chinese communities, universities, schools, and even provincial legislatures, as well as its relentless push to gain access to Canadian intellectual property rights (IPR). Cooperation in developing the oil sands had stalled once China realized that Canada intended to curb foreign acquisitions of its natural resources. Ministerial visits dried up, and in 2015 not one Canadian minister went to China. It seemed that the two sides were merely going through the motions with the once prized strategic partnership and with the various governmental dialogues that the two sides had established with much fanfare after 2009.[2]

In 2015, Justin Trudeau became prime minister, and once again a Trudeau was in charge of relations with China. Both sides considered that his father, Pierre, was the grand architect of the bilateral relationship, the father figure of recognition. Justin, the son, had spent time in China as a young boy, and pictures were circulated of him walking with his father on the Great Wall. Now, as prime minister, he promised to reset relations. After a decade of a Harper-led government, the Liberals were ready to wrest China policy back from the Conservatives. According to one member in the Canadian Embassy, "aside from Brian Mulroney and Stephen Harper, our China policy was made by the Liberals. They've owned China relations for over 30 years. That's how Beijing sees it, and their MFA is quietly welcoming the return of the Liberals."

In the fall of 2015, Prime Minister Justin Trudeau met with President Xi Jinping in Turkey at the G20 Forum. Xi praised Trudeau's father, Pierre, for having established relations forty-five years ago, and he declared: "That was an extraordinary political vision. China will always remember this." Trudeau, in turn, spoke of the strong relations existing between the two countries, and told Xi that Canada looked forward to establishing "a fresh approach":

> I'm well aware we have an opportunity to set a fresh approach to our relationship right now. I know that there are many opportunities for us to work together on economic, political and cultural ties ... [There are] many ongoing dialogues that we can improve and increase at all levels, whether it be the business level, at the diplomatic level, at the cultural level, and even at the political.

In early 2016, the two sides celebrated the forty-fifth anniversary of the establishment of diplomatic relations. It was a gala event in Ottawa with over 300 attendees, including the prime minister, several Cabinet ministers, Chinese diplomats, and senior Canadian government officials. According to one PRC account, "Prime Minister Trudeau spoke highly of the positive progress that had been made in bilateral relations over the 45 years since Canada and

China established diplomatic ties. He also recalled fondly his visit to China together with his father at a tender age, adding that [he] looked forward to visiting China again." Ambassador Luo Zhaohui pointed out that "Justin Trudeau carries forward his father's legacy," and he called on both sides to start negotiations on a bilateral free trade agreement, sooner rather than later. Luo said: "The two countries are creating new bright spots in cooperation in such areas as new energy, infrastructure development, and agriculture."

Luo emphasized that both sides "needed to walk the walk, and talk the talk." Planning began for an exchange of high-level visits: Prime Minister Trudeau to Beijing and Shanghai, and Premier Li Keqiang to Ottawa. In the previous chapter, we saw that such visits are benchmarks in diplomatic relations because they produce major agreements and "deliverables." Would this also be the case for Canada and China in 2016 as they repaired links? An agreement to begin free trade negotiations would be a positive start, as would cooperation in joint projects to transport Canadian oil and gas to west coast ports for delivery to China. Could the two sides get past what Ambassador Luo called "talking the talk," and instead, could they begin "walking the walk?"

Trudeau visited China in August 2016. I was there at the time, teaching at the Beijing Foreign Studies University. The dark clouds of the past few years were lifting, and the Chinese media were almost breathless with enthusiasm. According to one report, "he has curly hair, deep eyes, a handsome face and tight muscles. Today we introduce everyone to a Hollywood star – oops, that's not right – the Prime Minister of Canada." After meeting Trudeau, Jack Ma, the founder of Alibaba, China's giant online and mobile commerce company, proclaimed: "You can see and hear the spark, energy and confidence of Canada. We believe he is the future of Canada." My Beijing students decided Trudeau was handsome, young, and exciting. "He will change everything. He is even playing basketball with Yao Ming in Shanghai."

Chinese social media called him the "Little Potato," which was actually a term of endearment. "Trudeau," when translated into Mandarin, sounds like *teluduo* – similar to *tudou* or "potato." Now there were two Trudeau prime ministers – "Two Potatoes" – an

"Old One" and a "Little One." Would Justin, the "Little Potato," be able to restore the positive relationship between Canada and China that had existed under his father, Pierre, the "Old Potato?" The pro-government *Global Times* thought so: "During Harper's time in office, Canada-China ties were constantly disturbed by issues such as human rights ... The overall trend of bilateral relations was chilly. Trudeau is young and open-minded. He believes the world is developing, and developed countries should not remain bound to an old mindset."

Trudeau told Premier Li that he was "very happy" to be following in his father's footsteps, and Li announced that Canada and China were about to launch a feasibility study on the long-awaited free trade deal. They also decided to hold annual consultations at the prime ministerial level. Trudeau talked about cultural diversity – "diversity" being a code word for "human rights," the constant sore spot in relations with China. Li replied: "We have differences on some issues, this is only natural, but I also believe that we have far greater common interests between us. There is every reason for us to have a candid dialogue about differences."

In Shanghai, Trudeau spoke to a business audience about expanding trade. He announced that Canadian and Chinese companies had just signed fifty-six new commercial contracts and agreements, worth $1.2 billion. Canada was ready to contribute $250 million to join the Asian Infrastructure Investment Bank (AIIB), despite American opposition – a minor coup for China. Ottawa was opening seven additional visa application centres to handle the growing number of Chinese tourists expected to travel to Canada. Ambassador Guy Saint-Jacques welcomed this development, pointing out that PRC tourism to Canada had risen by 24 per cent in the first half of 2016, and only the Americans and the British were now travelling to Canada more often than the Chinese. However, the ambassador also told Canadians not to forget about human rights. He was worried that Chinese rights policy had moved backwards over the past three years, imposing further limitations on individual freedoms.

In his speech to the business crowd in Shanghai, Trudeau addressed human rights. I listened to him talk about freedom of expression, diversification, and good governance. In Beijing, he had told both Xi and Li that accepting a diversity of perspectives strengthened China and bilateral relations. "See, we're Canadians – we travel with our values and we don't hesitate to share them whenever and wherever we see opportunities ... In the global village we all have a stake in what happens here." The message that he delivered in Shanghai was that globalization, expanded trade, and human rights are permanently intertwined for all nations and cultures.[3]

Shades of Harper's speech in Beijing to the business community in 2009 when he said that trade opened the door to political liberalization. This was also Chrétien's Team Canada strategy redux, with trade triumphing over rights, but there was one difference – Trudeau turned out to be passionate about protecting gender equity, labour standards, environmental cooperation, and human rights. In the winter of 2016, Trudeau's "progressive agenda" had passed serious notice while everyone was awash in goodwill, but it would resurface a few months afterwards, becoming a major obstacle for negotiating any agreements with China.[4]

In my diary I wrote:

Am in Shanghai. The Trudeau visit looks good for Canada. We are on track again. The traders will be happy. As for human rights, Trudeau's heart is in the right place, but can he get the Chinese to sign on to his progressive agenda?

Li Keqiang arrived in Ottawa three weeks later, and marveled at Canada's fall display of colourful maple leaves – the Chinese call Canada "the land of red maple trees." Between the two visits, Canada and China had agreed to begin talks about an extradition treaty to return former Chinese nationals, now living in Canada, for criminal prosecution in the PRC. As an apparent *quid pro quo*, the PRC finally allowed a Canadian hostage, Kevin Garratt, to leave China after two years of detention. Both leaders committed to launching an economic and financial strategic dialogue, and Trudeau announced that the two countries would double their bilateral trade by 2025. At the annual CCBC Forum in Montreal,

Li reiterated his support for free trade, telling 700 members of the business community:

> During my visit, Justin Trudeau and I have reached consensus on further elevating the scale of bilateral trade. We have agreed to launch, as early as possible, the feasibility study for a China-Canada trade zone, which not only facilitates the expansion of China-Canada economic and trade cooperation, but also sends a clear signal of promoting trade liberalization and investment facilitation to the international community.[5]

The two sides issued a statement containing twenty-nine agreements, or "deliverables," to highlight their renewed engagement. They "welcomed the successful inaugural meeting of the Annual Dialogue between the Prime Minister of Canada and the Premier of China," and they reaffirmed "the goal of doubling bilateral trade by 2025." Two-thirds of the deliverables dealt with economic relations. The rest concerned a number of technical issues and the restoration of basic linkages. The key messages were "solidifying the new chapter in the strategic partnership" and "reaching an agreement to launch exploratory discussions for a possible free trade agreement." However, there was no mention of the PRC's request to begin extradition talks or of any action on the continuing Canadian concerns over human rights in China.

The Department said the 2016 Joint Statement "represented a widening of the links between the two sides, and brought relations back to a more encouraging level." Unlike the 2009 statement that was issued when Stephen Harper went to China, the 2016 statement was thin in content and avoided any reference to controversial political issues. For Canadians supporting Trudeau's intention to reset China relations, Li's visit was a let-down. There were no dramatic shifts in policy and no deliverables that could significantly alter relations. Free trade was going to be a long way off. It also wasn't likely that Canada would agree to an extradition treaty with China, not to a country that was escalating human rights abuses, using torture, and executing over 3,000 individuals annually.

Was Li's trip just diplomatic posturing by both sides, at best only marking time? Trudeau and the Canadian government did not speak about any "long game," aside from repeating that post-Harper relations with China were changing. According to one critical Canadian account, "Mr. Trudeau has yet to deliver a major speech or policy statement laying out his long game on China, and the Liberal government does not appear to share anything like a united vision. You hear different things about China from Foreign Minister Stéphane Dion, International Trade Minister Chrystia Freeland, and from the Prime Minister's Office." China specialist and University of British Columbia professor Paul Evans added: "We don't have a whole-of-country approach to China yet, or even a whole-of-government approach," and it appeared to many Canadians that Trudeau and the government were retreating from closer engagement with China.[6]

In the next few months, relations were frozen in time and space. Exploratory talks on trade were going nowhere, especially since Beijing was resisting Trudeau's progressive additions to any agreement. China also wanted better access for its state-owned enterprises to invest in Canadian natural resources, and more opportunities to acquire Canadian technology.[7] PRC agents were pursuing "fox hunts" in Canada, violating our sovereignty by forcibly retrieving former PRC citizens who were now living in Canada and were wanted for criminal prosecution back in China.[8] In a briefing note, the Department said that China's behaviour was presenting a "strategic challenge" to Canadian interests and values: *"The PRC promotes perspectives on governance, economic security, and human rights that diverge in fundamental ways from Canada's"* (emphasis added).

In Beijing, I wrote in my diary:

Human rights lawyers are disappearing. More talk about dangerous foreign influence seeping into education here. I've stopped teaching Canadian politics. Strangers are sitting in on my Beijing lectures. Now all my classes are being videotaped, and there's a camera placed outside my window directly looking into my room. I don't feel comfortable teaching here anymore.

In June, Foreign Minister Wang Yi visited Ottawa to initiate a new Canada-China foreign affairs ministers' dialogue. He insisted on meeting with Prime Minister Trudeau, although it was not normal Canadian diplomatic practice for foreign ministers to meet with the prime minister. During an Ottawa press conference, he accused a Canadian journalist of "arrogance" and "prejudice," because the journalist had asked Foreign Minister Dion a question about human rights. Wagging his finger, Wang berated the unfortunate Canadian reporter: "You have no right to speak on this. The Chinese people have the right to speak; you are arrogant and prejudiced."[9] Canadians didn't forget Wang Yi's undiplomatic remarks, spoken in front of Canada's foreign minister on Canadian soil. The image of his accusing face and wagging finger were circulated everywhere. China had become disrespectful, and even threatening.

In December 2017, Prime Minister Trudeau made his second official visit to Beijing. Exploratory free trade discussions had been continuing for some months. Were the two sides ready to announce the start of formal negotiations? Trudeau was hopeful that they could move forward "with the first trade deal that China will have with a G7 country. There is a coming together ... [T]his is going to be a big thing, not a small thing." They issued a Joint Statement on climate change and clean energy growth, and agreed to establish ministerial-level dialogues on environment and clean energy. They agreed that they would continue to have meetings at the prime ministerial and foreign minister levels, as well as hold regular dialogues on economic and financial security, national security, and the rule of law, but there was nothing on free trade.

Something was amiss. Had Trudeau just travelled over 20,000 kilometers for such meagre results? Diplomatic niceties had been observed for four days, and a few side agreements were made. But the big prize, the long-awaited trade agreement, was drifting away. It was an embarrassing setback. In Beijing, my students' love affair with the "Little Potato" was also waning. Almost two years had passed, and to them he was no longer the potential "Hollywood star," bringing "spark, energy and confidence" to the bilateral relationship. One of my students said: "He isn't like his father, the

'Old Potato,' after all. We think he is acting like any other foreign politician." In Canada, members of the China policy community were wondering what was happening. Had Canada decided to step back from closer engagement, or was this a Chinese decision? In my diary I wrote:

> The excitement over improving relations is gone. No more talk of the "Little Potato" in Beijing. The promised free trade agreement has vanished. Couldn't get a straight answer from the Embassy, and the Chinese MFA people aren't talking. The International Trade Minister stayed behind after Trudeau's visit to try to rescue the free trade talks, but no details. Ottawa cannot be happy.

There was no simple answer, although there were several possible explanations. The Chinese had no intention of adding Trudeau's progressive elements to any agreement, and they were upset that Canada had not agreed to discuss an extradition treaty. The MFA complained that Canada had become too critical of China and that it was becoming aligned with a growing American anti-China stance. Beijing was also resisting any new agreements that would force it to open more of its domestic economy to foreign companies. Fortified by Xi Jinping's mercantilist statements at the Nineteenth Party Congress in 2017, and celebrating the power of its growing economy, China was not interested in making concessions.

Canada was also hesitating. China's human rights abuses were escalating. As many as a million Uighurs were being "re-educated" in camps in Xinjiang designed to stamp out their religion and culture, and Canadians were appalled at this massive ethnic cleansing. The Department found there was lukewarm public support for a long-term trade agreement with China, if not substantial opposition. Even the powerful Canadian business community was advising Ottawa to proceed with caution. A stronger statement by the prime minister favouring closer links with China might have attracted more support, but after his second visit to China, Trudeau retreated from closer engagement, as Ottawa's attention was being diverted to renewed trade negotiations with the United

States. According to the Department, "our priority is to renegotiate the NAFTA accord, and then China. We can't do two big negotiations at the same time. We don't even have enough top negotiators." One ambassador claimed that Canada had lost the ability to negotiate, compared with the successful NAFTA negotiations twenty years earlier. Had we actually lost that skill, or was it the result of Canadian "naïveté" and an inability to listen? The *Globe and Mail* reported:

> Trade negotiation, once an elite art in Ottawa, is now a more mundane bureaucratic function ... Today the distance between the people who negotiate the deal and the person who signs it – the Prime Minister – is far greater, and many other people, among them congenitally cautious mandarins from Ottawa's "central agencies" and legions of hyper-partisan political staffers, stand between negotiators and the PM.
>
> We're also losing that most valuable of negotiating skills: the ability to listen ... These days, when the Prime Minister talks as he so often does about a "progressive trade policy agenda," it can sound like a lecture. Small states that need our largesse have to listen. China doesn't.
>
> The government seemed naïve about security risks, and flatfooted when asked how it could consider closer economic engagement with a country that capriciously imprisons foreign businesspeople.[10]

Almost two years had passed since Trudeau had assumed office, and his new approach to China had not produced the anticipated outcomes. The situation became complicated when American President Donald Trump decided to play hardball with Canadian exports to the United States by imposing tariffs on imports of Canadian steel for alleged "national security" concerns, threatening Canada's long-established American economic security blanket. That act, and an American-inspired tariff war with China, suddenly put Canada-China economic relations in jeopardy, sandwiching Canada between the two competing superpowers, and setting the stage for the emergence of the most difficult crisis in Canada-China relations since the establishment of diplomatic relations.

Two Elephants

For most of our long journey with China, the United States was Canada's ally, mostly supportive of our efforts to engage with Beijing, although the American government had officially opposed Canada's decision to recognize the PRC in 1970 and end *de jure* relations with Taiwan. Lingering concerns about American retaliation were reinforced by Pierre Trudeau's observation that relations with America were like sleeping with an elephant: "You have to be aware of every twitch and grunt of the beast."[11] President Gerald Ford's rebuke of Canada's decision to bar Taiwan from the 1976 Montreal Olympics, if Taiwanese athletes claimed to represent "China" when in Canada, may have been one of the last forceful US criticisms of Canadian China policy.

Canada wanted to preserve access to a vast American market that absorbs 75 per cent of Canadian exports. It had sought but never succeeded in reducing its dependence on that market by increasing its trade with China, Canada's second largest national trading partner. As described in conversation with one official, the Department understood what it meant to have a superpower as Canada's next-door neighbour: "We are living a charmed life, protected by American security; nearly almost all of our trade goes south, and both countries share a similar mindset with respect to China. On the other hand, we have to watch our step. At any moment the Americans can slap tariffs on us, like Nixon did in the 1970s, then with softwood lumber, and now with steel."

Official relations with America had soured in 2017 when President Trump accused Canada of unfair trade practices, imposed tariffs, and set out to renegotiate NAFTA. Hard negotiations, even name calling, by the Americans ensued, with Trump calling Trudeau "very dishonest and weak," someone "who makes false statements," and "Canada's worst president [*sic*]." He alleged that the United States was imposing tariffs on Canada, its closest ally, because of national security concerns, and he also claimed that Canada had gained a huge economic advantage in the old NAFTA. In fact, trade in merchandise and services between the United States and Canada had been more or less in balance during most of those two decades, although according to Trump, "NAFTA was one of the worst trade deals ever made." He railed against the tariffs imposed to protect Canadian dairy producers' market boards, while ignoring the massive support that the United States was extending to its own agricultural producers. In Washington, Larry Kudlow, director of the National Economic Council, claimed that "Canada has stabbed us in the back," and Peter Navarro, Trump's China policy advisor, said Trudeau was "one of those foreign leaders who deserve a special place in hell."[12]

When the new NAFTA, now called the United States-Mexico-Canada Agreement (USMCA), was signed in 2018, it contained a clause (Number 32) that gave Washington a potential veto over any major trade agreement that Ottawa might negotiate with China. This clause rankled Beijing, which was convinced that it was another American scheme to contain the PRC, and that Canada supported it. At the same time, relations between the United States and China were deteriorating as the Trump administration initiated a tariff-based trade war with China. Canada was thrust into a situation where its major ally, the United States, had turned protectionist and unfriendly, and a potential Canadian trade agreement with China wasn't happening, in good part because of American intervention. Relations with China rapidly cooled, to the point where they were now worse than when Justin Trudeau had taken office in 2015.

In my diary, I wrote:

> It's 2018. American protectionism has raised its ugly head. Unexpected, and driving a wedge in our relations with both the United States and China. Remember the Nixon tariffs back in the 1970s, and the threat of American protectionism? Thought that was long settled with NAFTA. Now we are back again with tariffs on steel. It's surely affecting our relations with China.

In December 2018, the Canadian government, acting on an official American extradition request, detained Meng Wanzhou, the CFO of Huawei, in Vancouver. The PRC reacted in near frenzy, arresting Michael Kovrig and Michael Spavor for allegedly spying, sentencing Robert Schellenberg to face the death penalty, and demanding that Canada release Meng immediately. The PRC also banned the import of Canadian canola, pork, and beef, worth over $3 billion annually. The Canadian government emphasized that it was bound by the legal requirements of its extradition agreement with America. Meng would be dealt with "according to the rule of law." The Chinese Foreign Ministry warned Canada of the "consequences" of allying with the Americans," that "the rule of law" was a cover-up for an outright political act by the Americans, who were attempting to stop Huawei from becoming the world's leading 5G provider. The MFA spokesperson issued a stern rebuke: "We hope the Canadian side will come to understand the full consequences of pulling chestnuts from the fire on behalf of the United States, and will not inflict more harm on themselves."[13]

Relations between Canada and China worsened, the hostages were not released, dialogue between the top leaders ceased, and Ottawa advised Canadians that it was not safe to travel to China. The Department reported to a newly formed parliamentary Special Committee on Canada-China Relations that "Meng's arrest is seen by Beijing as a US-directed blow to China's innovation agenda. Washington, for its part, remains wary of Canada's interest in China-led infrastructure or investment projects, illustrated most vividly by ongoing US efforts to minimize Chinese participation [by Huawei] in Canada's 5G network."[14]

Canada had little room to maneuver, since China was not likely to free the hostages or end its ban on Canada's exports, until Meng is released. Canada could not count on the United States for help, since the Trump regime was engaged in a long-term trade and political dispute with China. So Meng was an American hostage, stuck in Canada. Unless the United States decided not to proceed with her extradition, she could remain stranded in Vancouver for a long time, seriously compromising Canada's relations with China.

The *Globe and Mail* wrote:

Over the course of his mandate, Mr. Trump has insulted Canada, lied about our trading relationship, belittled the Prime Minister, imposed unjustified tariffs and sometimes acted as though this country holds no more importance to the United States than Belgium. But it's nothing compared to how China has treated Canada in its anger over the arrest of Ms. Meng ... It has shown a condescending disdain for Canada's obligations under the law, and it has insulted our country by accusing it of white supremacy – a feeble charge coming from a regime that has put almost one million Chinese Muslims in "re-education camps."[15]

In 2020, Canada was facing a China that flatly ignored Canadian requests to release the two hostages and to remove its arbitrary ban on canola and other key Canadian agricultural exports. Canada was also receiving paltry help from the Americans, whose request for Meng's extradition had created this crisis. With the two superpowers locked in a struggle for economic and political advantage, Canada had little leverage.

A Diplomatic Interlude

In earlier chapters, we saw how ambassadors on both sides played key roles in the bilateral relationship. Wang Dong headed the negotiations for recognition, and then served as ambassador in the early years of relations; in the 1990s, Zhang Yijun helped to restore relations after Tiananmen; Mei Ping provided a stable PRC presence towards the end of the Chrétien period; and Lu Shumin kept links from further fraying during the early Harper period. Canada had a steady stream of skilled ambassadors in Beijing, from the three "mish kids" in the 1970s – Ralph Collins, John Small, and Arthur Menzies – to Howard Balloch, David Mulroney, Guy Saint-Jacques, and Dominic Barton. Ambassadors are not supposed to make policy, but they have a public presence, and they speak authoritatively for their governments. Thanks to their familiarity with the local conditions where they are posted, they provide a nuanced perspective on relations. Whatever their message, ambassadors are spokespersons for their governments, and they are expected to carry out their duties in correct "diplomatic" fashion.

The two ambassadors, Lu Shaye for China and John McCallum for Canada, were exceptions. Lu spent two years in Ottawa until his abrupt departure in mid-2019, and he repeatedly made statements highly critical of Canada. Lu was one of the most "undiplomatic" diplomats that Canada had ever hosted from any country. The PRC had given him licence to speak harshly, and he did exactly that. At first, he was just critical of basic Canadian policy, loudly complaining about the prime minister's attempt to include "progressive" elements in the free trade discussions. Then, he said Canada was "discriminating" against China because of its rejection of Chinese state-owned company takeovers in Canada. The Canadian media became a target "because they pressured the Chinese government," and "they presented a negative view of [his] home country." When Canada asked China to release the hostages that China had taken in reprisal for the Meng detention, Lu exploded, saying that "this reflected Western egotism and white supremacy ... Western countries condescend to China and see it as an abnormal country." Canada is "arrogant," and "it practices double standards." The Department found him impossible to deal with, and Canadians quietly cheered when he was transferred to a posting in Paris.

John McCallum was the first political appointee as Canadian ambassador to China, and was a robust cheerleader for good relations with Beijing. It was an unusual appointment, considering that immediately prior to being ambassador, he had been minister of immigration, refugees and citizenship. He was always saying that Canada had to do "much more, much more, much more" (*geng duo, geng duo, geng duo*) with China. I was present at a CCBC roundtable in Toronto in December 2019, when he gave his report on current relations with China. He asserted that Meng might have a good case to make against extradition to the United States because, in his opinion, President Trump had politicized the matter by suggesting that a "deal" involving Huawei could be made between the Americans and China, which might release her. Then there would be no need to observe "the rule of law," which was Canada's rationale for detaining her for extradition. Canada could free her, and China could do the same with the Canadian hostages.

I was encouraged by this possibility. If the legal process was politically tainted, and if the Americans were planning a "deal" for Meng, there might be an opening whereby the Canadian government could free her. Was such a deal emerging behind the scenes, and were we among the first people outside our government to learn about this? Apparently not. McCallum repeated his message of liberation for Meng and the hostages twice more, in Markham and in Vancouver, and then he was fired "for comments inconsistent with the government of Canada." He had said too much, and in the government's opinion, he had undercut Canadian government policy. No deal was taking place, and he was excoriated in Canadian media, accused of "meddling" and of being "a rogue diplomat." McCallum then admitted that he had "misstepped."

There were puzzling aspects to this story. At the CCBC meeting, he had spoken with prepared notes. A government official who was present had not publicly objected to his remarks. A week earlier, McCallum had attended a meeting in Sherbrooke along with several other ambassadors, where they were briefed on the latest China policy – certainly about what they should or should not say publicly about the Meng situation. As a former minister in Trudeau's Cabinet, McCallum had a close political connection with the prime minister, and it was claimed that he could phone Trudeau without going through his foreign minister. It was "as if he never left Cabinet," and "as if he had been unofficially appointed as Trudeau's 'Minister for Canada-China Relations.'" He had retained vestiges of his former role as a minister, even attending Cabinet meetings. Given his political connections, it was a difficult decision for Trudeau to dismiss him.[16]

Can we lay all of the blame on McCallum? One senior official defended him, saying: "He tried to show that Canada's justice system was fair and impartial, and that Meng would be able to mount a strong defense." Another said he was receiving different messages from various parts of the government. The PMO, the foreign minister, and the Department were not always on the same China page, and the prime minister only stepped in at the end. At the Embassy in Beijing, it had not been smooth going for him, since career public servants and political appointees don't necessarily mix well. Ottawa, too, did not always appreciate his maxim of "more, more, more."

What did the behaviour of these ambassadors, Lu and McCallum, tell us about Canada-China relations? Two ambassadors acting badly: one rudely following his government's orders, the other "misspeaking" about an important policy decision. China was on the offensive over Meng's detention, and Canada, hemmed in by both China and the United States, was on the defensive, itself a hostage to big-power pressure. After fifty years of relations, this was not the outcome that Canada had in mind. Was this an epitaph for lost illusions about what Canada thought it had achieved with China?

I wrote in my diary:

> Am in Beijing. Are we in for a long period of poor political relations, with hostage taking, trade sanctions, and name calling? We just appointed our new Ambassador – Dominic Barton, replacing McCallum. The MFA responded coldly. Barton told me that his first priority is to get China to free the Canadians. No meeting with the MFA during this trip. Canadians are being shunned right now. Until the Americans decide what to do with Meng, there isn't much we can do.

At an Impasse

Both Prime Minister Trudeau and Foreign Minister Freeland asked for American help to free the Canadians, without success. Former prime minister Jean Chrétien offered to meet with China's leaders to discuss a possible exchange of hostages, but Freeland immediately rejected his proposal, stating that such an exchange violated Canada's commitment to the rule of law. Meng Wanzhou might eventually be freed; however, it had to be done through legal procedure, a process that could take months, if not years to resolve.[17]

Department officials said that, unless the Americans withdrew their extradition request, there was little Canada could do. "We are just marking time, waiting for an opening, looking for a path to move forward." Freeland said she was unable to talk with the PRC foreign minister: "I have repeatedly sought a meeting with Wang Yi, my counterpart. Thus far, this meeting hasn't happened. If Chinese officials are listening to us today, let me repeat I would be very happy to meet with Minister Wang Yi or speak with him over the phone at the earliest opportunity." In Washington, the Americans listened to the Canadian requests for assistance, but they chose not to intervene.

Meanwhile, relations with the PRC continued to deteriorate. In 2017, the two countries had created over forty bilateral dialogues and collaborative mechanisms, but by 2020 many were functioning poorly. According to a Department official, "it was as if the bilateral system had broken apart; a few mechanisms were working – in trade and culture, maybe environment – but no meetings at the leaders' level." In its Report to the Special Parliamentary Committee on Canada-China Relations, the Department stated that Beijing now posed "a long-term strategic challenge to Canadian interests and values," and in strong language not heard since Tiananmen, it denounced the Chinese government's actions:

Canada condemns the arbitrary detention of Canadians:

> The Government of Canada is vocal in expressing concerns about China's arbitrary actions against Canadians ... The Prime Minister, Minister of Foreign Affairs, the Canadian Ambassador to China, and Canadian diplomats around the world consistently reinforce the message that China's actions against Canadian citizens represent an unacceptable breach of the rules-based international order.

An unprecedented crisis in Canada-China relations:

> The bilateral relationship with China is in unprecedented crisis, with relations at their lowest ebb since they were established in 1970 ... While Canada has long framed its China policy through the lens of economic opportunity, it now needs to take account of Beijing's long-term strategic challenge to Canadian interests and values.[18]

China was punishing Canada with tactics that it also employed against other smaller countries with whom it had political disputes. As outlined in the report, "it did this with Norway after that country awarded the Nobel Peace Prize to a Chinese dissident in 2010. The PRC froze relations with Norway for six years, banned imports of their salmon, a huge loss, and Norway suffered additional retaliation. Canada is just one of many who are being bullied by China." At least a half dozen countries, including Norway, Sweden, New Zealand, South Korea, Japan, Australia, and the United Kingdom, are experiencing PRC behaviour "that tests the limits of the current rules-based international system."

The Department bluntly declared in its report: "The crisis has demonstrated Beijing's readiness and ability to use aggressive political and economic levers to punish Canada – a pattern observed in China's other bilateral relationships – and to propagate norms of international relations inimical to Canadian interests." A year had passed without freeing the hostages or ending the Chinese trade ban, and Ottawa said that it needed to rethink how to conduct future relations with Beijing. "Not just to 'reset' relations – that only brings us back to where we were before the crisis in 2018, and we were having problems with China then. No, we have to re-examine our strategy and go in a new direction. It's not 2004 anymore." In the final sentence of its Report to Parliament, Ottawa's message was explicit: "*The Minister of Foreign Affairs has indicated the need to explore a new framework for Canada-China relations*" (emphasis added).

Was it possible to find a way to end the crisis and restore relations? A return to the "normalized" Chrétien days was unlikely. The two partners were now too far apart, too asymmetrical. Canadians had been searching unsuccessfully for such a framework since the latter stages of the Harper period, when relations had soured. That search had enlisted many of Canada's top China specialists inside and outside government: the business community, academics, rights activists, and former government officials. In the four years after Justin Trudeau came to power, they met in Canadian think tanks, at conferences, in universities, and in board rooms, producing a half dozen proposals to help the government develop a new China strategy. In their view, Ottawa lacked the capacity to deal with the triple impact of American interference, Chinese aggressiveness, and rising Canadian public criticism of China. Their message was that the Trudeau government had to step up and take charge of the China file. The main objective was better management of the economic links between the two countries to support either a free trade agreement with China or phased-in sectoral arrangements. Other priorities included strengthening Canada's geopolitical presence in Asia, protecting Canada from China's aggressive intelligence activities, and continuing to hold China accountable for its human rights practices.[19]

Ottawa decision-makers were split. "Here in the Department there are those who want to move ahead with China and those who see risk in getting too close. Public criticism of China has increased, and this makes our politicians nervous. We are being insulted by Chinese diplomats ... The absolute priority is ending the arbitrary detentions of Michel Kovrig and Michael Spavor, and securing clemency for Robert Schellenberg."

With relations in crisis, should Canadians have blamed Prime Minister Trudeau? We can say that he made promises he could not keep and that relations with China in 2020 were worse than when he took office in 2015. Some members of the Department and the China policy community felt that Trudeau's hesitancy to confront China had added to the crisis. However, substantial blame rested on the actions of the two superpowers (the two elephants) – Washington with its punitive trade policies and its request to detain Meng, and Beijing for taking hostages with its aggressive behaviour.

In the first round of the Parliamentary Committee hearings, the Department provided a review of its China policy, which gave the opposition and informed Canadians a chance to question government policy. However, there was no breakthrough; the hearings did not end the Meng crisis, and they did not deliver a new framework for relations with China. Ottawa first had to extricate itself from the strategic competition between Washington and Beijing, be tougher with China, insist on reciprocity in the bilateral relationship, and carefully monitor Beijing's growing presence in Canada. In the interim, the best way to proceed was by cautiously preserving existing links in trade, education, and people-to-people exchanges. There would be no free trade agreement, but trade between the two countries was still expected to reach $150 billion by 2025.

During the hearings, Ambassador Dominic Barton remarked, "We're never going to be singing from the same hymn book as China, [but] we can have real discussions where we can argue and debate."[20]

Despite the political crisis, business was continuing at the same level; diplomats were carrying out their basic functions; and stakeholders in Canada and China continued their professional engagement, albeit with some uncertainty. Many collaborative networks were operating as before, especially in education, which continued to attract large numbers of Chinese international students. The Department reminded Canadians "of the importance of keeping channels of communication and cooperation open. Canada has remained open to visits and meetings with Chinese interlocutors. Our network of missions in China continues to provide valuable service and advice for Canadian travelers, businesses and organizations with a stake in the relationship."

Barton said that *he had a mandate to restore relations, with three priorities*: "First and foremost, secure the release of Michael Kovrig and Michael Spavor, and get clemency for Robert Schellenberg. That is the core. That's a priority. Second, promote and protect human rights. Third, echoing what Joe Clark had said after Tiananmen, 21 years ago: 'Deepen person-to-person relationships between the Chinese and Canadian people.'"

I wrote in my diary:

> The parliamentary hearings are solving nothing. It will take some time to restore relations and when we do, they will be different. Meanwhile, we have to rely on trade, education, and people-to-people ties to keep the links open. We had a good working relationship for 50 years, and there's no reason why we can't find a way to restore that. As Ambassador Lu Shumin said, "the pot is now on the back of the stove." How to make sure that the soup stays warm?

The Release of the Hostages

On September 25, 2021, Meng Wanzhou was allowed to return to China, and the two Canadians came home. The exchange was brokered by the US Department of Justice, in consultation with senior leaders in the three countries involved. Meng stepped out of an Air China airplane in Shenzhen to a hero's welcome, and in Canada, the two Michaels were warmly greeted by Prime Minister Trudeau and Foreign Minister Marc Garneau. By simultaneously exchanging the Canadians for Meng, Beijing was tacitly admitting that China's espionage charges had been trumped up and that the two Michaels had been political hostages. They had suffered cruel and unnecessary confinement in China. Michael Kovrig said that he had walked seven thousand steps every day in his tiny windowless prison room – or more than seven million steps in the over one-thousand days he was confined – alone with no visitors.

What happened to the two Canadians reinforced Canadian anger at China – that Beijing's leaders had gone beyond the boundaries of acceptable state behavior. A Nanos poll, taken immediately after their return, found that only 12 per cent of Canadians expected that future relations would be "friendly," and pollster Nik Nanos noted that, in the past decade, relations had plunged to an all-time low – that they were now "seriously damaged."[21]

Taking the longer view, would the return of the Michaels provide an opening for the renewal of relations with Beijing's leaders? Foreign Minister Marc Garneau commented: "Our eyes are wide open. We have been saying this for some time. There was no path to a relationship with China as long as the two Michaels were being detained. That has now changed."[22]

I wrote in my diary:

> The hostage release came without a warning. It was a surprise attack, but a good one. Now comes the hard part – how to restore fraying ties, how to make China more likeable, how to have a non-threatening relationship. As former ambassador Mulroney has said, "you don't have to love China to have relations with it."

Asked about Ottawa's position on China now that the two Canadians were released, Garneau said that the Department was continuing to develop a new strategic framework to reset relations. He said the framework would be based upon a four pillars formula, each pillar beginning with the letter "C" – coexist (keep engaging with China); compete (on trade); cooperate (on global issues such as climate change); challenge (on human rights and aggressive diplomacy).[23]

Shortly afterwards, PRC Ambassador Cong Peiwu delivered an encouraging PRC response at the annual CCBC trade meeting in Beijing:

> Due to differences in history, culture and social systems, differences between countries are inevitable. That being said, countries can realize common development by dialogue and cooperation on the basis of mutual respect and equity. The economic and trade cooperation over the past 51 years, since the establishment of diplomatic relations between China and Canada, has fully demonstrated that China-Canada pragmatic cooperation in various fields, based on complementary advantages and mutual benefit, has a strong momentum.[24]

Both sides were looking to restore links that had been damaged, and each knew that it was going to take time. Most Canadians now had an unfavourable view of China, and the state-controlled media there was portraying Canada as a weak, small country doing the bidding of the Americans. It would take time to change those images. Nevertheless, there was a palpable sense of relief. A cloud had lifted, and anti-China feelings in Canada began to subside. In conversation, members of the Department said that the taking of the hostages had turned China policy into an emotional issue: "Relations with China then became personal. People identified China with the cruel treatment of the two Michaels, contrasting that with Meng's luxurious lifestyle in Vancouver. Most of China's other human rights violations paled before that."

The Department was committed to developing a new strategy, but it wasn't about to reveal its content: "You can't expect us to publicize what we plan to do with China – or, for that matter, with any other country. Maybe a few details, but the point about strategy – and diplomacy – is that we always keep secrets, and we are dealing with an adversary that will tell us as little as it can. No openness there." Surprisingly, after the return of the hostages, Justin Trudeau also had little to say about developing a new strategic framework for China. This gave former prime minister Chrétien an opportunity to criticize the government's performance for the past three years. He had disagreed with Trudeau's decision to observe "the rule of law" during the hostage crisis instead of negotiating with Beijing to exchange Meng for the two Michaels. Chrétien felt that Ottawa had been too willing to follow the Americans on China policy: "Canada decided not to have trouble with the Americans ... We were the victim of the government of America. The United States forced us, and our government decided to go along with it, because they thought we had no choice ... We had a choice."

Chrétien said Canada had "lost three years" with China, and now "we have to talk":

> We have to talk. We have to exchange. We can disagree on politics, but we have to make sure that the benefits that are possible for us and the benefits that are possible for them should be respected ... Building a respectful Canada-China relationship is an obligation we all have.[25]

Future Relations

In the fifty-year history of Canada-China relations, there have been two major crises: Tiananmen and its aftermath, and then the two Michaels. Trade and people-to-people relations are the glue that has kept us together, even if the two countries are asymmetrical in many ways: in population size, cultural heritage, political system, geopolitical importance, and level of development. As China's economy grew and it became a superpower, virtually all of its relationships changed. Beginning in the mid-1990s, China became more assertive, and then, in the past decade, more aggressive towards Canada. And the world also changed. The Cold War ended, globalization and supply chains took root, and China became the dominant partner in virtually all of its relationships. During the Trump period, American relations with both Canada and China abruptly shifted, and by 2018 Canadian China policy was trapped between the two superpowers.

The hostage crisis was settled by the Americans: they created it, and they ended it. In all likelihood, our China policy, now and in the future, will go through Washington, and that may be an unpleasant truth for many Canadians. Some Canadians also think that Canada's leaders can tell China's leaders how to behave and that they will listen to us, but that had already stopped after 1989.

We may not succeed today in challenging Beijing's leaders on human rights, but we will keep trying. As Prime Minister Harper said in 2009, "we don't park our values at the door when we engage with China." When China's rights abuses reach unacceptable levels, as with the Uighurs and the Tibetans, in Hong Kong, or with repeated violations of due process inside China, we will join with other like-minded countries to register strong protests.

Canada's future China strategy should expand the positive links that we now have. After the return of the hostages, Ambassador Barton said: "China cannot be ignored where trade is concerned. Our companies need to engage China in support of our economic interests."[26] Canada will continue to expand its trade, international students from the PRC will continue to arrive, there is no shortage of Chinese immigrants, and the two million strong Canadians of ethnic Chinese origin will continue to travel to the PRC for business, tourism, and family visits.

Ottawa's management of China relations during the Harper and Trudeau periods lacked decisiveness. Former ambassador Mulroney said Ottawa had too many silos, failed to provide centralized direction, and had inadequate China expertise. Others have added that the Canadian government does have adequate China expertise, but in recent years this knowledge has not been well utilized by senior management. The Canadian China policy community criticized the core Ottawa government group – the PMO, PCO, and the Department – for ineffective leadership on the China file. That criticism was extended to both prime ministers – Harper for treating China as an antagonist and Trudeau for his hesitation to act. The government was also criticized for failing to consult with Canadians, unlike during the period of positive relations between 1986 and 2006, when it had a good sense of the public's views of China relations and was consulting widely with informed "outsiders" in government sponsored roundtables, conferences, and working groups. Canada must restore that lost linkage between government and the policy community.

While Canada no longer plays a leading role in international affairs, it can challenge China where our voice still counts, for example, by defending the freedoms of the Canadian citizens who are resident in Hong Kong, offering them safe haven in Canada, should they choose to leave. Canada is also expanding its role as a trading nation in Asia, in a combined market larger than China's, letting Beijing know that Canada supports those countries that are currently threatened by PRC expansion, for example, Japan, Australia, the Philippines, Indonesia, and Vietnam. At the very least, Canada should give moral support for Taiwan's right to exist as a nation, and we can hold China accountable in multilateral fora by waving the flag of good governance, commitment to the rule of law, and acceptable international behavior.

In the past we gave to China more than we received, in trade, development assistance, and freedom to travel in our country. We helped China to develop when over 80 per cent of its population lived below the UN official poverty line. But China doesn't need those benefits anymore, and today we don't have to treat China as a fragile state. Nor should we ignore its communist authoritarianism and its intelligence gathering activities inside Canada. Many Canadians now say that we have to be tougher with China to stop its threats to our sovereignty and to reclaim our self-respect as a nation. Beijing may retaliate when Ottawa acts more forcefully to protect its interests, but that is a price we can afford to pay. Relations are a two-level game – we can be firm and wary of China at one level, yet we can also combine that stance with more openness through expanded trade, education, and people-to-people ties. We can call this "our strategy of selective engagement."

In the future, Canada will reset relations with China, at least to where they were in 2015 when Justin Trudeau took office. Ottawa may create a new framework for its relations with Beijing, one that includes some of the observations made here. Engagement will continue, but basic trust has been lost, and Canadians will forever treat China with more caution.

I have written a final note in my diary:

Understanding China is an elusive concept. Caught up in our own cultural and ideological values, we often do not "get China right." After fifty years, China does not always behave in the way that we expected. Do we have the inclination and the resources to find a better way to deal with this emergent superpower? That is our challenge. Will I return once more? It would be the sixty-second trip. Maybe I've reached the end of a great journey that began in 1965. Learning about China and our relations with its government and its people has been as much a voyage in understanding my own culture and values as it was in learning about China. For that I am truly grateful.

Research Note

The main sources for this book are government documents and personal interviews. Comments by politicians and public servants are cited in the text or in the endnotes. While some are identified in the following list, many of the individuals in the Department whom I interviewed preferred to remain anonymous, and neither their names nor the dates of their interviews are identified.

Personal Interviews and Conversations

Canada

Arthur Andrew
Jack Austin
John Baird
Howard Balloch
Dominic Barton
Fred Bild
Kim Campbell
Pat Carney
Raymond Chan
Joe Clark
Ralph Collins
Stockwell Day
Earl Drake

Robert Edmonds
Michel Gauvin
Richard Gorham
John Hadwen
Andrew Halper
Alvin Hamilton
Michael Harcourt
Ivan Head
Don Jamieson
Sarah Kutulakos
Paul Lin
Mark MacGuigan
Paul Martin Jr.

Marcel Massé
John McCallum
Jean McCloskey
Barbara McDougall
Margaret Meagher
Arthur Menzies
Brian Mulroney
David Mulroney

Hugh Segal
Mitchell Sharp
John Small
Guy Saint-Jacques
Sarah Taylor
Pierre Trudeau
Michael Wilson

China

Cong Peiwu
Huang Hua
Liu Huaqiu
Lu Congmin
Lu Shumin
Mei Ping
Tang Fuqian

Wang Dong
Wen Yezhan
Yao Guang
Yu Zhan
Zhang Wenpu
Zhang Yijun

Government Documents

The Department of External Affairs, now Global Affairs Canada, granted access to classified and unclassified government materials. Most of these files are now accessible to researchers using Access to Information and Privacy (ATIP) legislation, which allows limited access to government materials. However, many of the classified documents used in this book remain redacted. The following files were especially helpful: 20-China-1-2, 20-China-1-3, 20-China-1-4, 4905-Human Rights-China-1-28, 7615-03-Asia-1-30.

Canadian Materials

Balloch, Howard. *Semi-Nomadic Anecdotes* (Lulu Publishing, 2013)
Cao, Huhua, and Vivienne Poy, eds. *The China Challenge: Sino-Canadian Relations in the 21st Century* (University of Ottawa Press, 2011)

Dobson, Wendy. *Living with China: A Middle Power Finds Its Way* (University of Toronto Press, 2017)

Evans, Paul M. *Engaging China: Myth, Aspiration and Strategy in Canadian Policy from Trudeau to Harper* (University of Toronto Press, 2013)

Hampson, Fen, and Mike Blanchfield. *The Two Michaels: Innocent Canadian Captives and High Stakes Espionage in the Us-China Cyber War* (Sutherland House, 2021)

Manthorpe, Jonathan. *The Claws of the Panda: Beijing's Campaign of Influence and Intimidation in Canada* (Cormorant Books, 2019)

Mulroney, David. *Middle Power, Middle Kingdom: What Canadians Need to Know about China in the 21st Century* (Allen Lane, 2015)

Potter, Pittman, with Thomas Adams, eds., *Issues in Canada-China Relations* (Canadian International Council, 2011)

Chinese Materials

Published materials by authors from the People's Republic of China on relations with Canada are sparse. Researchers in China do not have access to government documents or to interviews with PRC decision-makers, and they often have to rely upon Canadian sources. The following works provide a limited Chinese perspective on Canada-China relations:

Pan Xingming. *20 Shiji Zhong Jia Guanxi* [Canada-China Relations in the Twentieth Century] (Xuelin Publishing, 2007)

Song Jiaheng and Dong Linfu. *Zhongguo Yu Jianada: Zhong Jia Guanxi De Lishi Huigu* [An Historical Perspective on Sino-Canadian Relations] (Jinan Qilu Shushe, 1993)

Zhong Weihe, ed. *Report on Canada-China Relations* (Guangdong Foreign Affairs University, 2014)

Notes

1 Telling the Story

1 Interview with Pierre Trudeau. See also Jacques Hébert and Pierre Elliott Trudeau, *Two Innocents in Red China* (Oxford University Press, 1968). Note that all interviews were conducted by the author unless otherwise indicated.

2 Mao Zedong, "In Memory of Norman Bethune, December 21, 1939," in *Selected Works of Mao Tse-tung*, vol. 3, *1939–1941* (International Publishers, 1954), 104–5. For a Canadian perspective, see Roderick Stewart, *Bethune* (New Press, 1973).

3 On the Canadian presence in the Far East, see Charles J. Woodworth, *Canada and the Orient: A Study in International Relations* (Macmillan Publishers, 1941); H.F. Angus, *Canada and the Far East, 1940–1953* (University of Toronto Press, 2016); Arthur R.M. Lower, *Canada and the Far East, 1940* (Institute of Pacific Relations, 1941); John Meehan, *Chasing the Dragon in Shanghai: Canada's Early Relationship with China, 1858–1952* (UBC Press, 2011); Alvyn Austin, *Saving China: Canadian Missionaries in the Middle Kingdom, 1888–1959* (University of Toronto Press, 1986).

4 For an account of the difficult conditions in which Chinese labourers worked, see Julia Ningyu Li, *Canadian Steel, Chinese Grit: A Tribute to the Chinese Who Worked on Canada's Railroads More Than a Century Ago* [Feng gu Zhonghua hun: ji nian bai nian qian xiu jian Jianada tie lu de Zhongguo ren] (Paxlink, 2000).

5 See Paul M. Evans and B. Michael Frolic, eds., *Reluctant Adversaries: Canada and the People's Republic of China, 1949–1970* (University of Toronto Press, 1991), 65–9, 106–29.

6 Prime Minister Pierre Trudeau's conversation with Zhou Enlai, Beijing, October 10–12, 1973.

7 "Department" refers to the government body responsible for the implementation of Canadian foreign policy. Its name changed at least five times between 1970 and 2015, from the Department of External Affairs (DEA) to External Affairs and International Trade Canada (EAITC), the Department of Foreign Affairs and International Trade (DFAIT), Foreign Affairs and International Trade and Commerce (FAITC), and the Department of Foreign Affairs, Trade and Development (DFATD). It is now called Global Affairs Canada (GAC).

8 Interviews conducted May 1987 in Beijing by Jack Granatstein and B. Michael Frolic with State Councillor and former ambassador Yao Guang and former ambassador to Canada Yu Zhan. For the text of these conversations, see Chapter Five in this volume.

9 Earl G. Drake, *A Stubble-Jumper in Striped Pants: Memoirs of a Prairie Diplomat* (University of Toronto Press, 1999), 216.

10 Richard Fadden, speech at the Royal Canadian Military Institute, Toronto, March 24, 2010, and his testimony at the House of Commons Standing Committee on Public Safety and National Security, July 2010. Fadden was the director of the Canadian Security and Intelligence Service (CSIS). He said the CSIS had found evidence of "possible foreign political interference with certain Canadian politicians" attributed to the work of PRC agents. See Jonathan Manthorpe, *Claws of the Panda: Beijing's Campaign of Influence and Intimidation in Canada* (Cormorant, 2019), 247–56.

11 David Mulroney, "Ottawa Seems to Be Out of Ideas on Devising a New Kind of China Policy," *Globe and Mail*, June 19, 2019.

2 Diplomatic Relations

1 For Canadian relations with the PRC in the 1960s, see Paul M. Evans and B. Michael Frolic, eds, *Reluctant Adversaries: Canada and the People's Republic of China, 1949–1970* (University of Toronto Press, 1991). Published in the PRC as *Xin Kaiduan: Jianada Yu Zhong Hua Ren Min Gongheguo (1949–1970)* [A New Beginning: Canada and the People's Republic of China] (Henan Renmin Press, 1995). A previous account of the recognition negotiations can be found in B. Michael Frolic, "The Trudeau Initiative," in *Reluctant Adversaries*, 189–216. By permission, University of Toronto Press. For the American secret negotiations with China, 1969–72, see Henry Kissinger, *On China* (Allen Lane, 2011), 202–35.

2 Mao Zedong, "In Memory of Norman Bethune, December 21, 1939," in *Selected Works of Mao Tse-tung*, vol. 3, *1939–1941* (International Publishers, 1954), 104–5.

3 Richard Nixon said: "We seek an open world – open to ideas, open to the exchange of goods and people – a world in which no people, great or small, will live in angry isolation." *Foreign Affairs*, October 1967. For more on American views of China in the 1960s, see Norman St. Amour, "The American Factor, 1963–68," in *Reluctant Adversaries*, 106–29.

4 For previous Canadian attempts to establish diplomatic relations, see Paul M. Evans, *Engaging China: Myth, Aspiration and Strategy in Canadian Foreign Policy from Trudeau to Harper* (University of Toronto Press, 2014), chaps.1 and 2; and Paul M. Evans, "Epilogue: Canadian Recognition Initiatives, 1958–1968," in *Reluctant Adversaries*, 65–72.

5 Interview with Alvin Hamilton. See also Patrick Kyba, "Hamilton and Sino-Canadian Relations," in *Reluctant Adversaries*, 168–86.

6 President Lyndon Johnson was considering opening up to China in 1967, but then held back because of the war in Vietnam. See Michael Lumbers, *Piercing the Bamboo Curtain: Tentative Bridge-Building to China during the Johnson Years* (Manchester University Press, 2008).

7 For an account of Paul Martin Sr.'s attempts to admit China to the United Nations, see Don Page, "China in the United Nations, 1949–1971," in *Reluctant Adversaries*, 89–102.

8 Ibid., 97–8.

9 For Pierre Trudeau's 1960 visit, see Jacques Hébert and Pierre Elliott Trudeau, *Two Innocents in Red China* (Oxford University Press, 1968). In 1973, Zhou Enlai told Trudeau, "You visited China in 1960 … You said we were like a baby in adult's garments. You said that when we could run one factory, we would be able to run one thousand factories. So you are a prophet" (Conversations between Prime Minister Trudeau and Premier Zhou Enlai, Department files, 1973).

10 David Oancia, "Oancia, 2 Other Reporters Attacked, Spat Upon by Red Guard-led Mob," *Globe and Mail*, July 24, 1967, 1; and Charles P.B. Taylor, ed., *China Hands: The Globe and Mail in Peking* (McClelland & Stewart, 1984), chap. 3.

11 Anthony Grey, *Hostage in Peking* (Doubleday, 1971).

12 Trudeau, Ivan Head, and senior Department officials denied that Canadian intermediaries were secretly enlisted to explore engagement with Peking. Because of his personal connections with top Chinese officials, Paul Lin, a professor at McGill University, was singled out to act as a go-between for Canada and China. In interviews, Lin said he knew Ivan Head, "and I was in touch with him frequently." However, Lin did not directly admit to being an intermediary, and Trudeau claimed that he never met Lin. See also Paul Lin, with Eileen Chen Lin, *In the Eye of*

the China Storm: A Life between East and West (McGill-Queens University Press, 2011), chaps. 11 and 12.

13 The Right Honourable Pierre Elliott Trudeau, "Statement on Canadian Foreign Policy," May 29, 1968.

14 *De jure* are official relations, what Canada and Taiwan (ROC) had before October 13, 1970. *De facto* are unofficial relations without diplomatic recognition, what Canada and Taiwan had after Canada agreed to recognize the PRC as "China."

15 Materials from the files of the Chinese Ministry of Foreign Affairs. Presented by Ambassador Mei Ping, Lu Congmin, vice chairman of the Foreign Affairs Committee of the 10th National People's Congress of China, and Ambassador Chen Wenzhao, at "Past and Future in Canada-China Relations," a conference hosted by the UBC Institute of Asian Research and the Shanghai Institutes for International Studies, Shanghai, November 10–12, 2010. Chinese diplomats for the first time provided information from the closed MFA files about the PRC's negotiating strategy with Canada in 1968–70.

16 Interview with Robert Edmonds. See also Robert Edmonds, "Canada's Recognition of the People's Republic of China: The Stockholm Negotiations, 1968–1970." *Canadian Foreign Policy* 5, no. 2 (Winter 1998): 201–17. Until he was specifically instructed to do so, Edmonds could not talk with any PRC diplomats because in 1968 Canada did not have diplomatic relations with China. Similarly, at a Beijing diplomatic reception in 1975, I was chased into the washroom by a North Korean who wanted to shake hands and talk with me. Canada did not have diplomatic relations with the DPRK, and I had been told by Ottawa that under no circumstances could I have a conversation with a diplomat from any country with whom we did not have diplomatic relations. I had to sit inside the toilet cubicle and wait until he left.

17 On the difficulty of negotiating with the PRC, see Yafeng Xia, *Negotiating with the Enemy: US-China Talks during the Cold War, 1949–72* (Indiana University Press, 2006); and Richard H. Solomon, *Chinese Political Negotiating Behavior, 1967–1984: An Interpretive Assessment* (Rand, 1985)

18 Mitchell Sharp, House of Commons, July 21, 1969.

19 Some Canadians later said that a majority of Canadians had opposed the withdrawal of diplomatic recognition from Taiwan in 1970. However, there is little evidence to support that claim. Conservatives did criticize the government in the House, some Canadian companies worried about losing business with Taiwan, and most members of Canada's small ethnic Chinese community were pro-Taiwan. The majority of Canadians, however, had

no brief for the island and its authoritarian regime. Today, since Taiwan has democratized and its economy ranks in the top twenty globally, most Canadians have a positive view of Taiwan's right to exist as an independent nation.

20 House of Commons Debates, June 18, 1970.

21 For the text of the Joint Communiqué, see External Affairs, Government of Canada, November 1970, 378.

22 Mitchell Sharp, *Which Reminds Me: A Memoir* (University of Toronto Press, 1994), 203–4.

23 "Editorial: Canada-China Recognition: World Lesson in Realism," *Globe and Mail* October 14, 1970, 6.

24 *People's Daily*, October 13, 15, and 19, 1970.

3 The One-China Policy

1 See Xu Guoqi, "The Montreal Games: Politics Challenge the Olympic Ideal," in *Olympic Dreams: China and Sports, 1895–2008* (Harvard University Press, 2008), 164–96; Donald Mackintosh and Michael Hawes, "Trudeau, Taiwan, and the 1976 Montreal Olympics," in *Sport and Canadian Diplomacy* (McGill-Queen's University Press, 1994), 37–58; Lord Killanin, *My Olympic Years* (Secker and Warburg, 1983); James Worrall, *My Olympic Journal* (Canadian Olympic Association, 2000); and the Worrall Archives, University of Western Ontario.

2 Mitchell Sharp, October 17, 1972.

3 Paul Evans, "Canada and Taiwan: A Forty Year Survey," in *Transactions of the Royal Society of Canada*, sixth series, vol. 1 (The Royal Society of Canada, 1990), 165–88.

4 For an account of one Canadian ethnic Chinese community's perspective on recognition of the PRC, see Janet Lum, "Recognition and the Toronto Chinese Community," in *Reluctant Adversaries: Canada and the People's Republic of China, 1949–1970*, ed. Paul M. Evans and B. Michael Frolic (University of Toronto Press, 1991), 217–40.

5 Reply to Otto Jelinek, House of Commons Debates, July 5, 1976.

6 The Committee of One Million was a pro-Taiwan, anti-PRC organization with strong ties to the American Congress. Together with Madam Chiang Kai-shek's positive image in America, the Committee shaped pro-Taiwan opinion in the United States for several decades. See Stanley D. Bachrack, *The Committee of One Million: "China Lobby" Politics, 1953–1971* (Columbia University Press, 1976)

7 According to the minutes of the July 17 Cabinet meeting, Trudeau did have a conversation with Killanin.

8 *New York Times*, July 13 and 14, 1976; *Washington Post*, July 16, 1976; *Globe and Mail*, July 13, 1976; and Department files.

4 Development Assistance for China

1 Deng Xiaoping became China's "paramount leader" (*Zuigao Lingdaoren*) in the early 1980s. See Ezra F. Vogel, *Deng Xiaoping and the Transformation of China* (Belknap Press, 2011).

2 In the late 1970s, "Peking" became "Beijing" to reflect the correct pronunciation of the name in Mandarin.

3 Huang Hua was a Communist Party senior leader with a close connection to Mao Zedong. Huang was the PRC's first ambassador to Canada in 1971. He only served for four months before his appointment as the PRC's first permanent representative to the UN. He was foreign minister from 1976 to 1982, and vice premier from 1980 to 1982.

4 Paul Desmarais was head of Power Corporation and the Canada China Trade Council (CCTC). He was instrumental in establishing the CCTC, later renamed as the Canada China Business Council (CCBC), in 1993, Canada's premier China trade organization. For details, see Paul Lin with Eileen Chen Lin, *In the Eye of the China Storm: A Life between East and West* (McGill-Queens University Press, 2011), 205–7.

5 *Ziligengsheng* is the Chinese term for "self-reliance." It was used during the Cultural Revolution to show that China had to rely on its local resources and skills when foreign assistance was limited.

6 After leaving his position as foreign policy advisor to Pierre Trudeau, Ivan Head was president of the International Development Research Council (IDRC). Created in the early 1970s, it has focused on research, networking, and collaboration in scientific and technical assistance through small projects. The IDRC works at arm's length from the Canadian government. Its annual budget in 1980 was a few million dollars. Today, when combined with donor contributions, its annual budget is more than $100 million.

7 Jennifer Wilson, "A History of CIDA's China Program," Internal CIDA document, 2001.

8 Wei Jingsheng was one of China's leading dissidents. He put up a famous poster on the Xidan Democracy Wall in Beijing in 1979 advocating political modernization. Imprisoned from 1979 to 1993, he was released briefly, then imprisoned again until 1997, when he was deported to the United States. Wei is seen in the West as a symbol of the struggle to bring political liberalization to China.

9 Interview with Foreign Minister Mark MacGuigan. See also P. Whitney
   Lackenbauer, ed., *An Inside Look at External Affairs: The Memoirs of Mark
   MacGuigan* (University of Calgary Press, 2002)
10 Massé was appointed president of CIDA in 1981. Before that, he had
   served as clerk of the Privy Council during the government of Joe Clark
   in 1979. In his later career, he was deputy minister of foreign affairs, and
   he also represented Canada at the World Bank and the International
   Monetary Fund. In 1993, he was elected to Parliament and subsequently
   held several Cabinet appointments, including Intergovernmental Affairs
   and the Treasury Board.
11 Deng Pufang is Deng Xiaoping's son. He suffered a broken back at the
   hands of the Red Guards during the Cultural Revolution. A wheelchair
   user, he was flown to Ottawa in 1981 and had major surgery to enable
   him to sit properly and alleviate his pain. After his return to China, he
   became the head of the China Disabled Persons' Federation.
12 The best study of CIDA's partnership with Canadian universities is found
   in Ruth Hayhoe, Julia Pan, and Qiang Zha, eds., *Canadian Universities in
   China's Transformation: An Untold Story* (McGill-Queen's University Press,
   2016). For more information, see Cranford J. Pratt, *Canadian International
   Development Assistance Policies: An Appraisal* (McGill-Queen's University
   Press, 1994); and David R. Morrison, *Aid and Ebb Tide: A History of CIDA
   and Canadian Development Assistance* (Wilfrid Laurier University Press,
   1998). For the early period, see Máire O'Brien, "The Implementation of
   CIDA's China Program: Resolving the Disjuncture between Structure and
   Process" (unpublished PhD diss., York University, 2000).

5 A Canadian Trade Strategy

1 This chapter is an expanded version of B. Michael Frolic, "The China
   Strategy," in *The China Challenge: Sino-Canadian Relations in the 21st Century*,
   ed. Huhua Cao and Vivienne Poy (University of Ottawa Press, 2011),
   46–64. Reproduced with permission from the University of Ottawa Press.
2 Flora McDonald, "Who Is On Top? The Minister or the Mandarins," in
   Politics, Canada, ed. P.W. Fox and G. White (McGraw-Hill Ryerson, 1991),
   395–400.
3 Brian Mulroney, House of Commons Debates, October 11, 1985.
4 Brian Mulroney, *Memoirs, 1939–1993* (McClelland & Stewart, 2007), 311–12.
5 For the National Trade Strategy, see A.G. Blanchette, ed., *Canadian Foreign
   Policy, 1966–1976: Selected Speeches and Documents* (McGill-Queen's
   University Press, 1980), 44–5.

6 James Kelleher, Speech at the Sixth Annual Meeting of the Canada China Trade Council, 1985.

7 Mulroney, *Memoirs*, 439–45.

8 Interviews with State Councillor Yao Guang and Ambassador Yu Zhan, Beijing, May 1987.

9 For "Japan Inc.," the Japanese model of government-business partnership, see Chalmers Johnson, *MITI and the Japanese Miracle: The Growth of Industrial Policy, 1925–1975* (Stanford University Press, 1982); and Shōtarō Ishinomori, *Japan Inc.: An Introduction to Japanese Economics* (University of California Press, 1988).

6 Tiananmen Crisis

1 The best Canadian study of the Tiananmen military action is found in Timothy Brook, *Quelling the People: The Military Suppression of the Beijing Democracy Movement* (Lester Publishing, 1992). For a detailed American account, see Liang Zhang, Andrew J. Nathan, and E. Perry Link, eds., *The Tiananmen Papers* (Public Affairs, 2002).

2 Alan Gotlieb, "Romanticism and Realism in Canada's Foreign Policy," *Policy Options*, February 1, 2005, https://policyoptions.irpp.org /magazines/canada-in-the-world/romanticism-and-realism-in -canadas-foreign-policy/.

3 Interview with Earl Drake. See also Earl G. Drake, *A Stubble-Jumper in Striped Pants: Memoirs of a Prairie Diplomat* (University of Toronto Press, 1999), 181.

4 Jan Wong, *Red China Blues: My Long March from Mao to Now* (Doubleday, 1996), 244.

5 See Brook, *Quelling the People*. Figures for the number of people killed around Tiananmen Square vary from several hundred to over 1,000 deaths. The most reliable estimate is approximately 700, including soldiers. No one was killed in the Square on June 4.

6 Interview with Paul Lin. See also Paul Lin with Eileen Chen Lin, *In the Eye of the China Storm: A Life between East and West* (McGill-Queens University Press, 2011), 254–7.

7 Brian Mulroney, *Memoirs, 1939–1993* (McClelland & Stewart, 2007), 665–6.

8 John Fraser, "The Terror Is Remorseless," *Globe and Mail*, June 15, 1989, A7.

9 George Bush and Brent Scowcroft, *A World Transformed* (Alfred A. Knopf, 1998), 89.

7 Applying Sanctions

1 A detailed analysis of the implementation of the Canadian sanctions policy is found in Paul Gecelovsky, "Explaining the Canadian Response to the Tiananmen Square Massacre: A Comparative Study of Canadian Foreign Policy" (unpublished PhD diss., University of Alberta, 2000).

2 For a discussion of the effectiveness of sanctions, see Kim Richard Nossal, *Rain Dancing: Sanctions in Canadian and Australian Foreign Policy* (University of Toronto Press, 1994); and Lisa L. Martin, *Coercive Cooperation: Explaining Multilateral Economic Sanctions* (Princeton University Press, 1992).

3 According to the Department, "the decision not to proceed with the Canadian-financed television transmission facility in China had actually been taken before the crisis but had not been announced. Adding it to the June 30 sanctions list was a useful indicator of the new criteria for future project applications."

4 James Lilley, with Jeffrey Lilley, *China Hands: Nine Decades of Adventure, Espionage and Diplomacy in Asia* (Public Affairs, 2005), 335, 340.

5 George Bush and Brent Scowcroft, *A World Transformed* (Alfred A. Knopf, 1998), chap. 4.

6 Canada China Trade Council, *Special Report: Assessing Canada's China Policy: Is It Time for a Change?* (Canada China Trade Council, 1990).

7 Fang Lizhi was an astrophysicist and the former vice president of China's leading Science and Technology University. He inspired Tiananmen demonstrators with his liberal ideas, for which he had been repeatedly criticized in the past. He was accused of being one of the "dark hands" behind the Tiananmen protests. Forced to seek sanctuary in the American Embassy in Beijing on June 5, 1989, he remained there until June 1990, when the American and PRC authorities reached an agreement to let him leave China. He and his wife eventually settled in Arizona.

8 "Toast by the Honorable Brent Scowcroft, Assistant to the President for National Security Affairs, Beijing, December 9, 1989," *New York Review of Books*, June 23, 2011.

9 William Kirby, Gong Li, and Robert S. Ross, eds., *Normalization of US-China Relations: An International History* (Harvard University Press, 2005).

10 Earl Drake, *A Stubble-Jumper in Striped Pants: Memoirs of a Prairie Diplomat* (University of Toronto Press, 1999), 216.

11 Interview with Ambassador Bild. See also Fred Bild, "Canada's Response to China in the 1990s: A View from the Field" (unpublished paper, University of Montréal, 1996); Fred Bild, "Canada's Staying Power:

A Diplomat's View," in *The China Challenge*, ed. Huhua Cao and Vivienne Poy (University of Ottawa Press, 2011), 11–30.

12 The media had a field day. See Norman Endicott, "Three Stooges Take on the Dragon," *Globe and Mail*, January 28, 1992, A15; "Editorial: Theatre in Beijing," *Globe and Mail*, January 9, 1992, A14; and Ben Tierney, "MPs Say Belongings Stuffed into Plastic Bags," *Vancouver Sun*, January 8, 1992, A3.

13 On the advice of the PRC ambassador in Ottawa, the Chinese Foreign Ministry had invited the three MP's to "investigate human rights in China." Ambassador Wen Yezhan saw this invitation as a positive step to improve relations, but later he told Bild that he had made a mistake and had been punished for it.

14 House of Commons, Standing Committee on External Affairs and International Trade, February 13, 1992.

15 In the spring of 1992, Deng Xiaoping travelled to southern China, where he called for more radical economic reform to open up China to capital markets. The great surge in China's economic growth that followed has been attributed to Deng's remarks.

16 Brian Mulroney, *Memoirs, 1939–1993* (McClelland & Stewart, 2007), 996.

8 Team Canada Goes to China

1 The Team Canada Briefing Book, "Team Canada Mission to China One Year Later," (Canadian Communications Group, 1995). See also B. Michael Frolic. "Re-engaging China: Striking a Balance between Trade and Human Rights," in *Asia Pacific Face-Off*, ed. Fen Osler Hampson, Maureen Molot, and Martin Rudner (Carleton University Press, 1997), 323–47.

2 Jean Chrétien, *My Years as Prime Minister* (Alfred A. Knopf, 2007): 339.

3 Roy MacLaren, Speech at the CCBC Annual General Meeting, Beijing, November 1993.

4 Daniel Drache and Patrick Monahan, eds., "The Chrétien Era: A Red Book Audit," *Canada Watch* 9, 3–4 (February 2004): 5, 13.

5 Jack Austin had a distinguished career as a Liberal politician, public servant, and senator. He consulted on China policy with at least three prime ministers, beginning with Pierre Trudeau. In the 1990s, he served as president of the Canada China Business Council and played a key role in organizing the 1994 Team Canada visit.

6 Chrétien, *My Years*, 340–1.

7 Marian Botsford Fraser, "Canada's China Policy: Human Rights Be Damned," *Globe and Mail*, June 2, 1994, A25.

8 Barbara McDougall, "When Trading with Tyrants, Canada Can't Ignore Its Democratic Values in Dealing with China," *Toronto Star*, June 17, 1994, A27.

9 Rong Yiren, one of China's "red capitalists," established the China International Trust and Investment Corporation (CITIC) in 1979. He was vice president of China from 1993 until 1998. CITIC was one of CCBC's founding members, and it worked closely with CCBC to develop trade between Canada and China. Paul Desmarais was president of Power Corporation. He kept close ties with China's leaders, and he would often fly there in his private plane to discuss trade opportunities with them.

10 Team Canada Briefing Book.

11 Chrétien, *My Years*, 339–40.

12 Andrew Coyne, "How You Gonna Keep 'Em Down on the Farm after They've Seen Beijing?" *Globe and Mail*, November 14, 1994, A14; Thomas d'Aquino, "Letters to the Editor: Team Canada's Effort," *Globe and Mail*, November 21, 1994, A14.

13 *Wen Hui Bao*, October 1, 1994; *Jiefang Ribao*, October 12, 1994. For more on Li's visit, see Chapter Nine of this volume.

14 Howard Balloch, *Semi-Nomadic Anecdotes* (Lulu Publishing, 2013), 617–31.

9 Challenging China on Human Rights

1 For Canadian sources on human rights, see Pitman Potter, *Exporting Virtue? China's International Human Rights Activism in the Age of Xi Jinping* (UBC Press, 2021); and Andrew Lui, *Why Canada Cares: Human Rights and Foreign Policy in Theory and Practice* (McGill-Queen's University Press, 2012). See also Sonya Sceats and Shaun Breslin, *China and the International Human Rights System* (Chatham House, 2012); Ann Kent, *China, the United Nations, and Human Rights: The Limits of Compliance* (University of Pennsylvania Press, 1999); Rosemary Foot, *Rights Beyond Borders: The Global Community and the Struggle Over Human Rights in China* (Oxford University Press, 2000); and Ming Wan, *Human Rights in Chinese Foreign Relations: Defining and Defending National Interests* (University of Pennsylvania Press, 2001).

2 On the rise and fall of the Xidan Democracy Wall, see John Fraser, *The Chinese: Portrait of a People* (Collins, 1980), 203–71. For the 1982 Peking

University lectures, see B. Michael Frolic, *Sulian Shehui Xue Jieshao* [Introduction to Soviet Sociological Studies] (Peking University Sociology Department, 1982–83).

3 James A.R. Miles, *The Legacy of Tiananmen: China in Disarray* (University of Michigan Press, 1996), 13 and 22–3. See also Stijn Deklerck, "Human Rights in China: Tradition, Politics and Change," *Studia Diplomatica* no. 6 (December 2003): 53–108.

4 Information Office of the State Council, "Human Rights in China," *Beijing Review*, November 4–10, 1991.

5 Kent, *China, the United Nations, and Human Rights*, chap. 5.

6 Fred Bild, "Canada's Response to China in the 1990s: A View from the Field" (unpublished paper, University of Montréal, 1996).

7 The Supreme People's Procuratorate, or Procuracy, also translated as the "Prosecutor General's Office," is the highest national-level agency for both prosecution and investigation in the PRC.

8 The text of the June 25, 1993, Vienna Declaration and Programme of Action can be found at https://www.ohchr.org/en/professionalinterest /pages/vienna.aspx.

9 Liu Huaqiu's Vienna Conference Statement, 1993, is in Stephen C. Angle and Marina Svensson, eds., *The Chinese Human Rights Reader: Documents and Commentary, 1900–2000* (M.E. Sharpe, 2001), 390. See also Liu Huaqiu, "Proposals for Human Rights Protection and Promotion," *Beijing Review* 36, June 28–July 4, 1993.

10 Seven international human rights treaties, conventions, or covenants have been adopted by the United Nations. The PRC ratified five of them: economic, social, and cultural rights; elimination of racial discrimination; protection of the rights of women; convention against torture; and convention on the rights of the child. In 2020, it still had not ratified the covenant on civil and political rights or the convention on the rights of migrant workers and their families.

11 James K. Bartleman, *Rollercoaster: My Hectic Years as Jean Chrétien's Diplomatic Advisor, 1994–1998* (McClelland & Stewart, 2005), 207–12.

12 Jean Chrétien, *My Years as Prime Minister* (Alfred A. Knopf, 2007), 341. Balloch provides more details about the cardboard tanks. "The hotel had huge windows facing St. Catherine Street. Outside the windows and very visible from inside, protestors had erected the cardboard tanks as a memory to Tiananmen. The Chinese were livid and threatened that Li would not attend. In the end, the hotel arranged huge curtains to hide

the view of the city and the protests, so when Li was brought in he did not see the tanks."

13 The Department said that Canadian rights NGOs were "a loose cannon. Get them onside but don't give them a central role in policymaking." The NGOs were marginal participants in the bilateral dialogue, and the Chinese side wanted no part of them. The NGOs complained that the dialogue had failed to advance rights action in China because both governments were just paying lip service to real collaboration. (Interviews with Alex Neve, secretary general, Amnesty International [Canada], and Razmik Panossian, director of policy, programs and planning, International Centre for Human Rights and Democratic Development, 2005 and 2006).

14 Timothy Brook and B. Michael Frolic, eds., *Civil Society in China* (M.E. Sharpe, 1997). Published in the PRC as *Guojia yu Shehui* [State and Civil Society] (Central Compilation and Translation Press, Beijing, 2014). In the mid-1990s, aware of the positive role that civil society had played in the collapse of Soviet power, CIDA turned to civil society in China, establishing small projects at the local level that promoted "embryos of political participation." For Canada-PRC joint research on human rights funded by CIDA, see Errol P. Mendes and Anne-Marie Traeholt, eds., *Human Rights: Chinese and Canadian Perspectives* (The Human Rights Research and Education Centre, University of Ottawa, 1997); and Errol Mendes and Anik Lalonde-Roussy, *Bridging the Global Divide on Human Rights: A Canada-China Dialogue* (Ashgate Publishing, 2003).

15 Charles Burton, "Assessment of the Canada-China Bilateral Human Rights Dialogue," Report for the Department of Foreign Affairs and International Trade, 2006, http://spartan.ac.brocku.ca/~cburton/Assessment%20of%20the%20Canada-China%20Bilateral%20Human%20Rights%20Dialogue%2019APR06.pdf

16 The Canadian government has not disputed PRC sovereignty over Tibet, although it has criticized the PRC's sinification policies there.

17 Howard Balloch, *Semi-Nomadic Anecdotes* (Lulu Publishing, 2013), 541–3.

18 Chrétien, *My Years*, 343.

19 Charles Burton, cultural counsellor in the Embassy in the 1990s, said that trying to bring democracy to China resembled "a failed idealistic pursuit." He "had put five solid years" into various projects to build civil society, human rights, and democracy in China with disappointing results. "The issue is between those in China who want

no systemic political change and a larger group that understands the need for such change, but despairs how to bring it about" (Remarks at the Conference on Political Change in China, University of Toronto, April 4, 2008).

10 Stephen Harper Visits China

1 Speech at the National Press Club, Newsmakers Lunch, Ottawa, September 2005. In the 1970s, Lu Shumin was one of the first PRC exchange students in Canada. In this talk, he quotes Confucius. "When you reach the age of 30, you have reached maturity," Lu said. "I think this remark aptly describes the evolution of Canada-China relations that have just entered their 35th year ... China is ready to work with Canada to chart new territories – new areas of cooperation and mutual benefit; new areas of sharing and exchange; new areas of growth and development and build stronger and more dynamic relations in the years to come." The full text of the speech can be found at https://www.mfa .gov.cn/ce/ceca//eng/zjgx/t216314.htm.
2 Ibid.
3 Interview with David Mulroney. See also David Mulroney, *Middle Power, Middle Kingdom: What Canadians Need to Know about China in the 21st Century* (Allen Lane, 2015), 23–4, 263.
4 Falun Gong is a Chinese religious movement with a Buddhist heritage, combining meditation and breathing exercises (*qigong*). It reached a peak in 1999 in China when it had an estimated 70 million members. It was perceived as a threat because of its size, spiritual teachings, and independence, and it was banned by the Party. It has continued to promote its beliefs and criticize the Party from outside the PRC. See David Ownby, *Falun Gong and the Future of China* (Oxford University Press, 2008).
5 For the best account of the first six years of the Harper period, see Paul Evans, "Harper's Turn," in *Engaging China: Myth, Aspiration and Strategy in Canadian Foreign Policy from Trudeau to Harper* (University of Toronto Press, 2014), 60–82; Kim Richard Nossal and Leah Sarson, "About Face: Explaining Changes in Canada's China Policy, 2006–2012," *Canadian Foreign Policy Journal* 20, no. 2 (2014): 146–62; and Charles Burton, "Canada's China Policy under the Harper Government," *Canadian Foreign Policy Journal* 25, no. 1 (2015): 45–63. See also the work of Jeremy Paltiel and Wenran Jiang, who have written extensively on recent developments in Canada-China relations.

6 Tonda MacCharles, "Harper Downplays Rebuff; PM Denies Chill in Relations, but Indicates Chinese Cancelled Meeting over His Intention to Raise Human Rights Issues," *Toronto Star*, November 16, 2006, A3, Ontario edition; Brian Laghi, "China Snubs Harper: Cancellation of Meeting at APEC Summit Seen as 'Significant Rebuff,' Experts Say," *Globe and Mail*, November 15, 2006, A1; Geoffrey York, "Team Canada Man Sees Peril in Harper's Beijing Snubs," *Globe and Mail*, December 8, 2006, B10. The Chinese snub of Prime Minister Harper was reinforced by a *Xinhua* article about the Hanoi APEC meeting that put Canada and Harper's visit at the end of the article, preceded by a long discussion of Hu Jintao's meeting with the prime minister of Papua New Guinea.

7 Bo Xilai was the Party head in Chongqing and a strong contender for top leadership in China. In 2012, in a dramatic sequence of events, he was arrested, expelled from the Party, found guilty of corruption, and sentenced to life in prison.

8 Interview with Stockwell Day. See also Campbell Clark, "Hawkish Trade Minister's Beijing Trip Signals Policy Shift," *Globe and Mail*, April 8, 2009, A4, which reported: "Belatedly the Conservatives are coming to terms with China." Chinese social media commented: "Day is definitely coming for mendicant purposes. He needs China's money and turns friendly to China. When the crisis passes he will jump out to make trouble for China ... Every Western country comes to show friendship to us. They will be happy to empty China's pockets" (From a survey of Chinese media conducted by the Canadian Embassy, April 10, 2009).

9 David Akin, "PM's Chance to Make Up 'Lost Ground' with China; Visit to Focus on Climate Change, Trade, Tourism," *Ottawa Citizen*, December 1, 2009, A3. Peter Harder was the president of the Canada China Business Council. Prior to that, he had been deputy minister of foreign affairs and international trade, and an advisor to the prime minister.

10 Mulroney, *Middle Power*, 92.

11 For Chinese press accounts of the Harper visit, see *Xinhua*, December 1–4; *China Daily*, December 1–2; *Beijing Review*, December 3; and *Global Times*, December 2–4, 2009.

12 Lai Changxing was a Chinese businessman wanted in China for corruption. He managed to leave China, and arrived as a fugitive in Canada in 1999, and he then sought unsuccessfully to obtain refugee status. The PRC wanted him back to be prosecuted, but Lai managed to stave off extradition, and he remained in Canada for eleven years. Canadian authorities would not extradite him until China agreed not to impose the death penalty. After his return to China in 2011, he was

sentenced to life imprisonment. Canada's refusal to send him back to China until he had exhausted all possible legal procedures angered Beijing. During the Martin and Harper periods, the PRC continually complained that he was a Canadian hostage.

13 Mulroney, *Middle Power*, 94.

14 Jane Taber, "Harper 'Reaping What He Has Sown,'" *Globe and Mail*, December 3, 2009, https://www.theglobeandmail.com/news/politics/ottawa-notebook/harper-reaping-what-he-has-sown/article793423/. The Liberal leader added: "We've all had a wake-up call in Canada about how important China is, and Mr. Harper has taken a very long time to wake up." For Michael Ignatieff's comments, see "PM Doesn't Shy Away from Human Rights in China," CTV.ca, December 4, 2009, https://www.ctvnews.ca/pm-doesn-t-shy-away-from-human-rights-in-china-1.461131.

15 "President Hu Meets Canadian PM to Cement Ties," *China Daily* (*Xinhua*), December 3, 2009, http://www.chinadaily.com.cn/china/2009-12/03/content_9113104.htm.

16 The Canadian text of the Joint Statement can be found at https://www.canada.ca/en/news/archive/2009/12/canada-china-joint-statement.html. The Chinese text was published in *Xinhua*, December 4, 2009.

17 *The Canada-China Economic Complementaries Study*, May 2012, is archived at Global Affairs Canada. It can also be accessed at https://www.international.gc.ca/trade-agreements-accords-commerciaux/agr-acc/china-chine/study-comp-etude.aspx.

18 *Globe and Mail*, December 6, 2009. The transcript of Harper's speech in Shanghai on December 4, 2009, can be accessed at http://alicewong.ca/2009/12/. Ms. Alice Wong, member of Parliament for Richmond, British Columbia, and parliamentary secretary for multiculturalism, accompanied the prime minister on his visit to China.

19 SooToday.com, "Harper Meets Dude Named Rowswell. In China," *SooToday.com*, December 5, 2009, https://www.sootoday.com/local-news/harper-meets-dude-named-rowswell-in-china-5-photos-127131. The prime minister expected that the opening of the Canadian pavilion in Shanghai Expo would further reset relations. "Expo 2010 will be an opportunity for Canada to build stronger economic, diplomatic and cultural ties with our second largest merchandise trading partner."

20 Kate O'Keeffe, "Moody's Report Raises 'Red Flags' at 61 Chinese Companies," *Globe and Mail*, July 12, 2011; and speech by Foreign Minister Baird to the Canada China Business Council, June 29, 2011, when he said: "We have so much to learn from China. It is a clear priority for this Government and for our economy. I visited the Guangzhou railway

station. It's four times the size of Union Station. They can build these things in no time. It will take Toronto six years or more to redo Union Station." See Canada China Business Council, "Minister Baird Luncheon: Canada's Foreign Affairs Minister Calls Strengthened Ties with China a 'Key Priority,'" June 29, 2011, https://ccbc.com/fr/press-releases /minister-baird-luncheon-2/.

21 Michelle Shephard, "Explain Yourself or Resign, Critics Tell Top Spy," *Toronto Star*, June 25, 2010, A10; Susan Delacourt, "Olivia Chow Slams Spy 'Fiction,'" *Toronto Star*, June 25, 2010, A10; Anthony Reinhart and Colin Freeze, "Intelligence Controversy: NDP MP Olivia Chow Slams 'Baseless Spy Stories,'" *Globe and Mail*, June 25, 2010, A4; "What Richard Fadden Told the CBC," *Globe and Mail*, June 25, 2010, https://www .theglobeandmail.com/news/national/what-richard-fadden-told -the-cbc/article4322968/. This article is a transcript of a CBC interview conducted by Brian Stewart with CSIS director, Richard Fadden, who said: "Either by sending their people here, or by using their embassies, they try to exercise some control over these communities ... Representatives of these countries will sometimes just grab people by the scruff of the neck and send them back home so they can't continue their studies. We think that's a real interference with our sovereignty so we try to monitor this and stop it when we can."

22 Mulroney, *Middle Power*, 283.

11 Resetting Relations

1 Harper said: "We declined to even enter into a free trade deal with China after a pre-study. Canada is simply not in a position to get a good deal bargaining one-on-one with the People's Republic." He added: "We did not fall victim to the globalist delusion that because trade is usually beneficial in overall terms, it must be beneficial under any terms and for everyone." Stephen Harper, *Right Here, Right Now: Politics and Leadership in the Age of Disruption* (McClelland & Stewart, 2018), 109, 113.

2 For China's invasive activities in Canada, see Jonathan Manthorpe, *Claws of the Panda: Beijing's Campaign of Influence and Intimidation in Canada* (Cormorant Books, 2019); and the testimony of Richard Fadden at the House Standing Committee on Public Safety and National Security, July 2010. The testimony can be found at https://www.ourcommons.ca /DocumentViewer/en/40-3/SECU/meeting-28/evidence.

3 Bruce Campion-Smith, "Trudeau Talks 'Fresh Approach' with China While Xi Jinping Praises PM's Father," *toronto.com*, November 16, 2015,

https://www.toronto.com/news-story/6120153-trudeau-talks-fresh
-approach-with-china-while-xi-jinping-praises-pm-s-father/.

4 A drawing on Chinese Twitter showed Justin Trudeau with a red maple
leaf emblazoned on his back, bending over to kiss the hand of Mao
Zedong, who is lying in state. Trudeau is saying to Mao: "Let's talk about
money, not human rights, shall we?"

5 For Li Keqiang's speech, September 23, 2016, see Les Perreaux, "Chinese
Premier Wraps Up Ottawa Visit with Free-Trade Pitch, *Globe and
Mail*, September 23, 2016; and Giuseppe Valiante, "'Golden Decade':
Chinese Premier Calls for New Era of Canada-China Trade," *CTV News*,
September 23, 2016, https://www.ctvnews.ca/politics/golden-decade
-chinese-premier-calls-for-new era-of-canada-china-trade-1.3085925.
Li Keqiang's speech in Mandarin is posted on the CCBC website at
https://ccbc.com/pm-trueday-premier-li-ccbc/; Trudeau's remarks can
be found on the PMO website at https://pm.gc.ca/en/videos/2016
/09/23/pm-trudeau-attends-6th-china-canada-business-forum-and
-luncheon-premier-li. See also Joint Statement between Canada and the
People's Republic of China, September 23, 2016, https://pm.gc.ca/en
/news/statements/2016/09/23/joint-statement-between-canada-and
-peoples-republic-china.

6 *McGill online*, September 27, 2016; Nathan Vanderklippe, "Rules of
Engagement: China: How Far Is Too Far?" *Globe and Mail*, September 24,
2016, A1.

7 For PRC attempts to acquire Noranda Mining, Nexen Oil and Gas
Corporation, and Aecon Construction Group, see Gregory Chin, "An
Uncomfortable Truth: Canada's Wary Ambivalence to Chinese Corporate
Takeovers," *International Journal* 73, no. 3 (2018): 399–428.

8 The "foxes" are former PRC citizens living in another country. They are
wanted for criminal prosecution in China. PRC agents are the "hunters,"
who find these foxes and bring them back to China, often without
informing the host country.

9 Robert Fife, "Chinese Official Bristles over Human Rights," *Globe and
Mail*, June 2, 2016, A3. Wang Yi said: "Other people don't know better
than the Chinese people about the human rights condition in China, and
it is the Chinese people who are in the best situation, in the best position
to have a say about China's human rights situation."

10 David Mulroney, "Trudeau's China Setback Was a Self-Inflicted Wound,"
Globe and Mail, December 9, 2017, O11.

11 Address to Press Club, Washington, DC, March 25, 1969. Trudeau's
speech can be found at https://www.cbc.ca/player/play/1797537698. In

a later conversation, Trudeau said: "The elephant metaphor has followed me everywhere. The Americans did not really mind, and Canadians liked it. The elephant served us well."

12 American criticism of NAFTA for producing a large trade deficit with Canada was unfounded. In 2017, when Trump began his attack on NAFTA, the United States had a $23.2 billion deficit with Canada in goods. However, it also had a $25.9 billion surplus in services, producing an overall $2.8 billion surplus for the United States. In a September 2019 interview, Trump said that Trudeau was "easily Canada's worst president [*sic*] yet. Honestly, I think he's done a terrible job so far. He should be ashamed to call himself the President of Canada." "Donald Trump Calls Justin Trudeau 'Canada's Worst President Yet,'" *Burrard Street Journal*, https://www.burrardstreetjournal.com/trump-trudeau-canadas -worst-president-yet.

13 John Bowden, "China Warns Canada against Siding with US in Trade War," *The Hill*, May 31, 2019, https://thehill.com/policy/international /446329-china-warns-canada-against-siding-with-us-in-trade-war. While the detention of Meng, the CFO of Huawei, commanded immediate attention, it would also affect whether Canada would permit Huawei to participate in Canada's 5G network. By the end of 2021, Canada had still not made that decision.

14 Global Affairs Canada, "Note for the Special Parliamentary Committee on Canada China Relations," January 2020, Annex Seven. https:// www.ourcommons.ca/content/Committee/431/CACN/WebDoc /WD10653524/431_CACN_reldoc_PDF/DepartmentOfForeignAffairs TradeAndDevelopment-1-e.pdf.

15 "Globe Editorial: Why Canada's Relationship with China Cannot Rival Our Friendship with the United States," *Globe and Mail*, January 28, 2019.

16 Interview with John McCallum. See also Robert Fife and Steven Chase, "Canada's China Envoy John McCallum Says Huawei Executive Has Good Chance of Avoiding U.S. Extradition," *Globe and Mail*, January 24, 2019. Trudeau thanked McCallum: "For almost two decades, John McCallum has served Canadians honourably and with distinction. He held many positions in Cabinet over the years, including Minister of National Defense, Minister of Veterans Affairs and, most recently, Minister of Immigration, Refugees and Citizenship. I thank him for his service over the years." See Tonda MacCharles and Susan Delacourt, "John McCallum Resigns as Canada's Ambassador to China at Trudeau's Request," *Toronto Star*, January 26, 2019.

17 Chinese authorities detained Canadians Michael Kovrig and Michael
    Spavor on alleged espionage charges in December 2018, a few days after
    Meng Wanzhou was detained by Canada for extradition to the United
    States. In January 2019, Canadian Robert Schellenberg was sentenced to
    death by the PRC for drug crimes. In August 2020, two ethnic Chinese
    Canadians, Ye Jianhui and Xu Weihong, were also sentenced to death
    on drug charges. In September 2021, Kovrig and Spavor were finally
    released. None of the other Canadians had been executed.
18 Global Affairs Canada, "Note for the Special Parliamentary Committee
    on Canada China Relations," Annexes Six and Seven.
19 For discussions of Canadian China strategy, see Wendy Dobson and Paul
    Evans, *The Future of Canada's Relationship with China*, Institute for Research
    on Public Policy (IRPP) Policy Horizons Essay series (IRPP and Munk
    School of Global Affairs, 2015). See also Public Policy Forum, *Diversification,
    Not Dependence: A Made-in-Canada Strategy* (Public Policy Forum, 2018).
20 Peter Zimonjic, "6 Things We Learned from Dominic Barton's Appearance
    before a Committee of MPs," *CBC News*, February 6, 2020, https://www
    .cbc.ca/news/politics/dominic-barton-china-committee-1.5453779.
21 Steven Chase, "Poll Shows Hardening Position on China among
    Canadians," *Globe and Mail*, October 11, 2021.
22 Reuters, "Canada Foreign Minister Says Eyes Wide Open When It Comes
    to Normalizing China Ties," *Reuters*, September 26, 2021.
23 Ibid.
24 "Ambassador Cong Peiwu Attended the Canada China Business
    Council's 43rd Annual General Meeting and Delivered a Speech,"
    Embassy of the People's Republic of China in Canada, October 29, 2021,
    http://ca.china-embassy.org/eng/sgxw/202110/t20211029_10373585
    .htm. Cong repeated this message in a personal interview in Toronto on
    December 2, 2021.
25 See Christian Paas-Lang, "Chrétien Says Government Should Have
    Moved More Quickly on Release of Two Michaels," *CBC News*, October
    24, 2021, https://www.cbc.ca/news/politics/chretien-trudeau-china
    -michaels-1.6223107; and "Canada-China Brief: Joly Talks China, Chretien
    Questions Strategy and More," Institute for Peace and Diplomacy (IPD),
    October 2021, 6–8. Available from info@peacediplomacy.org.
26 Rena Li, "Why Canada Should Study Five-Year Plan," *China Daily Global*,
    September 30, 2021. See also CCBC and University of Alberta China Institute,
    "China's Economic Impact on Canada," October 2021: "Between 2011 and
    2020, Canadian goods exports to China increased by 50 percent, while
    Canadian goods exports to all other countries grew by only 16 percent."

Index